The Political Theory of Global Citizenship

In the context of increasing globalization and a shared, endangered environment, global citizenship is now firmly on the political agenda. Activists claim to be global citizens, teachers discuss education for global citizenship and political theorists debate whether the concept is coherent. In international politics, recent developments in international law and the erosion of state sovereignty have made it more plausible to think of a world community of individuals.

This book provides a comprehensive overview of the meaning of cosmopolitanism, and world citizenship, in the history of western political thought, as well as in the evolution of international politics since 1500. April Carter also explores possible interpretations of global citizenship today, examining issues such as global obligations, the theory and practice of universal human rights, migration and refugees, the development of European citizenship, the problems of citizenship beyond the nation state, and conflicts between regionalism and globalism.

The Political Theory of Global Citizenship goes on to consider how cosmopolitanism relates to different ideological and philosophical strands within political thought and international relations theory, and addresses the debate about global governance and cosmopolitan democracy. Finally, April Carter considers the critics of cosmopolitanism, including anti-imperialists, some feminists and postmodern theorists.

Providing an invaluable overview of earlier political thought, recent theoretical literature and current debates, this book also discusses recent developments in international politics and transnational protest. It will be of great interest to those specializing in political theory, international relations, peace/conflict studies and also to those already acting as global citizens.

April Carter is Adjunct Associate Professor in the School of Political Science at the University of Queensland. She is co-editor (with Geoffrey Stokes) of *Liberal Democracy and its Critics*, and her other books include *Peace Movements* and *Success and Failure in Arms Control Negotiations*.

Routledge Innovations in Political Theory

The Political Theory of Global Citizenship

April Carter

London and New York

First published 2001
by Routledge
2 Park Square, Milton Park, Abingdon, Oxon, OX14 4RN

Simultaneously published in the USA and Canada
by Routledge
270 Madison Ave, New York, NY 10016

Routledge is an imprint of the Taylor & Francis Group

First published in paperback in 2006

Transferred to Digital Printing 2006

Typeset in Baskerville by Taylor & Francis Books Ltd

British Library Cataloguing in Publication Data
A catalogue record for this book is available from the British Library

Library of Congress Cataloging in Publication Data
Carter, April
The political theory of global citizenship / April Carter
    p. cm.
Includes bibliographical references and index.
1. World citizenship. I. Title.
JZ1320.4 .C37 2001
323.6'01–dc21   00-068997

ISBN10: 0–415–16954–2 (hbk)
ISBN10: 0–415–39944–0 (pbk)

ISBN13: 978–0–415–16954–7 (hbk)
ISBN13: 978–0–415–39944–9 (pbk)

Contents

Preface and acknowledgements

There is now a rapidly growing literature on globalization, cosmopolitanism, global governance and cosmopolitan democracy. Since my own interest in exploring global citizenship was aroused in the early 1990s, more books and articles specifically on this topic have appeared.

The purpose of this book is to provide an overview of the idea of global citizenship from a number of perspectives. It traces the historical roots and evolution of the concept, and of associated cosmopolitan beliefs, in western thought. It examines how the duties and rights of global citizenship can be interpreted in the context of today's politics, and explores forms of citizenship that fall between national and global citizenship, with particular attention to European citizenship. Thirdly, it offers a theoretical examination of the existing literature on moral and political cosmopolitanism, cosmopolitan democracy and global citizenship, locating key authors within a range of ideological and philosophical positions in both political thought and international relations theory. The final chapter comments on some anti-imperialist, feminist and postmodern criticisms of cosmopolitanism.

This book is directed towards several kinds of reader. It summarizes a lot of material for students; and it engages with the arguments of colleagues. But it also discusses the activities and concerns of activists in global civil society, who are beginning to see themselves as global citizens, and refers to legal and institutional developments important to anyone interested in today's world. I have therefore given some weight to contemporary political events. I have also tried in the theoretical section to convey arguments and ideas – including those often elaborated in arcane language – in comprehensible English.

The terms 'global' and 'cosmopolitan' citizenship are now used interchange-ably in the literature. When discussing contemporary politics and theory I have generally opted for 'global citizen', unless discussing theorists who use 'cosmo-politan'. Until recently it was customary to speak of 'world citizens', and in the historical sections I have followed this usage. I have reserved 'planetary citizen' for a specifically ecological interpretation. Other forms of transnational or multinational citizenship are explained in context, and are not the same as global citizenship, though they may sometimes be seen as a stage towards it.

This book draws on my long-standing interests in political theory, in aspects of international politics and in social movements. I owe a debt to colleagues and postgraduate students in the Department of Government at the University of Queensland, who in recent years have encouraged me to extend my knowledge of aspects of both socialist and feminist theory. I am very grateful also to Katherine Welton, who enthusiastically chased up references and articles for me for the first part of the book.

I also owe a more formal debt to the Department of Government, which generously allowed me sabbatical leave to start work on the book, and provided me with some funding for research assistance at the same time.

Many people have given me helpful suggestions and information, including the Bradford School of Peace Studies Nonviolent Action Group, who commented on a very early paper, and Pat Arrowsmith, who provided materials on the world government movement and contemporary organizations for global citizenship. Miriam Griffin also gave me the benefit of her expertise on the Stoics. But I owe an especial debt to my former colleague Geoff Stokes, who worked with me on elaborating provisional ideas about global citizenship, helped with many references and commented on earlier articles on this topic.

Warm thanks are due to friends and colleagues who not only drew my attention to books and articles, but also spent time on reading earlier drafts of this book. I am therefore very grateful to Chris Vincenzi and Martin Leet, who gave me invaluable specialist advice on some chapters. Above all I owe an enormous debt to Margaret Canovan and Michael Randle, who read the whole book, and whose comments have greatly improved both the content and argument. Any remaining errors and deficiencies are entirely my responsibility.

April Carter
December 2000

Introduction

The idea of world citizenship is fashionable again. It is a very old idea, which goes back in western thought to the Greek and Roman Stoics, was revived in the Renaissance and elaborated in the eighteenth-century Enlightenment. It also had some currency in the middle of the twentieth century and immediately after the Second World War. But the term 'world citizenship' was not widely used – except by some dedicated believers in world government – after the consolidation of the cold war in the early 1950s. In the 1990s world citizenship, quite often renamed global or cosmopolitan citizenship, surfaced again.

Evidence of this revival comes from several sources. Individual activists for global causes may identify themselves as global citizens. One of four women who used a police boat to 'inspect' a Trident missile base in Scotland commented: 'Nuclear weapons are immoral and unlawful. It is right and proper that we as global citizens at last put the Ministry of Defence police boats to proper use – upholding the law.'[1] Activists also have a concept of a worldwide political constituency concerned with global issues: for example, Britain's *Guardian* newspaper ran an appeal in December 1999 addressed to the citizens of the world from the Parliament of the Canton of Geneva, supporting the call of 1,800 nongovernmental organizations for a moratorium on any extension of the powers of the World Trade Organization (WTO).[2] Journalists use the term 'global citizen' as a label for prominent representatives of global causes – for example *The Australian* headlined a report about Professor Ali Mazrui promoting Refugee Week: 'Global citizen seeks compassion for refugees.'[3] Education for citizenship in schools is also beginning to extend from national citizenship to global citizenship.[4] There is also growing political interest in the related ideal of global democracy. Charter 99, launched in the UK on 24 October 1999, called on the United Nations to reform international bodies, including the WTO, the World Bank and the International Monetary Fund, on democratic lines. The Charter claimed support from individuals in 92 countries and five continents by March 2000 and by organizations with global concerns such as Oxfam and Friends of the Earth.[5]

Moreover, social and political theorists have begun to think about global moral obligations and to debate ideas of world citizenship and global democracy. Since the 1980s debates about justice have not been confined to society within nation states, and a growing number of philosophers, such as Charles Beitz and Onora O'Neill, have examined obligations across borders and the possibility of transnational justice.[6] The most eminent theorist of justice, John Rawls, has also recently published his views on 'the law of peoples'.[7] Derek Heater and Richard Falk have been exploring for some time world citizenship as an extension of citizenship.[8] Martha Nussbaum has drawn on the Stoics and on Kant to reformulate eloquently an ideal of world citizenship, and Andrew Linklater has examined it from the perspective of international relations.[9] Approaching the problem of a political and moral response to globalization from a different angle, David Held has given prominence to the ideal of global democracy.[10] Arguments for global citizenship and global democracy have received powerful endorsement from Jürgen Habermas, whose theory of discourse ethics provides inspiration for Linklater and some other advocates of cosmopolitanism.[11]

This book examines the meaning of global citizenship in some depth in its historical evolution within the western tradition of political thought. It then explores evolving forms of global or transnational citizenship in practice in recent decades, including the development of a form of European citizenship. Thirdly, it surveys the recent literature on cosmopolitanism and global citizenship from a variety of theoretical perspectives, including debates about global governance and global democracy.

The idea of global citizenship is closely linked to the concept of cosmopolitanism. The Greek Stoics spoke of the cosmopolis, the city of the world, and the *cosmoupolites*, the world citizens. In the Enlightenment Kant distinguished between international society and international right between nation states (*jus gentium*), and 'cosmopolitan right', which relates to individuals and states coexisting, who may be 'regarded as citizens of a universal state of mankind (*jus cosmopoliticum*)'.[12] (Some commentators therefore prefer the term 'cosmopolitical' to cosmopolitan.)

The word 'cosmopolitan' has acquired a number of sometimes negative social connotations in different periods, but in today's political and international relations theory it is normally used to denote a model of global politics in which relations between individuals transcend state boundaries, and in which an order based on relations between states is giving way to an order based at least partly on universal laws and institutions. Cosmopolitanism also implies, following the Stoics and Kant, a moral position in which each individual should be valued as an autonomous being. Cosmopolitanism is linked to humanitarianism, in the sense that it suggests an active concern for others in need or distress, but differs from humanitarianism in stressing the dignity of those to whom one is offering aid. Cosmopolitanism is even more closely linked to a liberal belief in basic human rights, which all individuals should enjoy, but implies an ideal of a world community uniting in some sense individual bearers of rights. This does not imply all individuals are the same. Cosmopolitanism suggests awareness of cultural diversity, respect for other cultures and a desire for peaceful coexistence.[13] However, emphasis on tolerance of other cultures and on mantaining peace may at times be in tension with belief in individual rights – possible conflicts are explored in later chapters.

There are a number of reasons for the revival of interest in cosmopolitanism and global citizenship. The most obvious is the perception of increasing globalization – perceptions based in particular on the new technologies of communication, on the global nature of threats posed to the survival of the human race and of the planet by nuclear and chemical weapons and environmental degradation, and on the trend towards a global economy. While the thesis of increasing globalization, and in particular the claim that economic globalization is inevitable, is disputed, there is a general sense that we belong to one world, which has been mirrored in numerous international organizations, conferences and treaties that at least pay lip service to this sense of necessary unity.

There have also been important developments within international politics that have put cosmopolitan concerns back on the agenda. One of course was the end of the cold war, which also ended the division of the world into opposing ideological power blocs and suggested the importance of wider economic and environmental concepts of security. As a result the dominant paradigm in international relations theory ceased to be realism, stressing that the necessarily conflicting interests of nation states constitute the fundamental nature of international politics, and therefore the inevitably of war or military preparations to deter war. Instead there was a greater emphasis on liberal interpretations of world politics and a specific revival of interest in Kant.[14] The promise of 1991 of a more peaceful and cooperative world has been radically undermined by the revival of suppressed national conflicts, and economic and political insecurity has encouraged forms of xenophobia, religious antagonism and racism even in those countries benefiting from the global economy, in Europe and at the end of the 1990s in parts of Asia. Nevertheless, the 1990s saw much broader cooperation by the major states within the context of the United Nations and a number of important arms control and environmental treaties.

One way of conceptualizing international politics, used in this book, distinguishes between three possible models: anarchy between nation states, in which pursuit of conflicting national interest is paramount; an international society between states, in which conflict is moderated by a degree of cooperation to pursue common interests; and a cosmopolitan order transcending state boundaries and focusing on the rights of individuals. These models are associated with the theories of Hobbes, Grotius and Kant respectively (though it is arguable that Grotian interpretations of international law contained elements of cosmopolitanism).[15] The models can, however, overlap, both in theory and in actuality. Realist theorists who see international politics as anarchy can also note a degree of cooperation and law between states. More importantly for our purposes, a strengthening of international society between states may begin to undermine the sovereignty of states on which this model is based. Therefore international society may begin to shade off into a Kantian model of cosmopolitan community between individuals. This process is beginning to take place.

There has been growing international cooperation between states since the nineteenth century, and in the twentieth century there was an expansion of international institutions and international law. Therefore the framework for an international society has been in existence, but realists have questioned whether this framework has constrained states in pursuing what they see as their central interests. It has, moreover, not prevented major wars. It is also arguable that the way in which international bodies have been constructed and international agreements drafted ensures continuing freedom of action for states. Nevertheless, a growing number of international obligations and forums for continuous cooperation can be seen as strengthening the bonds of international society and gradually eroding state sovereignty. It is also possible to discern elements of an emerging cosmopolitan order.

This developing cosmopolitanism has been particularly striking in the area of international law. International law in the eighteenth and nineteenth centuries focused on obligations between states and upheld national sovereignty. In the twentieth century international conventions on individual human rights, and the principles of individual responsibility enunciated by the Nuremberg Tribunal at the end of the Second World War, indicated the emergence of a cosmopolitan spirit in international law, which could indeed be found in the writings of the early theorists of laws between nations, but most international law maintained the primacy of states. However, significant developments in international law during the 1990s indicated the extent to which international law is influencing decisions by national courts. For example, four women who damaged a Hawk aircraft due to be sold to Indonesia, on the grounds that it could promote genocide in East Timor, were acquitted by a jury at Liverpool Crown Court in August 1996. The judge allowed the women to ground their defence in international law and call witnesses representing the East Timorese opposition.[16] Moreover, individuals are becoming answerable to a global moral community. This assertion of cosmopolitanism strengthens the case for thinking in terms of global citizenship.

Perhaps the most significant indication of the cosmopolitan tendency in international law was the agreement by 120 states (out of 160) in July 1998 to a treaty to set up an International Criminal Court to try those who have committed genocide and aggression, war crimes and crimes against humanity.[17] The negotiations evolved out of the experience of the International Criminal Tribunals for the Former Yugoslavia and for Rwanda created earlier in the decade. A second development was the decision (affirmed twice in late 1998 and in March 1999) by the British House of Lords that the former Chilean military dictator Augusto Pinochet could not claim immunity based on the principle of national sovereignty and diplomatic immunity as a member of the Chilean Senate, and could be extradited to Spain to answer charges. The Lords based their ruling on the fact that torture had become an extraditable crime under international law in 1988.[18] General Pinochet was eventually allowed by the British Government to return to Chile on grounds of ill health and mental incapacity. But the Spanish judge who sought Pinochet's extradition had already taken up the cases of former dictators and generals in Guatemala accused of genocide, torture and state terrorism with the aim of demanding extradition to

Spain. The judge argues that Spanish law allows prosecution of genocide outside Spanish frontiers.[19]

The extent to which the world is moving beyond the principle of pure state sovereignty was clear by the early 1990s, when 'humanitarian intervention' within states to prevent genocide or other extreme abuses of human rights gained support, despite frequent criticisms from those holding a more traditional view of international politics. Advocates of cosmopolitanism may also be divided over military action for humanitarian purposes. The arguments for and against this approach were posed especially sharply by the war over Kosovo in 1999, because NATO acted militarily without UN authority and because of the strategy and weapons used.

A quite different reason for current interest in global citizenship within western political thought is the revived focus on citizenship since the 1980s.[20] There are a number of social and political concerns influencing this revival: a sense that pure liberal individualism needs to be supplemented by some awareness of social interconnectedness and political responsibility; a reaction even within the New Right to the idea of individuals solely as consumers;[21] and a regroupment on the left seeking to reinterpret ideals of equality, democracy and a public realm in a republican rather than a socialist language. Feminist critiques of mainstream political practice and theory have also focused on the inadequacies of earlier concepts of citizenship.

Political revolutions in the former Soviet bloc and the challenge of mass migration into the more affluent West also raised urgent questions about the basis of citizenship, especially in a re-united Germany. This is the context of Jürgen Habermas's reflections in the early 1990s on citizenship and the possibility of European and global citizenship.[22] The development of the European Union has made European citizenship a legal reality (for example the common European passport and right to free movement within the EU and rights to vote in all local and European Parliamentary elections in any EU country), although its political implications have still to be fully clarified. Green politics have also challenged traditional approaches to citizenship by stressing that environmental problems need international decisions. Fred Steward has argued for a concept of planetary citizenship: 'Citizenship of planet earth, then, embodies a new sense of the universal political subject beyond the context of the traditional nation state, and a refreshed awareness of equality in terms of our shared dependence on nature.'[23]

The concept of global citizenship has, however, also met with a good deal of scepticism. One basic objection to the concept of global citizenship is that the global conditions for citizenship do not exist and that the term is therefore at best metaphorical. David Miller argues that 'those who aspire to create transnational or global forms of citizenship ... either ... are simply utopian, or else what they aspire to is not properly described as citizenship'.[24] This is a cogent objection. There is still a lively debate whether there are in any real sense citizens of the European Union, despite the fact that this status was created by the Maastricht Treaty. This issue is debated later in this book. Since, however, there are very specific legal, institutional, political and economic bonds between EU peoples, and membership of the Union involves surrendering significant elements of national sovereignty, the EU is very much closer to creating conditions for citizenship than international bodies that cover the whole world. A rigorous definition of citizenship also raises the question whether it makes sense to talk about global citizenship except in the context of a fully established federal world government. If it does not, then the concept of global citizenship might well be described as 'utopian'. Whether it is really appropriate to speak in terms of 'global citizenship' is a question explored in depth in Part III.

Discussion of global citizenship presupposes a model of citizenship in the nation state. At a minimum, citizenship implies a legally and politically defined status, involving both rights (guaranteed by custom or law) and corresponding responsibilities. Historically, minimum rights have included personal freedoms and minimum obligations included the payment of taxes. The concept of being a citizen, as opposed to being the subject of a ruler, has also historically been linked to the right to participate in politics and belief in a fundamental legal and political equality between citizens. Until recently it has also of course been a privileged status, generally excluding the propertyless, women and indigenous peoples. During the twentieth century, as citizenship rights were extended, the nature of citizen rights also changed. The development of the welfare state led T.H. Marshall to his famous formulation of three kinds of citizen rights: civil, political and social. Marshall had in mind a historical progression from basic civil liberties to a widening franchise and evolving social welfare.[25] His formulation is still the starting point for many discussions of citizenship and is, for example, useful in examining the idea of European citizenship, which has given weight to social rights. But his 1944 essay did not envisage the claims of the second wave feminist movements or the movements of indigenous peoples in North America, Australia and New Zealand and other parts of the world, which have thrown up claims for new types of rights.

Apart from changes in the understanding of citizenship arising out of historical developments, there are also competing models of citizenship. There is a long-standing distinction between republican and liberal ideas of citizenship, the former implying a much stronger commitment to the political community and the latter allowing more scope for individual pursuit of private goals and with a more limited sense of necessary citizen obligations.[26] Socialist movements incorporated in principle republican rather than liberal ideals of democracy and citizenship, though with important differences of emphasis. Feminism has also engaged with the ideal of citizenship and promoted a number of differing interpretations of citizenship that would give women genuine equality.[27] These approaches to citizenship, and the extent to which they can incorporate the idea of a global citizen, are explored in the last part of the book.

One of the crucial elements in the definition of citizenship has been that it denotes membership of a specific political unit and that citizens are clearly distinguished from temporary foreign visitors and also from resident aliens. The element of exclusivity that has, historically, been built into the idea of citizenship might well suggest that global citizenship is an oxymoron. But the development of international law and the pressures of migration have challenged the exclusivity of the nation state and therefore the old concept of citizenship. The dissolution of former colonial empires, and pressure from would-be migrants from Africa and Asia, have also forced European countries to debate the implications of multiculturalism and to rethink their categories of legal citizenship, though often in a restrictive and discriminatory direction.[28] The potential for increasing migration among a skilled workforce, however, raises a case for a more generous view of citizenship rights and duties embodied in proposals for multinational citizenship.[29] Recent moves to extend dual citizenship, to give resident aliens ('denizens') full citizen rights, and to think in terms of transnational citizenship are discussed in Part II of this book.

The question of refugees who become stateless, a problem that affected millions in the twentieth century, has also challenged the adequacy of exclusive national concepts of citizenship and suggested the need for a global guarantee of minimum rights to those who lose their original citizenship. The development of League of Nations and United Nations provision for refugees and the evolution of international refugee law are also examined in Part II.

One of the central obligations of citizenship, in particular in the republican model, has been to fight for one's country against the citizens of other countries. This duty also underlines the particular loyalties associated traditionally with citizenship and the conflict between citizen patriotism and the universal commitments suggested by global citizenship. Indeed, cosmopolitanism has been associated with the quest to end war between nation states. From this perspective the idea of global citizenship is sometimes posited as an *alternative* to national citizenship, to signify a quite different kind of political allegiance.

But if national politics can be guided by cosmopolitan principles, then potentially national citizenship and global citizenship are not antitheses, but complementary. This position is suggested by Kant in his political pamphlets.[30] However, even if the principles governing national and global citizenship can coincide, in practice there is often considerable tension. Peace activists quite often claim to be acting as conscientious national citizens, even when they oppose a particular war, but they are necessarily giving priority to universal principles over the claims of immediate obedience to their government. Peace movements may therefore be seen as one important expression of people voluntarily acting as global citizens.

Transnational movements in support not only of peace, but also of human rights, preservation of the global environment or greater global economic equality are now often seen as vehicles for global citizenship. The development of a global civil society creates a context for citizenship action, just as civil society within the state is an arena for much citizen activity directed towards promoting the good of fellow citizens. In the absence of a fully developed framework of global govern-ance, individuals can choose to develop one aspect of the role of global citizen. Whether taking part in such movements necessarily exemplifies global citizenship is more debatable. These questions are considered later.

Bryan Turner has suggested one interesting alternative to trying to stretch the traditional concept of citizenship to embrace cosmopolitan goals. He agrees with theorists of global citizenship that, given the extent of globalization, the nation state is being undermined, and that, in any case, 'The nation-state is not necessarily the most suitable political framework for housing citizenship rights.' He notes that in Europe there is an increasing tendency to look to the European Court or the EU. Moreover, the state system is not well equipped to respond to the claims for aboriginal rights or the needs of refugees. Therefore he suggests that human rights provide a more universal, contemporary and progressive basis for responding to globalization.[31]

This book accepts the centrality of human rights, but suggests that the concept of universal duty suggested by the tradition of natural law complements the idea of human rights to underpin an evolving global consciousness. We now live in a world where international law and covenants on rights give moral principles some legal weight. Partly because the nation state is not the sole locus of decision-making and loyalty, we need a concept of citizenship that extends beyond it and takes account of global institutions.

There are, nevertheless, difficulties involved in an attempt to elucidate an ideal of global citizenship inherent in the ambiguities of cosmopolitanism. One frequent criticism, for example from conservative or communitarian theorists, is that social responsibility presupposes membership of a clearly defined community with its own values and obligations. One of the potentially negative connotations of cosmopolitanism, therefore, is lack of commitment to a specific polity and culture, or rootlessness and parasitism.[32]

Alternatively the claim to cosmopolitanism and world citizenship may be associated with membership of a privileged elite that happens to cross national boundaries. For example, the eighteenth-century *philosophes* formed an intellectual transnational elite. Nevertheless, although cosmopolitan attitudes can be elitist, since the eighteenth century they have been especially associated with popular movements.

A much more central objection is that today's cosmopolitan awareness is based on global economic trends, which are unifying the world but also exacerbating the gap between the world's desperately poor and the affluent, and destroying our natural environment. An optimistic interpretation from a neo-liberal perspective sees the spread of global markets as ultimately leading to greater wealth for the vast majority. Moreover, it can be argued that the global citizens *par excellence* are leaders of economic corporations, jetting round the world and living in similar hotels and meeting similar kinds of people. Falk quotes a Danish businessman, who, when asked if he felt more European than Danish, replied: 'Oh no, I'm a global citizen.'[33] These leaders *may* also develop a sense of citizenly responsibility – corporations usually support charities and are increasingly aware of environmental issues, at least in terms of public relations. But the logic of profit throws up numerous examples of western companies exploiting African or Asian consumers, or seizing their natural assets for drugs or new bio-technology, and it is also easier to ignore environmental standards in many poor countries.[34] There is therefore a conflict between one interpretation of globalism based on neo-liberalism and the emphasis on human equality suggested by liberal human rights doctrines and Kantian morality.

Cosmopolitanism from within the tradition of western political thought raises additional political difficulties, because of the role of western imperialism. It can be plausibly claimed that it is because the West has conquered most of the world by force of arms and superior technology in the past, and is asserting its present domination primarily through economic power, that liberal ideas and values are widely recognized, if less widely practised. Western corporations also control many aspects of global culture. Rejection of western beliefs has come both from governments, for example advocates of 'Asian values', and at a popular level from Islamic fundamentalism.

Postcolonial theory makes the more subtle charge that western universalism, even when voiced by groups in global civil society, is a form of cultural imperialism. Postcolonialism links up with western philosophical challenges to cosmopolitanism: the claim that it is based on a false belief in the possibility of universalism. A range of theorists loosely grouped under the label 'postmodern' theory have cast fundamental doubt on the possibility of establishing universal principles. Moreover, the attempt to establish universal rules as the basis of social order can be interpreted as a form of domination, privileging those who are presumed to observe these principles against all those who are different. Class, gender and racial domination may all be involved – some feminists have argued that only propertied white males are ascribed the rationality that makes them capable of understanding and acting in accordance with universal principles.

These considerations may undermine the attempt to discuss global citizenship today in a vocabulary that derives from western universalism, since the language may be taken to express membership of a privileged section of the world. A range of complex issues are raised by postmodern, postcolonial and feminist critiques of cosmopolitan universalism and these are discussed in the final part of the book. I argue that a form of universalism is possible, and that cosmopolitanism is not only a valid but a politically necessary stance, particularly for feminists.

This book is divided into three parts. The first traces the development of cosmopolitanism, including the evolution of international law and claims to world citizenship, in modern western thought and political practice. There are universalist principles to be found in many other cultural and religious traditions, and some books try to indicate the variety of perspectives for approaching a global consciousness.[35] But the focus here is on cosmopolitanism within western political thought, partly because this is the context familiar to me and most potential readers, but also because this is an intellectually and politically influential tradition that has shaped the evolution of international law and international institutions.

The Renaissance has been taken as a starting point, despite the great influence of classical Stoicism on the development of cosmopolitanism and the idea of world citizenship, because it is possible to trace a continuous development of ideas from 1500 to 1914. The story is not, of course, simply one of growing acceptance of cosmopolitan beliefs or uninterrupted progress in implementing them. Since the Enlightenment there has been a rise in nationalism (which may be compatible with cosmopolitanism, but often is not) and of racism, and wars have become increasingly destructive. Moreover, universal claims have some-times been used to justify the expansion of western economic and political power. This linkage can be traced in aspects of the evolution of international law, in much liberal thought – especially in the nineteenth century, and even in the attitudes and arguments of early transnational movements. But this survey also shows that strong cosmopolitan commitments provide a critique of imperialist practice in other parts of the world and assumptions of western superiority.

The second part of the book examines the emergence of various forms of transnational citizenship in the twentieth century. It begins with global citizenship within global civil society and the role of various transnational movements. The focus here is on citizenship as consciously assumed responsibil-ity, though the goal is often to secure the rights of others. Then it examines the legal and political extension of rights to stateless refugees (a key issue in early international law) and the impact of migration on dual citizenship and the emergence of a 'postnational citizenship' rooted in the rights granted by international conventions. The primary issue here is individual rights that transcend the state and rest on cosmopolitan principles. Thirdly, it examines the evolution of the EU and the debates about the meaning and reality of European citizenship, and whether EU citizenship is a step towards global citizenship or another barrier to it.

The last part of the book engages with concepts of citizenship in political thought, considering whether global citizenship can be incorporated into a range of theoretical approaches from liberalism to socialism, and assessing the validity of some republican and communitarian critiques. It then examines the implications of different models of international politics for global citizenship, and weighs up the arguments for world federalism, liberal global governance and cosmopolitan democracy. Thirdly, this section confronts the major contemporary challenges to cosmopolitan universalism from theorists of imperialism, from some strands of feminism and from postmodern philosophy.

Finally, I draw together my own conclusions about the possible meanings and validity of the concept of global citizenship and the value of cosmopolitan modes of thought and action. I suggest that although there are both utopian and rhetorical elements in claiming to be a global citizen, the phrase does denote a coherent understanding of a relationship between human rights and human duties and cosmopolitan beliefs, including a commitment to prevent increasing world poverty, and the destruction of ancient cultures and the natural environ-ment. It also denotes the complexity of individual links to international law and overlapping political institutions in a globalizing world.

Part I

Cosmopolitanism and international society between states, 1500–1914

Introduction: Roots of cosmopolitanism in the western tradition

Part I examines the major sources of cosmopolitanism and ideas of world citizenship in the modern western tradition from the Renaissance to the twentieth century. These ideas were held by a small number of intellectuals before 1700. The Enlightenment saw the strongest expression of intellectual cosmopolitanism and commitment to world citizenship, although this was not reflected in the politics between states. During the next century there were contradictory developments: an expansion of popular nationalism, on the one hand, and technological and social trends promoting closer links between governments and peoples, on the other.

This exploration of earlier understandings of cosmopolitanism reveals the different connotations of the idea of world citizenship, which are still relevant today, and also indicates some of its ambiguities. In particular it raises questions about the Eurocentric bias of western universalism, and throws light on the complex relationship between Europe's expanding economic, military and political power in the rest of the world and the evolution of cosmopolitan thought. Both these questions are central in today's debates.

The primary focus is on theoretical understandings of cosmopolitanism, articulated by leading thinkers such as Erasmus and Kant, and the recurring themes in cosmopolitan thought. These themes are: identification with all other human being as equals; belief that we share the earth in common; and commitment to peace and to tolerance of other religions and cultures. They are encapsulated in the concept of world citizenship. Most of these themes are also suggested by the closely linked concept of natural law, which suggests the duties we owe to others, though interpretations of natural law have tended to lead to the concept of just war rather than towards pacifism. By the eighteenth century there was a growing emphasis on the obverse of natural law – natural rights. Natural (or human) rights are also a powerful expression of the values embedded in the concept of world citizenship.

Each chapter sets these ideas briefly within their social and political contexts, in particular the nature of relations between rulers of states and how far an 'international society' existed between them. These first three chapters comment also on the development of international law and proposals for various forms of international organization, which can be seen as measures to strengthen a cooperative international society. But international law in its earlier expressions, and in its evolution today, can also have strong cosmopolitan implications by focusing on the rights of individuals and the duty to respect such rights. Part I also explores the development of intellectual, cultural and social movements and organizations across frontiers, facilitated in the nineteenth century through greatly improved communications.

A cosmopolitan consciousness, although prompted by awareness of globalizing social trends, has drawn heavily upon sources within earlier traditions of western thought. One influential source from the sixteenth to the eighteenth centuries – which has renewed appeal today – was the heritage of Greek and Roman Stoic philosophy, which embodied the idea of world citizenship. The original Stoic concept of the *cosmopolis* embraced all rational beings, including gods as well as men. But the Stoic legacy to us is its view of the human world. The teaching of the first Stoic thinker, Zeno, is summed up by Plutarch in a well known quotation:

> our life should not be based on cities or peoples each with its own view of right or wrong, but we should regard all men as our fellow-countrymen and there should be one life and one order, like that of a single flock on a common pasture feeding together under a common law.[1]

A brief discussion of Stoicism, which is relevant to understanding later cosmopolitanism, is therefore appropriate here.

The early Stoics wrote during the Hellenistic period, when the self-governing city states had been undermined by the development of the Macedonian Empire within Greece, creating a sense of moral and political uncertainty. Their attitudes may also have been influenced by the conquests of Alexander the Great, who incorporated many peoples with very different cultures under his rule.[2] The Stoics were not the only school of philosophy to arise in this period, and their beliefs were criticized by the Sceptics – these two opposing schools of thought were to be revived in the Renaissance, and both have their philosophical counterparts today.[3]

The Stoics are generally seen as rejecting key elements in earlier classical Greek thought, which distinguished sharply between Greeks and barbarians, and between freemen and slaves. Indeed the earliest Stoic philosophers, Zeno and Chrysippus, were described not as Greek but as Phoenician; and the later Stoic philosopher Epictetus had been a slave. Stoics did not, however, radically challenge the existing social order, which was based on slavery – two of the best-known Roman Stoics were Seneca, an adviser of the Emperor Nero, and the Emperor Marcus Aurelius.[4] But it is usually accepted that they did promote an ideal of human equality and brotherhood.[5] There is also some, inconclusive, evidence that the early Hellenistic Stoic thinkers believed too in the equality of women; and the Roman Musonius Rufus explicitly supported the education of women.[6]

The implications of Stoicism for politics were ambiguous. Stoicism is now often understood as an apolitical, individualistic stance of cultivating personal virtue and being resigned to the blows of fate. But it did frequently mean political involvement.[7] Although the Stoics were not associated with advocating revolutionary social change, they generally sought to alter social attitudes and the way people behaved, and therefore to influence public life. Martha Nussbaum suggests that Seneca's writings *On Mercy* and *On Anger* represented 'an argument in favor of replacing Roman norms of honor and manly aggression with new norms of patience and gentleness'.[8]

Although Stoicism is associated with belief in universal harmony and equality, as a doctrine of philosophers it also tended in its earlier expression to suggest that only an elite of the wise could belong to the *cosmopolis* – the city of the world. But this distinction between the wise few and great majority was rejected by the Stoic writers of the Roman Republic, who stressed the unity of the human race united by reason.[9] This tension between elitism and egalitarianism re-emerges in modern western cosmopolitan thought. The Stoic legacy also embodied a certain ambiguity about the connotations of world citizenship. The first Stoic philosophers had been influenced by the Cynics, who coined the term '*cosmoupolites*', and who probably designated themselves world citizens to denote their independence of any particular city, rather than the unity of humanity. Their views were generally unconventional and anarchistic. Baldry argues that the Cynics did not mean to suggest that cosmopolitanism meant being at home in every city, but rather that 'the wise man … is a vagabond with no fixed abode'.[10] But other commentators have claimed the Cynics held a more positive view of their relationship both with other human beings and with the natural world.[11] It is debatable how far the early Stoics also endorsed a concept of rootlessness, but the Stoic ideal of world citizenship is usually understood as an ideal of human unity. These differing interpretations of world citizenship are embedded in the later history of cosmopolitanism.

Generalizations about Stoicism are open to scholarly dispute. It was a complex doctrine spanning 500 years from Hellenistic Greece through the Roman Republic to the Roman Empire. Secondly, although some Roman texts survive, Hellenistic Stoicism is only represented by fragments, and knowledge of these depends on the evidence of later, sometimes hostile, authors. There is, moreover, scope for disagreement about actual translation and interpretation of these fragments.[12] But these difficulties do not invalidate the importance of Stoicism in the evolution of the idea of world citizenship. Nor do they affect the fact that Stoic philosophy inspired later thinkers with a belief in cosmopolitanism.

In addition to the concept of world citizenship, Stoicism promoted the tradition of natural law, belief in a set of universal principles applicable to all humanity, which all reasoning beings could understand. Elements of natural law can be traced to earlier Greek thought, but the Stoics elaborated on its role.[13] Chrysippus, Zeno's successor, claimed that: 'The natural law is king over everything, divine and human alike … it lays down the standards for right and wrong … .'[14] Indeed, some commentators have suggested that this is the most important Stoic legacy. Schofield, for example, argues that the idea of the *cosmopolis* was an attempt to retain the image of community and citizenship denuded of its geographical and social base, and can be seen primarily as a bridge between civic patriotism and the idea of natural law.[15] The Stoic concept of natural law, as formulated in particular by Cicero, influenced the development of Roman law and later European law. The concept of natural law was also incorporated into Christian canon law and adopted by the early theorists of international law.[16]

A second source of cosmopolitanism inherited by western thought derived from Christianity. Early Christianity had emphasized human equality, often finding converts among slaves and women and ignoring ethnic or political distinctions. Moreover, Christian beliefs and the idea of a universal Church provided a basis for asserting the potential worth of all human beings and a cosmopolitan view of the world. In the Middle Ages, the concept of an overarching Christendom provided a source of unity transcending state borders. In addition, the specific religious and political role of the Papacy inspired early writings that can be seen as precursors of later aspirations to perpetual peace and world government. Dante's *De Monarchia*, for example, is often cited as a contribution to such ideals. The Reformation was also significant in the development of a Christian humanism. A number of Protestant Christian Churches that emerged then, especially dissenting sects, have been influential in the modern period in promoting belief in human unity. The Quakers, Mennonites and others have also played a prominent part in movements opposing slavery, racial oppression and war.

The most important contribution of Christian philosophy to modern cosmopolitanism was, however, in incorporating and transmitting the universalist elements in classical Greek and Roman thought. Thomas Aquinas, for example, looked to the objective reason embodied in natural law to cover that part of humanity who did not embrace the Christian faith. Later Catholic philosophers at the beginning of the modern period elaborated the theory of just war and laid the bases of international law.

Some aspects of the medieval world were more conducive to cosmopolitan attitudes than the modern period in Europe. European Christendom was united by one faith (despite the distinction between the Roman and Byzantine Churches and a period of political rivalry between opposing popes), and there were overlapping religious and political jurisdictions between Church and king. There were also strong bonds uniting people across political borders. Peter Kropotkin celebrated the role of trade guilds and brotherhoods in creating solidarity, giving aid in case of illness, and defending their members as well as pursuing their craft and promoting commerce.[17] Paul Ghils finds the precursors of today's international nongovernmental organizations in the transnational religious orders. He also notes that in the Islamic world between the ninth and fourteenth centuries the role of transnational orders and brotherhoods acted 'as a counterweight to princely authority'.[18] But this premodern kind of social order, rooted in religion and based on princely rule, is ideologically and socially quite remote from the highly technological world in which cosmopolitanism is now being developed.

In the medieval period, despite the intolerance generated by Christian crusades against Islam, there was a significant exchange of ideas between the Islamic and Christian world. Islamic scholars made their Christian counterparts aware of the classical Greek heritage that had been lost to them, and Islamic thinkers (themselves drawing on the Greeks) influenced developments in Christian philosophy. Europe also drew on the superior mathematical, scientific and medical skills of Islamic civilization.

But Christians and Muslims frequently fought for power over the European continent. As the Ottoman Empire swept westward, starting in the 1300s, the Turks were seen as the major threat to Christian civilization, at least until the second unsuccessful siege of Vienna in the seventeenth century finally halted their advance. Religious belief could therefore easily become allied to power politics and to fear and hatred of alien cultures and beliefs.

The Stoic belief in human brotherhood, repudiation of cruelty and oppression, and advocacy of benevolence and charity provided a basis for the Renaissance rediscovery of cosmopolitan ideas in a classical, as opposed to a theological, tradition. The Renaissance humanists frequently drew upon both Cicero and Seneca to reject the sectarian intolerance associated with religious conflicts.

1 Citizens of Christendom or of the world?

Cosmopolitanism within an emerging state system

The emerging cosmopolitanism in Europe at the beginning of the modern age articulated some of the key themes associated with world citizenship to this day: rejection of war and systematic cruelty, desire to make friends across frontiers and identification with people from other cultures and countries as fellow human beings. Cosmopolitanism also took the form of a number of proposals for creating international organizations to secure lasting peace. Emeric Crucé, author of such a proposal, wrote in 1625:

> How pleasant it would be to see men travel freely across frontiers and communicate with one another without any scruples whatsoever as to nation, ceremonies, or other such formalities, as if the earth were, as it is in truth, a common city for all.[1]

Since this is the period which saw the ideal of a common Christian community under the Papacy destroyed by bitter religious wars, there is at first sight a certain irony in focusing on cosmopolitan legacies. Moreover, a clearly demarcated system of states emerged during the sixteenth and seventeenth centuries: Jean Bodin, often credited with first articulating clearly the concept of state sovereignty, published *The Six Books of the Republic* in 1576. Nevertheless, the emergence of modern Europe, which encompassed the Protestant Reformation and the bloody conflicts between Protestants and Catholics, also saw the development of pleas for religious toleration (at least between Christians). Arguments for legal toleration were sometimes religious – that the purity of beliefs depended upon their being held sincerely. But the main impetus was often political: to avoid violence between adherents of different doctrines. Although there are a range of possible reasons for advocating toleration as a policy, an attitude of tolerance is essential to cosmopolitanism, which values the mingling of different peoples and the ability to live harmoniously together. Secondly, the Peace of Westphalia of 1648, usually seen as the decisive event in the consolidation of the state system in Europe, also ended the Thirty Years War and so symbolized an end to religious wars. It therefore became possible to think of states belonging to an international society of Europe based on a shared heritage, common customs and legal agreements. The tradition of international law, which is playing an increasingly important role in promoting human rights and transcending national frontiers today, has its origins in this period.

In the period 1500–1700 cosmopolitanism was usually understood primarily in terms of either Christendom or Europe. The European voyages of discovery and the Spanish conquest of South America created some knowledge of the wider world, but often encouraged belief in European superiority to strange or barbaric customs. Nevertheless, there was a growing awareness of complex and varied cultures beyond European borders, and the concept of world citizenship was used rhetorically. Political theorists like Montaigne explored the implications of cultural diversity, and the writers on international law discuss the implications of relations with the non-European world. While this discussion was shaped by the economic and military ambitions of various European states, the universalist logic of natural law theory qualified claims to national interest and European superiority, provided a critique of crude exploitation and suggested the significance of natural or human rights.

This chapter begins by looking at a number of thinkers who can be broadly classified as cosmopolitan in their sympathies, and who are seen as important forerunners by later advocates of world citizenship. At the time they were unusual because they not only resisted religious intolerance, but also stressed the evils of war. The first of these thinkers is Desiderius Erasmus, symbol of Renaissance humanist scholarship, cosmopolitanism and (near) pacifism, who can be conveniently contrasted with the best-known advocate of *realpolitik*, Niccolò Machiavelli. Erasmus, who advocated religious toleration, also stands in strong contrast to the militant Protestant reformer Martin Luther. Erasmus was a Christian humanist whose vision was focused on Europe. A generation later, Michel de Montaigne, who was an admirer of Erasmus and is also often seen as an advocate of cosmopolitanism and a forerunner of the Enlightenment, was much more aware of the world beyond Europe. Montaigne's thought drew on the heritage of classical Stoicism (although he was also influenced by Scepticism and Epicureanism); his friend Justus Lipsius, advocate of European unity whose name is invoked by the European Community today, is more closely associated with the revival of neo-Stoicism and its conflicting cosmopolitan and statist political connotations.

Cosmopolitanism stresses links between individuals, the moral irrelevance of political frontiers and the goal of peace. It seems, therefore, to be opposed to the evolving tradition of international law, which attempted to transcend pure *raison d'état*, but remained rooted in the realities of international politics. International law focused primarily on regulating relations between kingdoms, principalities and republics (the concept of 'states' did not emerge fully until after 1648) and on rules for conducting war rather than how to end wars. Nevertheless international law, especially in this period, did also entail some concern about the treatment of individuals, did not endorse the wholly unrestricted sovereignty of rulers in their own countries, and asserted general moral obligations. The primary focus here is on Hugo Grotius, educated in the humanist tradition, influenced by Stoicism, and widely admired in the eighteenth century for his moral and political thought, as well as for his role in developing international law. The Grotian enterprise was to formulate a moral theory based on universal principles of natural law to refute the Sceptics. Although Kant rejected the Grotian concept of international society when formulating his more ambitious moral and cosmopolitan vision, and dismissed Grotius and later international law theorists in *Perpetual Peace* as 'sorry comforters',[2] international law theory did embody in the seventeenth century, as it does again today, significant cosmopolitan principles.

Indeed, because today we are gradually moving out of a world of sovereign states towards new forms of overlapping jurisdiction, there are elements in early international law that speak to us more directly than they did to the Europe of the eighteenth and nineteenth centuries. For example, the early international lawyers argued for the rights of refugees, on the grounds that all human beings need a home somewhere. They also laid the basis for claims to override national frontiers where crimes against humanity are being committed. So Grotius may be invoked in the context of debates about humanitarian intervention.

Thinkers who did not believe international law was a sufficient bulwark against the devastation of war adopted a more utopian approach of trying to subordinate sovereign powers to an international body. This desire to embody cosmopolitan principles in international politics is reflected in the plan for perpetual peace devised during the Thirty Years War by Emeric Crucé, who hoped to unite the states of the world in a voluntary 'federation'. This idea was independently restated within a more limited European context at the very end of the seventeenth century by the Quaker William Penn. These proposals foreshadow the more famous late eighteenth-century plans for perpetual peace.

Christian humanism and cosmopolitanism: Erasmus

If we look back at Erasmus of Rotterdam (1467–1536) from the vantage point of today, then he can readily be seen as a precursor of the Enlightenment, a man whose life revealed his rejection of narrow loyalties and his commitment to a community of scholars. It is therefore appropriate that the European Community chose ERASMUS as an acronym for its scheme to promote student mobility in Europe.[3] The Foreword of a recent biography on Erasmus comments: 'In our own times his attractiveness still lies for many in his being a European, not a sectarian or a national figure. Since he belongs nowhere, he belongs everywhere.'[4]

Erasmus did see himself as cosmopolitan, though whether this cosmopolitanism really extended beyond Europe is ambiguous in his own writings. Certainly he did not in his own life identify himself primarily with his birthplace. Nor, despite his admiration for some leading English scholars and periods of fruitful residence in England, can he be appropriately identified with the English reformers.[5] He was not focused on English problems but was a European, living and feeling at home in many different parts of Europe. He attacked the use of national affiliations, 'very stupid labels', which promote division. In *Complaint of*

Peace he noted: 'The English despise the French, for no other reasons than that they are French, the Scots are disliked because they are Scots. ... Why as men are they not benevolent to man, as Christians well-disposed towards fellow Christians?'[6] Sometimes Erasmus identified himself as a citizen of a '*Respublica Christiana*', though opposed to any suggestion of a Christian Empire.[7] At others his self-identification extended beyond Europe. He asserted in a letter to Ulrich Zwingli, who had invited him to become a citizen of Zurich: 'My own wish is to be a citizen of the world, to be a fellow-citizen to all men – better still a pilgrim. If only I might have the happiness of being enrolled in the city of heaven.'[8]

Erasmus's cosmopolitanism is open to the interpretation that it is based on a rejection of social ties. Augustjin argues that the letter to Zwingli denotes not cosmopolitanism, but 'a sense of independence closely akin to solitariness'.[9] Erasmus's biography can indeed be seen as illustrating his failure to belong anywhere. After being enrolled in monastic life as a boy, later he got permission to live his preferred life as a secular scholar, and he chose to avoid permanent attachment to any institution, whether court or university.[10] But he was not a marginal intellectual. His learning attracted not only the universities but many of the princes of Europe. He did sometimes act as adviser to princes, although this role could be in tension with his pacifist tendencies and his dislike of absolute power. He suggests, for example, that rulers should not go to war without the consent of the people through their representatives.[11]

Erasmus's brand of cosmopolitanism can be seen as elitist. He was a leading member of the select group of scholars who drew on the classical Greek and Roman heritage and who communicated across national frontiers and institutional affiliations. The group identified themselves as humanists, denoting the claims of the revived classical literature to provide a true education for the creation of a whole man. The humanists also associated their illuminating form of knowledge with civic engagement and social improvement.[12] The role of Latin as a universal European language, in which the humanist scholars usually wrote, also allowed for ease of communication and encouraged a sense that they were transcending frontiers.

Christian humanism embraced a diversity of positions. But Erasmus did have a good deal in common with several prominent contemporaries – in particular the Spanish humanist Juan Vives, the English churchman John Colet, who became Dean of St Paul's, and Thomas More, who became Chancellor to King Henry VIII.[13] More and Erasmus in particular were close friends and they combined to defend humanist argument and scholarship against its critics.[14] This group tended to share a belief in religious toleration and voice anti-war sentiments. But More abandoned his earlier support of religious toleration when Luther's conflict with the Catholic Church threatened both religious and political disorder, and he defended the burning of heretical books and even of Protestant heretics themselves.[15] More's anti-war sentiments are difficult to deduce from his most famous work, *Utopia* (1516), which has given rise to conflicting interpretations, but it is probable that he agreed with Erasmus in rejecting classical and feudal attitudes to martial glory and codes of honour. As a state official he promoted a military alliance between England and France in 1525, even though he probably favoured English neutrality.[16] Colet, on the other hand, preached more than once against war, including a sermon in 1513 in the king's presence on the moral dangers of war, which appeared to be a direct criticism of Henry's preparations for an imminent invasion of France.[17]

Erasmus argued strongly for both tolerance and peace. Indeed, his intellectual commitments kept him from taking sides in the major religious debates of his time. As a Christian who sought to revive the original meaning and spirit of the gospels, he was strongly critical of many practices of the Catholic Church; but when Luther in 1517 nailed up at Wittenburg his famous 95 theses challenging that Church, Erasmus declined to go the whole way and ally himself with the new Protestant reformers, remaining resolutely neutral. He did, however, deplore the outlawing of Luther in 1521 by the Edict of Worms and commented: 'The burning of his books will perhaps banish Luther from our libraries; whether he can be plucked out of men's hearts I am not so sure.'[18] As a result of his neutrality both sides attacked him: the Catholic Church put his writings on the Index of banned books, and Luther reproached him for his lack of zeal and commitment. But this very refusal to take sides enabled Erasmus to maintain a stance of religious toleration within Christianity.

Erasmus's hatred of war is expressed in varying literary styles in many of his writings, including the well-known *In Praise of Folly* (1517). But there are a number of texts in which he deplores the stupidity, brutality and wastefulness of war with directness and passion. His 1513 letter to Anthony Bergis comments on England's preparations for a continental war, wondering what 'can impel, I do not say Christians, but human creatures to such an extremity of madness and folly'.[19] The *Adages*, which first appeared in 1515, included a disquisition on 'War Seems Sweet to Those Ignorant of It' and attacked waging war on the Turks in the name of Christendom. *The Education of a Christian Prince* (1516) urges princes to go to arbitration over disputes and almost totally repudiates the possibility of a just cause for going to war. His best-known plea for peace, *Complaint of Peace*, was published in 1517 at the time of negotiations between England, France, Spain and the Holy Roman Empire on the future of Europe. In this work Peace speaks in her own person. Seven years later he commented sadly that he should write an epitaph for Peace.[20]

Erasmus was not, however, a totally consistent pacifist. In a letter known as *A Most Practical Deliberation About Waging War With the Turks*, written in 1530, he argues that Christians are clearly permitted to go to war and notes that Christians may legitimately wage war on the Turks, if they are deaf to appeals for peace and threatening Christendom. He therefore seems here to repudiate his anti-war stance. The literary devices employed in his anti-war rhetoric do indeed leave room for the reader to doubt whether they necessarily reflect his full position.[21] It has also been argued he moved towards support for just war theory.[22] But he does seem to have been close to pacifism in most of his writings – Grotius, when developing arguments for a just war, sees himself as explicitly refuting the pacifism of Erasmus.

Erasmus looked back to Plato and Seneca when discussing the possibility of restraint in the waging of war, and compares the classical period favourably with Christian practices in his own time, but one of his central arguments was that war was incompatible with true Christianity.[23] His views on war are linked to his repudiation of that strand of Renaissance humanism that, through its reliance on classical pagan sources, endorsed pure secularism – Machiavelli is the best-known example.[24] Erasmus's *The Education of a Christian Prince* (1516) addressed to Charles of Austria is exactly the kind of moral and Christian advice to princes that Machiavelli is subverting in *The Prince*.[25] Despite the tendency of much of this kind of literature to draw on classical sources, in particular Cicero's discussion of morality, *On Duties*, and Seneca's *On Clemency*, Erasmus here gives weight to Christian as well as classical wisdom.[26] Indeed Erasmus in this context explicitly rejected the heroes often used as exemplars for princes: 'When you hear of Achilles, Xerxes, Cyrus, Darius or Julius, do not be overwhelmed at all by the prestige of their names; you are hearing about great raging bandits.'[27] Erasmus and Machiavelli are therefore totally opposed in their assessment of the qualities required in rulers and in their reactions to war. Where Machiavelli admired the boldness of Pope Julius II in war, Erasmus detested his military conquests, and wrote a poem that compared Julius to the tyrant Julius Caesar.[28] Erasmus, therefore, stood for a brand of specifically Christian and pacific humanism. But, given his tolerance and cosmopolitanism, it is not surprising that the secularizing thinkers of the Enlightenment looked to him for inspiration.

Cosmopolitanism and neo-Stoicism: Montaigne and Lipsius

Montaigne (1533–92) was also claimed as an early *philosophe* during the Enlightenment.[29] He drew on different strands within classical thought – Stoicism, Scepticism and Epicureanism – that can be seen as reflecting either different stages of his thought or different facets of it. His own religious views are open to conflicting interpretations, as are his politics. He has, as Richard Sayce notes, been interpreted as both pious Catholic and atheist, monarchist and republican, conservative and liberal.[30] What is relevant here is the tolerance that Montaigne displays, in contrast to a tendency to fanaticism among many of his contemporaries in France at the time of the civil wars between Catholics and Huguenots. Quentin Skinner, who argues that Montaigne's Stoicism leads to a conservative emphasis on obedience to existing authorities, also notes the breadth of Montaigne's tolerance.[31] Sayce, who points to evidence of Montaigne's social and political conservatism, in the sense of opposing destabilizing change, elaborates as well on the evidence of his liberalism and cosmopolitanism.

There is a good case that Montaigne anticipated the Enlightenment sense of a common humanity transcending diversity of religion and custom, and the Enlightenment reaction against unnecessary cruelties. He attacked burning of witches and the use of torture, and claimed that the contemporary practice of slowly roasting a man to death 'under the cloak of piety and religion' was more barbarous than Brazilian cannibals, who 'roast and eat a man after he is dead'.[32] Montaigne shared with Erasmus a love of classical learning, and a hatred of war and harsh punishments. Montaigne too was widely travelled in Europe, seeking to adopt the customs of the country, although he spent most of his life in his native Bordeaux.

He travelled in his mind much more widely, anticipating the Enlightenment fascination with non-European civilizations. Nor did Montaigne assume European superiority; he commented on the positive warrior qualities of the Ottoman Turks, and on how the scientific, artistic and political achievements of Chinese civilization compared favourably with Europe. When dealing with less complex cultures, for example the native Americans, Montaigne enters imaginatively into their reactions to the first sight of Europeans and deplores their betrayal by European conquerors. Sayce finds in Montaigne a sense of the equality of mankind, even the superiority of unspoiled natural man as found in America to the 'Christian and "civilised" nations of Europe'.[33] Donald Frame agrees that Montaigne recognizes cultural pluralism and uses imaginative empathy to understand the values of others.[34]

Consonant with his sympathy for Stoicism, Montaigne also explicitly rejected claims to national or parochial superiority: 'I judge all men my compatriots and embrace a Pole as I would a Frenchman.'[35] He claims that this cosmopolitanism reflects his natural temperament, but he was of course aware of voicing a sentiment shared by contemporary writers seeking to combine Stoic and humanist ideas with Christianity.

Lipsius (1547–1606), who experienced the trauma of the civil war between Catholics and Calvinists in the Netherlands, deplored religious fanaticism and argued for religious compromise in the interests of political peace. This did not take the form of espousing official tolerance for a variety of Churches. Lipsius was prepared to argue for imposing uniformity in public religious observance (whilst claiming freedom for private religious beliefs and practices). This view can be related, as Richard Tuck argues, to a Stoic ethic of self discipline and cultivation of appropriate emotions.

The strand of Stoicism that both Montaigne and Lipsius found congenial was one that stressed that the wise individual should seek detachment from the passions and the affairs of the world. They did not look to Cicero, who maintained an emphasis on sacrificing the individual for the good of the republic, but took Seneca as their primary reference point. Lipsius wrote a dialogue on 'constancy', a virtue mentioned by Seneca but not Cicero, urging detachment from current conflicts. This detachment was linked to abandoning forms of passionate identification with a particular group and set of beliefs.[36]

Lipsius, therefore, also shared with Montaigne a belief in Stoic cosmopolitanism, and had one of his characters in the dialogue *On Constancy* (1594) attack the kind of patriotism that appealed to sentiments of reverence for one's motherland, when such sentiments are only appropriate towards real parents and towards God. In this dialogue the same character also claims: 'The whole world is our countrey, wheresoeuer is the race of mankind sprong of that celestial seed. *Socrates* being asked of what countrey he was, answered: *Of the world.*[37] (The reference to Socrates and the image of the celestial seed as the basis of the natural unity of mankind are taken from Epictetus.[38])

Montaigne and Lipsius expressed great admiration and sympathy for each other. Montaigne called Lipsius 'the most sufficient and learned man now living; of a most polished and judicious wit', and Lipsius said of Montaigne 'I have found no one in Europe whose way of thinking about things is closer to my own'.[39] Montaigne had a greater imaginative empathy with other human beings – he was therefore arguably more tolerant than Lipsius.[40] But Lipsius had a clearer vision of an ideal of European unity. In a study of the Roman Empire he drew the moral that Europe was 'racked by constant wars and rebellions' because it was divided into small and competing kingdoms. Instead he urged a new Europe united under one ruler to promote religious and political unity against the threat from the Ottoman Empire. Both Montaigne and Lipsius agreed that civil war was the greatest possible disaster and therefore opposed religious rebellion – Montaigne lamenting the war 'tearing France to pieces and dividing us into factions'.[41] Once it had broken out, restoring peace was a priority; Lipsius strongly urged that the war in the Netherlands should be ended by a negotiated peace, and that even a temporary truce created time for people to move towards agreement.[42]

Both Montaigne and Lipsius are usually taken to illustrate some of the ambiguities of neo-Stoicism. On the one hand, they espouse the cosmopolitan ideal based on belief in universal moral principles associated with classical Stoicism; on the other, they seem to uphold arguments that endorse 'reason of state', subordinating principles of justice to the need for ensuring internal stability. If they did opt for a pure Machiavellianism in their specific political proposals, this would be very difficult to square with a world view that was later to find expression in Kant. One response is to question their Stoicism and point to the element of Scepticism in their thought. A Scepticism about the existence of universal moral principles and emphasis on pursuit of self-interest as the root of human action clearly can provide a justification for pursuit of self-interest by states without regard for the claims of morality. The other response, which preserves their broad commitment to cosmopolitan ideas, is to question how much they agreed with Machiavelli. For example, Robert Collins has contested the view that Montaigne supported 'reason of state', though he may have been understood by his contemporaries as doing so.[43] Tuck argues that Lipsius developed a more limited doctrine than that of Machiavelli, justifying immoral or illegal action by rulers for the sake of preserving the state, but not for the sake of enhancing its glory and greatness, thereby retaining the distinction between a legitimate ruler and a tyrant.[44]

Whether or not Montaigne and Lipsius were wholly consistent in resolving the tensions between immediate political exigencies and a moral ideal, they do both illustrate the attractiveness of cosmopolitanism in a time of religious and political conflicts.

The law of nations as an expression of world society

Civil wars largely preoccupied Montaigne and Lipsius. But in a period when states were establishing their sovereignty, combining state interest and universal moral principles in politics between states proved to be the central problem, and one that still is a starting point for writers on international politics. One key issue is how far sovereignty should be seen as sacrosanct and how far cosmopolitan values should influence law and practice. The school of international lawyers who drew on earlier concepts of natural law attempted to find a middle way in addressing these issues. The figure we will concentrate on is Hugo Grotius, but first we should note his predecessors.

Three authors are often given particular credit for developing international law before Grotius. Two were Spanish Catholics – the Dominican Francisco de Vitoria (1485–1546) and the Jesuit Francisco Suárez (1548–1617) – and the third was the Italian Protestant who became Professor of Civil Law at Oxford, Alberico Gentili (1552–1608).[45] Both the Catholic theorists were engaged in the revival of the doctrines of Saint Thomas Aquinas and exposition of the significance of natural law. Suárez in *De Legibus ac Deo Legislatore*, published in 1619, argued that although a sovereign state constituted a 'perfect community in itself', each state is a member of a universal society based on the moral unity of the human race. The law of nations (*jus gentium*) was necessary to define how sovereign states should relate to one another.[46] Gentili developed the concept of the common interests of mankind to argue that it provided a justification for going to war: 'Look you, if men clearly sin against the laws of nature and of mankind, I believe that any one whatsoever may check such men by force of arms.'[47] He extended this claim to argue that sovereigns were subject to law, and that their subjects were entitled to protection as part of world society, thereby providing a justification for intervention in another state, provided the aim was to save subjects 'from immoderate cruelty and unmerciful punishment'. He therefore provided a justification for what we now call 'humanitarian intervention' as opposed to upholding strict respect for state sovereignty.[48]

Grotius acknowledged his debt to Gentili in the *Prolegomena* to *The Law of War and Peace* (1625) – though it has been argued that his debt was much greater than he acknowledged – and clearly drew on the work of Vitoria and Suárez. But by convention Grotius is usually regarded as the most influential figure and therefore his views are taken here as the basis for exploring cosmopolitan elements in international law.

Grotius (1583–1645) was born in Delft, as the Netherlands was becoming independent of Spain, and educated as a humanist classical scholar – his father had been a student of Lipsius. He was active in the politics of the province of Holland and in his early writings promoted a theory of republicanism, though in his better known work on international law he upheld the rights of sovereign monarchs and denied a right of rebellion to recover political freedom. He also had to confront the religious questions posed by divisions between Catholics and Protestants and divisions within Dutch Calvinism. Grotius tended to stress the common ethical basis of Christianity underlying doctrinal disputes and to urge tolerance of the practice of a variety of religious beliefs, and tolerance of disagreements within Calvinism itself.[49] But he did set limits to religious tolerance: in *The Law of War and Peace* he suggests that those denying the existence of a divinity concerned with human affairs 'may be restrained in the name of human society, to which they do violence without a defensible reason'.[50] This is linked to his belief in the role of religion in underpinning morality.

Grotius was deeply concerned with promoting peace within the state and preventing unnecessary and brutal wars between Christian states – this is scarcely surprising during the Thirty Years wars of religion. An eloquent passage in the *Prolegomena* to *The Law of War and Peace* seems to echo Erasmus: 'Throughout the Christian world I observed a lack of restraint in relation to war, such as even barbarous races should be ashamed of.' But he rejects the other extreme of 'forbidding all use of arms to the Christian'.[51] Unlike Lipsius, he did not look towards a united Europe to promote peace, being sceptical about the role of empires. As a Protestant he rejected aspirations of the kind voiced by Campanella to achieve European unity under Papal influence. His own solution is to resurrect and reinterpret the Roman and Catholic tradition of just war.

Grotius's interpretation of international law, focused primarily on his monumental analysis of the conditions of a just war, can be seen as an attempt to maintain cosmopolitan principles whilst giving due weight to the significance of the developing division of Europe into sovereign states. Whereas Erasmus tends to assume that the character and decisions of individual sovereign princes can directly impact on the condition of Europe, Grotius is inclined to define sovereignty as territorial, and to take account of a logic of conflicting interests between states.[52] So although Grotius wrote before the 1648 Treaty of Westphalia, he can be interpreted as providing a framework for the new European order and later international law premised on state sovereignty.

On the other hand, Grotius stops short of an absolute emphasis on the inviolability of territorial sovereignty; he also insists that all individuals are members of a world society and therefore upholds the right to intervene within states if the law of nature is being 'excessively' violated. He has therefore been a reference point for international lawyers in the 1920s writing in the context of the League of Nations and again in the 1990s when the wars in the former Yugoslavia made humanitarian intervention a key issue. He also suggests that when a ruler inflicts upon 'his subjects such treatment as no one is warranted in inflicting', the right of intervention is 'vested in human society' as a whole, although he recognized the danger of states using this right as a smoke-screen for pursuing their own interests.[53] Grotius here endorses the strong case for intervention adopted by Gentili, who upheld the principle of defending subjects of a ruler who have been 'treated cruelly and unjustly'. Gentili appealed to the authority of Seneca that 'the duty which I owe to the human race is prior and superior to that which I owe' to a sovereign who oppresses his own subjects.[54]

Because Grotius is poised between recognition of the political implications of the state system and a sense of a united humanity – his view of international society has been described as an intermediate position between Hobbesian realism and Kantian cosmopolitanism – there is scope to interpret his thought in either a realist or a cosmopolitan direction.[55] Indeed it is ambiguous whether the concept of international society denotes purely a society of states with certain common interests and obligations, or whether it suggests also a society embracing all the individuals in the world. Grotius clearly seems to be arguing for the latter view, both in his language and in his case for intervention to protect subjects against their sovereigns. The primary reason for ascribing to Grotius a significant degree of cosmopolitanism – his sense of a united humanity – has already been noted. This sentiment is given greater weight by his interpretation of natural law and by his explicit view that international law applies outside Europe in relations with peoples of other religions.

How Grotius understood natural law changed between his first work in international law, *The Law of Prize*, published posthumously in 1868, and *The Law of War and Peace*, published in 1625.[56] We will focus here on his later and more influential interpretation. Grotius sets out his theory of law in the *Prolegomena* to *The Law of War and Peace*. Unlike some of the Roman jurists, Grotius distinguishes clearly between the law of nature, which can be 'deduced from certain principles by a sure process of reasoning', and 'the law of nations', based on 'common consent' as evidenced by a core of agreement across different periods and varied cultures, and therefore based in 'the free will of man'. Both are distinct from law promulgated within particular states.[57]

Grotius, in defending the existence of natural law, which can be universally recognized and will have universal application, has to rebut the arguments of the contemporary Sceptics, an exercise that he undertakes by rebutting Carneades, the well-known classical Sceptic. Grotius appeals to the natural sociability of mankind, citing the Stoics, and the specifically human attributes of speech and the faculty of knowing and acting in accordance with general principles. 'This maintenance of the social order ... which is consonant with human intelligence, is the source of law properly so called.' Grotius then deduces some minimal precepts, such as abstaining from taking what belongs to others, making good a loss 'incurred through our fault' and the obligation to keep promises.[58]

Grotius then has to confront the question (inescapable at the time he wrote) of the relationship between the law of nature and the law stemming from the will of God. At this point he committed himself to a famous and much debated statement: that claims about the law of nature 'would have a degree of validity even if we should concede ... that there is no God, or that the affairs of men are of no concern to him'. This sentence has been used to suggest Grotius initiated a purely secular view of natural law. In a simple sense this is clearly wrong – similar statements that natural law does not depend on God's will can be traced to earlier Catholic philosophers who are summarized by neo-Thomists like Suárez.[59] Moreover, Grotius himself immediately notes that God, as creator of the universe, has implanted 'the essential traits' in human nature from which natural law derives. Nevertheless Grotius's statement was significant because, as D'Entreves observes, it challenged the view that will is the sole source of law, a doctrine being restated in his time both by Protestant theologians and by theorists of sovereignty.[60] He also associated the developing tradition of international law with a non-theological and hence a genuinely universal claim.

It is this genuine universality which also underlines Grotius's cosmopolitan outlook. In his early work on *The Law of Prize* Grotius upheld the right of the East Indies to trade freely with all nations at a time when the Portuguese were trying to enforce a trade monopoly in the area. This was certainly not a totally disinterested position, since the Dutch were trying to break the Portuguese monopoly for their own commercial purposes and had used force by seizing a Portuguese ship to make the point. Moreover asserting a universal right to trade can be seen as part of the history of western colonial expansion.[61] Nevertheless, Grotius did imply a two-way freedom for inhabitants of the Indies as well as for the Dutch. Grotius also here established a general claim to freedom of the seas held by mankind in common, a concept developed in late twentieth-century international law, when the 'common heritage of humankind' was a guiding concept in agreements on outer space, Antarctica and in the Law of the Sea.[62]

Grotius also discussed in *The Law of War and Peace* whether, at a time when the Spanish had imposed colonial rule in South America, in the name of converting the heathens to Christianity, various imperial practices could be justified. Although in favour of attempts to convert members of other faiths to Christianity peaceably, he argued that 'War cannot justly be waged against those who refuse to accept the Christian religion.'[63] He also followed Vitoria in arguing that discovery of a land by Europeans did not confer a title to ownership, upholding the validity of the property rights of the original inhabitants. This refusal to subscribe to the doctrine of *terra nullius*, which justified colonial occupation of 'empty' territory, has direct resonance for aboriginal claims to their land since the 1990s in courts in Australia. Moreover, Grotius had a genuine interest in indigenous peoples, and engaged in a number of studies on indigenous Americans.[64]

Another element of universality in Grotius's thought is his willingness to use a diversity of sources from a variety of cultures, and his condemnation of the tendency of the powerful to identify their own beliefs with the law of nature. Like other humanists, he drew freely on classical pagan sources, with an emphasis on Stoic thinkers. For example, he uses Marcus Aurelius when refuting Carneades and Chrysippus to uphold the view that the law of nature is divine in origin. (Unlike some of the other humanists, he draws indiscriminatingly on Plato and Aristotle as well as the Stoics, on Cicero as well as Seneca.) More surprisingly, he also drew examples from the non-European world, including Muslim practices and the cultures of South America.[65] Whilst Grotius has been criticized for failure to distinguish the important from the secondary in the range of sources and examples, his method indicates not only eclecticism but a desire to transcend his own culture in establishing the bases of international law.

Grotius was committed to a universalist view of the world and the applicability of natural and international law. For example, he claimed in *The Law of Prize* that 'the contention that one must have regard for one's fellow citizens, but not foreigners, is assuredly equivalent to repudiation of the universal bond of human fellowship, a bond which one cannot repudiate without being judged impious toward God Himself'.[66] But he did distinguish between the Christian and non-Christian world; the former united by their common obligation to divine law and the latter only through natural law, and suggested that 'we should be doers of good to all, but particularly to those who share the same religion'.[67]

He also gave weight to the claims of the state and the normal obligation of subjects to obey their sovereign. There is not a right of rebellion and active resistance can only be justified in the same kind of circumstances which justify other states intervening. But individual obligation to obey both natural law and God's commands, expressed through individual conscience, does entitle him to refuse to fight in an unjust war, not only if the cause is clearly unjust, but even where there is room for doubt, because 'disobedience in such cases is a lesser evil than slaughter of the innocent'.[68]

Whilst the state had primary responsibility for its own subjects, Grotius upheld the international obligation to offer asylum to refugees: a 'fixed abode ought not to be refused to Strangers, who being expelled their own Country seek a retreat elsewhere Provided they submit to the Laws of the State'. He even suggested waste land might be assigned to them. But there was a proviso: that the refugees had suffered undeservedly and had not acted injuriously 'to any particular Men, or to *human Society in general*'.[69]

The cosmopolitan elements in Grotius's thought do not extend to upholding the equality of human beings in social practice. In his early writings on international law he was prepared to endorse Aristotle's view that some men are slaves by nature. Although he repudiated this theory in *The Law of War and Peace*, he was still willing to argue as though slavery was justified.[70] He also accepted that the law of nations recognized that captives should become slaves, although the minimal ethics embodied in a universal law of nations could be transcended by agreements among particular religions or cultures – Christians had renounced taking captives into slavery in wars among themselves, as had Muslims.[71]

Grotius's main contribution to reducing the harm inflicted on human society by frequent and brutal wars was to elucidate what counted as just causes and to comment on limiting the actual conduct of warfare, but he did recognize the possible role of international conferences to resolve conflicts and the case for arbitration.[72] Although he did not envisage any form of international organization, his brief discussion of conferences between states was used by the Abbé de Saint-Pierre to introduce his own scheme for an international federation of states to promote peace (discussed below). It is to this strand of thought that sought peace and the realization of cosmopolitanism through a union of states that we now briefly turn.

International federation and peace

Schemes for European unity can be traced back to the Middle Ages. Dante's *On Monarchy*, written in about 1310, but not printed until the sixteenth century, is the best known. Dante sought to revive the Roman Empire and to link this new monarchy to the spiritual authority of the Papacy, which was to renounce its temporal power. Plans for unifying Europe politically were quite frequently aired in the sixteenth and seventeenth centuries, both by advisers to rulers and by individual idealists. Many of these plans had an element of *realpolitik*, designed in a way to give particular power and leverage to a particular country. Many also failed to embody a truly cosmopolitan outlook even in principle because their main purpose was to unite Christendom to wage war against the Turks. So the goal of peace within Europe was linked to destroying the threat from the Ottoman Empire and expanding European control. Erasmus, in criticizing plans for a war on the Turks, also commented: 'Most of us dread the name of World Empire, a title at which others seem to be aiming.' He suggested the danger of oppressive rule in an empire and that 'there is more safety in kingdoms of moderate power united in a Christian League'.[73]

A proposal for political unity that was genuinely cosmopolitan and based on a desire for a genuine and perpetual peace was put forward by the Frenchman Emeric Crucé (1590–1648) in his 1623 pamphlet *The New Cyneas*. The most radical aspect of his plan was that he looked beyond Europe and aimed to incorporate Turkey in his proposed association, and also Persia, China, Ethiopia and the East and West Indies.[74] All would send ambassadors to an assembly where decisions would be made by majority vote. His language reflects his cosmopolitanism, appealing to 'the basic similarity in men's nature, which is the foundation of true friendship and human society. Why should I, a Frenchman, wish to harm an Englishman, a Spaniard or an Indian?'[75] Crucé also emphasized the positive advantages of peace: an extension of religious toleration, greater freedom of travel, freedom of trade and reduction of poverty.[76]

Crucé set a precedent for a number of proposals for states to unite in a federation or confederation to promote peace: William Penn's *Essay Towards the Present and Future Peace of Europe* (1693), John Bellers' *Some Reasons for an European State* (1710) and the Abbé de Saint-Pierre's *Perpetual Peace* (1712). None of these plans was as ambitious as Crucé in trying to create a worldwide organization, and the first two still tend to link European unity to creating a bulwark against Turkish aggression – though not to a crusading zeal to roll back the frontiers of the Ottoman Empire.

Penn proposed all members of the League should be represented at an 'imperial parliament' to meet annually, to adjudicate on disputes between states that cannot be settled by other diplomatic means, and if necessary to enforce its decisions through combined force of arms. He suggests also weighted voting based on an assessment of the economic revenue of the member states. He hesitates whether to extend the membership of this European body to Russia and the Turks – qualifying an assessment of their voting power by the phrase 'if the Turks and Muscovites are taken in, which seems but fit and just'.[77] But he also notes that a possible advantage of such a league is the 'great security it will be to Christians against the inroads of the Turk', which seems to imply exclusion of the Ottoman Empire.[78] Bellers even more explicitly envisaged his league incorporating the recognized states of Europe (which did not yet include Russia) as a means of defence against the Turks.

The Abbé de Saint-Pierre's plan, on the other hand, included Russia in its various versions, and in its first edition also included the Turks. But as F.H. Hinsley notes in *Power and the Pursuit of Peace*, the focus of all three of these projects was on a distinctively European union as a culturally and politically more realistic goal than a world body.[79] Saint-Pierre did, however, envisage the possibility of an Asian federation also seeking peace, so it was not a vision hostile to the wider world. There are parallels with arguments today that the European Union can be seen as a potential exemplar of regional cooperation and internationalism, rather than as an extension of European power in the world and protection of European interests at the expense of other regions.

Conflicting legacies

The period 1500 to 1700 is a time of transition between a medieval society of overlapping jurisdictions, unified by religion and culture, and the emerging Europe of territorial sovereignty based on centralized state power. Erasmus, and to some extent even Grotius, still partially reflected this earlier world, normally writing in the universal language of Latin. But by the seventeenth century there was an emerging sense of national identity and an increasing tendency for scholars to write in their native tongue. Grotius invoked moral obligations towards individuals in the sphere of international politics, but looks forward as well to the eighteenth-century European world of sovereign states, pursuing state interest but maintaining a degree of cooperation and a core of common beliefs.

So it is possible to argue that there were two separate legacies from this period, which both became more clearly defined in the Enlightenment. The first was a legacy of international society between states, which engaged in quite frequent – if limited – wars of dynastic and territorial ambition, but moderated their behaviour in accordance with the customs and positive agreements that constituted international law between states, including some awareness of just war limits on acceptable methods of warfare. The second legacy was a peace-oriented cosmopolitanism, stressing links between individuals and moral obligations to all humanity. Hatred of war and a search for perpetual peace became a central theme in the Enlightenment. Some of the theorists mentioned in this chapter published their plans for peace at the beginning of the eighteenth century, and they provided a starting point for the most sophisticated and well-known proposal for perpetual peace, by Kant, published at the end of the century, in 1795.

Within the cosmopolitan legacy it is also possible to trace a gradual evolution from a predominantly European and Christian perspective to a view of the world which is more genuinely universal, and also more secular. This trend was of course to be fully developed in the Enlightenment. The humanist thinkers and exponents of international law both provided arguments for freedom to travel, freedom to trade and a sense that 'mankind' shares the earth in common, which were also dominant themes in the eighteenth century and have resonance today.

Contributions to cosmopolitan thought in the period before 1700 also reflected some of the ambiguities of universalist political and legal theories that present-day postcolonial and postmodern critics still detect in western liberalism. On the one hand, a plausible case can often be made that universal principles serve as a justification for pursuit of very specific western interests, as in calls for freedom of the seas, freedom of travel and trade. On the other, cosmopolitan aspirations by humanist thinkers often do attempt to transcend not only political but also cultural borders. This tension also becomes more explicit in the Enlightenment with the fact of growing European power over many parts of the world, and at the same time a growing awareness of other cultures and some concern about the abuses arising from various forms of colonialism and European settlement.

2 Enlightenment cosmopolitanism and world citizenship

The eighteenth century in Europe still influences our thinking about international politics, and provides the basis for three opposing models: international anarchy, international society and cosmopolitanism. This period saw the consolidation of a state system resulting in anarchy between sovereign states with naturally conflicting interests, but an anarchy tempered by a degree of order based on the pursuit of the balance of power, a model central to realist theory in international relations. It also saw the evolution of what can be understood as an international society between states, based on diplomatic conventions and common attitudes. International law in this period reflected this new order. The most important eighteenth-century theorist of international law, Emerich Vattel, moved away from the elements of cosmopolitanism in Grotian thought to stress the sovereign integrity of states and not the rights of individuals, and to promote correct diplomatic procedures and restraints on the conduct of war, rather than focus on the just causes of war. Vattel's approach to international law remained predominant until the twentieth century. The model of international society allows for cooperation as well as conflict between states and gives some weight to shared values, but with its emphasis on state sovereignty it is opposed to the more utopian aspirations of cosmopolitanism. But, despite the nature of the state system, a cosmopolitan emphasis on links between individuals across frontiers, the rights of all human beings, and the goal of world peace are also a significant feature of this period.

The Enlightenment remains a central inspiration for the idea of world citizenship and for cosmopolitan thought. The *philosophes* gave prominence to the Stoic concept of 'citizen of the world' and many viewed the Stoics with admiration. Charles-Louis Montesquieu, for example, commented: 'Never were any principles more worthy of human nature, and more proper to form the good man, than those of the Stoics.'[1] The Enlightenment thinkers are also associated with an assertion of belief in human equality and liberty, rejection of all forms of sectarianism and bigotry, and a sense of common bonds across national frontiers. Some of them specifically looked towards a possible world without war; all of them attacked cruelty and justifications for violence and oppression. They also tended to see the development of free trade across frontiers as a means of promoting peace and an exercise of world citizenship, though some were also sensitive to the ways in which trade, especially in the non-European world, could lead to exploitation. Today's debates about the problematic relationship between a global market and cosmopolitan goals were therefore prefigured in the Enlightenment.

Contemporary theorists responding to both globalization and nationalist xenophobia, have looked back for inspiration to the eighteenth century. Immanuel Kant is most frequently cited by today's cosmopolitans, because he has not only had a crucial impact on moral and political philosophy, but also had some influence on international relations theory, especially on issues of war and peace. Montesquieu too is often quoted for his cosmopolitan commitments. He is the inspiration for Julia Kristeva, looking for an alternative to racist and inward-looking tendencies in French nationalism.[2] He also figures, though less prominently than Kant, in international relations debates about the role of commerce and of liberal institutions within states in influencing less warlike foreign policies.[3] Tom Paine's advocacy of the rights of man and world citizenship has inspired John Keane, looking at the possibility of new forms of European citizenship transcending the fratricidal nationalisms of Eastern Europe.[4]

But there are many other significant intellectuals in this period who can be seen as cosmopolitan thinkers. In France, the centre of the Enlightenment, the essayist and satirist François-Marie Voltaire and the man of letters Denis Diderot are especially important; as are in America the political figures Benjamin Franklin and Thomas Jefferson. Thomas J. Schlereth in his study of cosmopolitanism in this period focuses primarily on the Scottish philosopher David Hume (together with Voltaire and Franklin).[5] The German dramatist Gotthold Lessing is often seen as promoting cosmopolitanism and religious tolerance, particularly in his best-known play *Nathan the Wise*, published in 1779. Adam Smith's major contribution to cosmopolitan thought was his economic theory arguing the benefits of free markets – commerce was widely believed to promote world peace. Jeremy Bentham devoted his reforming zeal linked to his utilitarian philosophy primarily towards English institutions, but extended his interests to international law and plans for perpetual peace. He was widely admired in Spain and Spanish-speaking countries in Central and South America, and his ideas strongly influenced nineteenth-century peace movements in the English-speaking world.

The major eighteenth-century political theorist who does not fit well into the cosmopolitan mode is Jean-Jacques Rousseau, who was opposed to many of the tenets of the *philosophes*, and can be presented quite convincingly as a lyrical exponent of patriotism who despised cosmopolitanism. Rousseau is, however, notorious for exploring apparently conflicting strands of thought; and he was also eloquent on the unnecessary barbarities of war, as the *Discourse on the Origin of Inequality* (1755) and the *Discourse on Political Economy* (1758) indicate, and shared the Enlightenment hatred of political oppression. But when Rousseau is taken as a model for political theory today it tends to be in order to support national citizenship against concepts of world citizenship (as we will see in Chapter 7).

Rousseau is usually seen as an important theorist in the republican tradition of political thought, which upheld citizen self-government against forms of monarchy and despotism. But in general the late eighteenth-century theorists who can be labelled republican, notably Paine and the Jacobins in their earlier speeches and writings, were explicitly cosmopolitan. The enlightenment cosmopolitan legacy was by the nineteenth century, however, embodied primarily in liberalism. Republican ideas were taken up by socialist movements.

There are of course potential pitfalls in referring back to the Enlightenment theorists to find a set of cosmopolitan ideas underlying today's cosmopolitan claims. Enlightenment rationalism and universalism are the central target of postmodern and postcolonial critiques that suggest that, far from promoting human liberation, they have legitimized forms of oppression. Even the humanitarianism of the Enlightenment is seen as suspect when viewed from the perspective of Foucault, who has explored how the end of cruel physical punishments coincided with new forms of social regimentation symbolized by Bentham's 'panopticon' prison, and how rationality implied the segregation and disciplining of those defined as 'mad'.[6] These issues are taken up in a later chapter discussing challenges to universalism and cosmopolitanism, but some of the tensions between universalism and cultural particularity, or between belief in rational European-style progress and admiration for quite different traditional styles of life, do already surface in the eighteenth century. Montesquieu's writings provide evidence of these tensions.

But there are more traditional problems in generalizing about a body of historical thought, for example the fact that there are major disagreements in interpretations of the Enlightenment.[7] In trying to identify central Enlightenment ideas it is important to note the oversimplifications involved in pulling ideas out of a body of thought. It is also important to note that the *philosophes* were not all in agreement on many issues, and that there was an evolution towards a greater radicalism. Peter Gay identifies three generations: Montesquieu and Voltaire, who set the agenda; Franklin, Hume, Diderot, Helvetius and others, who consolidated a scientific and anti-clerical perspective; and Holbach, Beccaria, Lessing, Jefferson and Kant, who were more engaged in issues of political economy, legal reform and practical politics.[8]

Moreover, individual thinkers could display prejudices that appeared to contradict their commitment to human equality and other cosmopolitan ideals. Voltaire's belief in tolerance, for example, is undermined by his sometimes vehemently anti-Jewish remarks – a contemporary Portuguese Jew, Isaac Pinto, an admirer of Voltaire, wrote to him to protest. Kant, despite his principled rejection of European colonialism in *Perpetual Peace* (1795), has been accused of being the author of crude national stereotypes and characterization of races in his anthropology.[9] Jefferson, author of the 1776 American declaration of rights, and Franklin, the campaigner against slavery, were both slave owners.[10] Less surprisingly, the advocates of universal rights were not so certain about the rights of women. Although many of the *philosophes* supported the higher education of women, Diderot and Kant specifically denied women intellectual and social equality.

The approach used in this chapter is to examine the key concepts and beliefs central to the Enlightenment that have a bearing on cosmopolitanism and world citizenship. It is not necessary that all the theorists linked to the Enlightenment agree on these issues, nor does it matter if there is some ambiguity or contradiction within the position of an individual theorist. Our search here is for the evolution of key approaches to world citizenship that have influenced beliefs and practices in recent years and that can be reinterpreted today.

But this chapter does explore tensions in these concepts that may be relevant to current debates, for example between assumption of European superiority and a respect for very different civilizations. It also notes some of the contradictions within eighteenth-century cosmopolitanism: for example that citizens of the world identified in particular with Paris and that the exponents of a common humanity tended to be a cultural elite – although Paine marks a shift towards a more democratic cosmopolitanism. It is also worth noting that cosmopolitan intellectuals often communicated in French, which in this period had replaced Latin as the universal language of Europe.

The cosmopolite or citizen of the world

An appropriate starting point for discussing the Enlightenment concept of the cosmopolite is the entry in that monument to the Enlightenment, the *Encyclopaedia* edited by Diderot and D'Alembert. The *Encyclopaedia* points to a light-hearted use of the term to indicate 'a man who has not any fixed abode' or 'a man who is not a stranger anywhere'.[11] The entry then gives two serious philosophical references. The first is to an 'ancient philosopher' (Socrates), who when asked where he lived replied 'I am a citizen of the universe.'[12] The second is to a famous saying by Montesquieu, which the *Encyclopaedia* simplifies to: 'I put my family above myself, my country above my family and the human race above my country.'[13]

Claims to be a world citizen in the eighteenth century were linked to an assertion of an overriding humanity. Diderot wrote to Hume: 'My dear David, you belong to all nations, and you'll never ask an unhappy man for his birth certificate. I flatter myself that I am, like you, a citizen of the great city of the world.'[14] Paine's statement is frequently quoted: 'I speak an open and disinterested language, dictated by no passion but that of humanity ... my country is the world, and my religion is to do good.'[15] Kant uses the term 'citizen of the world' when speaking of the anthropologist trying to understand fellow human beings.[16] But he also uses the term 'citizen of the world' to denote man as member of a species and comments on the potential of the human species as rational beings to develop out of evil towards the good. This can only be attained by 'a progressive organization of citizens of the earth ... as a system held together by cosmopolitan bonds'.[17] Kant asserted in *Perpetual Peace* that 'the peoples of the earth have thus entered in varying degrees into a universal community, and it has developed to the point where a violation of laws in *one* part of the world is felt *everywhere*'.[18]

There were also more specialized uses of 'cosmopolitan' or 'world citizen' to indicate enlightened intellectuals and their particular kind of lifestyle. *The Encyclopaedia* cross references 'cosmopolite' to '*philosophe*'. Franklin's American Philosophical Society, which was also a centre for scientific research, declared that 'philosophers are citizens of the world; the fruits of their labors are freely distributed among all the nations'.[19] Mathematics also provided a model of a world of the mind transcending mundane divisions. There was also a more general sense that men of learning or letters were part of this cultivated cosmopolitan elite. This understanding was reflected in Oliver Goldsmith's *The Citizen of the World; Or Letters from a Chinese Philosopher to His Friends in the East* (1762).

The cosmopolitans were almost all literally travellers. Montesquieu in *The Persian Letters* (1721) develops the theme that an enlightened man can feel at home anywhere: 'The heart is a native of any country; how could someone with a fine nature prevent himself from forming friendships? ... wherever I find men, I shall choose myself friends.'[20] But they tended to gravitate to the city that most embodied their ideals of philosophy and cosmopolitanism – Paris.

For our purposes it is important to note how the intellectual citizens of the world gave some social reality to their claims to both universalism and a shared solidarity, and thus prefigured what today is seen as the evolution of global civil society. One approach was the creation of purely personal networks of friends gravitating to key figures – Voltaire's 'literary government in exile' or Holbach's Parisian dinner table – and of corresponding across frontiers. But the central organizational bases were regular meeting places (for example the Parisian salons or the Edinburgh and London coffee houses) and clubs.[21] The Enlightenment thinkers also communicated through specialized societies with members in many countries, and a number of journals, like the *Nouvelles de la république des lettres et des arts* founded in 1778. These cosmopolitan journals supplemented the hundreds of national periodicals, in Britain and Germany especially, that promoted ideas among a like-minded readership.

The cosmopolitan spirit of these societies claimed, and often achieved, immunity from the quarrels between states, allowing individual philosophers and scientists to travel to 'enemy' countries in wartime. This sense that philosophy and science should transcend all political borders has sometimes been reflected in twentieth-century cosmopolitanism. This belief could also take utopian forms, as it did in Marie Jean Condorcet's goal of a transnational voluntary scientific body cooperating in an agreed and 'perpetual' plan of necessary scientific research.[22]

Because world citizens tended to travel the world, and because they often identified with Paris, the term 'cosmopolitan' acquired two of its pejorative meanings: rootlessness and superficiality. The claim to be at home anywhere and to belong to an overarching society could be seen as lack of patriotism and moral responsibility. Rousseau provided an early polemic contrasting 'that ardent love of fatherland that ... makes it unbearably tedious for its citizens every moment spent away from home' with the present situation, where there are no 'French-men, Germans, Spaniards, or even Englishmen – only Europeans'. He lamented that they all

> have the same tastes, the same passions, the same customs ... they will all tell you how unselfish they are and behave like scoundrels. ... Their fatherland is any country where there is money for them to steal and women for them to seduce.[23]

The claim to disinterested learning could be characterized as superficial sophistication, epitomized for Rousseau by Paris.

Some of the ambiguities of cosmopolitanism are embodied in the position of the Jewish financier and the Jewish intellectual. Whilst Jewish communities in Europe were subject to social and political discrimination and retained their own religious and social identity, a privileged minority gained a significant role as bankers to princes, and had connections across Europe.[24] The Jewish intellectuals, who began to emerge from the ghetto in the eighteenth century, did not have a clearly defined social role. Hannah Arendt has discussed the range of their possible positions, including those of the pariah and the parvenu. But during the Enlightenment they were often accorded a cosmopolitan status by the *philosophes* and were identified as true representatives of 'humanity', more enlightened and free of prejudice than others.[25] Moses Mendelssohn, who sought Jewish emancipation through embracing Enlightenment ideas, but (unusually) maintained his Judaism and tried to explain its values to the wider world, exemplified the Jewish intellectual who was accepted as a *philosophe* – the 'German Socrates' – despite his lack of formal education.[26] Lessing modelled Nathan the Wise – the subtle exponent of toleration and respect between Jews, Christians and Muslims – on Mendelssohn.[27]

The eighteenth-century intellectuals had to address whether or how far their cosmopolitanism was in conflict with patriotism. They naturally denounced xenophobic, aggressive and irrational expressions of patriotism, which they tended to identify with the uneducated: Lessing's 'the prejudice of the people'; or Hume's 'the vulgar are apt to carry all *national characters* to extremes'.[28] Voltaire noted the negative aspects of patriotism, and commented in his *Pocket Philosophical Dictionary*: 'It is sad that in order to be a good patriot one is very often the enemy of the rest of mankind.'[29] But Voltaire then drew a distinction between a patriotism seeking greatness for one's country at any cost and fostering hatred of neighbouring countries (which he suggested was a natural human impulse), and a restrained patriotism. 'The man who would want his country never to be larger, or smaller, or richer or poorer would be a citizen of the world.'[30]

Indeed, being a citizen of the world required being a responsible citizen of one's own country, as Richard Price argued in his *A Discourse on the Love of Our Country* (1789). Gay quotes the German scholar and novelist Christoph Wieland: 'Only the true cosmopolitan can be a good citizen.'[31] But the corollary was that a citizen of the world would oppose his own government if it were to contravene cosmopolitan principles at home or abroad.

Tolerance: freedom of thought and religion

The view that individuals should be allowed to maintain their own religious beliefs and practices was one of the tenets of the Enlightenment. Commitment to reason required belief in free speech and rejecting censorship of beliefs or opinions. Voltaire draws a comparison between slavery and slavery of the mind and comments: 'Without the freedom to explain what one thinks, there is no freedom among men.'[32] Goethe claimed that toleration was embraced by the best minds of the time as a 'watchword'. Reiss, after citing Goethe, argues that tolerance was not only a fashionable attitude but central to Kant's critical philosophy and the principle that every rational person should be able to engage in public debate.[33]

Individual tolerance and governmental toleration were important for the maintenance of peace and respect for the beliefs of others, and closely allied to a spirit of cosmopolitanism. Rejection of national prejudices, which divided human beings, was naturally allied to rejection of what seemed in the eighteenth century, in the light of recent European history, an even greater threat: religious intolerance. Locke's well-known essay *A Letter Concerning Toleration* (1689) was influential upon Enlightenment thought. Locke was arguing within a Christian context – despite references to Mohammedans and paganism – and primarily seeking freedom for dissenting Protestants. He excluded from toleration both atheists and Catholics, the latter for political reasons given Catholic countries were hostile to England. The Enlightenment philosophers were prepared to go further than Locke in denying the exclusive claims of Christianity itself, though they drew on his rejection of revelation as an adequate source of truth. Montesquieu, using the device of looking at Europe through Persian eyes, is caustic about the Papacy. But he also comments generally on the irrationality of many deeply held religious beliefs, for example taboos on certain objects or items of food.[34] The general tenor of his remarks, however, is not anti-religious but to urge the value of a multiplicity of religions, and some of his arguments suggest the social usefulness of religion to society and government.[35] Religious wars have been due to intolerance and the 'proselytizing spirit' passed on 'like a nation-wide epidemic' that results in doing violence to other people's consciences. Franklin's phrase 'blind zealots' indicates why religious enthusiasm often runs to extremes.

Enlightenment thinkers stressed both the dangers of religious zealotry and the irrationality of what they classed as superstition. Voltaire observes that 'It is superstition that has made rivers of blood flow since the time of Constantine.'[36] He attacks all religions based on revelation, which leads him to comment favourably on Confucius because he relied not on falsehood and violence, but on reason. The *philosophes* themselves tended therefore to reject specific religious commitments for a generalized deism. The Enlightenment emphasis on tolerance and the associated commitment to reason could veer towards positive hostility to religion. But it did mark a decisive rejection of policies designed to enforce religious conformity. Belief in tolerance also tended to undermine the claims of proselytizing Christianity as a reason for European colonization, though Enlightenment thinkers were not wholly consistent on this issue.

Rights of man and rejecting slavery

The link between identifying oneself as a world citizen transcending state boundaries and believing that all members of the human race are fundamentally equal goes back, as we have seen, to the Stoics. Even if the *philosophes* as world citizens identified themselves as an enlightened few, this is associated with a responsibility for asserting the fundamental humanity of all. In Paine's *Rights of Man* (1791), cosmopolitanism takes on a strongly egalitarian perspective and an emphasis on the universal nature of rights. Claeys comments: 'Mankind could now be understood as belonging to one universal fraternal community where all possessed equal rights and duties which upheld the fundamental dignity (a word of immense importance to Paine) of each.'[37] Cosmopolitanism of both an elitist and an egalitarian cast requires opposing the more obvious forms of oppression and inequality.

This commitment to the rights of individuals culminated in the declarations of rights by both the American and French Revolutions at the end of the eighteenth century. Respect for rights included opposition to practices such as torture and frequent use of the death penalty, widely practised in that century. The *philosophes* often concentrated primarily on opposing abuses in their own countries: Montesquieu attacked the burning of 'witches', heretics and homosexuals; Voltaire polemicized against specific cases of extreme cruelty and injustice; Jefferson's Virginia 'Bill for Proportioning Crimes and Punishments' opposed 'cruel and sanguinary laws'; and Bentham tried to reform the British penal code and end transportation. But this frame of mind was universalist in implication: John Howard, for example, specifically campaigned for prison reform in Europe as a whole.

Opposing cruelty and belief in rights logically required as a minimum the condemnation of slavery round the world. The Enlightenment philosophers therefore went much further than the Stoics in totally rejecting slavery, which also implied rejecting modified forms of slavery such as serfdom. Montesquieu's repudiation of slavery was unequivocal and Voltaire attacked it frequently. Anti-slavery societies in France and Britain had active support from leading intellectuals and Franklin presided over the Pennsylvania Society for Promoting the Abolition of Slavery. Paine was also noted for his opposition to slavery: in his 1775 essay 'African Slavery in America' he denounced both the Europeans for promoting corruption and war in Africa to further the slave trade and the inhumanity of the trade itself, which led to thousands of annual deaths, and he called on Americans to end the trade immediately.[38] The conscious cosmopolitanism of the anti-slavery crusade is especially interesting. Schlereth notes that the Englishman Granville Sharp, who became a corresponding member of

Franklin's Pennsylvania Society, believed that supporting abolition logically required that 'we ... consider ourselves as *Citizens of the World*'.[39]

Colonialism and aboriginal rights

Opposition to enslaving Africans tended to extend to criticism of colonialism, though the Enlightenment philosophers were less united on this issue. Montesquieu's views on the role of European countries in conquering distant lands indicate a tension – which still exists – between Enlightenment beliefs and respecting the autonomy of other cultures. In the *Persian Letters* he comments sardonically in Letter 75 on the hypocrisy of kings in invoking Christian principles of human equality in the freeing of the serfs and then making conquests 'in countries where they realized that it was advantageous to have slaves', forgetting their religious principles.[40] But in *The Spirit of the Laws* (1748), he suggests that instead conquerors could ideally remedy previous abuses or remove 'pernicious prejudices'. For example, he observes that the Spaniards could have imparted 'a mild religion' to the Mexicans, 'but they filled their heads with a frantic superstition. ... They might have undeceived them with regards to the abuses of human sacrifices; instead of that they destroyed them.'[41]

Kant dealt in some detail with colonialism and subjection of aboriginal peoples and explored how a cosmopolitan desire to travel the world could lead to the danger of exploitation. On the one hand, he asserts in *The Metaphysics of Morals* (1797) the right of 'the world's citizens' to visit anywhere and to try to make contact with indigenous peoples. But he then immediately qualifies this by asserting that there is no 'right to *settle* on another nation's territory' unless such a right is granted by a specific contract. He suggests there can be a right of settlement if it is far enough from inhabited areas to exclude intrusion upon them. But Kant then recognizes that nomadic peoples 'rely upon large tracts of wasteland for their sustenance', and stipulates that settlement is only justified if based on treaty and if there is no attempt to trick the native inhabitants into accepting it. Kant refers to the possible argument of bringing 'culture to uncivilised peoples' but explicitly rejects it as a justification for use of force and dubs it a 'plausible' excuse.[42] In *Perpetual Peace* (1795) he attacks the history of European conquest and colonialism in America, Africa and India, where '*visiting* foreign countries and peoples' is 'the same as conquering them'. Kant notes that when discovered these were looked upon as 'ownerless territories; for the native inhabitants were counted as nothing'.[43] He also comments on the wisdom of the Chinese and Japanese in placing restrictions on Western visitors.

Kant wrote with awareness of the Hottentots in South Africa and the 'native American nations'. It is interesting to compare his views with the Enlightenment spirit animating the instructions of the President of the Royal Society in 1768 to Captain Cook about the treatment of the natives of lands where his ships might call in. The instructions urged patience and stressed that shedding of blood would be 'a crime of the highest nature'. The most important point, however, was that these natives 'are the natural, and in the strictest sense of the word, the legal possessors of the several Regions they inhabit'. Therefore Europeans had no right to occupy the land without the inhabitants' 'voluntary consent'.[44] These sentiments were soon relegated to a minor, though continuing, dissenting voice to the dominant doctrine that Australia was *terra nullius* (belonging to no-one) and to the brutalities of the new British settlers.

Paine demonstrated his consistent cosmopolitan radicalism in opposing colonialism. For example, he attacked the East India Company in his 'Reflections on the Life and Death of Lord Clive' (1775) and the role of Lord Clive, 'the conqueror of the east', returning to England.[45] His attitude to the native Americans was sympathetic and admiring – he spoke of them as 'brothers' – and he took part in a delegation to negotiate with the Iroquois to discuss their position under the new republic. (Congress later repudiated the treaty.) But Paine did think modern societies were more advanced in the arts and sciences, and he did not openly oppose the widespread hatred felt by many white Americans for the 'savages'.[46]

Jefferson, despite his general cosmopolitanism, was less prepared than Kant or Paine to grant the rights of indigenous peoples. He argued that it was in line with natural law not only to take possession of uninhabited country but also to acquire rights to the land from native inhabitants by war or treaty, both of which are a basis for just ownership. Jefferson's position was of course influenced by the previous history of the colonization of America, but he was not prepared to look for ways in the present to provide some restitution to indigenous peoples. When the possibility of returning some land to the native Americans arose, Jefferson opposed it on the ground of the indivisibility of existing society unless the government had been delegated specific powers to hand back land.[47]

In general, however, Enlightenment thinkers opposed colonial expansion and oppression of people from non-European cultures. Edward Said contrasts this widespread view, which he ascribes to Diderot, Montesquieu, Voltaire and Rousseau, as well as to British theorists less associated with the Enlightenment (Johnson, Cowper and Burke), with the general implicit acceptance in the nineteenth century of an '*imperialist* and Eurocentric framework'. But even the Enlightenment anti-colonialists in Said's view still 'do not dispute the fundamental superiority of Western man or, in some cases, of the white race'.[48] Despite quite widespread eighteenth-century admiration for the character and culture of non-western peoples, and concern about their exploitation, this is probably an accurate assessment.

Migration, citizenship and rights of refugees

Cosmopolitanism, which in principle embraces all of humanity and strives to transcend national frontiers, necessarily supports the rights of individuals to travel. We have seen that the philosophers claimed this right for themselves even in wartime. But they also upheld a more general right to travel round the world and to be treated with hospitality. Kant made the principle of hospitality to strangers one of his definitive articles of *Perpetual Peace*, arguing that this did not require the residents of a country to offer active support to strangers (this cannot be claimed as a right, but depends on friendship), but that strangers should be guaranteed entry and security. Kant claims that there is a *right* to travel and to try to enter into relations with the inhabitants, because of 'that *right to the earth's surface* which the human race shares in common'.[49] One aspect of this right to travel is that it is a prerequisite of international trade, which the Enlightenment thinkers endorsed as an activity conducive to peace and the creation of cosmopolitan bonds. (We return to this issue in more detail later in the chapter.) But it also reflects the sense that all individuals have rights derived from their humanity that states should not abridge.

A more radical formulation of this claim requires a right not only to travel but also to choose where to live and to choose the state to which one wishes to owe allegiance. This means that states should not forbid their citizens to leave. Franklin commented: 'To keep People in England by compulsion, is to make England a prison ....'[50] Kant also insists, in *The Metaphysics of Morals*, that the state cannot treat a man like a piece of property and hold him back, and the migrant has the right to take his 'mobile belongings with him'. But Kant does give the state the right to control the subject's fixed property such as land.[51] Montesquieu and Voltaire both took the strong cosmopolitan position that it was the fundamental right of individuals to migrate to wherever they wished and they felt at home.

If there is to be a right of migration, then there also has to be an understanding among states that they will allow foreigners to reside in their countries. Jefferson in his elaboration of international law argued that the right of 'expatriation' was a natural right, but since this right had no concrete meaning unless two governments consented to let an individual leave and to receive the expatriate, it should be embodied in a treaty. The right to settle was also linked to the right to acquire citizenship. Jefferson opposed the 14 years' residence requirement for citizenship imposed by the United States, and argued, like many other Enlightenment theorists, that individuals should be free to choose their own governments, and that America should become a home for the oppressed.[52] Bentham was prepared to argue in his Catechism of Parliamentary Reform that resident aliens who were paying the appropriate taxes should have the vote. The French Revolution in its earlier stages reflected a cosmopolitan spirit, not only in the National Assembly's symbolic granting of French citizenship rights on 26 August 1972 to 18 famous 'citizens of the world' (including Paine, Priestley, Bentham and James Madison), but in its 1791 Constitution, granting resident aliens the possibility of citizenship after five years if certain other conditions were fulfilled. The 1793 Constitution was exceptionally generous, granting foreigners full political citizenship rights after only a year's residence.[53] But the nationalist element in the French Revolution was demonstrated by the suspicion of 'foreigners' during the Terror.

Insistence on an absolute right to migrate makes it unnecessary to take special account of the rights of those forcibly expelled from their countries, or those who flee from oppression or threat of violence and imprisonment. Although

Kant in *The Metaphysics of Morals* suggests that the state has the right to deport its own citizens for wrongdoing, or even to exile them totally, making them in effect outlaws, he does not pursue the implications of this for the obligations of other countries. The *philosophes* did not therefore specifically address the rights of refugees.

The theorists of international law Samuel Pufendorf, Christian Wolff and Vattel did, however, make provision for refugees. Their position was less cosmopolitan, since they emphasized the reality and benefits of state sovereignty. But they did envisage that states had mutual obligations within an international society, and that rulers had moral obligations under natural law towards individuals suffering extreme need. They therefore discussed the rights of foreigners to travel through or reside in another country, and recognized the plight of exiles, who had a right to live somewhere in the world. Obligation to fellow members of humanity was, however, tempered by prudence. A ruler needed to consider whether admitting refugees – particularly in great numbers – would strain national resources or disrupt society. Therefore no particular state had an absolute obligation to grant asylum, although rulers should give weight to the claims of human sympathy.[54]

International trade and world citizenship

The Enlightenment thinkers were eloquent exponents of not only the right to free movement round the world but also the freedom to trade. The value of trade in linking different peoples together and promoting interests in peace and peaceable as opposed to warlike values are common themes in the writing of eighteenth-century cosmopolitans. The developing theory of political economy stressed the economic advantages; Adam Smith is of course the best-known exponent of free trade, but many other members of the republic of letters took up arguments against mercantilism and in favour of widening commerce between different nations and different parts of the world with their diverse resources. These views were held by both those of a more sceptical and conservative inclination like Hume and Voltaire, and by radicals like Franklin and Paine.

Although economic arguments and the sense that peoples could create and share in a new prosperity were important, trade was also valued for its perceived political and sociological effects. Montesquieu argues in Book XX of *The Spirit of the Laws* on commerce that by bringing together diverse people trade was a cure for the most 'destructive prejudices', so helping to transcend irrational nationalism. Montesquieu also argued, as many later liberals did, that promoting trade meant promoting peace, both because it created strong bonds of common interest that made war irrational and because it promoted the kind of society that rejected martial attitudes and values. The role of free trade is one of the key elements in Bentham's proposals for peace, and Kant built the freedom to engage in trade into his requirements for promoting peace, this freedom to be guaranteed by the cosmopolitan right of 'hospitality'.

Schlereth points out that in the eighteenth century merchants engaged in international trade were often seen as forming their own cosmopolitan society, partly because they were of many nationalities. He quotes Joseph Addison on the experience of visiting the Royal Exchange in London, where he found himself among so many different national groups that he could imagine himself 'a Citizen of the World'.[55] Merchants were also seen as representing a cosmopolitan outlook and were sometimes referred to as 'cosmopolites'. This positive evaluation of the world traveller and merchant had become negative in America by the nineteenth century, and became associated with 'speculators, opportunists, and other such "operators" '.[56]

The optimism and enthusiasm with which the eighteenth-century philosophers viewed the prospects of opening up the world through trade reflected their sense that they were overthrowing the old regime in both politics and economics and moving into a new worldwide society. The benefits of trade were more obvious than the possible disadvantages. It is possible to claim, as Schlereth does, that the Enlightenment thinkers represented a rising bourgeois class and that their sense of belonging to the new progressive class was consistent with speaking in terms of universal principles. But even Paine, who came from an artisan background and spoke for the common man, shared the enthusiasm for world trade.

The belief in the cosmopolitan nature of world commerce is a theme of particular importance to current debates. Renewed interest in the idea of world citizenship at the beginning of the twenty-first century reflects a sense that global economic forces and technological possibilities have created a world society, but whether free trade and *laissez-faire* economic policies are promoting world harmony, or are a source of exploitation and radical economic inequality, is a crucial issue. It could of course be argued that the implications of the new commercial society did not become fully visible until the nineteenth century, when socialist critiques of liberal political economy were developed. Moreover, the thesis adopted by Lenin about the links between capitalism and imperialism only emerged around the beginning of the twentieth century, when Benthamite claims that commerce was more beneficial than colonialism could be countered by arguments that colonial expansion was essential to the continued health of monopoly capitalism. Since, however, many Marxist theories linking capitalism and war also now look outdated, and since exponents of unfettered commerce like Hayek find inspiration in the early political economists,[57] it is important to examine the qualifications that the Enlightenment thinkers inserted into their praise of markets.

Awareness of the potential benefits of a commercial society did not mean blindness to the costs that were also involved. If commerce promoted harmony between nations, it could promote individualist competition within a national society. Montesquieu notes that where the spirit of commerce dominates, 'they make a traffic of all the humane, all the moral virtues; the most trifling things, those which humanity would demand, are there done, or there given, only for money'. He then goes on to a balanced appraisal of the kind of morality produced by the spirit of trade, suggesting it 'produces in the mind of man a certain sense of exact justice', which is opposed to immorality like robbery, but also opposed to moral virtues that transcend purely private interest.[58] Moreover, Montesquieu recognized that commerce would operate differently in different cultural contexts: a leisured aristocratic class would promote a 'commerce of luxury' very different from the 'economic commerce' resulting from the English Protestant model of thrift and hard work.[59]

Even Smith, often presented as a symbol of the free market within and between states, approached the implications of the market with some caution. He arguably intended his *Wealth of Nations* (1776) to be read in the context of his moral philosophy in his *Theory of Moral Sentiments* (1759) and was highly critical of a view that human behaviour is motivated entirely by self interest.[60] Like Montesquieu, he noted negative as well as positive aspects of the commercial spirit, although Smith extends his understanding of commerce to early industrialization. He was also well aware that merchants and industrialists had the power and inclination to pursue their sectional interests rather than the public interest. So even though freeing commerce from certain state restrictions is a prerequisite for developing economic wealth and a basis for friendship among nations, Smith did not argue that free markets were an unmitigated blessing.

Kant saw that interests in trade could be linked to conquest for economic gain and could profit from slavery, as in the Sugar islands, though he also seems to suggest that reliance on violence is not ultimately profitable.[61] Kant does not show Montesquieu's sociological awareness of the limits of a commerce-oriented mode of thought and set of values, but it is obvious that his rigorous duty-based moral theory and his insistence on treating human beings as ends in themselves rejects a purely commercial spirit. It is therefore plausible to draw on Kant to critique reliance on an unfettered market or a pure utilitarianism and to argue for human welfare and environmental imperatives that should set the framework for trade and environment policies.[62]

International law and measures for preventing war

The Enlightenment philosophers of cosmopolitanism laid less stress on the role of international law than the theorists of international society, who made law central to their enterprise of creating rules of behaviour between states. International law and theories of just war were seen by some of the philosophers to legitimize the conflictual and immoral relations between rulers of states. This view is suggested by Montesquieu's comments in Letter 94 of *The Persian Letters*: 'this branch of law is a science which explains to kings how far they can violate justice without damaging their interests'.[63] Kant's dismissal of the most famous theorists of international law in *Perpetual Peace* suggests similar sentiments.[64] Indeed he sees them as providing justifications for military aggression. He also claims that rulers of states in a Hobbesian state of nature in relation to each other have never been influenced by the international law theorists to desist from military action.

But in fact neither Montesquieu nor Kant ignored the importance of rightly framed principles of international law and just war theory. Montesquieu went on in the *Persian Letters* to indicate that the principles of justice should be the same between citizens and nations, and to specify two just causes of war: to repel aggression and to help an ally who has been attacked. He concludes, 'this is what I call international law; this is the law of nations, or rather of reason'.[65] Kant does recognize the importance (as well as the difficulty) of international law in an international state of nature in *The Metaphysics of Morals* and discusses both the just war principles of *jus ad bellum* (just causes of war) and of *jus in bello* (just methods of warfare) as well as the principles that should apply to the ending of a war.[66] Kant relies heavily on a framework of international law in his proposals for *Perpetual Peace*. Kant's 'preliminary articles', which lay the foundations for a possible peace, contain moral and political prescriptions, but also imply what Kant himself calls 'prohibitive laws' accepted between states: for example independent states cannot be sold or inherited, and states should abstain from military intervention in the internal affairs of other states. Article 6 sets out prohibitions on certain kinds of conduct in the course of war (*jus in bello*).

Both Montesquieu and Kant appear to rely implicitly on some version of natural law, which had traditionally been the basis for international law theories, although in both cases their adherence to natural law is a matter of scholarly interpretation and dispute. Montesquieu's emphasis on the differences between the laws and cultures of diverse countries and his search for sociological causes of these differences can suggest he abandoned belief in universal general principles, but there are also indications that he did believe in some principles uniting all human beings.[67] Kant's explicit formulation contrasts civil law, international law or right (*jus gentium*) and cosmopolitan law or right (*jus cosmopoliticum*). The latter applies 'in so far as individuals and states, coexisting in an external relationship of mutual influences, may be regarded as citizens of a universal state of mankind'.[68] Kant goes much further than Montesquieu in addressing the need for peace. W.B. Gallie comments that the goal of perpetual peace has logically 'always been required by the idea of mankind as a single moral community. ... In this respect we might say Kant has paid the Stoic–Christian ideal of the unity of mankind the supreme compliment of taking its political consequences seriously.'[69]

The Enlightenment theorists adopted a range of positions on the possibility of promoting international peace. Voltaire is at his most cynical and pessimistic when looking at international politics. He played a part in diplomatic negotiations between France and Prussia in 1740 and again during the Seven Years War of 1756–63, and his experience of European power politics made him critical of the international law theorists. He is even more caustic about the starry-eyed theorists of European peace based on a federation of states like the Abbé de Saint-Pierre. Voltaire can be eloquent about the horrors of war, 'that crime that consists of committing so many crimes when called to the colours', and notes that it is not necessarily universal: 'Several American nations had never heard of this horrible sin before the Spaniards came, Gospel in hand, to attack them.' But there are no cures: 'Should a prince dismiss his troops, let his fortifications crumble, spend his time reading Grotius, in two or three years you will see whether or not he has lost his kingdom.'[70]

But many of the cosmopolites did believe that war could be tamed or prevented. Franklin wrote in 1783 to the President of the British Royal Society (of which Franklin was a member) 'rejoicing at the return of peace' between the two countries. He adds the hope that mankind will eventually 'have reason and sense enough to settle their differences without cutting throats; for, in my opinion, *there never was a good war, or a bad peace*'.[71] Jefferson, in his positions as Governor of Virginia, Secretary of State for the new United States and later President, drew on Vattel to promote principles of neutrality: 'To mitigate the horrors of war as much as possible', for example in treatment of prisoners; and to try to resolve disputes through negotiation or arbitration, or by measures short of war like economic pressure. Jefferson also proposed arms limitation – as an alternative to a buffer zone – in negotiations with the British about the Canadian border. Bentham was more optimistic that the causes of war were disappearing with the end of religious strife and feudal society and the growth of commerce, although he did recognize there might be need at times for a defensive war. In his *Plan for an Universal Peace*, published posthumously in 1843, he urged the major European powers, Britain and France, to undertake measures of both unilateral and multilateral disarmament, to end entangling alliances and renounce colonial ambitions. Fearing 'sinister interests' in foreign offices, he also relied heavily on the role of the press and power of public opinion.[72] Although Paine believed in fighting for a just revolutionary cause, he shared aspirations for an eventual European peace when 'quarrels among nations will be terminated by pacific methods and not by the ferocious horrors of war'.[73]

Kant's *Perpetual Peace* is the most sophisticated and complex of the many plans put forward in the seventeenth and eighteenth centuries (see previous chapter).[74] Kant was well aware of the realistic, Hobbesian arguments brought to bear by many in addition to Voltaire, and of Rousseau's biting critique of Saint-Pierre's reliance on self-interested monarchs binding themselves to end war.[75] He was also aware that peace could not be created by a single treaty, but if it were achieved it would be as the result of a long process of changing international values and behaviour.

Cosmopolitanism and a sense that one is a citizen of the world seem to suggest as a logical corollary that the goal should be to create a world state in which all are literally citizens. Kant provided some cogent arguments against this goal – the difficulties of making a world state a reality and the dangers of despotism if one could. Some commentators, however, believe that Kant's ideal goal is a world state, despite his arguments in *Perpetual Peace* and his proposal in this essay for a limited international organization of like-minded states that might expand over time.[76]

But in general the Enlightenment-century cosmopolites accepted the reality of the system of sovereign states. Their immediate goal was to create a cosmopolitan society, which in crucial ways transcended state boundaries through learning and exchange of ideas, through acceptance of universal humanitarian values, and not least by the cosmopolitan and civilizing effects of commerce.

Conclusion

There are several concepts of world citizenship to be found in the Enlightenment. The first two are marginal to the argument of this book. One is of the social outsider who becomes cosmopolitan because there are no satisfactory alternatives – the position of Jews in many European countries. In some cases this social positioning may result in genuinely cosmopolitan commitments, but this involuntary sense of world citizenship is not directly relevant to a political analysis. The second meaning assigned to world citizenship is a choice of life style, involving frequent travelling and a refusal to be fully associated with one particular country, whilst tending to move in very similar social circles. This way of life might be associated with the more negative connotations of cosmopolitanism such as rootlessness and lack of commitment. This life style could also, however, be linked to more serious understandings of cosmopolitanism, as in the case of some of the *philosophes*.

The third and fourth concepts of world citizenship are of much greater relevance to subsequent discussion. The third is based on membership of a particular profession or social group with interests that inherently transcend frontiers: for example scholars, scientists or writers. This understanding of being united by common professional interests became increasingly significant in the next two centuries and is one element in the creation of a global civil society. Such professional groups sometimes also specifically endorse cosmopolitan causes that arise out of their professional commitments. The fourth concept of world citizenship entails uniting across frontiers specifically to promote causes such as the abolition of slavery. There was the beginning of such activity in the eighteenth century, and these transnational movements became an important feature of nineteenth-century politics, challenging the existing order.

There is a final important, but contentious, interpretation of world citizenship, linked to professional activity: that of the merchant with worldwide interests, who is also a member of a group drawn from many nationalities. In the eighteenth century, when most thinkers accepted the beneficial effects of promoting prosperity and drawing the world closer together through freedom of travel and trade, this idea was relatively uncontroversial. Growing awareness in the next two centuries of the potential for world capitalism to create poverty and injustice, and its link with both direct and indirect forms of imperialism, has made the global entrepreneur a much more controversial figure. In today's debates about cosmopolitanism there are competing interpretations of the role of the global economy and whether the corporate executive should be seen as truly a world citizen (see Part III).

The Enlightenment period culminated in the American and French Revolutions and the two associated declarations of rights, which anticipated proclamations of human rights after the Second World War. The American Revolution and the subsequent Constitution of the United States and Bill of Rights could be seen as a realization of many (though certainly not all) Enlightenment beliefs. With their emphasis on protecting individual and minority rights against abuses of government power, they anticipated the rise of liberalism in the next century. The legacy of the French Revolution was more mixed. On the one hand, in its earlier stages the Revolution saw the expression of a cosmopolitan republicanism that looked back to classical Greek and Roman models but reinterpreted them in an eighteenth-century context. On the other, the Revolution heralded the coming of two new associated political movements, democracy and nationalism, which became potent during the nineteenth century and strongly influenced the twentieth. Because there was not a clear-cut demarcation between liberal and republican ideas and values in eighteenth-century thought, it can be argued that there were republican elements in the American Revolution and liberal elements in the French.[77] But their dominant legacies were to liberal and republican thought respectively.

Republicanism implied a self-governing people committed to political principles of individual freedom from domination, and the equal civil and political rights of citizens. Earlier republican theory usually limited citizenship to a propertied and educated elite, but the French Revolution extended it to all adult men. Republicanism also meant the willingness of all citizens to take up arms, if necessary, to defend their rights. But the goal was to extend the political principles of republicanism by force of example and argument, not to impose them on others by force of arms. Republicanism was therefore associated with a concept of patriotism, but not with a commitment to an ethnic or cultural national identity. Instead, as interpreted by the Scottish writer Andrew Fletcher, by Paine and by the French Jacobins in the early years of the Revolution, it was understood as a cosmopolitan creed and associated with being a citizen of the world.[78]

But Jacobin republicanism was corrupted into crusading nationalism during the course of the Revolution under pressure of hostile monarchies externally and fear of enemies within. The cosmopolitan tendencies of the French Revolution, for example the willingness to allow foreigners almost immediate citizenship, was transformed into intolerant xenophobia. During the Terror, Paine – the eloquent advocate of universal republican principles – was imprisoned, and Anacharsis Cloots, a self-appointed 'orator for the human race', was tried and executed as a Prussian spy.

Cosmopolitan republicanism ceased to be a significant force in the 1790s. Its democratic, egalitarian and universalist ideals were inherited by the new socialist movements of the next century, which embodied a form of cosmopolitanism. It is only in response to disillusionment with the socialist vision at the end of the twentieth century that republicanism has been resuscitated as a fashionable concept among political theorists. Liberalism, on the other hand, became the dominant progressive ideology of the nineteenth century and, although it often adapted to pursuit of national interest or took on an imperialist colouring, was the main repository for cosmopolitan aspirations and beliefs.

3 Internationalism, cosmopolitanism and challenges to them, 1815–1914

During the nineteenth century it was still common to view politics between states in terms of conflicting interests moderated by the balance of power. But the Concert of Europe, created at the end of the Napoleonic Wars by the representatives of the major victorious allies – Russia, Austria, Prussia and Britain – with the intention of securing order in Europe and holding periodic congresses, emphasized the important role also played by great powers in imposing a degree of order on international anarchy. Although the Congress system itself soon ended, the major European powers continued to try periodically to impose a new settlement, as at the 1878 Congress of Berlin on the 'Eastern Question'. Alongside this realist view of relations between states, there was also a developing sense of an international society between states. Formal recognition was enshrined in the growing body of work on international law, and in the acknowledgement of the importance of diplomatic rules in the Final Act agreed at the 1815 Congress of Vienna.

The comparative stability of Europe in the early part of the nineteenth century rested, however, on cooperation between dynastic empires and kingdoms and suppression of demands for democratic institutions or national independence. Movements for the overthrow of monarchical rule or for national self-government dramatically challenged the status quo in 1848, and although not all the revolutions were successful, the nationalism first unleashed by the French Revolution became in the latter part of the nineteenth century increasingly significant.

Popular nationalism also tended to undermine the cosmopolitan sentiments espoused by the *philosophes*, finding support among many intellectuals. The move from cosmopolitanism to nationalism was sometimes mirrored in the thought of individual thinkers, like the Russian *émigré* Alexander Herzen, who in the 1850s consciously abandoned his role as a member of an international community of political revolutionaries and accentuated his Russian identity and commitment to focus on reform inside Russia.[1] The rise of nationalist independence movements in Europe and their emphasis on national linguistic, cultural and historical particularity did not wholly reverse universalist aspirations and modes of thought. Many (though by no means all) liberals saw nationalism in Europe as a justifiable rejection of oppressive dynastic rule and a form of desirable political self-determination. Moreover, some nationalist theories, like Mazzini's invocation of a new Italy, were linked to liberal universalism – Mazzini expected a united Italy eventually to become part of a league of independent European states, replacing the reactionary Concert of great powers, which had subordinated Europe and prevented the emergence of new states.[2] Other nationalist ideologies were more inward-looking, and more inclined to anti-semitism or to define themselves in opposition to their historic oppressors or near neighbours.

The other major challenge to genuine cosmopolitan commitments in the nineteenth century was posed by imperialism. Imperialist attitudes influenced the thinking even of liberals predisposed to cosmopolitan views, for example John Stuart Mill, and appealed to a common European heritage superior to that of other peoples and cultures, however ancient their civilizations. In its cruder manifestations imperialism was linked to explicit racism. The political impetus for colonization came from great power rivalry and assertive nationalism. Nationalism as an expression of popular unity and desire for self-government is quite distinct from imperialism, and was invoked by Asians and Africans struggling against colonial rule in the twentieth century. But nationalist sentiments can also be used to justify imperial expansion. An alternative interpretation of imperialism, provided by socialists at the end of the nineteenth century, argued that it was a logical development of the global capitalist economy – although the exact role of finance capital, the search for raw materials and the securing of privileged markets in promoting imperialist policies was debated. By 1914 the imperialist scramble for colonies was seen by socialists, and many liberals, as one cause of the impending world war.

Although at some levels the nineteenth century seems to mark a retreat from cosmopolitanism, at others the period 1815–1914 saw much wider adherence to Enlightenment ideals and a strengthening of trends towards a consciousness of common interests between states and peoples. Liberal beliefs gained increasing ascendancy. Moreover, developing cooperation between governments was an expression of liberal internationalism, which created a richer conception of an international society between states. Thirdly, increasing liberal freedom within states encouraged a significant increase in transnational links between professional groups and social movements across state frontiers: liberal internationalism at a nongovernmental level. This tendency promoted a form of world citizenship. Each of these developments is elaborated below. This chapter also explores how far the challenge to the liberal economy posed by the growing socialist movement constituted a more radical form of cosmopolitanism.

Liberal internationalism: governmental and popular

There is a direct link between Enlightenment cosmopolitanism and the body of ideas that became known in the nineteenth century as liberalism. (The term 'liberal' as a political and ideological label was used in the 1820s to designate the rebels in Spain, and then gained currency during the nineteenth century.) The link with the Enlightenment was embodied in key figures like Jeremy Bentham in

Britain, who lived to 1832 and inspired a generation of reformers, and in Benjamin Constant in France, who died in 1830 and is recognized as a central figure in the evolution of liberal thought. But the link is also demonstrated by a continuity in many key ideas: belief in the primacy of reason, religious toleration, individual freedom, opposition to arbitrary government, hostility to militarism and support for international free trade.

Communications and travel became easier with improvements in shipping and the new technology of railways and the telegraph. By the end of the century the invention of the radio and of photography had created the basis for rapid and vivid transmission of news around the world, so that Kant's belief that what happened in one corner of the globe should be felt everywhere became technologically more possible.

International measures at a governmental level focused primarily on the promotion of communications, for example with the launch in 1874 of the International Postal Union, which came to include all the countries of the world. Governments also set agreed standards for transport by road, rail and sea, and negotiated the clarification and regularization of issues affecting trade and economic development, for example publication of tariff charges and promoting international agreements to protect industrial inventions (patents) and intellectual property (copyright). Thirty inter-governmental bodies were created before 1914, and 20 survived after the First World War.[3] These developments, which extended the limited concept of international society inherited from the eighteenth century into a liberal version of active institutional cooperation between states, were paralleled by an expansion of the role of international law, both in terms of actual agreements between states and in the academic study of international law.

International law became a major subject of study in European universities, and several specialist journals in French and German were created between 1869 and 1894. Moves to create a permanent Institute of International Law, composed of eminent legal scholars, and independent of governments, culminated in an inaugural conference in Ghent in 1873. Its aims were to encourage recognition of the principles of international law, to consider difficulties arising in interpretation and to provide, when required, expert opinion, and more generally to promote state respect for upholding peace, or if war broke out for observing the laws of war. The Institute also intended to inform public opinion on 'those principles of justice and humanity that ought to regulate the relations between peoples'.[4] Towards the end of the century there was also an increasing emphasis on law as the basis for promoting peace. Hinsley notes the formation in 1873 of bodies designed to codify international law in the USA – the International Code Committee – and in Europe – the Association for the Reform and Codification of International Law (in addition to the Institute for International Law already noted).[5] Therefore, although the dominant interpretation of international law stressed agreement between sovereign states, increased interest in international law by individuals and political movements suggested moves towards using international law as an instrument for constraining states to accept cosmopolitan principles.

The political upheavals of the nineteenth century meant that the principle of a right to asylum embedded, if precariously, within international law was frequently invoked. Most European countries did grant political asylum, though – with the exception of Britain until 1905 – governments discriminated between refugees on political grounds. The earlier practice of offering diplomatic asylum in embassies to those fearing persecution was largely abandoned by European countries. Their embassies made an exception, however, in countries suffering revolutionary upheavals, for example Spain from 1833 to 1875 and Greece in 1862, and also in China during the Boxer Rebellion. Because the European powers did not regard the Ottoman Empire as an equal sovereign state, and because they deplored its abuses of human rights, they did extend diplomatic asylum there. Latin American countries, interestingly, widely practised diplomatic asylum for political refugees and it was given status under international law, for example in the 1889 Montevideo Convention on International Penal Law.[6] This Latin American focus on diplomatic asylum was elaborated in the twentieth century and had particular significance in the response by Latin American embassies during the Spanish Civil War.

The Enlightenment pattern of intellectual cooperation and organization across frontiers continued. As intellectual life became more specialized, the republic of intellect was redefined in terms of professional interests, and found expression in international conferences and organizations. Scientific collaboration burgeoned in the 1850s and 1860s, with conferences on meteorology and statistics, chemistry, geodesy and botany. Specialist medical conferences were also held in this period on ophthalmology, veterinary science and pharmaceuticals. The growing number of scientific conferences after 1865 indicated the need for coordination, first supplied by the French-inspired *Alliance Scientifique Universelle*, created in 1876, and later by the German-initiated *Die Brücke*, founded in 1911 to foster intellectual and especially scientific links.[7] Pooling of resources to expand knowledge was promoted by international congresses of librarians, initiated in 1877, and by the decision to create an International Institute of Bibliography, arising out of the 1895 Congress.

Internationalism was manifested in the evolution of shared beliefs and practices and of a very wide range of economic, professional and humanitarian nongovernmental bodies, with 2,900 international meetings held between 1840 and 1914. This trend became pronounced after 1850 when the number of international bodies multiplied. The last quarter of the nineteenth century saw the rapid growth of international nongovernmental organizations – 130 were created in this period – and a further 304 organizations arose between 1900 and 1914. The proliferation of international nongovernmental bodies led in 1910 to the setting up of the Union of International Associations, which began to publish information on the range of international societies. These transnational links can be seen as attempts to create a world society between individuals transcending national boundaries and creating the nucleus of a global civil society.

The increasing ease of communication during the nineteenth century co-incided with the entry of wider sections of the population into political life, which had been heralded by the American and French Revolutions. So whereas until the 1770s cross-border communication occurred mainly between intellectual elites, the nineteenth century saw the rise of movements for social and political change, which established links across frontiers. The eighteenth century anti-slavery societies, which did mobilize popular support, developed into wider and more militant movements by the nineteenth century, with both the American and French Revolutions providing a catalyst for popular agitation, including slave uprisings in the Caribbean.[8] The philosophers of international law and perpetual peace had their ideas taken up after 1815 by the new peace campaigns, and prominent nineteenth-century advocates of peace like Cobden and Bright were known for their protest activities as well as their ideas. All these movements drew directly on the Enlightenment heritage and were predominantly liberal, though the anti-slavery movement was also at times radical republican and revolutionary. So whereas the previous chapter focused mainly on the ideas of philosophers, this chapter – though it does take account of the views of prominent liberal theorists – gives much more attention to political movements and social trends.

Can popular liberal internationalism be seen as a direct continuation of the cosmopolitanism of the eighteenth century? The idea of world citizenship was not invoked as frequently as it had been in the age of Enlightenment, although the label 'cosmopolite' was still occasionally used. For example, the *Ligue du Bien Publique*, reflecting republican ideas, started a multilingual monthly journal *Le Cosmopolite* in 1866 to campaign for a 'universal republic'. The switch in terminology does suggest a slightly different emphasis; whereas cosmopolitanism stresses membership of the world, internationalism suggests membership of a nation or state as a starting point for joining with people in other countries. But the political effect of transnational organizations and movements was to influence international politics in a direction that is clearly cosmopolitan. So this chapter treats popular internationalism as a manifestation of cosmopolitan commitments and charts in some detail the evolution of peace movements, predominantly liberal in inspiration and central to cosmopolitan aspirations. It also discusses the growth of feminist movements, which were also influenced primarily by liberal ideas, although there was an emerging if ambiguous maternalist ideology. Feminists often linked their campaign for women's rights with general cosmopolitan goals such as universal human rights and peace.

Some qualifications should be noted about this impressive development of professional and popular internationalism. It was still predominantly European and North American and the headquarters of international bodies were often in European cities. Moreover, these citizens' organizations were not always effective or long-lasting, and some were disrupted by the First World War. Only 191 out the 450 of the transnational nongovermental societies founded before 1914 still existed by the middle of the twentieth century, though some of them still play a role today, for example the Red Cross.

'Internationalism' at both a governmental and nongovernmental level primarily reflected liberal values, linked to globalizing economic and technological trends. The very success of liberalism, however, revealed the divisions within it: between support for the status quo and pressure for further radical change; and between an emphasis on the market and an emphasis on humanitarian values. In the most economically and politically developed countries liberal governments were coming to power. This meant that some liberal beliefs were more likely to be implemented, but also that radical cosmopolitan ideals were more likely to be espoused by popular movements or politicians in opposition than by governments. This split between those in power and those in opposition was most obvious on issues of war and peace and upholding human rights round the world. Liberals in or close to power were more likely to adapt to traditional military and diplomatic practices and to stress pursuit of national interest, whilst those more remote from power more often urged arbitration and disarmament or demanded respect for human rights. Liberalism also had to confront the moral and political demands of the new working class, calling for universal suffrage and moving towards socialist ideas.

Liberalism, cosmopolitanism and imperialism

Contradictory tendencies were apparent in liberal attitudes to both class and gender. But by 1914 many liberals had moved towards a 'social liberalism' that recognized the need for some state intervention to alleviate poverty and promote welfare in order to create a social and economic basis for equal citizenship. Liberal opinion also moved gradually towards recognition of women's civil and political rights. The most fundamental contradiction in liberalism in this period was the distinction many drew between Europe and parts of the world governed by settlers of European stock, and other peoples and cultures. Respect for the rights of others seen as fellow human beings was progressively consolidated in the European world, for example in moves towards less brutal penal punishments, prison reform and initial proposals to abolish the death penalty, as well as extension of political rights to the vote. Very different attitudes prevailed towards those outside this civilization. Whilst industrialization and an expanding market, both supported by liberals as progressive forces, were uniting the world, liberal attitudes tended to draw a sharp division.

Harold Laski has claimed that: 'The nineteenth century is the epoch of liberal triumph ... no other doctrine spoke with the same authority or exercised the same widespread influence.' Although liberals had to contend with a strengthened conservatism in the first half of the century, liberalism 'was the advocate of religious toleration; and it both broke the temporal power of Rome and ended the right of religion to define the boundaries of citizenship'.[9] Liberals advocated not only freedom of thought and conscience but also respect for individual civil and political rights.

This relative tolerance of religions within North America and Western Europe did not, however, suggest increasing respect for religions in other parts of the world. Even when adopting a universalist stance based on human rights, liberals could simultaneously appeal to distrust of non-Christian religions, as when the Anti-Slavery society combined with Baptist missionaries in the 1860s to protest against Indian indentured labour being sent to Jamaica, arguing in part that this meant the 'introduction of pagans and idolators'.[10] To the extent that many nineteenth-century liberals abandoned the Enlightenment opposition to colonialism, they also adopted a more intolerant attitude to non-European beliefs and practices than the cosmopolitan eighteenth-century thinkers. Even John Bright, who opposed many aspects of colonial policy, commented in an 1833 speech on India: 'We have seen how that wealth may be rendered available to England, and how the blessings of civilisation and Christianity may be spread abroad in that vast empire.'[11]

But it is important to note that hostility to non-western religions was prompted not only by forms of intolerance and prejudice, but also by Enlightenment principles. Liberals deplored what they saw as the superstition and cruelty of many religions and distrusted the reactionary effects of religious bodies having political power. The main examples of such religious dominance came from outside Europe. John Stuart Mill refers in his 1831 essay 'The Spirit of the Age' to the stifling nature of societies where religion prevented significant intellectual disagreement. 'These conditions exist among two great stationary communities – the Hindoos and the Turks … .'[12] Thus, as today's critics of Enlightenment universalism argue, commitment to 'reason' and progress could mean assertion of European superiority.

Nevertheless, there was some liberal awareness that religious toleration was a principle that should operate in favour of non-Christian religions. For example, in India during the 1830s Indian and British reformers linked to the newspaper *Friend of India* debated proposals for religious toleration as well as press freedom, law reform and local self-government.[13] There were Europeans sympathetic to non-western beliefs, for example scholars who studied alien cultures or belonged to the eccentric religious and social fringe. It is interesting that Gandhi – indoctrinated in India itself by western attitudes – read the *Bhagavad Gita*, and ceased to view Hinduism as a source of irrational superstition, through the influence of Theosophists when he was living in London in the 1880s.[14]

Liberal sentiment could also often be mobilized to oppose policies towards non-European peoples that were seen as exceptionally cruel and degrading. The campaign against the slave trade and use of slave labour, which had gained significant public support in both Britain and America by the end of the eighteenth century, made progress throughout the nineteenth century. This campaign may have been influenced by the Anglo-French rivalry in the 1790s, as C.L.R. James has argued, and was temporarily promoted by French Jacobins and by slave rebellions in the Caribbean.[15] Its success may also have been due partly to the declining economic advantages of the slave trade, as Eric Williams has claimed.[16] But the anti-slavery campaign was the first major transnational movement reflecting liberal universalist values. Abolition of legal slavery did not, however, end the system of shipping indentured Indian labourers to the West Indies and much later to South Africa. The Anti-Slavery Society in Britain was re-created in 1839 to oppose this new form of oppressive labour, but sustained opposition did not occur until 1900.

There were also protests against colonial abuses, for example against the cruelty with which Governor Eyre in Jamaica put down a minor rebellion in 1865 – a protest supported by Mill. Alexis de Tocqueville, distinguished liberal theorist, as parliamentary deputy and author of two reports on Algeria, condemned French military reprisals in that colony that created unnecessary misery.[17]

In Britain, many of those active in the campaign against the slave trade turned their attention in the 1830s to the fate of those living in colonized territories. The Aborigines' Protection Society was created in 1837 and a House of Commons Select Committee on Native Peoples sat in 1836–7. However, the economic and political pressures to consolidate colonial rule in India and to pursue white settlement of Australia and New Zealand overrode liberal concerns. Moreover, many prominent liberals endorsed these developments. British colonialism was seen as an instrument for extending the rule of law and promoting enlightenment.

In France, the other major European colonial power by the end of the century, moves towards imperialism were linked to the internal swings of domestic politics. After the Restoration in 1815 the government pursued an active policy of establishing a French presence in Algeria and West Africa. The new regime after 1830, although incorporating liberals like Guizot, failed to halt the process of colonization, though not encouraging it. Under Louis Bonaparte, France extended its empire in Africa and Indo-China, though the Emperor himself was more interested in European questions.[18] Tocqueville supported French control of Algeria on the grounds of promoting French national power and pride, and also supported sending more French settlers to Algeria, with the aim of creating eventually a liberal political system as opposed to military rule.

Tocqueville's view of racial differences was sociological. He strongly rejected the idea that there were innate differences between races that created a permanent racial hierarchy. His correspondence with Arthur Gobineau, an influential theorist of innate racial difference, makes clear the disagreements between the two men on this issue.[19] Their disagreement also indicates the future opposition of many liberals to the increasingly popular theories of white racial superiority in the heyday of empire and later in the evolution of fascism.

Towards the end of the nineteenth century those who adopted a broadly liberal stance were more likely than in earlier years to oppose various forms of imperialism, partly on the basis of a general opposition to expansionist wars and increasing armaments. In the USA the Anti-Imperialist League formed in 1898 drew on earlier opposition to US expansion (for example in Hawaii and Samoa) but was focused on resisting US government plans to annex the Philippines. The campaign drew on diverse ideological reasons for opposing imperialism, including liberal internationalism and belief that free trade and colonial conquest – which suggested exclusive control of resources and markets – were contradictory. The campaign had the support of some (though not all) American peace activists.[20] Ironically, racist considerations (fear of undermining white domination in the USA) encouraged one element in the opposition to imperialism. Other domestic concerns were about cheap colonial labour undermining work and wages, or corrupting American democracy.

British liberals became worried about the military implications of the race for colonies at the end of the century and opposed the imperialist policies of the Conservative Government in power from 1895 to 1905. When the Boer War broke out in 1899 a significant section of the Liberal Party sided with the rising Labour Party in opposition to the War. In addition liberalism as it entered the twentieth century was more sceptical about paternalist justifications of colonial rule.

Migration and freedom of trade

Liberals believed in the right of freedom to travel. Moreover, free movement of people was linked to freedom to trade. So, apart from restrictive legislation regarding aliens in time of war, the West European countries adopted a generally open policy for much of the nineteenth century. The home of *laissez-faire* liberalism, Britain, had (except in times of emergency) a relaxed open doors policy until 1905, at some stages waiving even the requirement that ships carrying immigrants should make an official declaration and that the immigrants should show passports.[21]

Migration took place on a much larger scale in the nineteenth century than it had before. Economic disasters like the Irish famine of the 1840s and political upheavals like the 1848 Revolutions precipitated people to leave their homes. General economic poverty and the possibility of a better life also encouraged migration within Europe to industrialized areas like the German Ruhr and the French coalmines, and to other continents: North America, Australasia and (South) Africa. Improved transport, such as the railways and the steam-ship, made migration not only quicker but safer. In addition government policies both in Europe and in the countries of the New World often encouraged migrants.

Restrictions on immigration date from around 1900 in many countries, reflecting a major increase in numbers of migrants, popular perceptions of the threat posed by migrants and in some case moves towards a welfare state, which encouraged stricter scrutiny of who might count as eligible. So although nationalism played a part in restrictions on immigration, it was also linked to incorporating the poor more fully as citizens of the state. In addition restrictions on immigration were linked to governmental moves from free trade to protectionism and trade union opposition to a flow of migrant labour that could undercut wages. In Britain all these factors contributed to the introduction of immigration restrictions in 1905.

Even where open door policies encouraged new migrants, labour movement pressures and pressure group agitation on national or racial grounds led to restrictions from the 1880s onward. The USA adopted a policy of encouraging immigration from Europe after the Civil War, a policy that brought profit to employers and steam-ship companies. But Congress responded to concerns about aliens becoming a charge on the public purse, and union opposition to contract labour, in 1880s legislation. Congress also passed three laws in 1882, 1884 and 1888 specifically designed to exclude all Chinese labourers and to deny those of Chinese origin the possibility of becoming US citizens. As Chinese immigration ended, another campaign began against Japanese labour, initiated by San Francisco unions in 1900 but soon supported by more prosperous groups in California.[22] The influx of immigrants from southern and eastern Europe was also seen as a threat to American culture and society by the Immigration Restriction League, founded by Boston intellectuals in 1894.[23]

Australia's policy was more explicitly geared to attracting people from Britain or Ireland, and major immigration from other parts of Europe did not take place until after the Second World War. During the nineteenth century some non-whites were allowed in for economic purposes. But by the 1890s anxieties about miscegenation, combined with the aspiration to create a new white civilization in an independent country as Australia moved towards federation, prompted laws allowing deportation of Chinese labourers and Pacific Islanders. As in Britain, limits on immigration were in part linked to protectionism and social legislation on behalf of labour, and the only opponents in parliament of White Australia policies were, in Manning Clark's words, 'two doctrinaire free-traders in the Senate'.[24]

Economic arguments for either free trade or protection varied over time, but a liberal tendency to support the principle of free trade was an extension of the eighteenth-century view that it promoted cosmopolitanism and peace. Many activists in the nineteenth-century liberal peace movements reiterated this belief. Cobden and Bright are the best-known advocates of this thesis in Britain, but J.S. Mill's early views on the close links between peace and trade, as expressed in the first, 1848, edition of his *Principles of Political Economy*, are often quoted: 'It is commerce which is rapidly rendering war obsolete, by strengthening and multiplying the personal interests which are in natural opposition to it.'[25]

To promote trade and industry, governments began the practice of holding international trade fairs, starting with the Great Exhibition in London in 1851 and in Paris in 1855. F.S.L. Lyons observes that 'by 1914 42 such international displays had been held in 30 different cities all over the world'.[26] These occasions were often used as springboards for international conferences and also suggested how human industry was bringing the whole world together. *The Times* described the opening of the 1851 Great Exhibition as 'the first morning since the creation … that all peoples have assembled from all parts of the world'.[27] The third international peace congress met in London in 1851 to coincide with the Great Exhibition at Crystal Palace.[28]

The belief that free trade led to peace was seriously questioned in the next few decades, even by some of its previous advocates like Mill, who became critical of the view that free trade automatically brought peace, and endorsed the need to use force in international politics to restrain aggressive and self-aggrandizing powers. In a speech on Britain's maritime power to the House of Commons in 1867 he rejected the 1856 Declaration renouncing the right to seize enemy property at sea as a 'blunder' influenced by the mood of the 1850s: 'The world was fresh from the recent triumph of free trade, fresh from the Great Exhibition of 1851, which was to unite all nations, and inaugurate the universal substitution of commerce for war. ... We were mistaken.'[29]

Although many liberals became sceptical about free trade's beneficial powers in preventing war, the perception of this connection retained its hold within the overall liberal tradition. Herbert Spencer, for example, was influenced by his belief that an aristocratic type of society geared to war had been replaced by a commercial society geared to peace, replacing status by contract.[30] Hobhouse, though differing from Spencer on domestic policy, argued that anti-imperialist liberal sentiments and concern for social reform led to a revival in belief in anti-militarism and the financial benefits of free trade.

A parallel was drawn between the peaceful benefits of free trade and international sport. Pierre de Coubertin, who campaigned successfully for the revival of the Olympics in Athens in 1896, expressed the belief that 'free trade' in athletes would be 'a great step forwards ... in the sacred cause of peace'.[31] The International Olympic Committee was created in 1894, and there were 26 international sporting bodies by 1914.

International peace movements

The transnational peace movements that existed from 1815 to 1914 were predominantly liberal in both their political ideas and their support, but at various times drew in republican and nationalist democrats and even anarchists and socialists.

Liberal peace activity, which began in the USA and Britain in 1815 after the Napoleonic Wars, drew heavily on the ideas formulated by liberal theorists, although its motivating force was often a religious pacifism. The first phase of the movement, covering the period from 1814 to the Crimean War of 1854–6, was dominated by American and British activists, who elaborated ideas to be found in Bentham, stressing the role of international arbitration. William Ladd's American Peace Union looked towards the settlement of all conflicts by 'a Congress of Christian Nations, whose decrees shall be enforced by public opinion that rules the world'.[32] The British movement added calls for disarmament, and, after the accession of Cobden and Bright to its ranks, made free trade as a means to peace a central plank of its platform. Cobden argued some institutions had a vested interest in war (for example the military), and shared Bentham's distrust of professional diplomats. 'As little intercourse as possible betwixt the *Governments*, as much connexion as possible between the nations of the world!'[33]

This English-speaking school of thought stressed international arbitration but did not advocate international organization with enforcement powers – Cobden was even more sceptical of such organization than Bentham.[34] The views held by Cobden and Bright were similar to those of prominent American peace advocate Charles Sumner, who also advocated free trade as a means to peace, although he was not so opposed to international institutions. Sumner, Senator for Massachusetts, urged America in 1849 to offer to the world 'a Magna Charta of International Law, by which the crime of War shall be forever abolished'.[35] In 1873 he introduced a motion in the Senate in favour of an international arbitration tribunal.

This Anglo-American approach to peace can be contrasted with a continental European emphasis on the need to create justice and democracy within dynastic states before peace is possible, a position argued by nationalist revolutionaries like Mazzini, and also by republicans. This, like all such generalizations, is an oversimplification – Cobden and Bright found allies in France in men such as Michel Chevalier and Frédéric Bastiat. But the views of prominent British peace campaigners did indicate their basic disagreements with European revolutionary movements.

British liberals did, however, experience their own tensions between avoiding war and securing rights and justice for individuals suffering oppression. Liberal internationalism could be mobilized to protest against the brutalities of despotic regimes, and was often harnessed to support for various nationalist movements trying to break free from the Ottoman or Austrian Empires. Liberals also attacked realist diplomacy, which ignored human rights in favour of maintaining a strategic alliance against a major enemy. Gladstone's philippics during the 1870s against Disraeli's policy of overlooking Turkish atrocities in suppressing a revolt by Christians in Bulgaria, because the Ottoman Empire was a bulwark against Russia, are a famous example. Gladstone was not alone in condemning the massacre of 15,000 Bulgarians: the Peace Society in Britain and its sister Women's Peace and Arbitration Auxiliary immediately organized deputations, public petitions and meetings. Plans were also made, with support from Florence Nightingale, to send medical relief to the Bulgarians.[36] The conflict between liberal emphasis on human rights and the impulse to intervene, on the one hand, and a realist diplomacy pursuing government economic and military interest, on the other, are both still extremely relevant today. Debates about intervention in Kosovo referred back to Gladstonian liberalism.

American advocates of peace faced their own difficult choice between war and peace when the Civil War broke out, and in particular when it became explicitly a war against slavery. At this stage prominent figures like Ralph Waldo Emerson, who in his 1838 lecture 'On War' had argued 'Trade, as all men know, is the antagonist of war. ... And learning and art, and especially religion, weave ties that make war look like fratricide, as it is,' supported the Union in the Civil War.[37] William Lloyd Garrison, founder in 1838 of the New England Non-

Resistance Society as well as ardent abolitionist, gave strong support to the Union during the Civil War after Lincoln's Emancipation Proclamation.

The other issue that divided American and British peace activists from continental Europeans was the desirability of seeking a supranational form of government. Victor Hugo, speaking to the third Universal Peace Congress in Paris in 1849, looked forward to 'the United States of America and the United States of Europe, holding hands across the sea'.[38] The revival of peace activity in the 1860s was linked to a more prominent role for continental European associations combining democratic demands with renewed calls for a federal Europe, and after the Franco-Prussian War of 1870–1 individuals from a larger number of European countries were drawn into peace activity. The holding of international peace congresses, less dominated by English speakers than in the first phase, revived in 1868.

The English-speaking organizations tended to maintain their focus on disarmament and arbitration, and the influx of lawyers and parliamentarians into peace activity in the 1870s and 1880s in due course provided weightier support for the goal of arbitration. American lawyers worked on draft codes of international law and found support among some educationalists, businessmen and politicians for formalizing arbitration. The National Arbitration League was founded in the USA in 1882. In 1889 parliamentarians from France and Britain formed the Interparliamentary Conference for International Arbitration, and in 1891 the International Peace Bureau was established to provide a permanent coordinating body for groups stressing arbitration and negotiations for disarmament.

There was a limited governmental response. The first Hague Conference of 1899 attended by 26 states, and the follow-up conference in 1907, attended by 44 states, embodied the goal of states negotiating to promote a more peaceable order. The first Hague Conference extended to war at sea the specific agreements on the humanitarian laws of war embodied in the 1864 Geneva Convention on treatment of the wounded and granting neutrality to military hospitals and ambulances. The first Conference also agreed on limited measures to create a framework for international arbitration, which were further developed after the First World War, but did not achieve the more ambitious goals of disarmament, for which many peace advocates had hoped. The 1907 Conference elaborated further on the Geneva Convention.

The growing nineteenth-century peace movement is of interest partly as an example of the role of popular movements in an increasing number of countries, which developed transnational links and created international organizations. By 1914 there were over 400 peace groups across North America and Europe (especially in Scandinavia and Germany) and also in Australia and Japan. Despite ideological divisions, and disagreements on specific political issues, the peace movement exemplified the sense that citizens of individual countries were also united in common interests as citizens of the world.

The movement included those inspired primarily by a religious (often nonconformist) ethic, who were most prominent in the early part of the century, and those emphasizing secular political arguments, who became more dominant in the latter part. The liberal and democratic peace groups were predominantly middle class, but the International Working Men's Peace Association, which supported disarmament, but not federalism, took part in the International League in 1868. (See below for socialist movement views on peace.)

In the second half of the century liberal peace activity involved increasing numbers of women. Beginning with the 1878 International Peace Congress, women won the right (earlier denied) to be delegates at national and international peace congresses and to speak publicly at them. The flamboyant Austrian Baroness Bertha von Suttner wrote a widely translated and influential novel, *Die Waffen Nieder* (Lay Down Your Arms), and she won the Nobel Peace Prize in 1905 for her campaigning in Europe. Margarethe Lenore Selenka from Germany mobilized mass support for demonstrations and a petition to the Hague 1899 Conference. However, although the transnational movement for women's suffrage promoted sentiments of international sisterhood, belief in women's maternalist commitments to peace and support for arbitration as an alternative to war, no international women's peace organization existed before 1914, and indeed many women suffragists were to support the war. The shock of the First World War, however, precipitated some prominent suffragists into organizing an International Congress of Women at the Hague, bringing together about 1,500 women from 12 countries and uniting women on both sides of the war as well as from neutral nations.[39]

Liberal feminism and maternalist internationalism

The emergence of an organized feminist movement dates from 1840, when American women active in the anti-slavery movement were refused the status of delegates at the International Abolition of Slavery Conference and decided to assert their own political rights, making contact with some radical women in Britain. Campaigns for the vote later spread to Australia and New Zealand, where women first gained the vote at the national level. Agitation for women's rights spread to most countries in Europe, though the political expression of feminist claims varied with the religious, cultural and political context. The only non-western country in which there was a significant feminist campaign before 1900 was Japan. Feminist protests began after the Meiji Restoration, but the 1889 Constitution banned women from political activity – though Japanese women managed to undertake some feminist agitation under the aegis of the Women's Christian Temperance Union in the 1890s.[40]

There were links between feminist groups in different countries that developed in the 1880s into the creation of international organizations. The Woman's Christian Temperance Union, founded in 1874 in the USA, embraced under the leadership of Frances Willard much wider reform goals, including the causes of women's suffrage and peace, and the World Woman's Christian Temperance Union created in 1884 set out to extend its international reach.[41] Leaders of the American suffrage movement launched the International Council of Women

(ICW) in 1888 to bring together women's voluntary associations in all parts of the world, to promote human welfare and respect for human rights and to encourage peace through negotiation and arbitration. (The ICW still exists and has extensive links to the United Nations.) But although the ICW stood for women's education, right to work and equal pay, it did not commit itself to votes for women, as this was a divisive issue among women engaged in social reform. As a result more radical feminists formed their own International Women's Suffrage Alliance in 1904. By 1914 it had members' organizations in 24 countries (Latin America was the only region where there was no support) and two of its leading members toured Asia between 1911 and 1913.[42]

Feminists often articulated the belief that women were naturally internationalist by virtue of their common exclusion from political rights and power. For example, the feminist Katherine Anthony noted: 'The disenfranchisement of a whole sex ... had bred in half the population an unconscious internationalism', which she forecast would soon become a conscious internationalism.[43] An explicit language of sisterhood become common in the 1880s among women in the temperance and suffrage campaigns.

The suffragists tended to invoke sisterhood when focusing on women's common wrongs, but also to appeal to a wider internationalism when opposing war. But criticism of war did often appeal to a belief in women's propensity to favour peace, either for biological or sociological reasons: women's natural biological predisposition to nurturing or their domestic experience.[44] Belief in women's special role could also be combined with a cosmopolitan appeal, as it was by Frances Willard, when she stressed the importance of internationalism: 'We must no longer be hedged about by artificial boundaries of states and nations.'[45]

There were, however, limits, both unconscious and conscious, to the effective cosmopolitanism of feminists, who were influenced by the class, national, racial and imperial assumptions of their own societies. For example, in Australia Aboriginal women were excluded from claims for the vote and many feminists adopted the rhetoric of white Australia. In the United States there were early links between feminism and the abolition of slavery, but later in the century suffrage campaigners often allied themselves in their rhetoric with the better educated American-born whites against recent immigrants and Afro-American voters.[46] Nevertheless, sense of their own exclusion often did engender sympathy for others who were oppressed: in New Zealand the suffrage campaign included Maori women, and suffragists in South Africa until the 1920s tried to avoid supporting racial policies.[47]

The specifically internationalist organizations tended to be predominantly white, which was unsurprising. But they also tended to assume that women from the most progressive nations should guide women from more backward and repressive societies. Leila Rupp argues that this embedded 'European imperialism' influenced not only the ICW and International Women's Suffrage Association, but also the 1915 Hague Conference. But she also accepts that there was an aspiration by the 1910s to become genuinely international in representation, and a partial recognition that some women in Asia or Africa had enjoyed certain rights denied in the West.[48]

Socialist internationalism

Feminists were often criticized by socialists for their middle-class bias. The growing political consciousness and organizational development of the working class in the West provided the basis of one of the most significant internationalist movements of the nineteenth century. Most attempts today to reconceptualize international politics draw on liberal views, either on a view of international law and institutions as a basis for a developing international society, or on a Kantian cosmopolitan approach. But there is an alternative source for cosmopolitan ideas – socialist internationalism.

Socialists had a more explicitly cosmopolitan vision than liberalism, which saw internationalism as an additional dimension superimposed on a general loyalty to the nation state, whereas the more radical versions of socialism aimed to transcend the nation state and create a socialist world. Both liberals and socialists focused on the significance of the global market. But whereas liberals typically saw this as a means of fostering transnational links and promoting friendly and peaceful relations, socialists saw global capitalism as an essentially exploitative system. Capitalism was, however, in the process of eroding the boundaries of the state. Marx foresaw these developments in the *Communist Manifesto*: 'The bourgeoisie has through its exploitation of the world market given a cosmopolitan character to production and consumption. ... we have intercourse in every direction, universal inter-dependence of nations.'[49] Marx and most socialists also hoped that this process was making common transnational interests between the exploited workers more significant than national ties. In practice resolution of nationalist issues in Europe caused ideological and political conflicts within socialism, but the ideal of worker internationalism remained potent until the outbreak of the First World War.

Socialism developed from a diverse set of radical and utopian ideas into an international political movement in the course of the nineteenth century, reflecting increasing industrialization and the growing strength of trade unions and socialist parties able to call upon a significant proportion of industrial workers. Despite well-known ideological differences between various strands of socialism, articulated with particular sharpness by Marxists defining themselves in opposition to all other schools of socialist thought, by the 1860s there was a sense of an international socialist movement.[50] The language of brotherhood and comradeship was built into the ethos of socialist activism. This sense of socialist internationalism was genuine, despite the bitter ideological, political and personal struggles that divided socialism. The First International, launched at a meeting in 1864, was destroyed in 1872 by the fundamental divisions between the Marxists, led by Marx himself, and the anarchists, in particular the followers of the flamboyant Bakunin.

The need for international cooperation and policy-making led to the creation of the Second Socialist International in 1889, although the extent of ideological rivalry between Marxism and a more reformist approach was reflected in the fact that two rival internationals were held in Paris in the same year, organized by Marxist and anti-Marxist socialist parties in France. (The Marxist congress, smaller but with stronger international representation – there were delegates from most countries in Europe, including Russia, and an American observer from the Seaman's Union and an Argentinian – is usually seen as the definitive event.)[51]

The Second International suffered not only from ideological disagreements but also from the fact that the labour movement in each country was shaped by its distinctive national context and problems. The first attempt at coordinated international action, simultaneous labour demonstrations for an eight-hour day on 1 May 1890, illustrated national variations in the radicalism of the movement, but did result in mass demonstrations and work stoppages in many countries – Germany was a notable exception. The protests were sufficiently impressive for May Day demonstrations to become an annual symbol of worker solidarity. The widespread trade union agitation coincided with a governmental conference on labour legislation in 1890, though it failed to agree on reforms. Unionists extended a degree of international solidarity to particular national struggles in the period up to 1914, though the defeat of the Swedish general strike of 1909 suggested a lack of really effective international support.

One possible objection to seeing socialism in this period as a cosmopolitan movement might be its class basis. But socialists aimed to create a world without class divisions and privileges and attracted many individuals from other classes, and their emphasis on economic and social equality for all fits with cosmopolitan beliefs. When, however, the language and strategy of class warfare implied willingness literally to destroy the capitalist class, then revolutionary socialism was not compatible with the emphasis on individual rights, tolerance and peace suggested by cosmopolitanism. This oppressive potential of socialist ideology became manifest after the Bolshevik Revolution in 1917.

Did socialist cosmopolitanism overcome imperialism? Trade union logic operated strongly, as we have noted, to block the entry of cheap non-European labour. But socialist parties generally opposed colonialism – though with qualifications. Although the International Congresses drew mainly on European socialist bodies, American socialists sent delegates and emerging South African socialist groups attended the 1904 and 1907 Congresses. Argentina and Uruguay were able to provide official representatives, and observers from Brazil and Chile attended the Second International. Despite flourishing labour movements, Australia and New Zealand were geographically too far away and ideologically too removed from Marxist social democracy to be linked to the Second International. Japanese intellectual socialism and trade union activity began in the 1890s, and despite divisions among socialist groups and intensifying police persecution, Japanese delegates attended both the 1904 and 1907 International Congresses. The President of the Indian National Congress attended the 1904

Amsterdam Congress, but industrial agitation in India had not yet resulted in trade union organization, and economic concerns were often linked to the wider struggle for national independence.

The International Congress voted in 1904 in favour of Indian self-government and also passed a more comprehensive resolution denouncing imperialist trade monopolies and oppression of colonial peoples and called for 'the greatest amount of liberty and autonomy compatible with the state of development of the peoples concerned, with complete emancipation the end to be sought'.[52] By 1907, however, the Congress was divided over their attitude to imperialism between those condemning it outright, and those seeking to improve conditions for the native peoples but to retain European control over the use and development of natural resources.[53]

Socialists did adopt a cosmopolitan commitment to oppose major war between capitalist states, but this position was undermined by nationalist allegiances. The International had engaged in serious debates about how the socialist movements should react to the threat of war, and this was a key issue at the 1907 Stuttgart Congress. One central question was whether socialist movements would commit themselves to a general strike in the event of war, but other issues included the case for national militias rather than standing armies, blocking taxes for war, and the revolutionary potential of war. The final resolution was a compromise that committed the working class of each country and their parliamentary representatives to 'make every effort to prevent the war by all means which seem to them most appropriate', but did not specify strike action.[54] The question of how to resist war and arguments for a general strike both arose again at the 1910 Conference in Copenhagen, where the Congress avoided commitment to industrial action but called on Socialist deputies to vote against war credits. An emergency congress was held in Basle in 1912 to protest against the Balkan war against Turkey. The congress scheduled for August 1914 in Vienna had to be cancelled. The International Socialist Bureau, the coordinating body of the International, did, however, meet on 29 July 29 1914 to discuss the crisis, after Austria had declared war on Serbia, and called on its members to step up their anti-war demonstrations and to demand arbitration.

As the crisis escalated into war the various socialist parties ceased to heed the calls of the International Bureau, though there were some attempts to keep internationalism alive. The headquarters of the International moved to neutral Holland, and there were two conferences of socialists from neutral countries in 1915 and 1916, and conferences between socialists on the Allied side and a separate conference between socialists from the Central Powers in 1915. However, the only truly international socialist conference bridging the warring parties and adopting a strong anti-war stance was the Zimmerwald Conference of September 1915, where Lenin played a significant part and which is often seen as a precursor of the Third (Communist) International that emerged after the Russian Revolution. This was, however, representative only of a minority of socialists. The women's section of the Socialist International maintained a more consistent anti-war stance than the International itself, and held a conference in

Berne in March 1915, which was convoked by the German socialist feminist Clara Zetkin and attended by women not only from Austria and Hungary but also from across 'enemy lines' – France, Belgium, Russia and Britain. However, activists in the Women's Socialist International were isolated from their own socialist parties and even more so from the great majority of women in their own countries.[55]

The failure of the Second International to act in a coordinated manner in 1914 is often attributed to organizational weaknesses within the movement, in particular the conservative nature of the large German Social Democratic Party and the divisions within French socialism. Other factors that inhibited international solidarity were opposing national perceptions of military threat (socialists often shared wider national fears about the aggressive and backward nature of states they would be fighting) and the extent of popular enthusiasm for war when it broke out. Socialist internationalism proved too weak to overcome popular nationalism and the realist logic of international politics.

Both liberal and socialist internationalism proved fragile in the period that culminated in the First World War: liberalism because its policy prescriptions proved inadequate and the proponents of liberal internationalism had insufficient weight; socialism because the international socialist movement was still politically vulnerable and because it was not internationalist enough in practice.

Conclusion

The record of internationalism both at a governmental level and between individuals within different states was therefore mixed. Despite the growth of cooperation between governments, conferences to discuss common problems and the evolution of international organization, states still gave largely unquestioned priority to national interest. Even the development of international law was double-edged. Despite increasing recognition of its significance, it was firmly rooted in respect for national sovereignty. Moreover, nineteenth-century jurisprudence rejected belief in universal precepts of natural law; it appealed instead to historical evolution or sovereign authority as the source of law. This positivist view was reflected in Lassa Oppenheim's celebrated *International Law* (1905), which defined international law solely in terms of custom and specific treaties. Liberal internationalism at a governmental level was also limited to the western world: different standards applied to those who were not white and did not share in European civilization.

Popular movements often incorporated a stronger sense of a shared humanity and aspirations to realize human rights and to create peace. But, although liberal movements quite often transcended nationalist prejudices, they did display marked national cultural differences in their view of the world, and also often tended to reflect imperialist and racist assumptions, though not in their cruder forms. Feminists, despite the ideal of sisterhood and a tendency towards a broader cosmopolitan idealism, were also often trapped within their class, national and racial identifications. Socialists, with their greater radicalism and strong internationalist emphasis, did make some progress towards working-class solidarity, but also failed to develop effective cosmopolitan commitments. Both nationalist and imperialist ideologies influenced many socialist and trade union leaders and their rank and file.

One issue of some importance in transnational cooperation is whether people can communicate easily. Although translation is possible at formal conferences, understanding and friendship are both more likely if people can literally as well as metaphorically speak the same language. The well-educated found a common language in Latin in the sixteenth century and in French in the eighteenth century. But by the nineteenth century a simple form of communication for those with less education and leisure seemed needed to unite the world, and there was a search for an international language. Forty in all were invented, of which three had some success. Volapük gained a following in German-speaking areas in the 1880s (it was influenced by the German language), to be superseded by Esperanto (invented in 1887). Ido, an alternative to Esperanto, was preferred by some linguists, but had less political success. Esperanto had acquired widespread support by 1914 among professional and peace bodies, and a Universal Esperantist Congress was held in 1905. Given the artificiality of any invented language – and its tendency to resemble some existing language in practice – the quest for a new world language could be seen as an example of the impossibility of cosmopolitanism divorced from specific national roots. But it did denote cosmopolitan aspirations.

What then were the legacies of this period to the future prospects for cosmopolitanism and world citizenship? We identified three major trends at the beginning of this chapter that are central to today's debates: economic and technological globalization; a corresponding development of liberal internationalism promoting a stronger version of international society between states; and the evolution of transnational networks and movements creating the nucleus of a global civil society.

Trends that tend to unify the globe are not, however, unambiguously cosmopolitan in their outcomes, if cosmopolitanism is understood (as it is here) to mean respect for the human rights and equal dignity of all human beings. One contradictory tendency, highlighted by socialists, is inherent in the logic of a global free market economy. Although this can have some of the positive tendencies identified by Enlightenment thinkers, the pressure to maximize profit and the growth of powerful economic corporations mean that in practice a global free market tends to be exploitative of vulnerable peoples and of the environment. As a result, the political division between exponents of *laissez-faire* and between those committed to give priority to social welfare and social justice, which was sharply defined during the nineteenth century, is still central to analysing cosmopolitanism today.

The second contradictory tendency is even more central to the meaning and political implications of cosmopolitanism: that is, the tension between the necessarily universalist goals and principles suggested by a vision of an essentially unified humanity and respect for the very considerable cultural and social differences that actually exist. Desire to promote one's own understanding of a universal good can lead to cultural insensitivity or even intolerance. Moreover, given the growing economic and military power of Europe – and later North America – over the rest of the world, promoting cosmopolitanism based on western traditions can be seen as a form of ideological imperialism. This chapter has argued that the association of liberal universalism with explicit support for empire is a denial of cosmopolitan principles, and on this issue many liberals in the nineteenth century abandoned Enlightenment ideals, But transnational movements with emancipatory and cosmopolitan goals did tend to reflect some of the assumptions of western superiority. The danger of a linkage between imperialism and universalism, and the rejection of this linkage by a fully articulated cosmopolitanism, emerges as a continuing theme in the next chapter and in Part III of this book.

Part II

Interpretations of transnational citizenship in practice

Introduction: Globalization

Implications for international society and cosmopolitanism

The trend towards globalism manifest in the nineteenth century has continued to intensify. There are disputes about globalizing trends, especially in the economic sphere, where it can be argued that the global nature of the pre-1914 economy based on the gold standard was reversed by wars, the inter-war depression and the later extension of the socialist bloc. Sceptics challenge the inevitability of economic globalization and the decline of the nation state, arguing that neo-liberal ideology and policies deliberately promote global capitalism and undermine controls upon it.[1] There is substance to this argument, and the nature of global capitalism today is often not, as we note below, conducive to cosmopolitan aims.

But at social and political levels the new forms of travel and communication have encouraged transnational cooperation across borders between citizens. There has also been a growth of governmental international bodies and a developing universalism in understandings of human rights to encompass the rights of women and the rights of people of all races. So the imperialism which had its heyday before 1914 was progressively challenged during the twentieth century both by rebellions within the colonized world and by growing liberal doubts in the West about the justification of empire.

The twentieth century, however, also threw up events and movements that halted or rejected both governmental internationalism and moves towards a world of global citizens. The rise of fascism embodied both nationalism and racism in extreme forms and threatened the liberal and internationalist institutions of the 1930s. Decolonization and often artificial colonial boundaries fostered the rise of new nationalisms and numerous wars to settle national frontiers. Moreover, the demise of the older European colonialism occurred alongside the rising economic and cultural domination of the United States, often reinforced by military power and political pressure.

Above all, the prospects of peaceful governmental internationalism were shattered by the two world wars and by the persistence of the cold war from 1947 to 1989. These conflicts did themselves constitute a form of globalism, but of a totally destructive variety. One long-term result of these wars, however, has been to strengthen a form of liberal internationalism. The horrors of the First World War gave urgency to earlier schemes for arbitration and international organization and led to the League of Nations. The League was destroyed by the Second World War, but the victors set up the new United Nations. The promise of this new body was then rapidly aborted by the developing cold war between the Soviet Union and the West.

Nevertheless, the end of the cold war gave a renewed impetus to the United Nations and led to a stronger emphasis on human rights. Global citizenship for individuals also seemed more relevant at the end of the twentieth century than at the beginning because of economic, technological and cultural trends that are summed up by 'globalization'.[2] Ease of movement has encouraged many individuals to travel more widely than ever before and has led to greater migration. Today's means of communication disseminate television pictures of happenings across the world; radios can be owned even in poor and remote villages; and the internet encourages individual and political interchanges. International nongovernmental organizations and transnational social movements flourish, creating what many observers have termed a global civil society.

Globalization in its present form does not, however, necessarily favour global citizenship. The increasing strength of a global capitalist economy means that wealthy and powerful multinational corporations strongly influence national governments and international bodies. The result of economic globalization is often economic and environmental exploitation. Freedom of movement round the world is largely confined to financial capital and to highly skilled professionals, whilst frontiers are closed to the poor and unskilled desperate for work – or they are allowed in as temporary labour, but denied any rights. Global culture is also dominated by the products and images produced by vast corporations and by the selective information disseminated by a few media companies.

At the governmental level the picture is also mixed. The integration of states into an international society with shared values has intensified since 1945, despite the cold war, and cooperation has extended to new areas like preservation of the environment. Governments of states have been willing to surrender a degree of autonomy by joining international organizations, signing a wide range of international agreements and acceding to a developing understanding of international law.

The genuine internationalism and commitment to cosmopolitan values of many governments is, however, questionable. States are reluctant to fund international bodies like the UN adequately, and are now giving proportionally less than in earlier decades towards assisting economic development. The needs of the global environment are frequently subordinated to perceived immediate national economic interests. Declared belief in human rights is often undermined not only by domestic violations of human rights, but also by restrictive immigration and asylum policies.

Nevertheless, governments are often constrained to make some attempt to treat both their own nationals, and migrants and *émigrés*, as having rights under international law, influenced either by domestic pressures or by world public opinion. Groups within global civil society do uphold cosmopolitan ideals, try to uphold international law, and lobby international organizations. Many individuals also choose to act as global citizens by volunteering to serve overseas.

This part of the book explores forms of transnational citizenship in practice in the present era. It does so by examining three facets of such citizenship: how individuals may respond to the moral and political duties implied by global citizenship; how far individuals can rely on the principles of human rights and the requirements of international law; and how far the evolution of international and supranational institutions can create a framework for a fully developed version of citizenship.

Chapter 4 looks at the expansion of global civil society and the various ways in which individuals choose to accept the obligation to act like citizens of the world by taking part in a number of transnational movements. Although individuals in the past have not necessarily seen themselves as global citizens, the effect of their activities has been to uphold cosmopolitan values. For example, peace campaigns in the period from the 1950s to the 1980s, which had the goal of saving the world from nuclear disaster, involved close transnational links between national movements. The idea of global citizenship in the sense of a universal moral commitment and political activity transcending national frontiers was therefore *implicit* in much peace activity – as it had been in the nineteenth century. By the end of the 1990s individuals in campaigns for peace, human rights, development or the environment were beginning to see themselves explicitly as global citizens.

Chapter 5 explores the rights conferred upon individuals under international law that go beyond the nation state. The focus here is on refugees and migrants. In relation to refugees the issue is whether under international law individuals without a country can claim the right as citizens of the world to be granted a home somewhere. In relation to migrants legal moves towards superseding national citizenship are dual citizenship, rights of denizens and transnational citizenship. Principles that should govern asylum for refugees and immigration policies are enshrined in international agreements but are implemented by national governments, and there is often a conflict between a generalized international duty and national calculations of what is possible. Issues of immigration and asylum have become increasingly controversial as the numbers seeking a better life or fleeing the threat of violence increase and as popular opinion in many of the more affluent countries hardens against admitting more strangers. One theoretical issue here is how far states can and should interpret scrupulously their obligations under international law: that is, how far states should become 'good international citizens'.[3]

The final chapter in this section explores the most significant attempt to date to transcend national boundaries: the European Union. Debate about citizenship of the EU is linked to its evolution into an increasingly supranational body, and raises key questions about the range of rights citizens of this new polity should enjoy. But the moves to consolidate rights for those within EU member states have also prompted measures to exclude the poor and the persecuted who hope to join this privileged society. Whether EU citizenship is therefore a move towards global citizenship or an obstacle to cosmopolitan goals needs to be examined.

4 Global civil society

Acting as global citizens

In the Enlightenment the world citizen was typically an intellectual, who travelled widely, met and corresponded with intellectuals in many countries, and advanced cosmopolitan views. In the nineteenth century transnational links bifurcated into occupational and professional organizations, on the one hand, and political movements on behalf of the oppressed, on the other. Since 1945 the quintessential global citizen is usually pictured as the activist in transnational social movements. But that does not mean that the earlier connotations of literally crossing national frontiers and of bonds of common learning and interests are wholly irrelevant.

The idea that travelling is an expression of cosmopolitanism is indeed debatable, partly because mass tourism, which often shields people from the society they are visiting, has nothing to do with increasing international understanding and may have harmful effects on the environment and local culture. But there are still forms of travel that are seen as means of promoting international understanding, for example exchanges between schoolchildren. The image of the wandering student or scholar is also still part of a cosmopolitan view of the world of learning. It is also sometimes encouraged by governments (in a more organized fashion) to promote friendly relations between their countries.

The development of informal networks and formal transnational organizations pursuing professional or social interests has become an increasingly important feature of international politics by the beginning of the twenty-first century. The growth of such bodies can be interpreted as the creation of a global civil society, existing at a different level from the relationships between nation states. The chapter begins by exploring the meaning of global civil society, and its implications for the nature of international politics.

It is not clear, however, that the existence of transnational associations necessarily means that those involved are acting as global citizens. In many cases they are primarily promoting their own particular concerns. Authors meet in international conferences to share their ideas and to call for states and international law to respect their rights to copyright and to an income from their writing; psychiatrists to debate the latest approaches to mental illness. In neither of these cases are the participants meeting for political purposes. Their specific commitments may, however, sometimes spill over into more explicitly political concerns. The International PEN issues protests on behalf of banned and persecuted authors, and international meetings of psychiatrists took up the issue of the abuse of psychiatry to silence dissenters in the former Soviet Union. Moreover, the universal nature of professional commitments, as in science, can be a basis for transcending national and ideological barriers. One important group to challenge the cold war in the 1950s on the basis of shared professional commitments were the scientists from the Soviet bloc, the West and nonaligned countries who met in Pugwash, Nova Scotia, in 1957 to discuss the dangers of nuclear power, how to control nuclear weapons, and the social responsibility of scientists.[1]

Campaigning transnational organizations are committed to global causes. The number and importance of voluntary bodies opposing oppression, or expressing practical solidarity with those suffering in other parts of the world, also grew significantly in the twentieth century. There are therefore many people round the world making links across national frontiers to demonstrate support for cosmopolitan ideals. Whether taking part in organizations frequently cited in discussions of global citizenship, such as Amnesty International, Oxfam and Greenpeace, really does constitute fulfilment of cosmopolitan duties needs, however, to be looked at in more detail.

This chapter considers first whether campaigners for human rights do necessarily promote cosmopolitan goals. It then explores how far solidarity across frontiers to promote social equality can count as global citizenship, taking the example of women's transnational organizations. Thirdly, it looks at a number of organizations offering aid and working for economic development. One of the issues here is distinguishing between charity and promoting social justice. Finally, the chapter examines briefly the role of some environmental organizations, which exemplify a concern for the global commons, are frequently cited as central to the development of global civil society and can provide a model of ecological global citizenship. These brief surveys cannot constitute proper case studies, but they do give some precision to generalizations about this kind of transnational activity.

Transnational movements usually involve political lobbying and protest and sometimes encompass more extreme forms of resistance. But they may also depend on individuals volunteering to offer direct assistance to those suffering from abuse, poverty or war, often in countries other than their own and sometimes at considerable personal risk. These volunteers may therefore be seen as global citizens in a strong sense, individuals and groups campaigning and fund raising at home in a weaker sense.

One way in which very large numbers can potentially demonstrate global consciousness is as consumers. In a global market the role of consumers can be politically significant. If they exercise their choice to boycott corporations with a reputation for exploitation of the poor or destruction of the environment, or to encourage trade that promotes economic development, then consumers are also acting politically. Consumer awareness is promoted by activists for global causes.

Global political activity, like all forms of politics, has numerous pitfalls. One central criticism many well-intentioned voluntary groups face is that they embody an unconscious cultural imperialism, trying to impose western beliefs on other peoples in the guise of universal principles. This issue is examined again in Part III of this book. But there are other problems. Where cosmopolitan campaigns seek to pursue their goals in the context of international conflict, they may frequently be accused of serving the interests of particular partisan interests. Transnational bodies may also be accused of sacrificing important principles in trying to fulfil their particular purposes. These issues are considered in the discussion of different types of cosmopolitan activity considered below.

Global civil society

The concept of civil society has become central to social theory since the 1980s, when dissident intellectuals in Eastern Europe looked to social networks initiated from below to provide a sphere of independence from the state and a basis for resistance. Since then the existence of autonomous social groups and institutions has been seen as essential to democratization both in remaining communist regimes such as China and in other authoritarian states. Democratic theorists have also argued that civil society is essential to liberal democracies, both as a barrier to an encroaching state, and because participation in voluntary bodies provides a political education and promotes responsible citizenship.

There is no agreement on a simple definition of civil society. The major question is whether it encompasses economic activity – both Hegel and Marx conceptualized civil society as the sphere defined by the market economy and its resulting individualism and socially divisive effects. But most theorists of civil society today see it as distinct from both the state and the economy. They focus instead on religious, educational, cultural and leisure institutions, professional bodies, interest groups and charities, and campaigning groups. But organizations arising out the economy to pursue group aims, whether federations of industrialists or trade unions, are usually included, as are consumer groups. Civil society also suggests very informal links – whether between friends neighbours, or fellow enthusiasts of a particular hobby.[2]

By no means all the activities and institutions of civil society within states, therefore, are explicitly political – indeed many are social, religious, cultural or professional. Choosing to join with others in these pursuits only has automatic political implications in a totalitarian (or semi-totalitarian) state where *no* social activity, or organization, independent of official control is allowed. In these circumstances, as Václav Havel argued eloquently in his essay 'The Power of the Powerless', adherence to norms of craftsmanship or professional or artistic integrity necessarily challenge the regime, and social solidarity is inherently a form of resistance.[3] But in a liberal state the value of many institutions of civil society is their freedom from governmental or partisan political influence. Nevertheless, autonomous institutions like churches or universities may be drawn into political action, for a number of reasons. They may feel obliged to debate on public policy when their beliefs or expertise are relevant. They may also have to defend their own principles and right to autonomy, or defend the wider political system that enables them to retain their integrity.

Civil society has until very recently been understood primarily within the context of the nation state, and its significance has lain in defining a sphere outside direct state control. This sphere may be oppositional if the state regime is hostile to pluralism or it may operate cooperatively within a liberal democratic system. But the nature of the state defines the role and nature of civil society.

The meaning of civil society when transferred to international politics, where there is no strong overarching central state, is clearly somewhat different. Some commentators who are sceptical about cosmopolitanism argue that the domestic analogy is wholly inappropriate at a global level, and that the conditions for a global civil society do not exist. They stress that instead of moves towards integration and cultural unity, the world is moving towards greater disorder.[4]

But civil society is a product of political activity. It may therefore exist alongside tendencies towards disorder, for example organized crime, and social disintegration both nationally and globally. Global civil society builds upon the autonomy of civil society bodies within their own nation states, and links them within a transnational realm independent of all nation states. Global civil society can also partially substitute for and precede world governance.[5]

The implications of global civil society must depend, however, on how it is defined and on the comparative economic and political power of groups within it. Just as the ideal of pluralism within the state can mean in practice the wholly disproportionate influence of business interests and a few other privileged interest groups on government policy, so at a global level organizations representing big business often have significant control over both international organizations and the governments within them. Moreover, by virtue of their economic activities, big corporations and investors structure the global environment in which states operate. So although business groups are recognized as part of national civil society in some definitions, and are among the nongovernmental organizations (NGOs) that play a recognized part at international conferences, it is misleading to identify them as members of global civil society. I exclude them in the rest of this discussion. (The problem of seeing top business executives and financiers as 'citizens of the world' is taken up in Chapter 7.)

At the other extreme, global civil society may be identified with social protest movements and with organizations providing aid. This is excessively narrow. The full political significance of civil society depends on it including the growing range of transnational trade union, professional, academic and artistic organizations, as well as the international nongovernmental organizations representing women, students or young people. During the cold war some international organizations in practice operated on behalf of western governments or the Soviet Union, but others remained genuinely autonomous.

What, then, is the relation of global civil society to the nation state? First, it can be seen as transcending nation state frontiers. Global civil society transcends state frontiers whenever transnational networks or movements correspond, hold conferences and plan common action to promote social interests that unite them. These transnational groups define themselves by shared characteristics or shared beliefs that, on this issue, are more significant than their citizenship and identity within their own states. This transnational identification need not necessarily conflict with national citizen loyalties, though it often implies pressing for political or social change within one's own society.

Secondly, global civil society poses a direct challenge to states when groups within one country ignore or oppose official policies to create links with citizens in other countries – in the most extreme case in 'enemy' countries – and when they jointly campaign against their governments in support of shared goals.

How does global civil society precede but promote world governance? Firstly, it can strengthen international society as opposed to anarchy between nation states. Friendship and cooperation between peoples are likely to encourage cooperation between governments. Here cosmopolitan sentiments may serve to strengthen a more limited liberal vision of governmental internationalism. Secondly, popular initiatives to promote universal humanitarian goals strengthen the political salience of principles of human solidarity or respect for human rights. Therefore global civil society underpins and promotes emerging international law. Thirdly, the role of many bodies within global civil society is to assist and lobby international governmental organizations to promote goals of governmental internationalism or cosmopolitanism. They may also monitor critically the operation of UN agencies or national compliance with particular international agreements. In all these ways global civil society is creating a context for strong forms of international law and global governance, although there is some danger of their independence being compromised by taking on semi-governmental functions and cooperating too closely with either govern- ments or international governmental organizations.

Although I have argued for a fairly broad interpretation of civil society, the focus of this chapter is on global organizations, networks and movements that embody cosmopolitan goals. They are an increasingly influential element in global civil society and represent most clearly the potential of global citizenship.

Campaigning for human rights: cosmopolitan principles and international law

Belief in universal human equality and human rights is a basic tenet of cosmopolitanism. Transnational organizations supporting human rights are often cited in discussion of both global society and global citizenship. For example, Richard Falk, discussing how global civil society promotes a world order based not on state interests but on the interests and rights of all human beings, suggests that Amnesty International and regional human rights bodies typify this move towards 'a law of humanity'.[6] An analysis of leadership for global citizenship by Barbara Crosby uses Amnesty International as one of its two case studies. She argues that we are 'being pulled towards world community, world citizenship', but have no clear understanding of what is involved in being a world citizen in the absence of world government. Studying the role of 'leaders in the global commons', those who build transnational organizations, will, she suggests, provide a partial answer.[7]

There are a number of other groups that play an important role in monitoring human rights worldwide and protesting about abuses – Human Rights Watch, which is based in the USA, is one of the most prominent. Lawyers also play a major role, as defence lawyers, as individual activists, and through national and transnational professional bodies, in drawing attention to and trying to rectify abuses of rights. An interesting example of a fusion of human rights and peace concerns is Peace Brigades International, which has since the 1980s provided transnational support for individual human rights campaigners in repressive and violent contexts in Central and Latin America and in Asia, where individuals upholding human rights may face harassment, imprisonment or even death. Volunteers from the Peace Brigades – 'unarmed bodyguards' – are able to offer protection to individuals and organizations at risk because they are foreigners, whose death would cause international publicity. They also lobby government embassies to take up individual cases. When the Brigades held their triennial general assembly in 1998 they had volunteers in Guatemala, Haiti, Colombia and former Yugoslavia.[8]

Amnesty International is, however, probably the best-known human rights campaigning organization, with a separate international secretariat and sections in many parts of the world, and is used here to exemplify transnational action to protect individual rights. Amnesty International was launched with an Appeal in 1961 by a British lawyer, Peter Benenson, and founded as an organization in 1962. Its remit was to uphold the rights of all people to enjoy freedom of belief, speech and publication and to engage in non-violent political activity. From the outset Amnesty's goal was to avoid partisanship in the cold war or favouring the North over the South, by supporting prisoners of conscience from the West, the communist bloc and the nonaligned world. Over time its remit was widened to oppose cruel punishments for all prisoners: it launched campaigns against torture and also against the death penalty in the 1970s.[9]

Amnesty mobilized its supporters to take part in symbolic demonstrations and to form local groups that would 'adopt' and campaign on behalf of particular prisoners. It also developed into a genuinely transnational organization with national sections as members, and with groups and individual supporters in over 100 countries by 1997. It maintains internal democracy through regular organizational conferences and attempts to avoid national or western bias by holding conferences in different parts of the world. An international secretariat was created in 1963 that recruited over time a genuinely international staff. Amnesty also tries to communicate in a number of different languages, although the primary language is English.

Amnesty appeals to individual governments to rectify abuses by letter-writing campaigns and sometimes through sending delegations. But its main focus has been on mobilizing international public opinion. It publishes detailed, authoritative and unemotional reports on the human rights situation in a range of countries, launches public appeals and issues press statements. Public opinion is used to bring pressure to bear on governments responsible for abuses.

Mobilizing public opinion is also a means of trying to strengthen international law. Crosby quotes Amnesty International's 1972–3 report, in which the Secretary-General wrote that 'international law "is virtually dependent on public opinion for its renovation and enforcement" '.[10] Amnesty bases itself on the UN Universal Declaration of Human Rights, in particular Articles 18 and 19 dealing with freedom of conscience and freedom of thought and expression. It works with the UN Human Rights Commission, on which it has had consultative status since 1965, supplying detailed information on human rights abuses and pressing the Commission to enforce human rights provisions existing in international law through monitoring and sanctions. Amnesty also works through other UN forums to strengthen international action on human rights as well as lobbying regional bodies like the Council of Europe (which has its own Convention and a Court to enforce it), the European Union Parliament and the Organization of African Unity.[11] In general, Amnesty has from the beginning argued the need for stronger international institutions to protect human rights. It therefore exemplifies the role of transnational bodies in strengthening international law and intergovernmental institutions. But its influence partly depends upon the extent to which governments have formally (if not necessarily in practice) endorsed international human rights law. Over 140 states have ratified the two UN Covenants on both civil and political rights and on social and economic rights.[12] Global civil society and international law therefore have a mutually reinforcing effect.

Amnesty has also played a role in strengthening global civil society. It has done so partly through its own organization and its campaigning success – Amnesty has influenced the release of thousands of prisoners, though it is difficult to determine whether its campaigns alone prompted governments to act.[13] It has also established links with a range of other nongovernmental bodies concerned with international law and humanitarian goals, including the International Commission of Jurists and the International Red Cross. It also works with Church, professional, trade union and student organizations, and is part of a worldwide community of national and transnational groups monitoring and campaigning for human rights.

Amnesty as an organization can be seen as a collective global citizen. It also provides a framework for individuals to act as global citizens, in the sense that they take an interest and inform themselves about international human rights, write letters of protest and attend meetings and demonstrations and provide funds for Amnesty's activities. Its supporters in liberal democracies are not called on to take risks or make sacrifices. Human rights networks in the Soviet Union and Eastern Europe in the 1970s and 1980s, however, did risk gaol or violent reprisals for protesting on behalf of political prisoners, as have human rights activists in Latin America and Asia. Such protesters act primarily as national citizens seeking to create a better polity, but insofar as they support human rights universally and appeal to international human rights charters they can also be seen as global citizens. The Argentinean human rights activist Emilio Mignone claimed that 'The defence of human dignity knows no boundaries.'[14]

Despite its impressive record of cosmopolitan achievement, Amnesty's policy is open to the criticism that it is biased towards the West, and does not take due account of the realities of developing countries. The human rights it espouses are strictly liberal ones, and some of its supporters have argued that it should recognize the importance of economic and cultural rights. The case for continuing to focus on civil rights was, as stated in its 1977 report, that in this area it was possible to 'achieve practical results'.[15] Moreover, protection from arbitrary detention, and from torture and execution, is important to even the poorest person and to people from all cultures.

Amnesty could initially be seen as gender-biased – its organization was at first dominated by men and most of its early prisoners of conscience were male. Feminist concerns have, however, had an impact on the international secretariat since the 1970s, for example in the language used in reports and in surveying the position of women in their reports in individual countries. Amnesty has in recent years given prominence to major abuses of women's rights, for example it published *Women in the Front Line, Human Rights Violations Against Women* in 1991 and a study of rape and sexual abuse by armed forces in Bosnia-Herzegovina in 1993. A 1995 Amnesty video is entitled 'Women's Rights Are Human Rights'. Nevertheless, campaigning on the specific rights of women has been primarily the province of women's organizations, to which we shall now turn our attention.

Women's rights and transnational solidarity

There are numerous transnational networks and organizations camapaigning on issues affecting women, and their numbers and influence have grown as a result of the new wave of feminism in the 1970s. But the women's groups that already existed before the Second World War – some of them with their origins in the late nineteenth century, and others founded in the inter-war years – saw the importance of establishing women's rights unequivocally in international law at the time of the founding of the UN. They were building on the work of transnational organizations that had put pressure on the League of Nations to embody in international law women's rights at work and the right of married women to a clear national status to avoid the danger of statelessness. A few feminists were included in the national delegations to the 1945 conference to create the UN in San Francisco. Their efforts to ensure that the UN was committed to women's rights were supported in particular by Latin American feminists, who had gained strength in campaigns in the 1930s. As a result several clauses of the UN Charter referred to 'fundamental freedoms for all without distinction as to race, sex, language or religion'.[16] Latin American women also played a decisive role in getting the UN to commit itself in principle to proper representation of women within its own organs. Feminists pressed in addition for an independent UN Commission on the status of women reporting to the Economic and Social Council.

The well-established women's transnational bodies based much of their work within the UN and continued to do so after the 1970s, whilst the new feminist networks were more likely in the 1970s and 1980s to concentrate on cross-border links between women and grass-roots campaigns, though many also made use of UN declarations and conferences. The older groups like the International Council of Women and International Alliance of Women (the renamed International Women's Suffrage Alliance) and professional groups like the International Federation of Business and Professional Women and International Confederation of Midwives engaged, Deborah Stienstra argues, in what could be described as 'interest-group activity', representing their members' views both to member governments and to the UN and lobbying at both national and UN level. A number of religious women's groups also fell into this category. Of these established groups, 25 enjoyed some kind of consultative status with the Economic and Social Committee of the UN, and many had this relationship with specialized UN agencies like UNESCO, UNICEF and the ILO. Among their achievements was the launching of International Women's Year in 1975 and the UN Decade for Women 1976–85, monitoring the position of women within the UN and giving prominence to particular issues such as the problems of elderly women and women with disabilities. However, Stienstra notes that these women's organizations failed to provide the kind of technical expertise and information that Amnesty International is able to offer to the Commission on Human Rights.[17]

Whereas many of the earlier transnational bodies represented the interests of particular sections of women, many of the post-1970s feminist groupings were focused on particular campaigning issues. These included contraception and abortion rights, women's health, sex tourism and violence against women. The new feminist campaigning tactics were also more dramatic and more radical. Attention was focused on the oppression of women through the 1976 International Tribunal on Crimes Against Women in Brussels attended by about 200 women from 40 countries.

There was also a significant difference in organizational style, with many of the new feminists rejecting centralized and formal structures in favour of more flexible networks and frequent transnational conferences and workshops. The new feminism emphasized the importance of providing information and fostering channels of communication. During the 1970s the Women's Information and Communication Service (ISIS) and Women's International Network (WIN) were created. The development of feminist research and publishing also had an international dimension, in academic conferences and in four international feminist book fairs between 1984 and 1990, attended by thousands of women.

Some of the new feminists were highly critical of a strategy of working through the UN, but the UN Decade for Women and UN governmental conferences provided a context for a large number of feminist meetings and activities, and women's groups met alongside official UN governmental conferences. Moreover, the Convention on the Elimination of All Forms of Discrimination Against Women (the Women's Convention) agreed during the UN Decade, and ratified by 78 countries by the end of the Decade, provided a focus for campaigning activity. The International Women's Rights Action Watch (IWRAW), launched at workshops at the Nairobi NGO forum to mark the end of the decade, is committed to work for implemention of the Convention. By 1998 this network had 5,000 individual members and groups in all continents.[18]

The campaign groups of the 1970s and 1980s were more likely to be explicitly feminist than the earlier women's bodies, though they reflected at an international level the range of feminist approaches within western countries – liberal feminism, socialist feminism and radical feminism. There were also some feminist transnational anti-militarist networks linked to the rise of the peace movement in the 1980s. During that decade feminist theorizing began to reject the earlier political labels and to raise new questions about women's identity and the possibility of treating women as a universal 'class'. These new approaches were in part a response to the influential strands of post-structuralism and postmodernism in social theory. In this guise they had more significance for feminist academics than for women campaigners. But new feminist thinking was also strongly influenced by developments within transnational women's conferences, when women from Asia, Africa and Latin America – as well as from non-white minorities in the West – strongly challenged the assumption of western feminists that they could speak for all women.

White 'imperialism', which was implicit in the late nineteenth-century women's liberal organizations, was unconsciously carried over into the lobbying bodies at the UN. Despite the role of Latin American and a few prominent Asian women at the foundation of the UN, the international work of the established bodies, largely funded by a predominantly western membership, tended to be the preserve of 'a group of increasingly elderly, white, middle-class women from First World countries'.[19] Though many such organizations had some third world representation, the full-time executives and the voluntary officers tended to be white. Western feminists' dominance in shaping policies at transnational meetings was first bitterly challenged at the 1975 Mexico City tribune of nongovernmental organizations and at later conferences. It was argued that western feminism was itself a form of cultural imperialism, and that women were not necessarily united by gender, when they were divided by major economic and political issues and by their religious and cultural inheritance.

During the 1980s women's campaigns developed in Latin America, Asia and Africa and these groupings formulated their own priorities. Women Under Muslim Laws, founded in 1984, represented women from Muslim communities round the world; Latin American and Caribbean women had regular conferences in the 1980s; and the DAWN network, created after a 1984 conference on women and development in Bangalore, links women from the South in research and campaigns. Western feminists also became more sensitive to non-western priorities and engaged in dialogue with women from developing countries at various international conferences. There continued to be disagreement over some contentious issues, such as circumcision of girls in Africa (which some feminists saw as genital mutilation and a form of torture) and women's position under Islam. But participants agreed on a wide range of policies at the major NGO forum at Nairobi in 1985, attended by 15,000 women from 150 countries at the end of the Decade for Women, and at the UN Conference in Beijing in 1995. The importance for women of challenging economic oppression and promoting genuine economic development was incorporated into feminist programmes. At Beijing participants recognized that violence against women 'cut across cultural and geographic boundaries', although the primary manifestations of such violence varied in different cultures, from dowry deaths in India to domestic violence (sometimes resulting in death) in Japan and the West.[20]

Established transnational women's organizations and the newer feminist networks do promote global citizenship in a number of ways. They encourage cooperation across boundaries, promote knowledge of worldwide issues affecting women and provide channels for large numbers of women (and some men) to associate themselves with activities focused on promoting women's formal rights and actual security and status.

Women's transnational activity has always had a cosmopolitan commitment to opposing injustice against women everywhere. But as we have seen, until the 1970s the understanding of universalism tended towards an often unconscious bias towards the commitments and priorities of western women. Since then the transnational dialogue has promoted a greater awareness of the variety of circumstances women face, and encouraged a sense of universal solidarity which allows for different formulations of women's needs.

Feminism has also always tended to make links between the improvement of women's position and general social progress. Some feminist demands designed to improve the health, education and welfare of women were seen as also very directly benefiting children and raising social standards. Recent awareness of the crucial role women can play in economic development, widely accepted by economists and aid institutions, illustrates well this long-standing feminist position. But even where claims to women's rights required attacking the (unjust) privileges of men, feminists have often believed that redefining men's and women's social roles will also have advantages for men.

Some feminists have also argued that introduction of womanly values into public life should benefit humanity as a whole, particularly in encouraging the creation of a more peaceful world. This belief has been important in women's transnational peace campaigning. Even if the political realism of this aspiration is questionable, women's peace activity does embody a truly cosmopolitan goal.

Women's transnational organizations have also operated to strengthen international law and the attention given by UN agencies to women's issues. The report of the 1985 Nairobi conference was endorsed by the UN General Assembly, which passed a resolution requiring implementation and regular reviews of progress every five years. After 1990 the UN coordinated activities within many different agencies with the aim of achieving the goals set out at Nairobi. Thirty-three sections of the UN secretariat and of UN agencies joined this new system and more UN resources were devoted to women's issues.[21] There was a particular emphasis on women and economic development.

Transnational action for aid and development

Giving material aid to people in distress in other parts of the world has roots in nineteenth-century philanthropy. The practice has grown in response both to the speed with which news is transmitted and relief can be transported, and to a growing sense of global responsibility. Until the 1940s offering practical aid was seen as the responsibility of voluntary charitable bodies, often operated by religious organizations. During the First World War the unofficial American Commission for Relief in Belgium worked with groups from other neutral countries to distribute food in German-occupied areas with the agreement of both sides.[22] After the war the Society of Friends provided famine relief in the new Soviet Union.

During the Second World War there was widespread famine due to the destruction caused by fighting, the unwillingness of occupying German armies to divert resources to the local population and the British blockade of supplies to occupied countries. The International Red Cross warned of a humanitarian disaster in Greece in September 1941 and the Red Crescent in Turkey organized supplies for some months until the transport ship sank. Pressure from the Red Cross and some western governments persuaded the British in 1942 to allow wheat from Canada through the blockade of Greece, to be distributed by the neutral Swiss and Swedish Red Cross Commissions. Within Britain itself several organizations sprang up to relieve famine in Europe during and immediately after the war. The new UN, however, also assumed intergovernmental responsibility, setting up UNRRA (the UN Relief and Rehabilitation Administration). Voluntary agencies worked alongside the UN body in war-devastated Europe in which was to become a familiar pattern of cooperation between the UN and voluntary aid organizations.

There has been a significant growth in provision of aid both by national governments and international agencies. But the former have often been justly criticized for gearing their aid to national political goals or to supporting business interests, and the latter are vulnerable to the criticism that they spawn a bureaucracy of highly paid careerists.[23] This discussion focuses entirely on the voluntary aid agencies, which tend to spend much less on administration, and whose workers generally accept modest salaries and often take considerable risks.

Since 1945 numerous nationally based voluntary groups and explicitly transnational organizations have sprung up to try to alleviate suffering round the world. Some aid bodies have been formed in response to a specific emergency, but many more have adopted a permanent mandate and have well-funded and well-supported organizations. There are two distinct forms of aid (though some organizations like Oxfam are involved in both): short-term aid in response to natural or social disasters, such as earthquakes or war; and long-term action to overcome deep-rooted poverty in many parts of the world. The first is primarily an expression of humanitarian concern – though it can have wider political implications and reflects a sense of global solidarity. The latter was originally conceptualized as aid, which has overtones of charity, but many groups and individuals involved have come to see it as an issue of global social justice. Development aid has also raised basic questions about western assumptions of knowledge and expertise and the need for the poor to have a voice and central role in activities designed to assist them.

Providing temporary relief to those suffering as a result of natural or human disasters can involve millions of people in offering donations and organizing collection of funds or supplies, as well as mobilizing smaller numbers of skilled professionals and administrators to work on the spot in demanding and sometimes dangerous conditions. This kind of operation normally involves national governments, international agencies and voluntary groups that appeal for funds from the public. This response to disasters like floods and earthquakes arguably falls into the category of humanitarian gesture, but can also be interpreted as a form of human solidarity and a cosmopolitan sense of what unites people across frontiers.

Although essentially apolitical, transnational relief efforts may raise questions about the efficiency shown by national governments, for example in the Armenian earthquake of December 1988 and in the major earthquake in the Marmara region of Turkey in August 1999.[24] On the other hand, there were also positive political implications in both cases. The rapid response by expert teams from the West to the Armenian earthquake underlined the potential for further *détente*, and friendship between the peoples of the USSR and the West, at a time when Mikhail Gorbachev was attempting to pursue a more conciliatory policy towards the West. One interesting element in the international response to the Turkish earthquake was the immediate response of Greek volunteers offering practical aid, setting aside long-standing political enmity between the countries. Turkish volunteers reciprocated when, soon after, Athens suffered from an earthquake. Arising out of these expressions of solidarity in which voluntary bodies took the lead, the Greek and Turkish governments presented a joint resolution calling for a UN international rescue team for earthquakes.[25] So humanitarian action can potentially strengthen international society and undermine ideological or national hostilities. (Human disasters do not of course necessarily evoke sympathies that override political conflicts – the 25,000 deaths in the Armenian earthquake did not reduce the severity of the conflict between Armenia and Azerbaijan over the enclave Nagorno Karabakh.[26])

Providing relief to those suffering as a result of wars between states or civil war, despite its obvious humanitarian basis, can raise many political issues. The proliferating aid agencies may be in competition with one another for funds and a high-profile presence in disaster areas (though they do quite often coordinate emergency relief). Relief may be seen as providing indirect support to governments or guerrilla organizations waging an unjust war – and may involve direct support if relief supplies are seized by those engaging in the fighting (an increasing problem in the 1990s).[27] Conversely, offering aid – even to civilians – may be conceived as a gesture of support for their political and military cause. Oxfam Canada, for example, made a grant in 1971 to an organization controlled by the guerrilla independence movement fighting in Mozambique, FRELIMO, as an act of solidarity.[28] Moreover, individual volunteers offering their services have to decide whether their position is purely humanitarian – providing food to the hungry or medical care to the sick and wounded – or whether they also have a political responsibility to act as witnesses to human rights abuses. On this issue the more radical *Médecins sans Frontières*, set up by French doctors in 1971 during the Biafran war, diverged from the apolitical stance of some of the longer established humanitarian bodies like the Red Cross. *Médecins sans Frontières*, which won the Nobel Peace Prize in 1999, saw its mission as 'witnessing', being close to those in danger and attacking violations of rights. It is now a transnational organization with 23 offices worldwide and about 2,500 volunteer doctors, medical workers and other experts in the field.[29]

The problems facing aid organizations, whose aim is the long-term eradication of poverty, arise primarily from the fact that aid is being given by groups and individual volunteers from the developed North to people in the very much poorer countries of the South. Charity, when the donor is permanently richer and more powerful, is, however well intentioned, always liable to suggest patronage. Maggie Black discusses the 'tension between the obligation of compassion of the donor, and the obligation to the dignity of the receiver'.[30] Moreover, when aid is being given to developing countries, the problems of cultural imperialism also arise: the donors and volunteer workers may impose their ideas about development with insufficient knowledge of local conditions or respect for local wishes. These issues were widely debated within aid bodies from the 1960s.

By the early 1970s the aid community had already recognized that one source of poverty was the fact that the terms of trade benefited the industrial goods of the West over the primary products of the developing countries, and had begun to encourage local communities to produce handicrafts for sale in the West at fair prices to provide jobs. The high-profile British organization Oxfam (which during the 1970s took some not wholly successful steps towards creating an international Oxfam) also began to buy from cooperatives that did not rely on child labour and did not exploit their workers. Nevertheless Oxfam, which had initially often supported local development projects associated with missionaries or other Britons living overseas, was open to the charge of a concealed colonialism. During the 1970s it moved towards working through local people and allowing them to define their own priorities: the focus was at the village level. Oxfam supported the Bangladesh Rehabilitation Assistance Committee, which in the early 1970s promoted local reconstruction with appropriate technology and materials and cheap loans, encouraged agricultural and fishing cooperatives and sought 'integrated development' involving family planning, health care, literacy and a role for women's groups. Oxfam also accepted the philosophy adopted by the US organization 'World Neighbors', which worked in Central America, and focused on training local villagers to spread knowledge of agricultural techniques.[31]

By concentrating on work at a local level and responding to people's own assessment of their needs, voluntary agencies by the 1980s had rejected attempts to promote western-style development through a local elite. But many members of the aid community became increasingly convinced that poverty and development had to be understood within the context of political oppression, environmental degradation and structural injustice.

Aid bodies began to focus on the appalling burden of debt incurred by many developing countries in the 1970s, and the need to stop crippling interest payments on these debts. They also focused on the role of multinationals and of international agencies like the IMF and the World Bank, commenting critically on 'structural adjustment programmes', imposed as a condition of further loans and aid, which required ending food and housing subsidies and other welfare supports for the poor in the interests of market efficiency. During the 1990s increasing attention was given to the impact of the World Trade Organization – on increasing 'liberalization' of the global market, which campaigners argued made it impossible for governments of developing countries to limit the role of western multinationals and to protect their producers.

Can aid agencies be seen as channels for global citizenship? Despite the problems of benevolence arising out of inequality and the dangers of liberal neo-colonialism, charted above, individuals offering money or time to help others in distant parts of the world are putting into practice a belief in the essential unity of humankind. As the aid organizations have become more involved in public education or in political lobbying, some of their supporters have been drawn into political activities to further their cause. Those who actually volunteer to spend months or years abroad are most clearly acting as global citizens. They may take considerable risks in earthquake areas or war zones, and have to adjust to varied and austere conditions.

Volunteers might sometimes have been sent partly in order to provide young school leavers with chances for travel and adventure as well as service – this was part of the ethos of the early years of the British Voluntary Service Overseas (VSO) programme launched in 1958. The result was a political education for the volunteer as well as practical service, which might promote greater cosmopolitan understanding. But VSO has since switched to sending professionals with specialized skills.[32]

Aid organizations do play a clear role in promoting both transnational links between peoples and helping to create an international society between governments. Like other NGOs they often work with the UN and its agencies, and exert pressure for the UN to act more decisively to deal with crises. Aid organizations also contribute to the debate about the most efficient and most democratic ways to offer aid, criticize the negative effects of international bodies like the World Bank, and press governments to act to remove obvious impediments to economic development. At the G8 summit in Birmingham in 1998 mass demonstrations to demand cancelling of debts to the poorest states, backed by a coalition of aid organizations and Churches, met with some official sympathy, though by no means all government pledges on debt relief have been met.[33]

NGOs have also begun to achieve some response by world financial institutions. In response to NGO lobbying, the World Bank set up its Inspection Panel in 1993 to look into claims that the Bank had acted contrary to its own guidelines and procedures.[34] The aid organizations and their allies have had less success in influencing the policies of the World Trade Organization (WTO), created in 1995, although it now provides a forum for civil society bodies.

By the end of the 1990s the WTO had become the symbol of the negative power of globalization, of a global economy dominated by multinational corporations with more resources than many small states and able to ensure the richest and most powerful states – especially the USA – acted on behalf of corporate interests. When the 135 members of WTO met at Seattle in 1999 to discuss a further round of liberalization for the millennium, aid organizations joined with diverse groups – socialists and anarchists, trade unionists, Churches, consumer activists and environmentalists – to articulate their opposition or to engage in mass demonstrations. Over fifty thousand protesters took part in street demonstrations in Seattle, and the major themes over four days were human rights, trade union rights, protecting the environment and opposing biotechnology.[35] Two visions of a global world order symbolically confronted each other: global capitalism given support in international law by the WTO; and an aspiration to a world in which people have control over their own lives and resources, conserve the environment and raise their living standards within a just international framework. *Le Monde* summed up this confrontation in its front-page headline on 30 November 1999: 'Les citoyens du monde s'invitent à l'OMC [WTO]'.

This symbolic contrast is of course over-simplified. It ignores the extent of disagreement and diverging interests among national governments, and official western concern for the developing countries – though many critics argue that the latter is a matter of lip service, rather than effective support for policies that would protect the poorer parts of the world. It also ignores the very varied goals and strategies of the protesters and their contradictions. At the extreme, the minority of 'deep ecologists' at Seattle see human beings as the source of the planet's problems and endorse anti-humanist positions (for example welcoming AIDS as a means of population control).[36] There are, moreover, difficult policy issues. At Seattle demonstrators against child labour had the support of the US government, which was under pressure from American unions. But many involved in development feared that requiring trade sanctions against countries with poor protection for workers would, in practice, make these countries poorer and increase labour exploitation, and would also favour trade by the richer countries able to afford stringent standards.[37] Nevertheless, the great majority of the protesters were united in opposition to what WTO stood for and in favour of a more egalitarian and environmentally friendly world.

Green activists and world citizenship

Groups that campaign for a better environment can be seen as a quintessential expression of global civil society and world citizenship. Lipschutz, for example, comments that: 'One political space in which global civil society is particularly visible is that surrounding environmental politics.'[38] Paul Wapner sees environmental groups like Friends of the Earth and the World Wildlife Fund as contributing significantly to global civil society.[39]

There are a number of reasons why this is so. The first is that environmental issues naturally tend to cross state boundaries: polluted rivers often flow through several countries; acid rain generated in one country destroys forests in another; climate change is truly global in its effects.

Secondly, since the 1970s green campaigns have tended to grow in numbers and had a significant impact on international law and institutions. Environmental issues often transcend the right–left divide in western politics and command support from wide constituencies. Campaigners for the environment have also stressed transnational action and influenced world public opinion. Green campaigns have often also managed to combine scientifically informed analysis and political lobbying with spectacular protests that capture worldwide publicity. Greenpeace International exemplifies this varied campaigning style. Greenpeace grew out of a number of autonomous groups in North America, Britain and New Zealand trying in the early 1970s to develop a green lifestyle, which cooperated informally, for example to oppose French nuclear tests in the Pacific. The Vancouver Greenpeace Foundation then set up Greenpeace International, which has gone on to wage numerous well-reported protests, including against the transport of nuclear waste and against later French nuclear tests.[40]

Thirdly, although there are many western groups protesting on a wide range of environmental issues both nationally and internationally, green concerns are not simply a response to western affluence. During the 1980s many dissidents took up ecological issues in the Soviet Union and Eastern Europe, appalled at the ravages of the Soviet style of economic development. The environment and bio-diversity are also becoming central to politics outside North America and Europe. The poor in developing countries often suffer most from economic activities like logging, which destroy their environment, from multinationals taking control of their indigenous species and from climate change. There are therefore local, national and transnational groups working to preserve the environment. Examples in India are the Chipko campaign by villagers in the Himalayas to save trees from logging, and a well-publicized national campaign is resistance by the people living in the Narmada valley in India to the building of a dam that would flood their valley, which has been supported by Booker Prize-winning novelist Arundhati Roy.[41] In Africa a movement launched by Wangari Maathal has inspired women first in Kenya and then throughout Africa to plant over 20 million trees in 20 years.[42] An example of a transnational network is the Asian Pacific People's Environmental Network operating out of Penang, Malaysia.[43]

Although green concerns can conflict with immediate needs for jobs and development, there is a growing linkage between environment and development issues. This is well illustrated by the campaign in India against genetically modified crops, which it is feared will make the poorest farmers dependent on multinationals like Monsanto, and push them into crippling debt. Monsanto had started planting GM cotton crops in India in 1998, but was forced to stop by mass protests leading to government action. Environmentalists and farmers' organizations argue that traditional methods and ecological knowledge can produce crops more efficiently than genetic engineering and at the same time empower the farmers. In March 1999 a mass campaign, *Bija Satyagraha*, was launched against patenting seeds.[44]

Green politics has encouraged a theoretical re-evaluation of the concept of citizenship. Fred Steward, quoted in the Introduction to this volume, has argued that it requires both a sense of global community and a strong sense of individual social responsibility. It also invokes a concept of rights that includes rights to health and a good environment. Steward suggests that green politics also results in 'an enhancement of civil society in relation to the state'.[45] Andrew Dobson, reflecting on the meaning of 'ecological citizenship', argues that it implies a greater emphasis on obligations than on rights, and 'these obligations are owed primarily to strangers, distant in both space and time'. He also claims that, unlike mainstream theories of citizenship, which focus on the public political sphere, ecological citizenship encompasses the private sphere and is expressed in day-to-day decisions on energy use, recycling of waste, and so on.[46] Steward too focuses on the importance of an ethic of responsibility exercised through consumer choice. Both authors stress that 'green citizens' have direct obligations beyond fellow human beings to other species and to the planet itself: Steward speaks of a 'duty of care' and Dobson of 'the virtues of care and compassion'.

Consumers as global citizens?

Even for those who are not full-time workers or volunteers who go overseas, taking part in campaigns often involves spending a good deal of time in political lobbying, protests or fund-raising activities. Campaigns rely also on a wider circle of members and donors who play a more minimal role – who might be seen as signing on as global citizens but sometimes in a fairly passive sense.

There is, however, another way to support campaigns for rights, social justice and preservation of the environment that involves minimal extra effort or expenditure, but may have a significant economic and political impact. This is the role of the consumer as global citizen.

Economic boycotts have a long history as part of movements for social justice both within and between states. The best-known recent international example is the widespread boycott of South African produce (extended to banking, sport and other activities) during the apartheid era. But in the past such boycotts were exceptions, closely linked to particular campaigns. There is now a growing tendency for people to regulate their day-to-day purchases in accordance with a set of related principles: for example to favour organic foods over those heavily sprayed with chemicals, to buy 'fair trade' goods where the profits return to the poor farmers and handicraft workers, and to boycott companies accused of exploiting poor countries or supporting repressive regimes.

In the context of the vast increase in tourism there are also important questions about its impact on the local society and environment. In some cases tourism can involve direct exploitation, as in the case of travel agents promoting child prostitution. Voluntary groups began to campaign on this issue in the 1990s and argue for action to be taken against it both by governments in countries attracting such tourism and by governments in the countries where such tourists come from.[47] As a positive alternative to both mass tourism and exploitation there are companies that offer to provide 'eco-tourism' that does not damage the environment and respects the way of life of indigenous peoples.

Making political choices in day-to-day life is not limited to shopping and going on holiday. How individuals invest their savings can be a way of trying to support just causes rather than supporting powerful financial and corporate interests, which promote injustice or environmental damage. One tactic used since the 1970s is to become a shareholder in major corporations by a small investment, and then to use the annual company meeting to protest against its policies. For example, British campaigners against levying high interest on third world debt bought single shares in Lloyds Bank to stage a spectacular protest that disrupted the annual general meeting in November 1995 and attracted widespread publicity.[48] The emphasis here is on political protest in a corporate setting.

The alternative is to ensure that one's own savings are channelled in a positive direction. Ethical investment schemes offer savers a way of preventing their funds supporting companies engaged in activities such as arms manufacture to which they have moral and political objections. There are also schemes to channel investments directly into helping the poor who cannot normally get access to credit – the best-known example is the Grameen Bank, founded in Bangladesh, but there are also initiatives in the West.[49]

There are some objections to recognizing politically conscious consumers as serious global citizens. Buying fair trade coffee or saving with an ethical investment fund need not mean making any differences in one's life style. It could therefore be seen as a means of pacifying one's conscience at no cost, or as a form of radical chic. More importantly, it is questionable whether such gestures have a major impact on the economic system. Companies may embrace and undermine environmental and other concerns, for example by claiming to produce 'green' products that are not genuinely eco-friendly. A radical critique suggests that western consumers need to do more than purchase selectively, and totally alter their lavish life style to achieve goals of social justice and preservation of the environment.[50] A less radical position might suggest that the significance of consumers acting politically depends upon their supporting alternative institutions.

On the other hand, it would be sweeping to deny the increasing significance of consumer action, especially in relation to specific issues. Perception of consumer fears about genetically modified (GM) crops in 1999 forced many supermarket chains and some food manufacturing companies to alter their policy on stocking GM foods, and put giant multinationals like Monsanto onto the defensive.[51] Moreover, becoming more aware of the implications of consumption and investment may lead to growing political awareness and more fundamental life style changes. The role of consumers is one important aspect of many cosmopolitan campaigns, and a way of bringing in wider numbers.

There is also a link between consumer action, the response of retailers, and groups active on global issues. For example, Greenpeace, cooperating with Brazilian environmental officials, was able to prove how wood illegally logged in the Amazon rainforest was being sold (without their knowledge) by the London furniture store Heal's.[52] A small environmental group working from London, Global Witness, has campaigned successfully to spotlight the trade in diamonds from areas of conflict like Sierra Leone, where they have been funding the rebels. The UN imposed a ban on trade in diamonds from rebel territory in both Sierra Leone and Angola, and the International Diamond Manufacturers' Association, faced with the threat of a boycott and publicity similar to earlier campaigns on the fur trade, agreed at its July 2000 Congress to certify rough diamonds in exporting countries. The campaign was helped by widespread publicity about children in Sierra Leone mutilated in the conflict. A network of churches in the USA had considered a total boycott of diamond engagement rings before the Diamond Congress met.[53] De Beers, which controls 60 per cent of the world market, has responded to the threat.[54] British Foreign Office Minister Peter Hain commented that 'the twenty-first century consumer increasingly demands the right to know. The voice of civil society cannot be ignored.'[55]

Conclusion

We have noted a tendency towards convergence of transnational campaigns on rights, development and the environment, and awareness of the relation between these and preventing destructive conflicts. This tendency has also been linked to a sense that active participants within them are taking upon themselves the role of global citizens and encouraging others to do so. Oxfam, for example, is promoting the ideal of global citizenship and organized a conference in June/July 2000 to promote the values of this ideal in the classroom. The organization suggested that a global citizen is someone who consciously adopts this role and is committed to social justice, diversity, sustainable economic development respecting the environment, and to a peaceful world.[56]

In the light of the discussion so far, is it possible to determine how far activists in and supporters of transational campaigns can be seen as global citizens? There is clearly a spectrum of degrees of commitment and activity. In addition different models of global citizenship are involved.

The great majority of those who take part in particular campaigns almost certainly see themselves as national citizens first and foremost, with an additional concern about international issues and the fate of individuals in other parts of the world. They may often criticize particular government policies, but believe that if their country took a more internationalist stance that this would be in its long-run interests and would benefit its status in international society. If so they are operating within a long-standing liberal tradition (explored in the previous chapter) and it therefore seems debatable whether labelling this liberal cosmopolitanism 'global citizenship' really denotes a new role.

But the fact that many issues, such as the degradation of the environment and the nature of the economic system, are inherently global means that worldwide action is needed to alter them. A global consciousness and transnational links are central to any campaign. So even those who stand within a liberal tradition of seeing themselves as citizens of their own state, but with cosmopolitan concerns, may increasingly tend to see themselves as having a dual set of moral and political obligations, both national and global. In that case the concept of global citizenship, though partially rhetorical, is far from meaningless. In addition those who focus on their responsibility to the global environment can be seen as developing a new notion of planetary citizenship.

A minority among those who campaign or work for cosmopolitan causes probably do see themselves primarily as global citizens, rejecting identification with their own state and committing themselves to a life of opposition to governments. Some anarchists do desire to subvert both states and international governmental organizations, and to create alternative forms of global community. But the majority of those who serve in transational bodies or support cosmopolitan campaigns almost certainly understand global citizenship as contributing to the possibility of a new kind of world order based on international law and institutions.

Moreover, as noted earlier, the very fact of numerous voluntary transnational bodies creates a kind of global society crossing national borders and undermining the state. New technology can often assist such groups. Greenpeace is experimenting with solar panels to power small satellite transmitters, which would enable campaigners to transmit pictures of illegal logging, or protests at military bases, to its own website and to the media. Sending emails *en masse* can also influence corporations and governments.[57] The internet greatly aids transmission of news and coordination between individuals and groups in different countries, although these include far right racist groups as well as the kind of campaigns discussed here.

There are enormous advantages in a changing technology altering the role of television, which may challenge the extent to which perception of news has been controlled by a few media giants like the Murdoch empire and CNN. But the fact that people may cease to view common news programmes may also make it harder for the cosmopolitan global organizations to make an impact. A former deputy director of Greenpeace UK reflected on the danger that fragmentation of the mass media will also mean a decline in the effectiveness of Greenpeace, Amnesty International or Oxfam to influence consumers and citizens.[58]

Other important factors are, as we have seen, the extension of international law and the role of international institutions. These create a new legal and political framework for individual activity and also place constraints upon governments of states. So there is at least an embryonic world order, within which organizations of global civil society play an important role. The possible danger for global organizations is that they will be compromised by close cooperation with international organizations and become increasingly professionalized and hierarchical internally. There are also dangers of voluntary bodies wasting funds and becoming inefficient – both major problems for international governmental organizations. If so, voluntary agencies may cease to represent the interests of the most disadvantaged and lose their oppositional edge. But it is also likely that new groups will arise to take on these functions.

The final caveat, which relates to a central theme of this book, is that – as the protesters at Seattle recognized – the kind of economic globalization associated with neo-liberal ideology and policies generally operates to nullify the goals of the transnational bodies considered in this chapter. This is particularly obvious in the case of green concerns. Moreover, although there are eloquent advocates of the benefits of free trade for developing countries, the kind of aid and campaign groups discussed here are convinced that neo-liberalism and institutions embracing such policies (frequently the World Bank and the IMF and now the WTO) are making the poor much poorer.

The present global economy also impinges seriously on human rights and the position of women. In part this is because it erodes any social and economic rights, for example rights to food and education, which governments might once have provided. But it also leads to a direct loss of personal freedom for millions. Kevin Bales has estimated that at the end of the twentieth century 27 million people were slaves, a few in a traditional form of slavery, but the vast majority of those sold into effective slavery to escape starvation. These include child labourers and large numbers of women and girls sold into prostitution.[59] Many of the latter are likely to die, some on the journey and many others because of the scourge of HIV/AIDS. It is indeed an irony that Anti-Slavery International, with its roots in the anti-slavery campaigns of the nineteenth century, is still active today.[60]

5 Global or multinational citizens?

Refugees and migrants

The previous chapter focused on individuals and organizations who voluntarily assume global duties and can therefore be seen as in some sense fulfilling the role of global citizens. The purpose of this chapter is to look at the other side of the coin, and to examine how far the moral rights of individuals to be treated as fellow citizens of a world community have recently been either recognized or respected in practice. The focus here is on the right to settle in other countries. Issues of asylum for refugees and of immigration are both extremely topical. They are a barometer of the extent of governmental or social oppression and discrimination in various countries, and of the gap between rich and poor areas. They also provide a crucial test of how far governments and public opinion in the more liberal and affluent parts of the world respect the human rights of individuals, and how far they are willing to act on Crucé's sentiment that the earth should be seen as 'a common city for all'.

The right of individuals to find somewhere to live safely, if they can no longer feel at home in their country of birth, and the right to travel to other parts of the world and perhaps settle there, have been central to the evolving theory of international law and to cosmopolitan thought. For example, following Grotius, two prominent eighteenth-century theorists of international law upheld the rights of refugees and of aliens. Vattel, despite his support for state sovereignty, argued that 'Banishment and exile do not take away from a man his human personality, nor consequently his right to live somewhere or other,' though the exile cannot claim an 'absolute right to choose a country at will'.[1] Wolff claimed that foreigners, regardless of religion, should be able to study in 'our schools and academies' and be able to 'stay with us, for the purpose of recovering health' and should be subject to the same property laws as citizens.[2] Enlightenment cosmopolitanism was committed to the right to travel – provided travel did not result in abuse of the inhabitants of those lands.

Early international law was partly engaged in interpreting moral rights based on the concept of natural law, although it also built on existing customs and specific agreements. By the twenty-first century, human rights in general, and specific rights, such as the right to asylum, have been progressively incorporated into international conventions to which many (but not all) states have formally acceded. In practice, however, governments may ignore their international obligations. But even the existence of a Declaration or Convention gives added weight to individuals and groups appealing to the moral rights of refugees or poor immigrants.

Despite the development of international law with a cosmopolitan focus on individual rights, appeals for asylum highlight the conflict between the claims of a common humanity and the political realities of a world in which, even in an age of globalization, the legal right to cross frontiers is still controlled by states. Ernst Tugendhat has commented that the right of asylum is one 'which is both national and international in its very content'.[3]

Since the First World War the phenomenon of large numbers of refugees forced to flee from their homes has become a major feature of international politics. Specific international conventions and newly developed international institutions have attempted to meet the basic needs of these displaced persons, but at the beginning of the twenty-first century many long-standing refugees still lack a proper home and new waves of refugees are created by civil war and persecution.

Mass migration for primarily economic reasons has been a significant element in globalization. It reflects the pressures within a global economy to recruit labour when needed, and for the impoverished to seek a better life. Mass migration creates greater cultural diversity within the host states, and results in links between immigrant communities and their countries of origin. It therefore tends to promote social activity across borders and to challenge exclusive identification of a 'nation' with the legal and political structure of the state. But in this area, as in others, globalization also stimulates a nationalist reaction, and therefore leads to pressure to restrict migration.

Where immigration is restricted, but many elsewhere are desperate to find work, then illegal immigration is likely to flourish and to be promoted by criminal gangs. The terrible human costs of this trade in illegal migrants was spotlighted by the discovery of 58 Chinese who had suffocated whilst being smuggled by a Dutch lorry driver into Britain in June 2000.[4] Illegal immigration can also result in virtual slavery for the men and women involved, who have no legal rights in the country where they find work and face deportation by the police. So migration often demonstrates some of the most negative aspects of globalization.

But the fact of widespread migration has promoted both academic and political debate about the relationship between the rights of citizens and the rights of foreign migrants. Migration has encouraged the extension of dual citizenship in recent years, despite the legal anomalies that can arise from this status. The existence of large numbers of resident aliens has also led to a dialogue about extending the democratic rights of 'denizens' and stimulated reflection on the concept of 'post-national' or transnational citizenship.

Refugees: the right to asylum and international aid

Treatment of those who are banished, or who flee persecution in their own country, is a basic test of how far governments and peoples are prepared to uphold universal human rights. As we have seen, the rights of refugees were recognized in principle by the early theorists of international law. Although flight and exile have always occurred, the term 'refugee' was coined to cover the 200,000 Huguenots escaping from religious persecution in France in 1695.[5] After the First World War, in response to the plight of millions of displaced people, the League of Nations initiated some measures to encourage governments to cooperate in finding humanitarian solutions. John Hope Simpson commented: 'New means of rapid communication have meant for the refugee that to a certain extent the world is his asylum and the world is concerned with his fate.'[6] After the Second World War, refugee rights were enshrined in international law in the 1951 Convention Relating to the Status of Refugees (supplemented by the 1967 Protocol extending its scope), and over 110 states had signed both by 1993.[7]

But on the other hand, as Hannah Arendt argued vividly in *The Origins of Totalitarianism*, the refugees' lack of any effective legal rights, once they ceased to belong to a particular state, and the tendency of state officials to shuttle them from one country to another, illustrate the emptiness of rights based purely on moral universalism.[8] Pierre Hassner has more recently reflected on how the plight of 'refugees without refuge', who, 'because they are citizens of nowhere' are 'potential citizens of the world', raises the question 'whether citizenship can be based on universal human rights alone'.[9] Even international law offers very limited protection so long as governments retain discretion to accept or refuse entry. For refugees to acquire a meaningful status as citizens of the world, they need effective protection from international institutions. But despite some steps in this direction in the twentieth century, to be a refugee is often to lose one's basic rights and to be cast into a precarious limbo. Indeed by 1998, 50 years after the Universal Declaration of Human Rights recognized that everyone has a right to leave and return to their own country, and the right to seek and enjoy asylum from persecution, a contributor to the *UN Chronicle* deplored the tendency of states to interpret the 1951 Refugee Convention not as 'an individual right but a political offer on the part of the host country'.[10]

The position after 1918

The numbers of people forced to flee persecution rise in times of political upheaval such as revolutions and the redrawing of national boundaries. It is not therefore surprising that when a large number of new states were created in Eastern Europe out of old Empires after 1918, and when communist and later fascist revolutions turned sections of the population into ideological or ethnic enemies, that millions of people became 'displaced persons'. Many became stateless because the drawing of state boundaries in 1919, and in some cases later redrawing of boundaries due to political turmoil, left their nationality unclear, especially if they were not living in their birthplace when new states were created. Many more were displaced by revolutions and had their nationality withdrawn by the new government for ideological or ethnic reasons. This category included Russians, Armenians, Hungarians, Germans and

Spaniards. The practice of withdrawing nationality from suspected enemies of the state was initiated during the First World War, and practised on a much wider scale later. Some managed to find asylum, but many lived a precarious existence as people with no clear status, at the whim of arbitrary authorities and liable to deportation. For example, an estimated minimum of 350,000 out of the one and a half million Russians who fled after the 1917 Revolution were still stateless in 1942.[11]

The problem was exacerbated after 1918 by the tendency of states to impose much stricter controls on any form of immigration than in the past. Some governments also excluded categories of people for ethnic or ideological reasons – for example some Latin American countries restricted the entry of Jews and Argentina refused to admit radicals fleeing from Franco's Spain.[12] The unwillingness of states to grant asylum and eventual naturalization to hundreds of thousands of stateless people was not surprising. Fear that refugees would engage in political agitation or terrorism, or be instruments of alien powers, was one reason for restrictive policies. Reluctance to take on government obligations to provide for the welfare of destitute exiles – especially when economic depression struck at the end of the 1920s – was another factor. So was fear of popular opposition to entry of large numbers of foreigners.

But since the League of Nations had been created to further the humanitarian goals of international society, it had a potential role in helping the stateless. The Covenant of the League did not make any provision for refugees, but faced with human catastrophe the League did begin to act. Initially it created a Commissioner for Russian Refugees. This role was filled by the Norwegian polar explorer Fridtjof Nansen, who also had diplomatic experience and had assisted in repatriation of prisoners of war and the relief of famine at the end of the First World War. After his death, the Nansen International Office continued his work from 1931 to 1938. A second High Commissioner for Refugees was created in 1933 to deal with refugees from Nazi Germany. The International Labour Office also had a refugee section. Finally the League coordinated all its efforts for refugees under a single High Commissioner in 1939, just before the Second World War brought an end to its work altogether.[13]

Nansen organized an international conference in 1922 that agreed on the provision of a certificate of identity that would enable refugees to travel legally across borders. Governments issued the document, which was valid for one year. The rights of those holding a 'Nansen passport' were strengthened in 1926, when another conference agreed that the pass include a return visa. But not all governments endorsed the system – though by 1929 over 50 had signed the 1923 agreement – and immigration officials could refuse to recognize the passport.[14] The other limitation was on the categories offered the Nansen passport. It was originally only issued to Russians, though the passport was extended later to Christian refugees from the Ottoman Empire and some other groups. Fascist Italy blocked an attempt by the League in 1927 to provide a uniform travel document for all stateless people, and the League Assembly later decided against offering the Nansen passport to German refugees, though an alternative document was created for Jews deprived of their nationality by the Nazis.[15]

The 1933 Refugee Convention codified arrangements, agreed in 1928, that gave the High Commissioner responsibility for determining who should qualify for refugee status and vouching for them to governments. In effect the Commissioner became a consul for the refugees.[16] The Convention also ruled out forcible repatriation of refugees to a country persecuting them, and set out rules for the fair treament of refugees inside countries, for example in relation to welfare and education.

But the League's role was limited almost entirely to diplomacy and administration. With the exception of aid to Russian refugees, it did not spend funds on providing food, medical care or shelter. This task was undertaken by a wide range of voluntary bodies, including the Red Cross, the Quakers, the Roman Catholic Church and the Save the Children Fund. There were also a number of organizations that gave aid to particular national groups, for example the Armenian Refugees' Fund and Russian Famine Relief Fund. Many of these voluntary bodies combined to appeal to the League in 1921 to appoint a High Commissioner for refugees, in order to help clarify the legal position of 800,000 refugees then in Europe. When the Commissioner was appointed, 16 of these nongovernmental organizations formed a committee to advise him.[17]

The position since 1945

After the Second World War the scale of the refugee problem became even greater, but the United Nations did make rather more sustained efforts than the League to grant them some aid and protection. Millions were uprooted during the war as evacuees, forced labourers, prisoners of war and exiles. At the end of the war, redrawing of German and Polish frontiers, and the contested creation of Israel, resulted in a mass exodus. But the United Nations Relief and Rehabilitation Administration (UNRRA), created in late 1943, offered aid to countries destroyed by war and was later succeeded by a number of UN specialized agencies, including the International Refugee Organization, created in 1948, which set up refugee camps for the displaced. In 1951 the UN High Commission for Refugees (UNHCR) was created, and at the same time the 1951 Convention Relating to the Status of Refugees provided a general definition of a refugee (which was not linked to ethnic origins as in the inter-war period), stressing a well-founded fear of persecution on racial, religious, national, social or political grounds. The Convention also laid down the principle that refugees cannot be returned against their will to a country where they may be persecuted, and set out standards for their treatment within countries offering asylum. The Convention only applied, however, to those who became refugees before 1951 and was limited to Europe, so the 1967 Protocol established true universality, but this universality was based on a narrow definition of the status of refugee.[18]

Experience of masses of people being displaced for other reasons led to two regional agreements that broadened the definition. The 1969 Convention initiated by the Organization of African Unity (OAU) specified external aggression, occupation, foreign domination or internal political turmoil as reasons for refugees to flee their country. The 1984 Cartagena Declaration on Refugees, issued by Central American states and Mexico, included the OAU categories, but added massive violation of human rights. In addition the UN General Assembly has asked the UNHCR to step in where a crisis exists, even if the groups are not covered by existing definitions of a refugee under international law – for example to offer aid to large numbers displaced within their own countries such as the Kurds in Northern Iraq. There has also been a tendency for national authorities and judges to extend the definition of persecution. Canada, for example, has given asylum to women suffering rape or domestic violence.[19]

In order to become a refugee it is necessary to leave one's own state. But communist states and other repressive regimes have often refused to allow their citizens to leave at all, or have only released selected categories. Thus the right to freedom of movement for migrants and refugees, granted under the Universal Declaration of Human Rights, has often been denied. These restrictions have also, of course, restricted numbers of potential refugees.

The assumption in the early 1950s that the work of the UNHCR would shortly be finished proved much too optimistic. Some problems, such as the Palestinians condemned to live in refugee camps, remained intractable: 2.8 million were still registered with the UNRWA in 1995.[20] Moreover, numbers of refugees rose rapidly in the 1970s due in particular to external and civil wars in southern and central Africa, Vietnam, Laos and Cambodia, the Lebanon, and the Soviet invasion of Afghanistan. After the disintegration of the Soviet control over Eastern Europe and the break-up of the USSR itself by 1991, and as a result of the fratricidal wars within the former Yugoslavia, the number of refugees in Europe soared to an estimated 1.9 million in January 1995. But at this time there were 6.75 million in Africa, due to numerous wars in the continent and the genocide in Rwanda, and 5 million in Asia. The UNHCR, therefore, was responsible for 14.5 million refugees in 1995, as well as another 13 million displaced within their own countries. Although voluntary organizations still play a very important part in providing both short-term and long-term aid, the emphasis has changed significantly since the inter-war years, when governments regarded charity as a private matter.

The sheer number of refugees is threatening the international system created for their protection. The UNHCR 1995 Report deplores the declining commitment to the right of asylum and 'a growing readiness to ignore long-established protection principles and humanitarian norms'.[21] The political motivation behind offering asylum has also changed. During the cold war the West was disposed to welcome the usually relatively small numbers of political dissidents who escaped from communist regimes, were forcibly exiled or allowed to depart. Indeed the USA, until the 1980 Refugee Act, defined refugees in relation to people escaping communism.[22] Providing asylum publicized both the repressive character of communism and the liberal rights prevailing in the West, and therefore had political value. These considerations prevailed even when refugees fled in large numbers, as they did after the suppression of the 1956 Hungarian Uprising. The flight of refugees from Vietnam after the victory of the communist North created greater problems. Some western states – especially the USA – did offer asylum, but neighbouring Southeast Asian states proved reluctant to accept huge numbers. Many of the Vietnamese boat people interned in Hong Kong were forcibly repatriated to Vietnam on the grounds that the Hong Kong immigration authorities defined them after investigation as 'economic migrants' rather than refugees. But 200,000 were still in the refugee camp when it was closed down in June 2000.[23]

The great majority of refugees flee to neighbouring countries, which are themselves often extremely poor. But a minority of refugees from Africa and Asia, and those from the former Soviet bloc, have sought refuge in the developed world of North America, Western Europe, Japan and Australia. Numbers of applicants for asylum to OECD countries rose from 116,000 in 1981 to 541,000 10 years later and to about 700,000 in 1992, then falling to 330,000 by 1994.[24]

The EU and restrictions on refugees

The members of the European Union in particular became increasingly restrictive in their asylum policy during the 1990s. As the numbers coming to EU countries increased in the late 1980s – from 70,000 in 1983 to over 200,00 in 1989 – attitudes to asylum also began to change.[25] There was no longer a political bonus in offering asylum, and concerns about financial cost became more salient. Collinson comments that the 'moral, legal and humanitarian bases of refugee policy in Western Europe – particularly its emphasis on asylum – are only now really being put to the test'.[26]

In addition, as the EU has moved towards total freedom of movement within its borders and extended the range of rights available to members of other states within the Community, it has become more unwilling to admit strangers, especially those in distress. This dual logic was expressed in the Schengen Agreement of 1985. The Dublin Asylum Convention, agreed in 1990, which came into force in 1997, specified that only one EU country – the one in which the refugee first arrived – would consider granting asylum. Moreover, EU Ministers agreed in July 1993 to classify large parts of the world sufficiently safe to return asylum seekers there, even if the refugees claim persecution. The decision by Germany in 1993 to end its previously liberal policy towards accepting refugees, partly because of the large numbers from Eastern Europe seeking asylum, also encouraged the rest of the EU to tighten up asylum policy. Britain, for example, passed the 1993 Asylum Act designed to speed up proceedings and send asylum seekers back to a country designated 'safe'.[27] European governments have also adopted measures such as fining airlines that carry asylum seekers without official passports from their country of origin. The goal of uniform procedures within the Union can itself be used to make asylum policy less liberal. The British Home Secretary, Jack Straw, went to an EU Justice and Home Affairs meeting in October 1999 with the aim of curbing British judges who adopt 'an over-liberal approach' in interpreting asylum.[28]

It is ironical that the EU, the most impressive example of institutions, laws and agreements that secure rights across national borders, should also act to curb universal rights and even a weak concept of global citizenship. But it is not only the logic of regional supranationalism that is at work here. The increasing lack of sympathy for human beings in distress is also spurred by a rise in xenophobic nationalism throughout the EU, particularly in the two states that have played a central role in promoting the Union – France and Germany.

One element of stricter rules on asylum has been an increasing tendency to categorize refugees as illegal immigrants. But refugees may by definition often be unable to secure official papers from the government oppressing them. Refugee organizations suggested that from 1994 to 1999 between 500 and 1,000 asylum seekers, some seeking to travel to North America, had been prosecuted in Britain for possessing forged documents. The High Court trying three test cases ruled in July 1999 that the British Government was contravening its obligations under the Geneva Convention on refugees, since Article 31 states that asylum seekers should not be penalized for illegal entry.[29] Another measure to limit asylum has been to redesignate political refugees as economic migrants – particularly when they come from poor areas. It is true that the distinction between escaping governmental or social persecution and escaping from conditions of extreme poverty is not always clear-cut, and that in some cases people only escaping poverty have no doubt sought asylum. But the tendency of EU governments to treat asylum as part of an immigration policy means that concern for universal human rights becomes wholly subsidiary.[30] The Italian Government was strongly criticized when in August 1999 it decided to treat as illegal migrants about 7,000 Gypsies from Kosovo, who were fleeing from violent reprisals by Albanians (who accused the Gypsies of collaborating with the Serbs). During the NATO intervention in Kosovo Italy had created a special 'humanitarian status' for Kosovar refugees, which it now revoked.[31] If asylum and migration policy are merged, then questions about the treatment of all immigrants, and whether the country of immigration observes due process and respect for the rights of immigrants, become even more important.

Migration and the spectrum of citizenship rights

Changing patterns of migration and national policies

Economic migration rose rapidly in the decades before 1914, but increased even more dramatically in the later part of the twentieth century. By the 1990s an estimated million people migrated each year. A rapidly growing population and striking divergence between the prosperous and poor parts of the world (where the population has also grown fastest) are two major reasons.[32] The developments in communications, which both inform the poor about wealth elsewhere and make travel easier, have also encouraged people to leave their homeland to seek a better life. The scale of migration reflects, therefore, one of the positive effects of globalization, that it creates a sense of 'one world' – although the information conveyed by the media to would-be immigrants may be misleading.[33] But it reflects even more strongly the damaging effects of the present global economy on the living standards and environment of the majority of the poor.

Governments' willingness to allow migration has often been influenced by racial or ethnic factors. Before 1914 governments were beginning to restrict immigrants on these grounds, but in the inter-war years explicitly racial and ethnic policies predominated. The USA set strict quotas biased towards migrants from North and West Europe; Canada, Australia and New Zealand favoured the British and West Europeans; and Latin American countries favoured people from Italy, Spain and Portugal. The onset of economic depression and widespread unemployment led governments to discourage immigration even further.

The readiness of countries to welcome economic migrants depends to a considerable extent on the demand for labour. Although there is an international elite of the highly qualified who move from one well-paid job to another in different countries, the vast majority of migrants offer cheap and less skilled labour. During the 1950s and 1960s, therefore, the main flow of economic migrants was to North America and Western Europe. Britain and France drew particularly on their previous empires – migrants came from the Indian subcontinent, sub-Saharan Africa and the West Indies, and from North Africa respectively – whilst Germany attracted guest workers from Turkey and Yugoslavia in particular. After western economies slowed down in the 1970s, more foreign workers were attracted to the oil-rich Gulf States and the rapidly developing economies in parts of Asia.[34] But towards the end of the 1980s economic migration into Western Europe rose again, and in the 1990s many more were seeking entry.

In the 1990s, however, Western Europe treated wide-scale immigration as a problem to be controlled rather than a potential economic benefit. Fear of floods of migrants from the former Soviet bloc as well as from Africa, and the belief that relaxing border controls within the EU requires a strong common policy of effective external controls, have both influenced attitudes. In addition to seeking common intergovernmental action within the Union, the EU has encouraged states that may be sources of migration to enter into agreements to curb illegal migration and tighten up border controls. (The name of the 1991 'Conference on European Cooperation to Prevent Uncontrolled Migration' signalled the EU agenda.) In effect the EU tried to create a buffer zone in Central Europe and to get governments there to prevent migrants reaching the West.

Prosperous Asian countries were more welcoming to immigrants, and willing to turn a blind eye to illegal border crossing for most of the 1990s. But the crisis in financial institutions, which undermined economic stability in Asia in 1997, meant a fall in demand for outside labour in countries with previously buoyant economies. For example, Malaysia, which had provided work for thousands of Indonesian labourers, launched 'Operation Go Away' to deport 10,000 immigrants a month. But since Indonesia was suffering even more severe unemployment, thousands continued to cross the border illegally into Malaysia. When illegal migrants rioted in detention camps in March 1998, Prime Minister Mahathir bin Mohamad denied claims that there were human rights abuses in camps for those waiting to be repatriated.[35]

Migrants' rights and issues of citizenship

The degree to which economic migrants enjoy either basic human rights or the rights of citizenship varies enormously. At one end of the scale there are illegal migrants, desperate for work, who may take great risks in entering their destined country. Mary Robinson, the UN Human Rights Commissioner, drew attention to the fact that hundreds of Mexicans trying to cross into the USA die each year, and in May 2000 the UN sent an investigator to the Mexican border to look into vigilante killings of Mexicans by Texan ranchers.[36] When migrants reach their destination they live on the fringes of society, open to exploitation by unscrupulous employers and vulnerable to harassment and deportation by the police. Their position is similar to that of refugees who elude initial frontier controls, but they have even less claim under international and national law to make a case for staying, though they may have a right to appeal against deportation.

Illegal immigrants therefore enjoy virtually no rights at all, though if they can stay long enough, with the help of members of their ethnic community, they may qualify for the periodic amnesties granted by governments to those who have entered illegally in the past. Many Western European governments have offered amnesties to tens of thousands of illegal entrants. But, as noted above, countries in the EU have tended since the 1990s to impose stricter curbs on illegal immigration. The US amnestied 2.7 million in 1989. Moreover, in the US the many thousands of Mexicans who have illegally crossed the border, and not gained any recognized status, have been able to send their children to school and gain some welfare benefits.[37] Right-wing political candidates have threatened to remove these rights.

Even migrant workers who enter legally may have very limited rights, depending on the policies of the host government. The Gulf States, for example, when they let in large numbers of foreign workers, subjected them to extremely harsh conditions. The migrants required government permission to do specific jobs and to change their place of work; they were denied the economic right to own property or businesses and access to social services; and they were also denied political rights to hold public meetings or form trade unions.[38] Some Western European countries – Germany, Switzerland and Belgium – created the category of 'guest worker' for unskilled migrant labour, which only allowed temporary residence and no citizen rights. Some guest workers always intended to return home, but over time others were allowed permanent residence. Their children have claimed rights of citizenship in Germany, with some success (see below).

At the other end of the spectrum from illegal migrants, and the poor and unskilled admitted on a temporary basis, are those who are allowed to enter as permanent residents with the expectation of gaining full citizenship. The countries that have historically relied on a flow of migrants to boost their population, like the USA, Canada and Australia, tend to be most open to granting citizenship, though states generally allow the possibility of long-term residents acquiring full citizen rights. However, states like Israel and Germany, which have been willing to open their doors to all those claiming to be Jews or Germans respectively, have not in the past recognized rights of citizenship based on residence. A number of European states – including Germany – that have traditionally stressed ties of blood, '*jus sanguinis*', slightly modified their position in the 1990s.[39]

But allowing migrants to *change* their nationality, and identify totally with their new country, still involves restriction of choice. It may become difficult to visit relatives in one's native land and there may be financial penalties, such as problems over inheriting property or losing pension rights in one's country of origin. Moreover, renouncing one's first nationality may be seen as abandoning one's culture and identity. Many in the Turkish community in Germany, for example, whilst desiring citizen rights in their country of residence, do not wish to give up all their links to and rights in their land of origin.

A cosmopolitan stance on migration suggests that there should be a distinction between nationality and citizen rights, and that people should potentially be able to enjoy civil, social and even political rights in more than one country. A general right to 'be treated equally' wherever one goes can be seen as an ideal of global citizenship, although one that is extremely remote. Alastair Davidson comments that, 'while it should function as a light on the hill, it is still so far off as to be very dim'.[40]

There are, however, some international bodies that do create cross-border rights. The UK grants resident citizens of Commonwealth countries civil and political rights, including the right to vote in national elections. These rights are extended to the Irish, treated like a Commonwealth country since 1949. This position arises out of Britain's imperial history and decolonization. However, since the 1960s the right of people in former colonies to enter Britain has been drastically curtailed. The European Union is a new experiment in regionalism that has created a new status of European citizenship. This experiment is examined in the next chapter.

The long-established legal provision that allows individual citizen rights in more than one country is dual citizenship, although this is only a limited extension of the concept of national citizenship. An alternative approach, which is also emerging in law and political practice in the West, is to grant a wide range of citizen rights to foreign residents. The case for 'denizens' rights' has been argued by Tomas Hammar and a number of other experts on migration, such as Rogers Brubaker and Zig Layton-Henry.[41] Rainer Baubock has also explored approaches to including immigrants in democratic politics.[42] From a slightly different perspective, Yasemin Nuhoglu Soysal has argued that there is an emerging form of 'postnational' or transnational citizenship, which grants rights not on the basis of belonging to a particular state (or states) but on the basis of international recognition of universal human rights. These three approaches, which represent different points on a spectrum from national citizenship towards a version of global citizenship, are considered below.

Dual citizenship

In the past, dual citizenship has often been almost accidental, for example as a result of being born outside one's parents' home country. But it has become a more systematic response to migration. People may be granted dual citizenship if they leave their country of origin to live and work in another country, where both states favour the concept of dual citizenship. Where there are close ties and frequent migration between two countries, citizen rights may be extended automatically by the host country. Normally, however, individuals have to apply for citizenship within their country of residence after some stipulated period.

Dual citizenship can cause problems. It has, for example, sometimes meant that men became liable for military service in both countries. Conversely dual citizens may be seen as a potential security risk. Other considerations are: dual citizenship may legalize kidnapping a child by one parent returning to his or her country of origin; it may lead to dual voting rights, which is questionable on democratic grounds; and there may also be questions about which state should extend diplomatic protection.[43] Perception that dual citizenship created undesirable legal complexities led the Council of Europe in 1963 to formulate a Convention to reduce multiple nationality and dual obligation to military service. But only 11 countries had ratified this convention by 1990,[44] and restricting dual nationality only strictly applied to nationals of other ratifying states. Some states that grant citizenship on the basis of residence rights have been happy to continue to extend dual citizenship. France, for example, allows Portuguese and Spanish immigrants dual citizenship – although it signed the 1963 Convention, it does not apply the Convention to nationals of non-signatories like Portugal, or countries that have only signed the chapter relating to dual military obligations, like Spain.[45]

Moreover, the position in Europe has changed since 1963. The position of women has also altered, so that women who in the past would on marriage have usually taken the nationality of their husband are now often able to retain their own nationality and may also confer it on their husbands. Children of mixed marriages are also likely to inherit their mother's nationality as well as that of their father. A Council of Europe Resolution in 1977 supported this dual citizenship for children (at least until they came of age), which led the Swedish Government to suggest in 1981 that the Council of Europe should re-examine its general position on dual citizenship.[46] At that time only France and Sweden supported making dual citizenship easier. Nevertheless, by the end of the 1980s it was estimated there were a total of 3 to 4 million people with dual citizenship in Europe – statistics are not exact.[47]

There have been further changes within Europe since the end of the 1980s. Notably, the obligation to military service has since the end of the cold war been abandoned in a number of countries. Several national governments have also changed their previous position that opposed allowing naturalized citizens to keep their original nationality. Sweden set up a Parliamentary Commission on Citizenship, which reported in 1986 that in principle immigrants in Sweden should be allowed dual citizenship. States with a policy of normally restricting citizenship to those claiming ethnic ties have in some cases also reconsidered their policy on dual citizenship. Switzerland decided to allow dual citizenship in 1990 and the Netherlands in 1991.[48]

The public debates in Germany have been most widely reported, partly because Germany had welcomed large numbers of immigrants, but had very low rates of naturalization. An international conference in West Berlin in 1989 noted that nearly 5 million had lived in Germany for 20 to 30 years without acquiring full citizen rights. The German government was strongly opposed to dual citizenship, whilst the Turkish government was happy for its nationals to acquire it – but not for them to renounce their Turkish links. By contrast the German government offered citizenship unconditionally to those of German descent in the Soviet Union or Eastern Europe, even if they spoke no German.[49] In the context of rising hostility to immigrants and asylum seekers, the Social Democratic Party called in 1993 for the extension of dual citizenship, which would 'send a signal to our foreign residents that we fully recognize them as human beings'.[50] Once in power the Social Democratic Government introduced legislation to liberalize the procedures for long-term residents – in practice particularly Turks – to acquire German citizenship and for children born in Germany to acquire dual citizenship. The legislation was attacked by the right wing in Germany, but passed in amended form early in 1999.

In general, countries that lose many of their citizens through emigration favour dual citizenship, while the prosperous states that receive immigrants may be more hesitant. The changing attitudes in Europe are therefore significant, though their significance is offset by the clampdown on immigration from outside the EU. Countries with a history of encouraging immigration, such as Australia and Canada, are also more likely to grant dual citizenship.

Dual citizenship is open to interpretation in different ways. It may not mean having active rights in one's country of origin when living abroad. Hammar notes that Spanish and Latin American law allows for 'sleeping citizenship', which can be invoked by a returning national.[51]

One of the arguments for dual citizenship is that increasing numbers of immigrants in North America as well as Western Europe are reluctant to seek naturalization, and may therefore lack some basic rights, in particular political rights. But it is arguable these rights can be secured without engaging in the legal complexities of dual citizenship and allowing for people to move between several countries in their lifetimes.

Denizens' rights

Long-term or permanent residents, who have sought employment in another country, become effectively part of the population of their adoptive state.

Hammar has adopted from earlier English usage the term 'denizens' to denote the status of privileged aliens who have both rights and duties in their country of residence, but lack the full rights of citizenship. He limits the term to legal permanent residents who do not need to renew their work or residence visas periodically (though they may in fact leave for economic or other reasons). His well-known thesis is that the existence of millions of denizens in North America and Western Europe, who cannot vote or stand for office, poses a problem for democracy.

In the case of Western Europe the special rights granted to citizens of member states of the European Union means that only migrants from outside the EU would count as denizens. Although denizens have enjoyed in varying degrees civil, social welfare and employment rights and pay taxes, they have typically lacked political rights. This is no longer wholly true, since a number of European countries – such as Sweden, Norway, Denmark and the Netherlands – have extended the right to vote in local elections to non-EU residents. A debate about allowing foreigners from outside the EU to vote in local elections – EU citizens have had this right in principle since 1992 – revived in France at the end of 1999.[52] But denizens cannot vote or stand as candidates in national elections (except for Commonwealth and Irish citizens in the UK), though Hammar hopes that rights of participation at a local level will encourage immigrant involvement in political parties and pave the way for national participation. If this goal were achieved, then denizens' rights would be virtually identical to those of citizens (depending on arrangements for diplomatic representation), but a distinction would still be maintained between formal nationality, with its symbolic associations, and specific rights and duties.

The moves towards granting some political rights to denizens reflects changing policies in Europe since the Second World War. In the 1950s and 1960s 'guest workers' were seen as temporary migrants, and subject to severe legal restrictions. They could not bring their families to join them, and did not enjoy the basic civil freedoms of movement, assembly or association. Nor could they freely change their jobs. They could not therefore join trade unions. But during the 1970s, when restrictions on numbers entering were imposed, many European governments passed laws extending a range of citizen rights to migrants already in the country, many of whom also gained the status and security of permanent residence.[53] Migrants were able to apply for their immediate families to join them. They also became eligible for many welfare rights, such as education, health care and social security, though, given disparities in welfare provision in different countries, the precise benefits and conditions for eligibility varied. In general, migrants also became free to apply for all available jobs, though many countries exclude non-citizens from some or all civil service posts and sometimes from public legal roles.[54] There may also be problems about the acceptability of some professional qualifications.

By the 1980s those countries that had previously withheld civil and political rights from immigrants (for example France and Belgium had denied the right of association) lifted some of these restrictions. Thus, in general, migrants acquired legal rights to due process (though with variations between countries in relation to deportation), rights to freedom of religion, and rights to free speech and assembly and association, so that they could join unions and political parties. During the 1970s and 1980s there was also an expansion of organizations representing migrants, in some cases fostered by the state, which represented migrants' interests, assisted integration into the host society, and offered various social services. Migrant organizations have also helped to maintain the religious and cultural heritage of their ethnic groups, and in some cases have received public funding to do so. There has also been, therefore, an extension of recognized cultural rights.[55]

From this perspective migrants in Western Europe now enjoy almost all the rights of citizens, and some rights specific to their immigrant status. Moreover, not only permanent residents, but also legal temporary residents, have access to many of these rights. A similar pattern applies in North America and Australia. There has therefore been a historical shift in the willingness of western societies in general to grant an assured status to large numbers of resident aliens. Soysal points to the draconian treatment of temporary migrants towards the end of the nineteenth century in many countries – her generalizations do not apply to the UK. Such migrants might have no claims to protection in the workplace or to state welfare, such as poor relief, and were often subject to strict supervision by the police and deported for minor misdemanours or as it suited government economic policy.[56] This situation changed especially after the Second World War, with a marked movement towards ensuring migrant rights since the 1950s.

Soysal notes that unlike the movement from civil to political rights to social rights assumed by Marshall, who saw political rights creating pressure for welfare, denizens have tended to acquire social rights and rights at work before gaining any political rights.[57] This progression has also been noted by commentators on the evolution of European Community citizenship.

Postnational or transnational membership

Both Hammar and Soysal focus on the extension of rights of residents who are not citizens. But whereas Hammar is still thinking primarily in terms of rights in the context of residence within nation states, Soysal sees herself as transcending this territorial basis for claiming rights, and is arguing for a fundamental rethinking of citizenship. She is challenging the 'nation-state model' to argue that there have been 'fundamental changes in the relationship between the individual, the nation-state, and the world order'. Her alternative model is 'postnational membership', in which 'the individual transcends the citizen' and which provides a 'transnational status for migrants'.[58]

The exclusivity associated with citizenship of a particular state is, she argues, giving way to an international system in which individual rights are guaranteed under international law. The increasing interconnection between states, including mass migration, and an increasing emphasis on the universal rights of individuals, mean that the role of the state has changed. States still have direct responsibility for how individuals are treated, but the rules and norms are set at an international level. Soysal cites the Universal Declaration of Human Rights and the European Convention on Human Rights, noting that many countries have incorporated these into their constitutions. She also lists the large number of more specific international agreements, at both UN and European levels, covering the rights of migrants as workers, rights to family reunification, cultural rights, and prohibition of religious, racial or gender discrimination.

These developments in international law also mean that if governments come to power with an agenda of restricting the rights of denizens or seeking to repatriate them, they can be challenged in national and international courts. She also notes that migrant organizations increasingly appeal to these universal norms and international legal rights. She cites a number of examples relating to calls in the late 1980s and early 1990s for political and cultural rights, for example Turks in Berlin demanding teaching in Turkish in schools on the grounds that use of one's mother tongue is a human right.[59]

Soysal is careful to deny that she is charting some irreversible historical progression towards transnational citizenship, noting that both economic and political factors – for example a scaling down of welfare – can undermine some of the rights of denizens. She also takes due note of the rise of identity politics and nationalism. But she argues that regional identities are undermining nation states, and that 'as particularist identities are transformed into expressive modes of a core humanness, thus acquiring universal currency, the "nation" loses its charisma'.[60] Soysal's thesis is not that a strictly global citizenship is emerging, but that the position of migrants demonstrates the emergence of multiple membership in a variety of societies and the acceptance of multiple identities, with 'intersecting complexes of rights, duties and loyalties'.[61]

There are several major qualifications that need to be noted about the thesis of an evolving transnational membership. Even states that ratify international conventions may opt out of some provisions – for example Britain did not ratify the fourth Protocol for the European Convention on Human Rights, which would have ruled out the 1968 Immigrants Act, which effectively made Asian citizens expelled from East Africa stateless.[62] Moreover, even the formal rights that are guaranteed to migrants may be very significantly eroded in practice. Soysal notes that there is an 'implementation gap', but does not elaborate in any detail. This gap is, however, of very considerable importance for many migrants. There is, for example, a major discrepancy between the legal right to be joined by one's spouse and children and the actual difficulties and delays experienced by migrants from the Indian subcontinent living in Britain.[63] Moreover, fear of illegal immigration may result in police harassment of legal residents.

But a gap between international norms and actual implementation at a national or social level may be partially bridged over time. Soysal's thesis is that an international framework now exists that has set totally new standards, and that this framework is being strengthened. So it is then relevant to ask whether transnational citizenship will in future apply to many migrants in practice. The main beneficiaries of denizens' rights in Western Europe, for example, are primarily those who arrived in the 1950s and 1960s and their children. As European states seek to restrict legal migration from other parts of the world - except for family members of denizens – the number of denizens is likely to fall. Hammar indeed specifically notes that the present situation of large numbers of partially or wholly disenfranchised denizens in Western Europe will soon end, but argues that there will continue to be international migration.[64]

If this trend of the most developed countries cutting back on legal migration continues, then transnational citizenship loses much of its significance. Falling birth rates and ageing populations in Western Europe may mean that immigrants – at least those with needed skills – will increase in numbers again. But it seems probable that states committed to international and regional agreements on rights of migrants will offer virtually full citizen rights to strictly defined categories only, whilst dealing harshly with those attempting illegal entry, and denying opportunities to many who most desperately need them. Some other states may continue to accept short-term unskilled labour to whom they offer no rights at all.

Moreover, it can then be argued that the link that, it is often suggested, exists between the nation state and generous provision of social rights has not really been broken.[65] Although the developed West has extended these rights to some migrants, this has been because each state has ensured that relatively few migrants will in future be able to take up these rights. Offering social rights to existing denizens serves to integrate them better into society.

These considerations do not totally invalidate the thesis of postnational or transnational membership – the trends that Soysal has charted, including increasing unwillingness of new migrants to abandon their cultural identity and the greater reliance on human rights and international law, are clearly significant. But, as she notes, there is still a tension between a strengthening of nationalism and a focus on safeguarding the nation state's borders, on the one hand, and a move away from purely national citizenship towards 'a new mode of membership anchored in the universalistic rights of personhood',[66] on the other.

Soysal seeks to underpin her thesis by reference to the status of refugees. She observes that refugees are effectively 'stateless' (though they may have UN passports) and so are granted rights as individuals. She claims that: 'Universal personhood as the basis of membership comes across most clearly in the case of political refugees, whose status in host polities rests exclusively on an appeal to human rights.'[67] But as we have seen, there is a striking gap between international norms of human rights and the actual practice of both nation states and the EU towards refugees. Whilst Soysal recognizes that states have recently often denied asylum, for example in the case of Gypsies from Romania repatriated by the German Government in 1992, she suggests that they do tend to accept some responsibility for promoting human rights elsewhere. In the case of the Gypsies, the German Government promised funds to help the Romanian government to 'reintegrate' the refugees.[68]

Transnational responsibilities of governments?

There is indeed a trend for states to try to anticipate the problem of waves of political refugees, and of mass migration due to poverty, by pursuing policies designed to prevent human rights abuses or encourage economic development. Governments have been concerned (though very selectively) with both issues since 1945. But there is now a much greater awareness of the links between crises in other parts of the world and the implications for mass movement of peoples. This response may result in genuine international cooperation to protect human rights or promote economic development. But it may be a rationalization for doing very little.

Interestingly the UNHCR has supported moves to pre-empt refugee movements, by such measures as international monitoring of human rights, and of the position of those already displaced, and peace keeping operations.[69] There are clearly strong arguments for trying to ensure people can live safely and freely within their home countries. But there are also dangers that implementation will in practice undermine human rights. If humanitarian intervention involves military action, as in the attacks on Serbia to secure the rights of Kosovan Albanians, the resulting immediate destruction and long-term health, environmental and economic effects may themselves constitute a major denial of many people's rights. There may even be a danger that fear of a flood of refugees will encourage military intervention.[70] Attempts to create 'safe areas' in Iraq and the former Yugoslavia also raise questions about whether safety can be assured – the UN failed abysmally in 1995 to protect civilians at Srebrenica in Bosnia, where the conquering Bosnian Serb army executed an estimated 7,000 men and forced all the women and children to flee.[71] At a less dramatic level, the UNHCR emphasis on repatriation as a solution raises many questions about the ability of international bodies in practice to safeguard the rights of those who return, even if there is some degree of international monitoring.

International attempts to promote economic development as an alternative to migration merge into general policies of economic aid. They are then subject to the political and ideological difficulties and disagreements about methods of providing aid and the strings attached to governmental assistance. However, this approach may be linked directly to migration policy if, in order to assist economic development, states sponsor programmes of training personnel admitted for short periods. Germany reached an agreement of this sort with a number of Central European states in the early 1990s.[72]

Where support for international action to promote human rights or reduce poverty is primarily inspired by a refusal to grant asylum or entry rights to foreigners, it is difficult to interpret such policies as evidence of growing commitment to global norms. On the other hand, genuine commitment to uphold the rights of people in any part of the world, and to prevent extremes of poverty and disease, does suggest an acceptance of universal principles and of global responsibility. In practice these motivations may coexist, especially in government policies and within international governmental organizations like the UN. But even if governments undertake genuinely constructive international action – as opposed to policies that are themselves a breach of rights or an extension of economic exploitation – it clearly cannot be a total substitute for accepting the rights of refugees and the legitimacy of migrants seeking to escape immediate poverty. So policies on asylum and immigration remain a crucial test of respect for individuals on the basis of universal human rights and of the development of forms of transnational citizenship.

How governments respond to their international obligations to support rights and economic justice in other parts of world, and how they implement policies on asylum and immigration are tests of how far states can be said to act as 'good international citizens'. This ideal clearly tempers cosmopolitan commitments with safeguarding legitimate national interests, but suggests that the governments of the West could devote significantly more of their considerable resources to economic aid and support for refugees than at present. It also suggests that limits set on numbers of asylum seekers and migrants should not be determined and implemented in a way that clearly reflects racist and xenophobic attitudes. By these standards the countries of Western Europe are very far from qualifying as 'good international citizens'.

Conclusion

There are two distinct aspects of global citizenship that may be involved in a discussion of refugees and migrants. Firstly, those individuals who are forced to flee extreme persecution, or are expelled by their own governments, have a claim under international law to be treated as fellow human beings and allowed to find a new and safe home. They are in danger of falling into the category of displaced persons stripped of all effective rights. But by virtue of their stateless-ness they should from a cosmopolitan perspective be treated as citizens of the world, with rights to travel, to work and to be guaranteed basic civil liberties. Similarly, economic migrants who are escaping severe poverty are staking a claim to be allowed the opportunities to make a decent life for themselves and their families and to be treated with respect as fellow human beings.

The second aspect of global citizenship that is relevant is that demonstrated by those who voluntarily assume a duty to aid those in need. As we have seen, voluntary bodies have played, and continue to play, a very important part in providing food, shelter and medical aid to those displaced by war or repression. These groups have also had an important political role in promoting and strengthening international law and international action by governments and international bodies like the UN. In addition to specifically transnational relief agencies and campaigns, there are many national voluntary groups that lobby on behalf of the rights of refugees and immigrants, and try to make their governments live up to obligations under international law.

Therefore, whether refugees or poor migrants – who are treated increasingly in Europe as an overlapping category – are treated as global citizens depends to a significant extent on the activities of groups who accept cosmopolitan commitments. These groups include refugees and migrants who are granted asylum or entry, who often then become involved in promoting the rights of others. There is also a framework of international law that provides some – though inadequate – support for both those seeking human rights and those accepting global duties.

6 European citizenship

Bridge or barrier to global citizenship?

The evolving concept of citizenship within the European Union (EU) is relevant to global citizenship for a number of reasons. It indicates how citizenship as a legal and political status may be extended beyond the nation state, and the potentiality for multiple forms of citizenship. Moreover, advocates of cosmopolitan democracy often see increasing European integration as a step towards global governance. But examining citizenship of the EU also suggests the complexity of establishing an extra-national concept of citizenship. More importantly, evidence of the exclusionary nature of EU citizenship – for example in relation to new immigrants – also suggests that regional integration may be a barrier to developing a genuinely global citizenship.

Whether there is a coherent concept of citizenship to be extracted from examination of the EU is hotly debated. Despite the federalist vision of the founders of the Community, for a long period the EEC was primarily an economic free trade area and any rights granted to nationals of member states derived from the logic of freedom of movement for workers and ensuring fair competition between states. Even since the 1990s, when there have been more determined moves towards economic integration and political unity, and the introduction of the concept of European citizenship in the 1992 Maastricht Treaty, sceptics argue that European citizenship is far from being equivalent to citizenship within the nation state. In particular, the EU is very far from being democratic.[1]

In response to these doubts, theorists who do see a significant concept of citizenship evolving in the EU argue that, despite the cumulative and rather *ad hoc* nature of EU moves towards political unity and political representation, it does represent an important model of citizenship beyond the nation state. Given the impact of globalization and the changing world we live in, the overlapping jurisdictions and loyalties created by the EU are indicative of the need to rethink the meaning of citizenship.

This chapter begins by charting the historical development of the concept of European citizenship and examining the present legal and political position. It then explores some of the peculiarities of the present legal and political status of 'citizens of the Union', and the extent to which there is a dimension of economic and social citizenship. This analysis raises the question whether a stronger form of European citizenship is likely to emerge as a result of moves towards a federal Europe. An alternative approach is to consider whether different and more flexible models of citizenship might be more appropriate to the political and cultural complexity of Europe. Finally we engage in a wider inquiry about the compatibility or otherwise between European citizenship and global citizenship.

The evolution of European citizenship

The idea of European citizenship has evolved gradually as the institutions of economic and political cooperation have developed. This evolution has been marked by a widening of the membership of key institutions over time and by continuing tension between a federalist impulse and pressures to maintain national veto rights and an intergovernmental structure. Extending membership has tended to weaken moves towards integration, but the advocates of integration made considerable progress in the 1990s, despite the influx of new states, putting the idea of European citizenship more firmly on the agenda.

The initial steps towards European economic cooperation reflected the federalist aims of key figures like Jean Monnet and Robert Schumann. The European Coal and Steel Community (ECSC) was created in 1951 by France, West Germany, Italy and the Benelux countries to promote the economic recovery of Western Europe and resolve the historic enmity between France and Germany. The ECSC, which was a compromise between Monnet's supranational goal and the more limited concept of a customs union, created a directing High Authority, a European Court of Justice, a Common Assembly drawn from members of the six national parliaments, and a Special Council of Ministers. When the member states founded the more wide-ranging European Economic Community (EEC) in the 1957 Treaty of Rome they used the same institutional structure.

The federalist impulse was generally maintained by the policies of its bureaucracy, the European Commission, although the Commissioners in charge of various departments were nominated by national governments to ensure representation of all member states. The judgments of the Court of Justice in Luxemburg, which became part of an expanding body of European law, have also required national governments to accept the primacy of EC law and the principle of 'direct effect': that Community law imposes both rights and obligations on individuals, independent of national legislation.[2] But the strength of the intergovernmental Council of Ministers, in which the requirement of unanimity gave one dissenting state a right of veto, acted as a brake on integration throughout the 1960s and 1970s. The accession of Britain and Denmark in 1973 strengthened opposition to any form of federalism. (Ireland, admitted at the same time, was more amenable to integrationist policies.) The introduction of the European Monetary System in 1979 did, however, prepare the way for monetary union.

The European Parliament, a crucial institution for the development of European citizenship, was composed of nominees from national parliaments until direct elections to the Parliament began in 1979. But, even after this increase in democratic authority, the Parliament continued to play a fairly minor role. The problem of the 'democratic deficit' is one of the issues frequently raised in debates about European citizenship.

During the 1980s, despite the fact that Greece, Spain and Portugal became members, there were significant moves towards further integration. The President of the Commission, Jacques Delors, began in 1985 to call for the realization of the goals of the founders of the Community: a complete internal market, monetary union and a defence union.[3] An Intergovernmental Conference met in 1985 to consider amendments to existing treaties, and the 1986 Single European Act, which was the outcome, came into force in 1987. The Act increased the scope for majority voting in the Council of Ministers – thus reducing the power of individual states to veto policy – formalized cooperation on foreign policy, which had begun in 1970, and gave the European Parliament a wider role. A deadline of December 1992 was set for creating a complete single market within the Community. Recognition of the social and political as well as the economic role of the Community, and of moves towards integration, was reflected in the tendency by the later 1980s to refer not to the EEC but to the EC – the European Community.[4]

The pace of integration quickened in the 1990s. The Maastricht Treaty of 1992 (strictly the Treaty on European Union) endorsed economic and monetary union, to be introduced in stages, with a common European currency by 1999. Britain and Denmark were allowed to opt out. The Treaty included amendments to the Treaty of Rome and formally renamed the EEC the European Community, which retained its distinct legal personality although it was part of the wider union. This union included two separate 'pillars': on Common Foreign and Security Policy; and on Justice and Home Affairs. These are not part of Community law and therefore not within the jurisdiction of the Court of Justice, one of the key institutions in promoting Community law and creating a sense of European citizenship.

Parliament gained from Maastricht enhanced powers of 'co-decision', the procedure whereby it has joint responsibility with the Council of Ministers and can in the last resort, if agreement with the Council is impossible, exercise by majority vote a veto over proposed measures. Its existing right of co-decision over the Community budget was extended to legislation. The Treaty also increased the power of the European Parliament directly in relation to the Commission, making the appointment of Commissioners subject to parliamentary approval and giving it the right to question nominees. These parliamentary controls over appointments gained in political relevance in 1999 after exposure of the corrupt practices of some commissioners resulted in the enforced resignation of all 15 members of the Commission in March 1999.[5]

Further negotiations in the Intergovernmental Conference, the institution used for framing treaty amendments and also a forum for articulating federalist visions of Europe, led to the Treaty of Amsterdam, signed in 1997. Apart from legal streamlining of the heritage of earlier treaties, Amsterdam increased the scope of parliamentary 'co-decision'. Amsterdam failed, however, to address questions about how voting in the Council of Ministers should be weighted and about the number of Commissioners, both important issues in the light of the growing membership of the Union.

In 1995 three neutral European states – Sweden, Austria and Finland – joined the EU despite some reservations about their ability to agree with the majority (who are members of NATO) on foreign policy and defence issues.[6] Cyprus also began negotiations on entry in 1998, while Malta had earlier expressed interest and Turkey has sought, so far unsuccessfully, to be deemed a suitable candidate for admission.

The end of Soviet control over Eastern Europe in 1989 also led many of the newly liberal states to seek membership as part of their drive to become part of the West. The EU entered into negotiations with Poland, Hungary, the Czech Republic, Estonia and Slovenia in 1998 – the European Commission having judged that these countries had made sufficient economic and political progress to be incorporated into the Union. Five other Eastern European countries are already linked by Europe Agreements, which allow forms of economic and political cooperation, and negotiations for possible future entry began in 2000.

There is an obvious tension between the extension of EU membership envisaged and moves towards political federalism. The introduction of the common European currency in 1999 under the control of the recently created European Central Bank based in Frankfurt highlighted increasing economic integration. Moreover, the decision by EU defence and foreign ministers in December 2000 to set up a joint European crisis intervention force, able to act without the United States, indicated the possibility in the future of stronger military integration.[7]

But the prospect of a much larger membership creates problems for further political integration, despite pressure from some German political leaders in mid-2000 for moves toward a European constitution, European president and stronger parliamentary powers. The French President also called for more rapid integration, without specifically endorsing the German proposals.[8] Some commentators have argued for a concentric circle model of development, in which the inner core is the most highly integrated. There is already some precedent for this model, for example Britain's and Denmark's initial decision to opt out of the monetary union. The Maastricht Treaty also distinguished between areas that should be integrated and areas like foreign policy that should remain intergovernmental.[9] The EU summit in June 2000 appeared to endorse the idea of a 'two-speed Europe', and the prolonged negotiations at the Inter-Governmental Conference in Nice in December 2000 kept open this possibility. The Nice Conference, designed to pave the way for admission of 12 prospective new members in future, extended the range of issues that could be decided by qualified majority voting and agreed, with difficulty, on a new system of weighted votes for each country in the EU Council (including for prospective members). Advocates of a move towards European federalism were disappointed by the summit. A constitutional clarification of the relationship between the EU, nation states and regions within states was deferred to a further conference in 2004.[10]

How does European citizenship fit into this complex picture? A symbolic gesture towards such citizenship was the introduction of a European passport in 1985. The uniform colour and size and reference to the European Community immediately identify passport holders as belonging within the European Community, and one purpose was to promote a sense of shared identity. But the passport can also be seen as a symbol of the persistence of national interests and national identity within the EU, since it can only be issued by national governments and the proposal for such a passport, first discussed in 1974, took years of negotiation to achieve. The European flag, which had been adopted by the Council of Europe in 1955, was introduced as a Community symbol in 1985 by the Commission.

The aspiration to promote a sense of popular identification with elitist European institutions was expressed in the 1975 Tindemans Report, which discussed bringing Europe 'close to the citizens'. The Committee for a People's Europe set up in 1984 submitted two reports in 1985 and 1986. The Committee's title was intended to denote a single common constituency for European institutions, as opposed to a diversity of 'peoples'. The Committee endorsed the European passport and proposed widespread use of the flag. More significantly, some of its provisions relating to European citizenship were incorporated in the Maastricht Treaty, which sets out the legal basis of Union citizenship.

Maastricht recognized the status of 'citizenship of the Union'. But this was not meant to imply that Europeans belonged to a supranational polity. The Treaty specifies that the union should respect the identity of nation states, whilst the British Government had ensured there were no references to federalism. The Treaty does, however, specify a number of civil and political rights, some of which already existed within the EC and others which it created. Firstly, all citizens of the Union enjoy the rights guaranteed under the European Convention on Human Rights. The EEC committed itself to respect these rights in a 1977 Joint Declaration on Fundamental Rights, which became part of Community law. Secondly, Maastricht reasserted the principle of freedom of movement and residence within the Community (subject to limitations) and the principle of non-discrimination on the basis of nationality or gender. The Treaty also reasserted an existing political right to petition the European Parliament. The specifically new political rights were: the right to appeal to the Ombudsman set up by Maastricht; the right to vote, when living in another member state, both in local elections and in European Parliamentary elections; and the concomitant right to stand as a candidate in local and European elections. European citizens also gained the right to diplomatic protection from the Community, which in practice means that when they are abroad, if there is no national embassy or consulate in the country, diplomats from other member states have a duty to respond in the light of reciprocal arrangements to be made between member states.

Limits of European civic and political citizenship

The central ambiguity in the legal definition of European citizenship, as many commentators have noted, is that Article 8 of the European Community Treaty, as amended at Maastricht, reads: 'Citizenship of the Union is hereby established. Every person holding the nationality of a Member State shall be a citizen of the Union.' Therefore nation states, which have their own nationality laws, determine who can count as a European citizen. Long-term residents in Europe, who are not nationals of the relevant states, remain 'third party nationals' with a different status.

This emphasis on the continuing role of nation states in determining citizenship also explains what many analysts see as a major weakness – the inability of those European citizens, who exercise their right to move freely within the Union, to vote in the national elections of other EU states. Moreover, the Maastricht Treaty, when providing for the right to vote in local elections of other countries, did not attempt to harmonize national practice. This right is therefore dependent on the varying national regulations concerning length of residence and residence in a constituency. In addition the Directive implementing local voting rights allows states to make a number of exceptions – for example if the local population of non-nationals exceeds 20 per cent of nationals of voting age, long terms of residence may be required. The Directive also allows states to bar non-nationals from standing for local executive posts.[11] Similar exceptions apply to European parliamentary elections, where national governments can limit the number of non-nationals on lists of candidates.

In addition to exceptions provided for in EU rules, some countries began to impose additional barriers to non-nationals voting in local elections. Both France and Spain, for example, made this right dependent upon reciprocal arrangements with other countries. Some regions in Germany and Luxemburg failed to allow EU non-nationals to vote in their local elections. Questions of implementation can, however, be referred to the Ombudsman, who reported numerous complaints on this topic at the beginning of 1996.[12]

It is not only the political rights of European citizenship that are attenuated. Some of the civil rights set out in principle are hedged by significant qualifications in practice. From its inception the EEC's goal of a single market implied freedom of movement not only for goods, services and capital but also for labour, and in 1968 workers gained the right to take up jobs in other countries. This right was qualified in Article 48 of the Treaty of Rome by limits 'justified on grounds of public policy, public security or public health'.[13] States can also exclude non-nationals from public service.

But over time the Court of Justice has extended the definition of 'worker', for example to those not fully employed provided they have insurance, and has developed a fairly inclusive definition of a worker's family.[14] The Court has also buttressed the right of free movement by requiring that migrant workers and other travellers enjoy basic civil rights, such as the right to compensation if criminally assaulted, and the right to follow proceedings through translation or the right to use their own language if they have to appear in court. It has also endorsed migrants' property rights, including the right to a mortgage to buy a home.[15]

As a result of moves to abolish internal frontier controls, the Community issued Directives in 1990 requiring that the right of free movement should be extended beyond workers to students, pensioners and others. This right was, however, significantly qualified by the requirement that those moving must be financially independent, with medical insurance and an assured income or guaranteed welfare benefits from their own state.[16] Siofra O'Leary argued in her 1996 survey of European citizenship that the economically active, whose right of free movement was guaranteed by treaty, were therefore in a different category to those not in work, whose right of residence depended on the fulfilment of conditions determined by national governments, and who could be deported if they failed to meet requirements. She noted that students are particularly likely to run into difficulties if their grants run out whilst they are completing a course, and that disabled students might not be able to afford the required level of medical coverage.[17] The limits on genuinely free movement of students runs counter to EU programmes to promote mobility of university students and student and teacher exchanges.

Ray Koslowski notes, in an article on the role of EU migrants, that European citizenship is 'segmented citizenship', compared with a federation like the USA where rights are immediately transferable between states of the union. He does observe that EU migrants can potentially hasten integration, since they have agitated for political rights and cases before the Court of Justice can extend migrants' civic and social rights.[18] But he also comments on the degree of popular hostility to ratification of Maastricht displayed in the French referendum and nationalist fears – linked to the extension of rights of EU migrants – of a loss of state sovereignty. So he concluded that rapid extension of political rights seemed improbable.[19]

The Commission in its 1995 report on Maastricht commented that the ambitious concept of Union citizenship had 'not yet produced measures conferring really effective rights: the citizens enjoy only fragmented, incomplete rights which are themselves subject to restrictive conditions'.[20]

Social and economic rights as a component of EU citizenship

The discussion so far has focused on civil and political rights, but since the 1900s social and economic rights have often been seen as an essential component of citizenship, and necessary to a genuine assertion of civil rights. As Elizabeth Meehan has pointed out, in the EC the creation of a framework of economic and social rights, enforced by the Court upon member governments, preceded political rights, thus reversing the historical order within nation states.[21] Therefore it is possible to argue that a form of European citizenship was well established before Maastricht, even though it grew out of the logic of equal competition within the boundaries of the Community. The Community has also endorsed moves towards consultation between management and workers and limited forms of industrial democracy, so it can be seen as putting a concept of industrial citizenship on the agenda.

There have been several impulses behind the evolution of Community policies on social and economic welfare. Provisions on 'social security' (as defined in EU terminology) have been designed to ensure that freedom of movement for workers is not inhibited by losing social security benefits, and the Court has adjudicated on when migrants can also claim benefits in the host country. Community 'social policy' seeks to promote better working and living conditions for citizens within their own nation states, and to promote equality of standards across the EC. It has been animated both by the need to promote economic efficiency and employment, and by a degree of shared ideological commitment to a welfare state and workers' rights. When the Social Chapter, which included provisions for a minimum wage and parental leave, was drafted for inclusion in the Maastricht Treaty, only the British Conservative Government insisted in 1991 on opting out, thus forcing its exclusion from the main treaty. The British Labour Government's endorsement of the Social Chapter in 1997 enabled it to be incorporated in the Treaty of Amsterdam. But despite the EU's strengthened role in social policy since 1997, EU legislation must 'take account of the diverse forms of national practices', and although many measures can be agreed by qualified majority voting in the Council of Ministers, there are some issues on which unanimity is still required.[22] It is therefore debatable how far a specifically social dimension of citizenship is directly created at a European level. Preambles to Community legislation affirm a goal of common standards, but there is still considerable diversity between states in welfare provision.

The Community has considered various measures to give weight to the economic rights of workers within Community legislation and practice. These include worker representation on company boards, obligatory consultation with workers within companies on key issues, and European-wide collective bargaining. The Commission has tried a number of times since the 1960s to introduce forms of worker representation or requirements for worker consultation, both in national companies and in European multinationals operating in several EC countries. But these proposals aroused strong resistance from the European employers' federation (the Union of Industries of the European Community) and from some national governments that saw them as an additional burden on their industries. But there was also opposition from trade unions, which saw the proposals for worker representation as too weak, and from governments (such as Germany) with their own well-established institutions of co-determination, which feared that EC proposals would in fact dilute them.

Only limited progress on Europe-wide worker representation or consultation was achieved in the 1990s. The Social Chapter provides for 'dialogue between management and labour' and also allows for these 'social partners' to take responsibility, if they so request, for implementing directives arising from their agreements. But one reason why the British Conservative Government opposed the Social Chapter was the provision for giving workers a right to representation.

When the British Labour Government accepted the Chapter it specified that directives proposing worker representation required unanimous – not qualified majority – votes. This ensured that EU directives on this issue will probably be blocked in the future.

A Directive on instituting works councils in Euro-companies (with over 1,000 workers and based in at least two countries) was passed in 1994, which provided for management and unions to negotiate what form it should take. As a result over 350 companies set up works councils, but by 1998 only one (the French-based Danone) gave the European Works Council a specific role in social and employment policies. The rest were purely channels for providing information and general consultation.[23]

Another possible channel for workers rights to be strongly represented at European level would be through trade union influence on EU decision-making. Trade unions have used Community policy to press for raising of national benefits to workers, and at times the Commission has been accused of working too closely with trade unions. But a corporate model of trade union bargaining has not so far developed at EU level, although since Maastricht there have been some signs of a move towards collective bargaining. The European Trades Union Congress strengthened its own position in relation to its national affiliates in 1991, and two agreements between 'peak' union and employer organizations resulted in EU Directives on parental leave in 1995 and on the rights of part-time workers in 1997. Opponents of the parental leave Directive, however, contested it by arguing that the peak private sector employers' body, the Union of Industries, did not represent all sectors of industry or the enlarged EU.[24]

It is still debatable how far workers' rights will be consolidated within the EU. John Grahl and Paul Teague argued in 1994 that European economic citizenship 'cannot transcend national practice', although they recognized the trend toward extending EU powers in labour market, trade, industrial and employment policies and (after Maastricht) in monetary union. They suggested that there were four areas in which the EU could contribute to economic aspects of citizenship: (1) labour market regulation promoting employment rights; (2) retraining and vocational educational – already part of EU policy – as well as promoting acceptance of different national professional qualifications; (3) regional economic and social policy, where corporatist trade union bargaining might flourish; and (4) generating employment, which is essential to ensure full citizenship and prevent permanent exclusion from economic life.[25]

If the Community has had a limited impact on workers' rights, it has done much better on the rights of women. Legislation on women's rights, for example on equal pay and equal treatment, has been less controversial in the Community as a whole than workers' rights, though resisted by the Thatcher Government until a series of European Court decisions obliged Britain to fall into line. During the 1970s the Community could claim to have pioneered legislation on sex equality, and to be in advance of most member governments, though ironically the Commission's own employment policies were referred several times to the Court on the grounds of sex discrimination.[26] Certainly feminist pressure groups, and bodies such as the Equal Opportunities Commission in Britain, could use EC legislation to appeal to the European Court with some success on issues of equal pay, non-discrimination at work and access to security benefits.

In the 1980s the Commission turned its attention to promoting a single market and general workers' rights and gave less attention to sex equality, but the Court continued to adjudicate on issues affecting women. There was some progress in the 1990s in general Community policy, for example on the issues of parental leave arising out of the Social Chapter. The 1997 Amsterdam Treaty incorporated the requirement of equal pay not only for equal work, but also for work of 'equal value' – a clause that is important since women often do not do the same jobs as men. The Treaty also endorsed positive action, allowing for provision of 'specific advantages in order for the under-represented sex to pursue a vocational activity or to prevent or compensate for disadvantage in professional careers'.[27] Equal treatment is an important element in the EU's employment policy – the 1998 guidelines to member states specify the need to strengthen equal opportunities. But it has been argued that the Court of Justice, which earlier played an important role in promoting women's rights, tended in the 1990s – although it upheld women's right to pregnancy leave – to adopt a more cautious and restrictive attitude.[28]

Despite the strengthening of women's legal rights, their effective position can be undermined by developments in the economy threatening traditionally female jobs or encouraging an expansion of ill-paid, insecure part-time work. Ursula Vogel argues that deregulation of the European market could therefore 'primarily and adversely affect women'.[29]

The special status of workers within the EU could also, of course, lead to large numbers of unemployed men (also affected by a changing economy) losing their effective economic and political European citizenship. Issues of class and gender therefore intersect and raise wider questions about the understanding of citizenship, considered below in relation to passive citizenship.

Is EU citizenship really citizenship?

A number of theorists have made a strong case that EU citizenship is not at present in any significant sense a genuine form of citizenship. The case that 'citizenship of the Union' has no real basis starts from the assumption that citizenship requires a close linkage between rights and duties, political status and cultural identity. Exponents of this view include Siofra O'Leary, Hans Ulrich Jessurun d'Oliveira and Percy Lehning. But several of the key arguments against the existence of EU citizenship can be qualified to suggest that they are not totally compelling. One possibility is that the dynamic of the EU will lead to federalism and a political culture uniting diverse traditions, so creating a context for full citizenship. Jürgen Habermas speculates that 'In a future Federal Republic of Europe' national traditions could be 'connected with the overlapping consensus of a common, supranationally shared political culture of the European Community'.[30] There are also theorists who claim that EU citizenship is already becoming a reality, provided a more flexible concept of citizenship is adopted, and if questions of identity are separated from citizenship. Maurice Roche, Elizabeth Meehan, John Keane and Etienne Tassin suggest alternative models.

The most fundamental objection to the existence of true Union citizenship at present is that the status of being a European citizen is entirely dependent upon being a citizen of one of the various member states, and that nation states have autonomy in defining their (varying) rules about how citizenship is acquired. This is a significant limitation on the reality of EU citizenship, especially for those who are already living within EU territory and aspiring to become EU citizens. Some national requirements, where citizenship is generally based on birth not residence, make becoming a EU citizen very difficult. Moreover, the right of individual member states to determine nationality was reiterated in a Declaration attached to the Maastricht Treaty. However, as O'Leary notes, the Court of Justice has stipulated that national policy must be compatible with the goals of Community law.[31]

A second and related argument about the primary role of nation states is that rights accruing to individuals within the Union are not based directly on their relationship with the institutions of the EU, but depend on member states providing for and respecting these rights. This point was made by a European Parliament working document on citizenship, which commented that under Maastricht citizens of member states acquired rights in other EU member states, but 'The Union has virtually no obligations towards them.'[32] The same applies to their rights if they travel outside Europe. Despite the 'European' passport and the provisions for diplomatic protection, in reality protection abroad depends upon national governments (and on possible reciprocal arrangements with other national governments).

There is one obvious objection to the thesis that nation states are still the channels for citizenship rights, and that is the rulings of the Court of Justice on the principles of 'primacy' and 'direct effect'. The primacy or supremacy of Community law over national law was established by a Court ruling in 1964 that states had, by accepting the Treaty of Rome, also accepted 'a permanent limitation of their sovereign rights'.[33] The principle of direct effect, based on its ruling in the Van Gend En Loos case (1962), went further by asserting that: 'Independently of the legislation of Member States, Community law ... not only imposes obligations on individuals but is also intended to confer upon them rights which become part of their legal heritage.'[34] Therefore the Community makes not only states, but also individuals, subject to its laws and has a form of constitutional law distinct from the more limited abrogations of sovereignty under international law created by treaties between states. Some national courts, however, in particular the German and Belgian Constitutional Courts, have begun to challenge rulings of the EC Luxemburg Court.[35]

The third objection to the reality of European citizenship relates to the political dimension. The basic argument is that there is no real link between European voters and the European Parliament, despite direct elections since

1979. Elections are organized nationally for national candidates under differing electoral systems. The conduct of European elections suggests that national issues often predominate over European ones. Sometimes purely local issues may arouse more interest – Karlheinz Neunreither notes that in the 1994 European elections in Germany, where *Länder* held elections on the same day, there was more debate on bicycle lanes than on the future of Europe or the Bosnian conflict.[36] The European elections also suggest a considerable degree of apathy among European voters. The average turnout in 1994 was 58.5 per cent (raised by compulsory voting in Belgium, Luxembourg and Greece), but dropping to 35 or 36 per cent in some countries. In 1999 the average turnout fell to 43 per cent (130 million out of a possible 298 million voted).[37]

Opinion polls also suggest that a significant proportion of the electors in member countries do not identify as European citizens – although there is significant variation between countries – and many also oppose the extension of European citizen rights to nationals of other EU states resident in their country.[38] This evidence leads some commentators to conclude that there is not yet a European '*demos*' or 'people', only 'peoples'.[39]

One possible reason for lack of interest in European elections could of course be the perceived ineffectiveness of the European Parliament. Although voters may know little about the EU and its institutions, and by now underestimate the potential importance of the Parliament, commentators on the democratic deficit in the EU generally agree that the Parliament, although its powers are now much greater, is still unable to ensure that the Commission – let alone the intergovernmental Council of Ministers – is democratically accountable. So European citizens cannot be expected to exercise their democratic political rights fully until their representatives can be seen to make a difference to their lives.

The fourth objection to EU citizenship having any conceptual or practical validity is that, although the Maastricht Treaty refers to citizens' duties, in practice there are no duties attached to being a citizen of the Union. There are only duties to member states. This was one of the key arguments put forward in 1974 by Raymond Aron, when he pointed out that there was no obligation of military service to the European Community.[40] Aron saw military service as a defining citizen duty, but this very French and republican perspective is highly debatable at the beginning of the twenty-first century. Since he wrote, many European countries have abandoned conscription and France itself has abandoned its historic commitment to military service by all its male citizens.[41]

The European Union may be very gradually moving towards an integrated military defence – the aspiration of the architects of the Community, but aborted in 1954, when the French Parliament refused to ratify the 1952 Treaty creating a European Defence Community and common European army between the six members of the ECSC. (The Western European Union created in 1955 has never played a major military role.) But if a new European security system does emerge it seems likely to be based on a modern technology that does not rely on mobilizing huge reserves of conscripts, and to be based on professional armies. As Martin Shaw has observed, since the end of the cold war, and in the light of major cultural changes, 'the historic European link between conscription and citizenship seems set, therefore, to be cut'.[42]

But even if military service is seen as inappropriate to European citizenship, some conception of duties is not. So long as no one pays taxes directly to EU institutions there is no sense of a direct obligation on individuals to maintain them. Mandatory voting for European elections in all countries would impose a minimal duty, but is unlikely to be introduced since only a minority of countries have compulsory voting.

A fifth argument is that the rights of Union membership are qualified by the fact that *not* all these rights are *exclusive* to EU citizens. Hans Ulrich Jessurun d'Oliveira claims that one of the central aspects of citizenship is to distinguish between those who truly belong to the polity and those who do not.[43] This is not true of EU citizenship, since the central right of free movement within EU borders is given to many who are not nationals of member states, for example European Free Trade Association (EFTA) state nationals. In addition, all residents in the territory of the EU have the right to address the European Parliament and the Ombudsman. Moreover, in some countries it is now national policy to grant local voting rights to residents who come from countries outside the EU, and the 1992 European Convention on the Participation of Foreigners in Public Life at Local Level requires signatories to grant this right.

The notion that exclusivity defines citizenship is, however, contestable. It has been common national practice to extend civil rights to foreign residents and to require certain reciprocal duties, like payment of taxes. Extension of specifically political rights is more rare, but by no means unknown, as illustrated by the example of Irish citizens enjoying voting rights in the UK.

Finally, citizenship is usually linked not only to legal rights and duties but to some sense of cultural identity. Cultural identity can be linked to a shared history, language, religion and various symbols, though even in a national identity these are often either artificially constructed or highly debatable. The idea of a European identity based on, for example, the influence of the Roman Empire, the role of Christianity or the evolution of liberalism is even more contestable, partly because of the conflicts between Christian Churches and the different borders within Europe that can be drawn on these kind of grounds. Moreover, in the last two centuries the significance of linguistic and national difference has been much more marked than a sense of European unity.

But the identity of nation states is now much more problematic because of migration, which has created religious and cultural pluralism; because of the increased status of many historically and culturally defined regions within established states like Britain, France and Spain; and because of the declining power of the state. Moreover, the fact of migration between member states of the EU – though still limited – encourages diversity and a sense of European citizenship. It is also possible to follow Habermas in rejecting a nationalist identity for the state as both dangerous and outmoded, and to argue for the promotion of a constitutional patriotism based on a specifically political culture.[44] But Lehning argues that, given the persisting strength of national identification, there is no prospect of a European civic identity or European sense of solidarity. There is no European *demos* at a cultural level any more than at a political level.[45]

Therefore, from this critical standpoint it can be concluded that European citizenship is not a truly political category and does not suggest the kind of individual values and attitudes associated with active citizenship. Rather it is a passive status and still defined by the Community's original goals, an 'economic citizenship' at best.[46] Even at this level the limits to freedom of movement (discussed above) undermine the claim to citizen status.

The case that European citizenship is an illusion rests implicitly, and often explicitly, on the assumption that for true European citizenship to exist the EU must be a federal state. The Union would then inherit all the attributes of a nation state. If this is the assumption, then clearly there cannot yet be European citizens, since the EU – although it has supranational elements – is clearly not yet a federation. Some commentators stress its fragmented nature and lack of coherent direction. For example, Pierson and Liebfried conclude: 'What is emerging in Europe is a multi-levelled, highly fragmented system in which policy "develops" but is beyond the control of any single authority.'[47] Others suggest the EU has a distinctive structure. John Kincaid argues that it is a 'confederal federation', with a confederal system of government but operating in a federal mode in its spheres of competence. He concludes that its confederal structure makes it difficult to grant to EU migrants all the rights enjoyed by nationals, and notes the exclusions in the Maastricht provisions for local voting rights.[48]

Of course, one response to the model of citizenship within a European federation is to point to the degree of integration that has already been achieved, and to argue that, despite nationalist resistance in many member states, the EU is gradually evolving towards greater supranationalism. Apart from the Maastricht and Amsterdam Treaties and changes relating to EU institutions, there have been political changes in the strengthening of Europe-wide trade unions and transnational political parties. MEPs organized themselves early on into ideological blocs within the European Parliament and parties formed loose federations. Since Maastricht, socialists, Christian Democrats, liberals and greens have formally become recognized European parties, to which national parties are affiliated. The aim envisaged in the Treaty is that they should 'contribute to forming a European awareness and to expressing the political will of the citizens of the Union'. Despite negative evidence about their success in achieving these aims in Euro-elections to date, over time European parties may gain in influence. Moreover, despite the lack of a clear-cut European identity, there is also *some* evidence that there are people who do identify as Europeans. Perhaps not surprisingly migrants to another member state are likely to adopt this identity. Meehan cites the example of middle-class Britons abroad who feel 'European.'[49]

So although European citizenship is not yet a fully developed legal status or related to a clear identity, the position may change quite radically in the next two or three decades. Ulrich Preuss comments that 'at present the duality of national and Union citizenships clearly displays the predominance of the former over the latter. But ... political developments may enrich the status of Union citizenship ... .'[50] The widening of the EU might tell against this prediction, but significant extension of membership in the 1980s and 1990s did not halt the renewed impetus towards greater union. However, the vision of a future federal Europe is still highly questionable, and the EU seems likely to remain a hybrid system.

The case that EU citizenship is a genuine form of citizenship

Therefore the main arguments for the possibility of a genuine European citizenship depend upon invoking different models of citizenship, not predicated upon a sovereign state. Maurice Roche examines the erosion of the nation state by the forces of economic globalization and claims that 'post-nationalism' is 'an historical reality'.[51] He also agrees with Elizabeth Meehan that the Community has developed civil and social rights ahead of substantial political rights. The evolution of the European Union is, Roche argues, a continuation of earlier European experience that encompassed both city states and empire. Europeans will be 'both united and divided in their political loyalties and identities' as in the past according to 'the three factors of *locality* ... *nationality* and *Europeanness*'.[52]

Meehan too draws on earlier historical examples of citizenship, for example in the city state, and on the separation between nationality and legal citizen rights in the Roman Empire. She also stresses that citizenship need not be fused with two other distinct categories: legal nationality and national identity. Instead people may have sense of multiple identities and enjoy more than one level of citizenship. The Roman Empire provided a remarkable example of a conquering power extending a range of citizen rights to its new subjects.[53] Initially, as Rome expanded within Italy in the fourth century BC, it developed a dual Latin citizenship, which enabled men to be citizens both of Rome and of their native city. Further expansion within Italy led to the introduction of two levels of citizenship, political and civic, the latter excluding political rights but endowing those who came under the sway of Rome with equality before the law and the right to claim this Roman second level of citizenship. These citizens also enjoyed dual citizenship rights, retaining their local status as citizens.[54] This practice continued until the end of the Roman Republic in the first century BC.

Meehan suggests that one possible model for EU citizenship is a 'neo-imperial' model recognizing the pluralism of institutions and a dual national and (more limited) European status, though the EU is of course a voluntary union of states and not the result of imperial conquest.[55] The other possible model she envisages is a 'neo-national' one, with a European dimension 'added-in'.[56] Writing in 1993, she thought that in view of the limits on measures to promote citizenship and the proposed enlargement of the Community, this was rather more probable. But she suggested that the role of civil society groups might affect the precise nature of European citizenship that emerges and move it beyond the 'neo-national' model.

The increasing strength of European civil society, within the context of the Maastricht Treaty providing a legal framework for a minimal European citizenship, can be seen as the primary basis for an evolving European citizenship. John Keane suggests that transnational links between businesses and trade unions, political parties and social movements, and personal networks create the 'habitat' of the new European citizen. This kind of citizenship is based on increased physical mobility and ease of communication, and combines a sense of national identity with a rejection of crude nationalism. Whilst recognizing the threats from both extreme nationalism and the domination by multinational corporations seeking to control their workforces and manipulate consumers, Keane is cautiously optimistic about the potential of citizenship rooted in European civil society.[57]

Civil society could be one element in a model of European citizenship based on the concept of a shared public space. Etienne Tassin, in an interesting essay, 'Europe: A Political Community?', rejects the proposition that Europe can draw on a coherent historical, cultural or philosophical identity, and also rejects a concept of a European political community analogous to a nation state based on a common will and defined by a hierarchical structure of power.[58] Instead he argues for a Europe defined by a politically organized public space in which all citizens can participate. This public space is characterized by pluralism, people with differing cultural backgrounds and beliefs. Tassin also emphasizes the importance of breaking the link between citizenship and nationality, seeking the ending of ethnic nationalism in favour of a concept of European fellow-citizenship. Therefore he wishes to extend European citizenship rights like voting in local elections to resident aliens not from EU countries.

One major objection to the idea of a democratic European public space is that the central medium of communication, a common language, is lacking. Dieter Grimm has rejected the possibility of 'a European public' or 'a European political discourse', so long as there are no newspapers, radio or TV programmes that unite all Europeans. In the EU in 1995 there were 11 languages, and even the two languages that are most used within EU bodies, French and English, are foreign languages for over 80 per cent of the people within the Union.[59] Widening of the EU will of course multiply the number of languages within it. Will Kymlicka picks up this problem of a shared language, commenting that understanding a foreign language for purposes of tourism or business is not the same as the more sophisticated understanding needed for political debates. Elites can transcend language borders, but if the aim is maximum political participation, then people are much more likely to take part if the debate is in their native language.[60] Habermas, in a comment on Grimm, suggests that English could become 'a second first language' if it were taught systematically in schools, so making common communication possible.[61] But this suggestion does not fully meet Kymlicka's point about the high level of fluency needed for political discussion.

Tassin's concept of public space is both abstract and idealized – especially as it is based on a strong concept of direct participation as opposed to representation. It is not clear by what institutional mechanisms all citizens can exercise their obligation to participate. There is, on the other hand, much more scope, given the nature of EU institutions, for orthodox pressure group lobbying of the Commission and Parliament, which is already well established. There is also potential scope for representing interests or opinions through various processes of consultation. There is a maze of hundreds of official advisory committees in Brussels on aspects of EU policy. They are, however, appointed by member governments, and the majority of members are civil servants, though both official and private sector experts are included. But a pioneering small-scale study concluded that these committees were less effective than informal lobbying as channels of influence.[62]

One strand in Tassin's argument is that the creation of a European institutional space needs to be supplemented by breaking down the nation state from within, by giving renewed recognition to the political role of regions. This idea is taken up by a number of commentators, although not necessarily in such utopian terms – Tassin cites Proudhon and Denis de Rougemont. Roche argues that post-nationalism implies that sub-national as well as supranational levels grow in importance and that some citizen rights may be enjoyed at a regional level.[63] Kincaid also notes that many regions have reasserted their distinctive identity and there is a case for representing regions as well as nation states.[64] Moreover, the Committee of the Regions created by the Maastricht Treaty, which is made up of 'representatives of regional and local bodies', has a secretariat in Brussels and enjoys formal advisory powers. It can be consulted by the Commission or the Parliament and can issue its own 'Opinions' where regional concerns are at stake in EU policy. If regions acquire enhanced influence, then citizens of the Union may identify with their regions as well as – or sometimes instead of – their nation states. So the role of regionalism enhances the argument that European citizenship is necessarily based on multiple affiliations and loyalties.

The worth of European citizenship: passive not active citizens?

The discussion in the previous section focused primarily on whether at present European citizenship exists in legal and political terms. This debate raised the question whether there is a European 'people' in cultural terms, but did not address the economic and social conditions that empower people to exercise fully their formal civil or political rights. To the extent that the EU has extended the minimum social rights of those living in member states, and guarateed no loss of social rights to those who opt to work or live in other Community countries, citizens may be said to enjoy their rights in actuality. But this claim has to be assessed not only against the social and economic rights guaranteed but against the broader economic, social and ideological trends.

Since the 1970s the evolution of the global economy has not only set in motion forces that undermine the nation state, it has also resulted in a move away from industrialism towards reliance on new technologies. As a result there has been substantial unemployment, particularly among working-class men. There has been a rise in women's employment, but often in part-time, low-paid and insecure jobs. Consequently the goal of full employment that underpinned the post-war welfare state has been replaced by quite widespread joblessness and the evolution of a significant underclass of those either permanently out of work or in the margins of temporary employment. These economic factors, combined with other social trends such as a growing number of pensioners and single-parent families, have put a severe strain on the welfare state.

The rise of the New Right in the 1980s was one response to these problems, which sought solutions in creating cheaper labour by reducing wages and cutting back on welfare entitlements. This approach, adopted most enthusiastically in the English-speaking world led by the USA, did stimulate more investment and cut back unemployment, but at the cost of cutting wages, and reducing workers' trade union and other rights. Although Christian Democrat and Social Democrat governments in Western Europe were more resistant to this extreme liberal ideology, they experienced growing unemployment, and in practice they did scale down generous welfare provisions in the 1980s and 1990s. So EU attempts to promote social welfare and workers' rights, for example through the Social Chapter, are in the context of falling standards within some of its member states.

The problem of long-term unemployment is particularly significant in relation to European citizenship, since most commentators agree that workers still gain preferential treatment in regard to freedom of movement and maintenance of social rights within the EU. It is, moreover, very unlikely that the unemployed and socially marginalized will take an active political interest in the Union or even exercise their right to vote for and lobby the European Parliament.

But even if relatively full employment and a generous understanding of social rights can be secured in the future, it is arguable that European citizenship will remain a predominantly passive form of citizenship. If the analogy with the Roman Empire is pursued, it is relevant to note (as Heater does) that in Imperial Rome from the first century AD citizenship became less significant as a real badge of status and rights, and class became more important.[65] When the Emperor Caracalla decreed in the fourth century AD that almost all men in the now vast Empire (except for slaves) should become citizens, this meant that they had to pay taxes and did not endow them with corresponding effective rights. Citizenship in a meaningful sense implied a privileged elite (even if in the Roman Empire it became an unusually large elite).

Today citizenship has lost its privileged status within nation states (except in relation to aliens). The dimensions of social citizenship in principle compensate (at least partially) for effective class, gender and racial inequalities, but emphasize a view of citizens as recipients of benefits rather than as political agents. As a result of the social emphasis in European citizenship it might also therefore be argued that it will necessarily remain a passive form of citizenship, a question of civil and social rights rather than active political influence, and a legal status not a moral and political ideal.

A distinction should be made here between welfare rights and economic rights to employment, to trade union membership and to a voice within workers' places of employment. Whilst the former may reinforce dependence on welfare authorities, the latter help to empower workers, both by enabling them to have the dignity and independence of a job and by giving them channels of influence over their conditions at work. But ensuring the right *to* work depends upon political action to surmount the economic trends of deindustrialization discussed above, whereas strengthening rights *at* work depends upon overcoming employer resistance and ideological views hostile to trade unionism and workers' representation within companies. Whilst the EU has made tentative moves towards promoting economic rights, they are (as noted above) so far still limited in their effect.

Widening of the membership of the Union seems to make the political content of European citizenship even more nominal. Those who have become EU migrants (and their numbers are likely to increase as a result of new countries joining the Union) might be one exception. They have a special reason to feel European and to desire a European status, and to agitate for uniform rights across the Union. But it is necessary to distinguish here between the professional middle classes, whose qualifications, linguistic abilities and other advantages enable them to move between jobs and European countries by choice, and workers seeking jobs abroad who may (especially if they come from poorer states) be raising money for their families and their future, like genera-tions of economic migrants before them. The former are much more likely to use the Court of Justice and agitate directly for their civil and social rights, and to seek full political rights. Some politically aware workers may, however, operate through trade unions or socialist parties and thus indirectly promote European consciousness.[66]

The second exception to the conclusion that European citizenship is a passive status, based on receipt of rights granted from above, are those who are committed to active politics within a European framework. There are a few committed to promoting European Citizenship as such: groups like ECAS (Euro-Citizen Action Service) and VOICE (Voluntary Organizations in a Citizen's Europe) began campaigning in 1992.[67] Other groups may focus on securing greater rights for their class or gender, as in the case of trade union or feminist activists. They may also be concerned with upholding human rights within the Community or with health, consumer protection or environmental issues. Organizers and activists in pressure groups or social movements represent quite a wide spread of interests and ideals, but they are self-selected minorities, and are in one sense an elite, albeit an elite operating from below rather than from above. But insofar as they *choose* to be politically active at a European level, they are an elite of *active* citizens, strongly contrasting with general popular apathy about the EU or European-wide issues.

Therefore, whilst there are a number of rather different groupings who might be categorized as active European citizens, the vast majority of the peoples of Europe remain passive, and only enjoy partially realized European citizen rights.

European citizenship and global citizenship

There are a number of ways in which the EU can be seen as a stepping stone towards cosmopolitanism and a more developed concept of global citizenship. The record of the EU suggests how regional cooperation and organization may promote principles necessary to a just and peaceful world. Firstly, it demonstrates that nation-states can curb pursuit of national self-interest and xenophobic nationalism within a wider political framework and in pursuit of common goals. Despite frequent disagreements, the evolution and day-to-day operations of the EU indicate willingness to compromise and a commitment to close and continuous collaboration.

Secondly, the EU strengthens cosmopolitan principles by implementing them internally. It endorses (via the Council of Europe) the European Charter on Human Rights and in addition – as we have seen – seeks to implement throughout the Union a range of social and economic rights. The EU also tries to reduce poverty and inequality between its member states, providing economic assistance to less developed regions. In addition it has responded to environmental concerns, creating a European Environmental Agency in 1990 and legislating on air and water pollution and waste disposal.

Thirdly, the Community was created after the Second World War with the explicit aim of preventing another war in Western Europe, in particular between France and Germany. This aim has been achieved and it is possible to see the EU as an embodiment of Kant's vision of a confederation of liberal democracies creating a zone of peace, which would gradually extend to other states. (It could, however, be claimed that the cold war division of Europe also helped cement cooperative relations between the EC countries. Although common membership of NATO did not prevent Greece and Turkey going to war with one another in 1974 – both countries were then outside the EU and neither then qualified as democracies.) Incorporation of Eastern European countries within the EU is intended to enlarge the zone within which both liberal democratic institutions and peaceful relations can be consolidated. The brutal wars within the former Yugoslavia indicate, however, that there are regions where this pacifying process has no impact – at least in the short term.

Finally, the EU sometimes promotes world order through its regional role in global politics. Falk has suggested that regions can both moderate the forces of 'negative globalism' associated with the free market economy and promote positive global values.[68] The EU has arguably played some role in resisting potentially harmful scientific developments in food, for example by challenging sale within its borders of hormone-injected US beef. It has also offered favourable trade arrangements to over 70 developing countries in Africa, the Caribbean and the Pacific (with former links to EU members as colonies) through the Lome Convention, originally signed in 1975 and since renewed periodically. These arrangements are challenged by the free trade regulations adopted by the World Trade Organization.[69]

The EU is not, however, regarded as a champion of global economic justice either by developing countries or by NGOs. It has a rather stronger claim to make a positive contribution on environmental issues. The EU as a body has endorsed a number of international environmental conventions and played an active part in some international environmental conferences, such as the Kyoto conference on climate change.

The EU also offers two possible models of citizenship appropriate to a global as well as a regional level. If a concept of citizenship is accepted that does not assume a single political locus of citizenship rights, duties and loyalty, but accepts a multiplicity of relevant political levels, then the EU provides an interesting model of this new kind of multi-layered citizenship in practice. It also embraces a wide range of cultures. But the EU does in addition offer supranational political institutions to which individuals have some direct relationship, as in the European Parliament and Court, thus giving European citizenship a dimension that advocates of global democracy believe is needed at the world level. Preuss speculates that the EU may in future confer Union citizenship directly on migrants and refugees inside its territory, so disconnecting citizenship from membership of nation states.[70] Therefore the EU can be seen a precursor of global citizenship.

There are, however, cogent reasons for doubting whether the EU really shows the possibilities of global citizenship. One set of reasons is based on the nature of the Union itself and the bases for unity within Europe. The other reasons arise from the logic of European integration as necessarily exclusive of the outside world.

Despite the growth of the EU over time, admission to the Community has always been contingent upon new members meeting the criteria set by its founders. Therefore members of the EU must endorse a free, capitalist, market, they must be comparatively well developed and have attained a level of economic stability. (Some EU members include poor regions and classes, but poverty is measured by European rather than global standards.) They must also be parliamentary democracies evidencing a reasonable degree of respect for civil rights and political rights. These criteria excluded Spain, Portugal and Greece until the 1980s and have been used to discriminate between countries of the former Soviet bloc.

Moreover, although concepts of common European cultural identity are questionable, there is some significance in the historical legacy of both the Roman Empire (bequeathing the common Latin language) and of Christendom (despite divisions between Churches). There is also a shared heritage of a struggle for civil and political rights and of common learning and modes of thinking, demonstrated particularly clearly during the Enlightenment. Moreover, a cosmopolitan European consciousness, as we have seen in earlier chapters, has been developing since the Renaissance and a European civil society began to evolve at the end of the eighteenth century. So despite numerous European wars, and the divisiveness of nineteenth- and twentieth-century nationalisms, there is some substance to a European identity. There have also been aspirations to unite Europe politically ever since its evolution into distinct nation states. There is therefore a cultural, political and ideological basis for EU institutions and EU citizenship that is unlikely – despite globalization – to apply on a world scale.

The economic success and civil liberties enjoyed by those living inside the European Community have always attracted both those fleeing from persecution at home and the much large numbers unable to earn a living in their impoverished countries. But as the numbers seeking refuge or jobs in member states increased due to the disintegration of the Soviet bloc and pressures in North Africa and other parts of the world, members of the EU became less welcoming. This growing reluctance to open European doors to the unfortunate by the 1990s had a number of causes, including growing unemployment and a significant rise in right-wing nationalism in many parts of Europe.

But the logic of integration within the Union also encourages exclusion of people living outside its borders. The extension of civil and political rights and the provision of social rights also suggest the need to limit enjoyment of them. Opening up internal frontiers has coincided with attempts to strengthen controls on external frontiers. Therefore promoting European citizenship has been at the expense of governments recognizing the rights of refugees or being prepared to allow large-scale immigration either from the former Soviet bloc or from other continents. The Schengen Agreement of 1985 and Convention of 1990 illustrated this dual logic. Indeed, the EU is arguably in contravention of some international treaties on rights of asylum.[71]

The EU position on 'third country migrants' and its record on receiving refugees has been discussed in more detail in the previous chapter. Its relevance here is to highlight the fact that European citizenship is a privileged status to be maintained by preventing large numbers of non-Europeans gaining its benefits. The EC Commission has endorsed policies encouraging the return of African nationals and unskilled Polish migrants, and in a 1991 report commented on the danger of the Community being 'swamped by persons seeking the social rights granted to asylum applicants'.[72] Where migrants have been long established inside member states of the Union they have become (in principle) the recipients of civil and social rights, but not of political rights. But in practice they are often subject to discrimination if they come from Africa or Asia and are more likely to be unemployed. Despite official Commission and Council statements against racism and xenophobia, there have been no common European policies to combat racial discrimination, though by the end of 1999 the Commission was considering directives to harmonize legislation on race equality.[73] Illegal migrants are in a much worse position and subject to extreme economic exploitation and often harassment by police. The failure of members of the Union to grant genuine equality and rights to non-European migrants demonstrates graphically how far European citizenship is from a genuinely cosmopolitan ideal.

There is, however, another way of viewing the EU. It can be seen as a model not of global citizenship *per se*, but of regional development that other regions may emulate, even if their governmental cooperation and regional institutions take a rather different form. The development of such regionalism might make the eventual strengthening of world order politically more realistic. So indirectly European integration might create conditions more conducive to global citizenship.

There are indeed other regional institutions – for example the Organization of American States, the Organization of African Unity and the Asia-Pacific Economic Cooperation forum – already in existence. But these regional groupings lack many of the political and economic advantages of the EU, so it is very doubtful whether they will evolve into stable and economically developed regions demonstrating effective respect for democratic principles and human rights in the foreseeable future.[74]

In conclusion, aspects of the EU and evolving EU citizenship do suggest a potential for global cooperation and global citizenship. But many of the policies of the EU indicate that regional integration, and a strengthening of the rights of EU citizenship, are in conflict with cosmopolitan principles and recognition of the rights of all individuals as citizens of the world. Habermas, who believes that a developing public sphere and steps towards federalism in Europe *could* create prospects for global citizenship, is also fully aware of the opposite dangers:

> If the federative project aimed only to field another global player with the clout of the United States, it would remain particularistic, merely endowing what asylum-seekers have come to know as 'Fortress Europe' with a new – that is, an economic – dimension.[75]

Part III

Global citizenship today

Theoretical and political issues

Introduction: From 'world government' to 'global governance'

The purpose of this final part of the book is to examine global citizenship, and related concepts of global governance and cosmopolitan democracy, in the context of contemporary social theory.

As a background to this discussion it is relevant to glance at how the specific idea of world citizenship fared in the changing circumstances of the twentieth century, and to consider briefly how world citizenship was linked to the goal of world government in the political movement that had an impact after 1945.

The idea of world citizenship was quite widely used in the 1930s and 1940s. For example, a biography of Mahatma Gandhi attempts to sum up his ideas and activities in the title *Gandhi: World Citizen*.[1] Virginia Woolf invoked the concept in 1938, when discussing women's lack of psychological investment in war and nationalism, claiming that: 'As a woman I have no country. As a woman I want no country. As a woman I am a citizen of the world.'[2] The phrase is used in a more negative sense in the film *Casablanca*, when Humphrey Bogart asserts his cynical lack of patriotism and role as bar owner by claiming that he is 'a citizen of the world', the world of drinkers.

During and immediately after the Second World War world citizenship as an ideal was closely associated with belief in the need for federal world government. For example, the New York-based Conference on Science, Philosophy and Religion organized a series of symposia on such topics as 'Approaches to World Peace' (held in 1943) and 'Foundations of World Organization' (1950). Norman Cousins argued in a 1943 paper, 'The Making of World Citizenship', that this ideal, held by eminent forebears such as Confucius and Paine, has become a possible in an interconnected world. He saw world citizenship being realized within the context of a world government.[3] The 1943 Conference, which looked at trends underpinning world citizenship and possible world government, also noted the dangers of American ideological imperialism and recognized the contribution of Asian cultures to promoting attitudes conducive to peace.[4]

After the United States dropped the atomic bomb on Hiroshima and Nagasaki in August 1945, and the testing of the H Bomb by the USA and the USSR in 1952 and 1953, campaigns for peace and world government gained a new urgency. H.G. Wells had foreseen the possibility of atomic bombs in his 1913 novel *The World Set Free* and became committed to the idea of world government. After 1945 many eminent scientists and intellectuals, religious leaders and some trade unionists, businessmen and politicians gave their support to world government for reasons summed up in the slogan 'One world or none'.

Campaigns for world government sprang up in the USA, Britain and many countries in Western Europe. UNESCO opinion polls in the late 1940s found a surprising degree of popular support for the idea: 42 per cent in the USA, 44 per cent in Britain, 45 per cent in France and 46 per cent in Germany.[5] By 1950 the World Movement for World Federal Government had member groups in 22 countries, parliamentary groups in 11 countries and an estimated 156,000 members. Local government bodies in several Western European countries and in India had adopted the Charter of Mundialization and declared themselves world territory.[6]

Most campaigns for world government envisaged strengthening the United Nations and progress through governmental agreement. But there was also a radical wing that called for a people's convention of delegates who had been popularly elected. In Britain this approach was promoted by the Crusade for World Government, headed by the Labour MP Henry Usborne. The most dramatic assertion of the reality of world citizenship was staged by Garry Davis, who destroyed his American passport, declared himself a world citizen, and in September 1948 camped in the area temporarily declared international UN territory for the meeting of the UN General Assembly in Paris. His goal was to highlight the inadequacy of the UN and he called for a true world government.[7] His register of world citizens had gained about one million signatures from 78 countries by 1950.[8] Davis continued to travel with his own 'world passport', mobilizing support and issuing copies of his passport, until 1958, when he issued his final communiqué as the symbolic 'First World Citizen'.[9]

The movement for world government reflected some of the political uncertainties of the eighteenth-century schemes for confederation about the scope of its membership. The main problem was whether the Soviet Union should or could be included, given the unremitting hostility in this period of the Soviet leadership to any supranational schemes. The movement also suffered from the drawback of many nineteenth-century cosmopolitan campaigns, that it was dominated by North Americans and Europeans. The only Asian countries represented strongly were Japan, India and Pakistan; and from Latin America only Argentina had world federalist groups. Many peoples at this time were of course still under colonial rule.

Despite disagreements about the scope of the powers a world body should enjoy, and divisions between groups over the appropriate strategy, the movement for world government and world citizenship did have significant support. But as the cold war became permanent, and United Nations-sponsored negotiations for world disarmament proved totally abortive, many who had been active in urging world government turned in the later 1950s to campaigning directly against nuclear tests and weapons and pressing their own governments to take action to curb the nuclear arms race.

The idea of world citizenship did still have some adherents. A 'Parliament of the Mondcivitan Republic' met in Vienna in 1959, and by 1963, when a second Parliament met in Cardiff, claimed several thousand self-declared world citizens in 60 countries. Mundialization of cities also continued, especially in Japan, where Tokyo became the sixteenth Japanese city to declare in favour of world government in 1964.[10] But despite these initiatives, world government as a popular and newsworthy cause was superseded by other peace campaigns.

Not until the end of the cold war did the goal of some form of popular representation in accountable world institutions gain new adherents. The model of a federal world government has, however, been largely replaced by the concept of global governance and proposals for reform of existing institutions to promote greater accountability to the people of the world. Instead of a single world sovereign, global governance denotes the multiplicity of international and regional bodies that already exist, and also the role of business corporations, nongovernmental organizations and social movements. The problem as it is defined by Charter 99 in its newsletter *Global Citizen* is how to make the formal international organizations accountable. The Charter urges greater openness, independent information gathering and independent scrutiny, and sees a major role for the UN and the World Court.[11] A number of groups have proposed either direct popular representation in a Second UN General Assembly, or direct representation of civil society groups.

Connections can also be made between today's cosmopolitan idealism and its manifestations at the end of the Second World War. For example, the work of Eleanor Roosevelt, as the chair of the UN Commission on Human Rights, in drafting the UN Declaration was celebrated at a 1998 conference by a paper entitled 'Eleanor Roosevelt: Global Citizen Ahead of Her Time'.[12]

The concept of global citizenship, and its relationship to human rights and global obligations, as well as to international law and global institutions, are all issues discussed in Part III. But the focus in the following chapters is on *theory* rather than political campaigns. Chapter 7 traces the debates in mainstream political theory about the possibility of and prospects for both moral and political global citizenship. Starting from the dominant ideology in the world today, liberalism, it then explores Kantian and Habermasian approaches that include many elements of liberal thought but suggest a more critical stance on the dominance of the market, before assessing the implications of socialist theories for global citizenship. Finally, after examining the contradictory attitudes within contemporary republicanism towards global citizenship, it debates some republican and communitarian criticisms of cosmopolitanism.

Chapter 8 starts from the perspective of international relations theory, examines realist, liberal and Kantian interpretations of international politics – including constructivism – and analyses what scope they provide for a concept of global citizenship. It then comments on different possible models of global regulation – world federalism, liberal internationalism and cosmopolitan democracy – and their apparent practicality or desirability. Thirdly, this chapter examines the problems of controlling the global economy. It also examines the claim that cosmopolitanism today is a political expression of US and western imperialism.

Chapter 9 starts by assessing more subtle arguments, for example by post-colonial theorists, that cosmopolitanism is an ideological form of imperialism and that cultural diversity makes universalism both undesirable and impossible. This view is explored in relation to debates about human rights, before discussing from a feminist standpoint whether cultural relativism is a valid position. The chapter then discusses conflicting cosmopolitan and postmodern strands within feminist theory and their implications for a feminist concept of global citizenship. Finally this chapter looks at the issues raised by postmodern-ism in philosophy and international relations, and two possible responses that advocates of cosmopolitanism have advanced.

7 Global citizenship in contemporary political thought

This chapter examines the idea of global citizenship in the context of prominent traditions of political thought about society, politics and citizenship within the state and about the global order. The dominant tradition today is indisputably liberalism, especially in the light of the global economy and the collapse of the Soviet bloc. The starting point for discussion is therefore the evolution of liberal views of citizenship, and liberal moral and political perspectives on international politics. But the contrast between different strands within liberal thought and practice is also extremely significant. I focus in particular on the conflict between liberals who stress the centrality of free markets, and liberals who believe that social justice is necessary for the full realization of liberal values. Neo-liberal views chime with economic globalization, which this ideology actively promotes, but I argue that there is not a satisfactory concept of citizenship involved. John Rawls is the central theorist of liberal justice and has recently extended his views to relations between states. I compare his minimal concept of global citizenship with the more radical and activist model endorsed by Richard Falk, who stresses environmental and peace issues and the role of global civil society.

Liberalism is, however, only one source for developing concepts of global citizenship. There are other theories that embrace many elements of liberalism, but are aware of the negative effects of reliance on the market and more committed to active citizenship.

One is Kantian cosmopolitanism, as interpreted today. Kant has provided inspiration at three different levels: his moral theory endorsing cosmopolitanism; his views on the relationship between historical developments promoting globalism and the role of political action; and his views on international institutions. Three recent cosmopolitan theorists who have been influenced by Kant are discussed here. The American philosopher Martha Nussbaum, who has become one of the most eloquent advocates of world citizenship, focuses primarily on Kant's moral cosmopolitanism, which she links to Stoic philosophy. (In another capacity she has also been instrumental in promoting measures of economic growth that reflect the social welfare of that society.) Karl Jaspers, the existentialist philosopher writing on cosmopolitanism in Germany after the Second World War, draws on both the moral and historical elements in Kant in developing his own understanding of the philosopher as world citizen and the

imperative to seek world peace. Andrew Linklater, whose writings on international relations embrace both Australian and British perspectives, combines
moral, historical and institutional considerations, and draws not only on Kant
but also on Habermas to support global citizenship.

Habermas rejects the vision of globalization projected by neo-liberals, whose
ideal he characterizes as an ultimate market equilibrium based on the mobility of
all factors of production. Even if this goal is feasible, Habermas argues that it
envisages a long period of transition 'which would see not only a drastic increase
in social inequalities and social fragmentation, but the deterioration of moral
standards and cultural infrastructures as well'. This process also undermines the
value of democracy within states.[1]

Moreover, Habermas is the most influential theorist of deliberative democracy, which is inherently applicable to units smaller and larger than nation states.
Habermas himself sympathizes, as we have noted earlier, with the ideals of both
European and global citizenship – though he has not written in much detail on
the latter. This chapter comments very briefly on key aspects of Habermas's
overall social theory and its relationship to deliberative democracy, before
elaborating on his approach to transnational and global citizenship. It also notes
that the concept of a 'public space' has proved attractive to theorists who
embrace cosmopolitanism.

The most incisive critique of liberal capitalism from within the western
universalist tradition of thought has, of course, been provided by socialism, and
in particular by Marxism. From the late nineteenth century the socialist
movement also provided the most powerful political alternative to liberalism,
despite the pressures to compromise with capitalist realities and the divisive
effects of nationalism. Moreover, the socialist movement has embraced as an
ideal (if by no means always as a reality) an active form of cosmopolitanism.
Therefore, despite the widespread contemporary disillusionment with socialism,
it is important to explore how socialists today view global citizenship.

Commitment to social democracy results in an internationalist rather than a
cosmopolitan view of global politics. Supporters of social democracy today tend
to reject the thesis of inevitable globalization, and to argue for a restoration of
social democracy within a strengthened nation state and reorganized framework
of international economic bodies. The alternative is to accept that globalization
is probably irreversible, but to look for forces of transnational resistance that may
undermine this system. The first approach suggests a form of global citizenship
exercised through national governments, the second a radical version of global
citizenship through participation in global civil society.

The recent revival of republicanism in political theory, which since 1989 has
appealed to some former socialists, has underlined weaknesses in liberal ideology
and advocated an ideal of active citizenship. Republicanism today has, however,
an interestingly ambiguous relationship with cosmopolitanism. For some political
theorists, for example Alastair Davidson writing in an Australian context, it
provides a basis for supporting forms of transnational citizenship. But for others,
for example David Miller, it provides grounds for forcefully debunking global

citizenship and imprecise globalist aspirations. Hannah Arendt, the most distinguished recent theorist of republicanism, also provides an important critique of cosmopolitanism.

Cosmopolitanism may be rejected by conservatives and nationalists, but the focus here is on communitarianism. Michael Walzer, who is linked to the communitarian school of thought in the United States, has engaged in critical debate with Martha Nussbaum. This chapter concludes by considering both republican and communitarian criticisms of cosmopolitan morality and the claims made by Miller (who also endorses a qualified nationalism) and by Walzer that global citizenship cannot be a form of citizenship.

Liberal citizenship, governmental internationalism and cosmopolitanism

In order to formulate contemporary models of liberal citizenship, and the links between liberalism and cosmopolitanism, a highly simplified historical summary is in order. Early liberalism developed in the seventeenth century, in the context of a market society that undermined previous traditional hierarchy. Liberal theory focused on the individual as the primary unit of analysis and represented society and government as the outcome of a social contract between rational individuals pursuing their individual interests. Liberals argued primarily for civil rights, qualified freedom of conscience and government based on consent.[2] Some liberals have continued to stress the links between individual freedom and free markets and the dangers from state control, a view revived in neo-liberalism. The logic of capitalism has, however, often come into conflict with the values of liberalism. In domestic politics an alternative version of liberalism, sometimes dubbed social liberalism, has recognized that markets also have negative consequences and therefore endorsed some state intervention in the economy, and the importance of granting social rights and trade union rights to buttress civil and political equality.[3] Liberals differ not only in their attitudes to the market, but also in their attitudes to democracy and political participation. Until the twentieth century some liberals opposed extending the franchise to the propertyless poor and to women. All liberals are aware that centralized democratic power can be oppressive, and therefore emphasize constitutional and legal safeguards for individuals and minorities. But whilst some see individuals almost entirely as recipients of rights pursuing their personal interests, others give weight to social and political obligations and political participation. As noted in Chapter 3, liberalism has generally been linked to internationalism in foreign policy, and is open to extending citizenship beyond the state.

I suggest that there are three models of citizenship in the state that can be found in liberal thought. The first seeks to maximize individual freedom of choice and is linked to market or neo-liberalism. The second model gives more weight to individual moral and political responsibility towards a shared society. The third emphasizes individual obligations, as well as rights, and the value of political activism. All three can be extended to a version of 'global citizenship'.

The first suggests a global market, run in accordance with rules set by global bodies, in which individuals act primarily as entrepreneurs and consumers. The second fits a liberal governmental internationalism, in which individuals exercise political influence primarily as voters for national governments. The third is compatible with a focus on global civil society and cosmopolitan values.

The first model, which assumes that individuals are primarily concerned with pursuing their economic interests and private lives, has its roots in Hobbes' psychology. It also shares with Hobbes the assumption that individuals will only pay taxes, or fulfil other obligations that are against their personal interests, under compulsion. Whilst market liberals reject both Hobbes' view that individual rights must be subordinated to the requirements of public order, and his commitment to centralized power, in favour of civil liberties and constitutional checks and balances, they do agree with Hobbes that active popular involvement promotes irrationalism and disorder. They favour representation, not direct participation, and hope that individuals will play a minimum role as potential, but often apathetic, voters in the conduct of public affairs. Friedrich Hayek is the major theorist of neo-liberalism.[4] Similar views on democracy (not on neo-liberal economics) can be found in the major theorist of elitist democracy in the 1940s, Joseph Schumpeter, who did not believe most voters were well informed or equipped to do more than judge between competing leaders, and saw a degree of political apathy as a sign of political stability.[5] A more extreme interpretation, drawing on the same theoretical roots, resulted in the theory of 'economic democracy', in which individuals are seen as consumers of politics, who often have no rational incentive even to take the trouble to vote.[6] Since the 1980s New Right ideology has encouraged policies that treat individuals primarily as consumers in all spheres of life, whether as students, patients or beneficiaries of government services. Citizen rights are tending to become consumer rights.

Neo-liberalism as an ideology has promoted the thesis of economic globalization, and belief in free markets has always tended to transcend state frontiers. This tradition is therefore well suited to endorse a version of global citizenship. The Enlightenment saw traders, or an international business class, as global citizens *par excellence*. Herman Gunsteren suggests that the emergence of this class, which is 'multilingual, multicultural and migrant', is 'a real development of world citizenship'.[7]

Moreover, the very limitations of neo-liberal individualism, and of the passive model of citizenship within the state, become advantages: individuals can see themselves as bearers of rights in a global context; they cannot be expected to undertake very specific duties at a world level – although a future global tax (additional to state taxes) is not unthinkable; and since citizenship is not central to individual identity, the absence of a global culture is not a problem.

There are, however, several major objections to seeing this as a satisfactory model of global citizenship. The first is that it is a primarily economic conception, so individuals are first and foremost entrepreneurs or consumers, pursuing profit and cheap goods and services. There is no sense of mutuality of obligations or of belonging to a common society suggested by the concept of citizenship. Moreover, neo-liberals reject the concept of social justice and oppose an active role for the state – or international bodies – in transferring resources or curbing market forces.

In principle Hayekian precepts suggest that curbs on monopolies, rules to ensure genuinely free markets and freedom of movement for labour as well as capital could result in a more equitable world. But in practice distrust of governmental controls, and the actual power of multinational corporations to shape the rules, plus the enormous social problems posed by mass migration of labour, mean that neo-liberal beliefs endorse the most affluent exploiting the rest of the world. Enlightened businesses may be aware that in the long run it is in their interests to maintain the environment, and avoid extreme poverty and political instability.[8] But the logic of economic competition works in the opposite direction. Moreover, a mode of thought giving rational priority to pursuit of self-interest, from Hobbes through to the present theorists of rational choice, suggests a necessary conflict between immediate individual interest and longer-term collective interests.

Furthermore, in political practice, the New Right's individualistic neo-liberal ideas have in both the USA and Britain coexisted with a strong commitment to nationalism. Nationalism provides the sense of community and identity so notably lacking in the neo-liberal landscape, but also tends to result in stringent immigration policies and distrust of international organizations and courts, which presume to tell 'us' what to do. Neo-liberalism, therefore, is global in its economic perspective, but nationalist in its explicit politics, and doubly opposed to cosmopolitanism as interpreted in this book.

The second model of liberal citizenship draws on the mainstream of nineteenth-century liberal thought. Its central exponents are John Stuart Mill and today John Rawls. This model does give some weight to the duties of citizenship as well as to rights. It also argues for government action to ensure that individual rights and opportunities are not denied by the operations of the market. Thirdly, it gives more weight than does neo-liberalism to the political aspect of citizenship.

This version of liberalism believes that individuals have the capacity for reason, which not only enables them to conduct their private lives intelligently, but also potentially enables them to pass rational judgements on political issues. To do so, however, people may need political education that may be fostered by taking part in local politics or civil society. Liberals also assume that individuals possess the capacity for a moral intelligence, which can encourage them to be socially responsible. The emphasis on free thought, free speech and free assembly safeguards religious and cultural freedom, but also creates a framework for political debate and action. The ideal liberal citizen therefore exercises the right to vote rationally and with a sense of moral responsibility.[9]

The universalist basis of this version of liberalism has fostered support for international institutions that create a framework for international law. Moreover, liberal respect for universal principles of justice has given legitimacy to individual citizens who oppose their own governments, as liberal movements against colonialism and unjust wars have demonstrated.

Mainstream liberal theory also provides a basis for arguing that states endorsing liberal democratic principles are inherently less likely to go to war unless facing direct aggression. A more limited version of this thesis, widely accepted in the 1990s, is that liberal democracies – though they may wage war with vigour on states ruled by dictators – do not wish to fight each other.[10] The spread of liberal democracy therefore creates a zone of peace. Both approaches suggest that the liberal democratic citizen is committed to the global implementation of human rights and favours the creation of a peaceful global society.

Rawls, who provided an impressive philosophical defence of liberal principles in *A Theory of Justice* (1971), has now met criticisms that his theory was focused almost exclusively on justice within the state. In that work, Rawls did consider the arguments for a just war, and support strictly non-violent civil disobedience against unjust wars. But he did not tackle issues of rights and equality at an international level. The *Law of Peoples* (1999) develops the universal implications of his earlier theory and examines how ideally relations between peoples should be arranged. By his choice of the word 'peoples', rather than states, Rawls is rejecting a realist concept of states operating without moral constraints, and also rejecting the view that states are wholly sovereign and unaccountable for the way they treat their own citizens. But his framework is drawn from the precepts of international law and a concept of international society, and he explicitly rejects a 'cosmopolitanism' that focuses primarily on relations between individuals throughout the world.[11] Rawls is therefore providing a version of liberal internationalism for the beginning of the twenty-first century.

The purpose of the essay is to extend the argument of *A Theory of Justice*, which explored how rational individuals engaging in a hypothetical social contract would design a truly just society. In *The Law of Peoples* Rawls imagines a contract between peoples to create a just international society based on respect for the independence and equality of all peoples and for individual human rights, though these rights are 'a special class of urgent rights' such as freedom from slavery and security from extreme discrimination and violence against particular groups, and not coterminous with all the rights of citizens in a liberal democracy. This contract would be sustained by countries honouring agreements and providing assistance to societies burdened by oppression or extreme poverty. Although liberal democracies provide the ideal basis for such an international society, and Rawls refers to the thesis that liberal democracies maintain peace with each other, he recognizes that some societies have independent traditions. In line with a liberal respect for pluralism he argues the need to recognize different interpretations of liberalism, and more importantly to show tolerance for other cultures and forms of government, with the central liberal proviso that *they do not violate fundamental principles of decent government and human rights*. In the case of those states outside the pale of international society, there is a duty to bring pressure to bear to stop atrocities and to try to assist them to achieve a better political and economic way of life. If outlaw states initiate aggression, then the principles of just war should determine the response.[12] Rawls rejects radical proposals for redistribution of resources between the rich and poor parts of the world, and in general is not critical of the operations of the global market.

Rawls is proposing a 'realistic utopia' and not prescribing policy choices. As a result he does not address crucial immediate issues, such as immigration or the spread of nuclear weapons. He also abstains from making specific suggestions about international organization, though he envisages the possibility of a variety of bodies based on international cooperation or closer 'federal' ties. But he is categorically opposed to a world government, citing Kant's fears of world dictatorship.[13]

There is a concept of global citizenship to be found in Rawls' essay, but it is an extension of the role of ordinary citizens within a liberal democracy and a very attenuated concept. The citizen within the state has a responsibility to think like a legislator, and to vote against candidates and governments who support unreasonable policies. Similarly citizens have a responsibility to think like foreign policy-makers and to reject politicians who violate the principles that should underpin international society. This responsibility towards the law of peoples is therefore exercised within a national setting.[14]

A more activist interpretation of how individuals as citizens within the state can act as global citizens, not incompatible with Rawls' position, is to argue and lobby for their governments to pursue liberal foreign policies: for example refusing to sell arms to dictators or supporting human rights in other countries. Liberal theory has also justified non-violent disobedience where governments seriously contravene liberal principles – a position adopted by Rawls himself, as we noted earlier. So global citizenship can be exercised as a facet of national citizenship.

The third model of liberal citizenship is more strongly critical of the market than are mainstream liberalism and Rawls himself, and therefore leans closer to socialism. It also lays greater stress on the duties of citizens and on political activism and self-realization through politics, and therefore also leans towards republicanism. In its present-day manifestations it has also been influenced by feminist and green ideas and tends to favour social movements. But this model is firmly rooted in the liberal tradition of civil rights under the rule of law and representative democracy. Elements of this model can be found in the 1960s critics of elitist democracy, arguing for political participation and sympathetic to forms of democracy at places of work.[15] These theorists, however, assumed that democracy is confined within national boundaries. In more recent democratic theory the writings on civil society and associative democracy reflect contemporary concerns and are more open to transnational interpretations.[16] But the model can be deduced most clearly from the role of political activists in social movements.

This model is linked to the tradition of liberal cosmopolitanism explored in Chapter 3. Liberal belief in individual rights and rejection of cruelty and oppression, both inside the state and at a global level, encourages the development of and respect for international human rights law. Liberal commitments to tolerance of religious and cultural diversity have in the past favoured open immigration policies and generosity towards refugees. They have also prompted engagement in movements against war and oppression. Taking part in transnational social movements is, as noted in Chapter 4, a central model of global citizenship.

This third model of liberal citizenship is strongly opposed to neo-liberalism both domestically and, more importantly here, globally. Movements concerned with world poverty, the environment or human rights frequently criticize the activities of powerful multinationals and call for national and international political intervention to curb global economic power. They therefore see many members of business elites not as global citizens but as global oppressors. This sharp theoretical distinction is suggested by Richard Falk, who contrasts economic globalization 'from above' with transnational activism 'from below'. Falk does not totally reject global market forces, but his approach seeks 'to identify and regulate adverse effects and correct social injustices'.[17] The potential of social movements to constrain the operations of the global economy is, however, necessarily limited.

A response compatible with liberalism is to turn to reform of international institutions like the World Bank in order to strengthen the economic powers of the state. However, the perceived decline of state power may also lead to proposals for direct individual representation in global bodies, one aspect of David Held's idea of cosmopolitan democracy. Falk is sympathetic to this idea, but develops a slightly different concept of 'normative democracy' to encapsulate the principles that he believes are emerging from and should unite global civil society, and that should constrain global institutions, Many of these are liberal principles: for example consent, the rule of law, respect for rights, accountability and transparency. But he also stresses political participation and a restored emphasis on 'public goods' in relation to health, welfare and the environment and means to fund them.[18]

Falk is cautious about suggesting specific reforms to international bodies, particularly if this involves proposing more centralized global bodies as world federalists did. His emphasis is therefore on globalization from below and he also notes the utopian element in global citizenship. He suggests this concept is not spatial, like traditional citizenship, but temporal. The global citizen is 'reaching out to a future to-be-created' and becomes 'a citizen pilgrim' on a journey towards a country yet to be established, and in the process of creating a future global community.[19]

Falk therefore adopts a position between an international politics based on liberal internationalism, in which nation states cooperate within international institutions, and a more cosmopolitan order, in which individuals relate directly to international law and global political institutions. The latter is more often associated with a Kantian ideal.

Kantian approaches to global citizenship

In Kant's own writings it is possible to discern an active model of citizenship within the state that combines republican and liberal elements – though liberal elements predominate. In addition there is a moral universalism that obliges individuals to think like citizens of the world. Although Kant's name is used to symbolize a cosmopolitan model of world politics, in which relations between individuals (not between states) are central, his own theory is poised between a political recognition of internationalism between states and moral commitment to an overarching cosmopolitanism.

Thus Kant himself does see citizenship primarily in terms of the state. The good state is one governed by laws rather than by men, in which active citizens have a responsibility for electing governments and also a responsibility to engage in public debate about the correct policies to be pursued. Kant does not envisage participatory democracy. He does believe that in a good 'republic' the citizens will, when necessary, bear arms, because this will help to ensure that the state goes to war only in a truly just cause. From a political standpoint, therefore, citizenship is primarily national, but with a dimension of influencing the state to act in accordance with universal principles that should govern an international society.

But as moral beings individuals have a duty to obey universal imperatives and to comprehend the bonds that unite them to all human beings. Kant's moral theory argues that human beings should always treat all others as ends in themselves, not as a means to an end. Morality requires individuals to be autonomous: they should be their own 'law-makers', and they should act out of duty, not upon a utilitarian calculation of consequences. Moral duties are not bounded by state frontiers; individuals have universal obligations. These obligations are set out most clearly in the discussion of the reciprocal obligations of hospitality. People ought to extend hospitality to strangers. But there is also a moral requirement on individuals when travelling to respect those in the lands they visit, not to open the door to commercial exploitation and political conquest.[20]

Kant's primary argument for a cosmopolitan politics is a moral one. Although there are differences between personal and political morality, politics is governed by principles of 'right' that require states to create conditions for individuals to act freely and autonomously. This means that they should not be subject to arbitrary coercion but governed under the rule of law in a republic. It also means that they should not be subject to arbitrary violence, which cannot be guaranteed as long as wars between states continue and there is no global rule of law. So there is a moral obligation to work towards world peace, even though we cannot be sure if this goal is attainable. Even if it is a pious hope, 'we must simply act as if it really could come about'. By trying to give it reality through gradual reforms we may bring the goal closer.[21]

The moral case for cosmopolitanism is still central. Kant is also relevant to debates about global citizenship today, however, because of his view that the historical changes in international society are creating conditions in which utopian cosmopolitanism might gradually be realized. International society may, he suggests, be changed both by unifying economic and technological trends drawing the world closer together, and by the recent experience of increasingly devastating wars.[22] Some of the language used by Kant suggests a 'mechanism of nature' (or a hidden hand) promoting necessary human unity, but history is not moving towards an *inevitable goal*. He concludes that it is impossible to be certain the ideal of perpetual peace will be achieved. But the existence of objective trends means that it is our moral duty to work towards the goal of world peace, 'which is more than an empty chimera'.[23] The way forward is through an expanding confederation of states that embrace constitutions based on popular representation and the rule of law, and that will create a zone of peace, which may gradually encompass more states. (For further discussion of the nature of this confederation, see Chapter 2.)

Many of today's exponents of cosmopolitanism and global governance combine a moral appeal with an assessment of new political possibilities. Martha Nussbaum develops the moral dimension of Kant's cosmopolitanism in her defence of world citizenship. She is particularly interested in the implications for personal conduct, noting Kant's own commitment to observe the courtesies of hospitality to a guest when he was himself on the verge of death.[24] She is also interested in seeing how the Stoics' understanding of the psychology of individual passions, for example the possibility of reducing anger, might strengthen Kant's approach. This psychological emphasis relates to her interest in education and the possibility of combating the politics of nationalism by providing a cosmopolitan education. This is the theme of her essay 'Patriotism and Cosmopolitanism', in which she argues that American children should learn more about the geography, ecology and cultures of other countries and be encouraged to think about their obligation to respect the rights of others. The stance she recommends is 'that we should give our first allegiance to no mere form of government, no temporal power, but to the moral community made up by the humanity of all human beings'.[25]

This emphasis on education of the emotions and of the intellect to achieve cosmopolitanism has of course political implications. Nussbaum believes that cosmopolitan education will have important political and economic consequences. She suggests, for example, that Americans should, if they take Kantian morality seriously, 'be troubled' by the fact that the whole world cannot achieve American standards of living without ecological disaster.[26]

Karl Jaspers, though he is seldom mentioned in today's debates about global citizenship, is an interesting example of a philosopher who tried to be a world citizen in both his philosophy and his personal and political life, whilst simultaneously stressing his obligations as a citizen of Germany. Therefore he exemplified the ideal of the politically engaged and cosmopolitan philosopher upheld by Nussbaum, who looks to the Stoics for such a model.[27] Jaspers' opposition to the Nazi regime, which denied him his university post and the ability to publish, and threatened him and his Jewish wife with deportation, strengthens this claim. His position in the debates about NATO and armaments in the 1950s, in which he opposed calls for Germany neutrality, was more controversial.[28] But he did engage in public argument about the immense dangers of nuclear weapons and the problems of the cold war.

After the Second World War, and his immediate engagement in questions of German guilt and the basis for a new German politics, Jaspers considered his philosophical responsibilities. He writes in his 'Philosophical Memoir' that he had two tasks: 'to clarify the moral premises and real conditions of politics in my own mind, and secondly, to take my bearings on political thought from the anticipated standpoint of a world citizen'.[29] He also tried to popularize philosophy: 'My aim was the kind of philosophizing that can be accessible and convincing to man as such, not the esoteric business of a few aristocrats.'[30] This enterprise was important partly because, as Jaspers suggests Kant understood, philosophers cannot alone provide the moral and rational influence on politicians necessary for pursuit of peace. 'Effective leadership can be provided, not by individual philosopher kings or supermen, but by the truth which comes to light in public discourse and intellectual contention.'[31]

An illuminating brief discussion of Jaspers is provided by Hannah Arendt's essay 'Karl Jaspers: Citizen of the World?', in which she presents as sympathetically as possible Jaspers' philosophical approach designed to provide a basis for world citizenship.[32] The philosophical basis for human solidarity is 'limitless communication'. This communication requires those who enter into it to renounce the binding and exclusive claims to the truth of any single philosophy or tradition. Jaspers stresses the value to him of Hindu and Chinese thought as well as of his own European tradition, and sees philosophizing as trying to 'make universal communication possible', which requires 'a conscious view of the entire philosophy of mankind'.[33] Arendt claims that 'faith in the comprehensibility of all truths *and* the good will to reveal and to listen as the primary condition for all human intercourse' is central to Jaspers' philosophy. Truth can only be revealed through reasoned communication; and this communicative truth is in Jasper's words 'what binds us together'.[34]

Jaspers' emphasis on moral human unity is paralleled by his fear that nuclear war will destroy human beings altogether. This awareness influences his comments on Kant's *Perpetual Peace*. Kant suggests that bitter experience of wars and disaster leads men towards recognition of the need for peace. The threat of nuclear war creates much greater urgency and intensifies the fear. But fear alone will not change people's behaviour or international politics. What is required is a reasoned response and 'the resolve of the innumerable human beings who set the course of history'.[35] Elsewhere Jaspers argues that, however minimal the influence of individuals, each person has some 'responsibility for the whole', and has some power, however little.[36] Like Kant, Jaspers is strongly aware of the force of realist arguments about the inevitability of conflicts between states, but also believes that it is necessary to avoid despair.

Arendt claims that Jaspers rejects Kant's philosophy of history, as suggested in the 'Idea for a Universal History', that human beings are driven towards perpetual peace by a hidden force. But Jaspers did agree with Kant that people have to act as though the goal of giving political expression to human solidarity, which logically implies peace, is possible. Arendt summarizes: 'Just as, according to Kant, nothing should happen in war which would make a future peace and reconciliation impossible, so nothing should happen today in politics which would be contrary to the actually existing solidarity of mankind.'[37]

Jaspers adopts for internal politics Kant's concept of democracy, a 'republican manner of government', and addresses the institutional and social issues involved in trying to realize a politics based on respect for the dignity and self-realization of each citizen. He also suggests that the democratic idea – 'the idea of reason' – should ideally extend from the nation to the international community.[38] He looks towards a limitation of national sovereignty and an extension of international law and the eventual possibility of a world federation founded on law, since humanity does not want to perish. 'What was done on a small scale when governments were first instituted might be repeated with an international confederation.'[39] In the foreseeable future he argues that it is essential to maintain the UN, despite the cynical manipulation of its institutions by the great powers, because, however badly it operates, it is 'a tool to serve peace in unpredictable fashion' and provides a framework for the future when 'a stable peace of organized law' may be attained.[40]

Linklater, who also develops several aspects of Kant's thought, notes that one model of global citizenship is a recognition of a universal moral dimension. He suggests that one view of cosmopolitan citizenship today, therefore, is that ethical obligations to humanity as a whole can transcend obligations to fellow citizens. 'This is the essence of the Kantian conception of world citizenship.'[41] This view of global citizenship does not link it to the development of global institutions, and certainly does not envisage any kind of world federal government.

Kant does not, however, rely on moral imperatives alone and recognizes the need for political action by states to strengthen international society. Therefore, Linklater suggests, Kant provides a bridge to a second concept of cosmopolitan citizenship, which rejects the adequacy of a purely moral dimension, and looks to a specific political framework in which to give citizenship substance. One drawback of the moral perspective is that it implies compassion and wide-ranging (if not precise) duties for individuals who see themselves as global citizens, without any corresponding rights. But citizenship usually suggests a set of specific rights.[42] Moreover, citizenship requires at least some clear-cut duties. Therefore those who believe it is 'morally desirable and politically possible to uncouple citizenship from the state' look for new transnational political arrangements.[43] This is clearly Linklater's own preferred position. He discusses how far the EU provides such a framework, notes the very limited version of citizenship embodied in the Maastricht Treaty, but comments on proposals for a stronger European citizenship.

Whilst Kant is one of the theorists on whom Linklater draws, his model of cosmopolitan citizenship is more directly indebted to Habermas. He describes it as a 'dialogic approach' and he asserts the need to 'develop communication communities in which the vulnerable can contest the ways in which they are treated'.[44]

Habermas and European or global citizenship

Habermas provides a basis for developing a strong concept of cosmopolitan citizenship for a number of reasons. Kant's universalism has come under sustained attack in recent decades from theorists adopting versions of postmodernism, and Habermas has made the most impressive theoretical attempt to uphold universalism in today's context, whilst rejecting any kind of metaphysical system. His theory, focused on the conditions for equal access to participation in reasoned discourse, suggests the need for 'dialogic communities' at various political levels. Moreover, Habermas himself is highly critical of exclusive nationalism and sympathetic to forms of citizenship transcending the state.

Widespread belief in universal principles, which can be ascertained by and applied through reason, a belief typified by the Enlightenment, is, Habermas suggests, a product of modernity. (It does of course have roots in classical Greek philosophy that influenced modern thought.) But the very processes of modernity, which have eroded both tradition and religion, have meant that societies are no longer united by shared and unquestioned beliefs. Instead, individuals have to develop moral beliefs in communication with other members of their society. When a shared culture no longer provides social cohesion, then the ability to communicate still provides a unifying factor.[45]

Habermas elaborates on the conditions that can enable individuals to reach moral agreement. Individuals must recognize certain rules of argument, such as the different kinds of claims to validity inherent in appeals to objective external truth, moral rightness and personal sincerity. They must also believe that when they enter into discussion their own interests and needs will be taken into account, not suppressed.

Habermas's theory of democracy follows logically from his theory of rational discourse.[46] The requirements of respect for other individuals and recognition of their legitimate interests, as well as the commitment to be a part of a shared society, are embodied in constitutional rights and duties. The centrality of reasoned speech in framing common policies is embedded in the concept of deliberative democracy. Habermas argues that his ideal of deliberative democracy contains elements of liberalism in its institutional framework and of republicanism in its emphasis on the inherent value of participation in political deliberation. But it does not have such a limited view of citizenship as liberalism or unrealistically assume the degree of political community and commitment to the public good required by mainstream republicanism.[47] Deliberative democracy does not presuppose that all policy is based on agreement reached through discourse, since a reasoned consensus that can be conclusively accepted and justified by all concerned is an ideal that can never be fully achieved, and agreement in practice depends upon shared assumptions and elements of political culture (lifeworld). Where consensus is impossible, deliberative democracy allows for compromise of interests based on fair bargaining. It also allows for deliberation in a number of spheres – within both parliamentary bodies and 'culturally mobilized publics' based in civil society.[48] The deliberative model of democracy can therefore apply at various political levels. It can be decentred within the state and it can transcend state borders – and in some of his writings Habermas envisages that the latter may occur. But before it can do so there must be a common political culture emerging from a civil society and public communication across national frontiers.[49] Habermas rejects a philosophical approach of arguing from a preferred moral position what should happen, so in envisaging transnational democracy he sees himself 'reconstructing' elements of an existing process.[50]

Transcending state borders is related to developing a non-nationalistic concept of citizenship within the state. Habermas notes that the concept of the nation has both cultural and political roots, but distinguishes between citizenship understood as national identity, a status granted by birth, and citizenship as voluntary membership of a political community. The tension between an 'ascribed nation' and a 'voluntary nation of citizens' who generate democratic legitimacy can be resolved if the state constitution 'gives priority to a cosmopolitan understanding of the nation as a nation of citizens over an ethnocentric interpretation'.[51] The increasing cultural pluralism of society also suggests the need to replace nationalism by constitutional patriotism. Social cohesion requires not only secure civil and political rights but equality promoted through welfare rights and cultural rights. The possibility of democracy within the state is, however, challenged by global economic trends undermining state borders and welfare provision. Thus one solution is to create supranational regimes.

How far does the EU provide this supranational framework? Habermas wrote a number of commentaries on this question during the 1990s. He notes that there is economic integration and supranational administration, but no political integration beyond the level of the nation state. 'The technocratic shape taken by the European Community reinforces doubts as to whether the normative expectations one associate with the role of the democratic citizen have not actually always been a mere illusion.'[52] But there are some grounds for hope, if a public sphere in which deliberation occurs develops, and through its influence on public administration can impose some social and environmental limits on the economy. If decision-making bodies become more open and accountable and if social movements can ensure key issues are on the public agenda, then 'European-wide public spheres may emerge'.[53] Picking up this theme again he argues that, 'Given the political will', the EU could 'create the politically necessary communicative context', and that even the requirement of a common language, which would be English, could be achieved through education.[54] There is not yet a European people united in solidarity, but just as in the nineteenth century nation states created a political culture, this process can potentially be repeated in Europe.[55]

On global citizenship Habermas is even more tentative. But he does note that the world public sphere that Kant identified 'today will become a political reality for the first time with the new relations of global communication'. So global citizenship is no longer 'merely a phantom' and can be seen as part of a continuum with state citizenship.[56] A global consciousness also exists, demonstrated for example by the UN Earth Summits, however limited the impact of such meetings on the actual behaviour of the governments of great powers.[57] Historical trends and a changing consciousness may make possible the development of supranational forms of global governance. In an essay analysing Kant's *Perpetual Peace* in the light of the past 200 years, Habermas suggests the possibility of reforming the United Nations and the development of cosmopolitan democracy.[58] His argument here is taken up in the next chapter.

Given that deliberative democracy is designed to operate in contexts where there is considerable inherited cultural diversity, it seems inherently suited to forums where people from differing world cultures deliberate. Shared political understandings can develop though a process of debate. There are also pressing common concerns such as global warming. Even if people approach global problems initially from different perspectives, the need to address them can create a shared basis of information and agreement on political strategies, as social movements indicate.

The role of social movements in creating a cosmopolitan public sphere is stressed by the philosopher James Bohman in his reflections on Kant from a Habermasian perspective. Taking up Kant's point that publicity constrains governments to pursue justifiable courses of action, Bohman argues that what are required are self-critical debates about issues of public concern, which becomes cosmopolitan when networks of communication and the audience transcend national boundaries. A developing cosmopolitan public sphere renews democracy within the state and through the associations of international civil society. There is a role for official transnational institutions – Bohman refers to the European Parliament – but he sees as even more crucial the development of transnational institutions to organize public debate and decision-making by world citizens.[59]

Socialism and global citizenship

Socialist theorists today are actively engaged in debates about economic globalization, global governance and global civil society, and it is possible to deduce two main positions on global citizenship within contemporary debates.

To simplify drastically a complex tradition, two main strands of socialism emerged in the twentieth century: social democracy and variants on revolutionary socialism. Social democracy suggests a strong concept of citizenship within the state and a more limited version of global citizenship within an international socialist context. Revolutionary socialism has implied a stance of pure resistance until a new social order is achieved, and the violent overthrow of existing authorities.

Whether armed struggle can ever be seen as compatible with cosmopolitan goals, which suggest non-violent methods, is a large question. I am excluding from discussion here guerrilla movements. Advocacy of action through global civil society for socialist goals can be seen as a version of global citizenship. (I also ignore here the question of citizenship within regimes established by revolutionary socialist movements, since the Soviet Union no longer exists and the regimes within China and Vietnam are being influenced by their increasing openness to the global economy. Cuba and North Korea are also, for different reasons, in a process of change.)

The evolution of social democracy within the West led to a form of citizenship that was based on a wide range of rights, including not only a strong concept of welfare as an entitlement, but also economic rights to be exercised through trade unions and representative bodies within companies. (In practice social liberal and social democratic programmes may not be wholly distinct, but social democracy suggests a stronger role for trade unions and for the state.) The duties of social democratic citizens reflect the range of their rights. To maintain and extend social democracy it is necessary that citizens willingly pay high taxes and that workers actively support its key institutions: trade unions and socialist parties. Sweden, the European state that has come closest to embodying a strong model of social democracy, has also relied on a defence policy requiring military service by all male citizens, and the republican belief in a citizen rather than a purely professional army has been an integral part of socialist thinking in much of Europe. Early in the twentieth century the democratic importance of citizens taking up arms was articulated by the French socialist Jean Jaurès.

The primary goal of social democrats has been to promote greater equality and prosperity within the nation state, but they have maintained some commitment to international solidarity with the poor and oppressed elsewhere. Socialist movements have in principle opposed wars between capitalist states (though in practice the Second International failed to do so in 1914), and some unions and parties have resisted wars by imperialist states against colonial rebels or socialist countries, like the newly created USSR in 1919–20 or North Vietnam in the 1960s. The cold war brought some western governments with social democratic aspirations into confrontation with the Soviet Union, but Sweden remained formally neutral. Sweden also played a prominent role in trying to promote arms control between the Soviet bloc and the West, and with other Scandinavian countries has been more generous and radical in its aid to developing countries than many liberal governments. In international politics, therefore, social democracy adopts positions similar to those adopted by radical liberals in social movements.

Two models of global citizenship are therefore suggested by social democracy. The first is global citizenship as an additional dimension of national citizenship. Since, however, social democratic governments concerned about social justice at home are more likely to take it seriously at a global level than liberal regimes, there is greater potential for social democratic citizens to contribute to global welfare through government policies. The second model of social democratic global citizenship is an actor in global civil society, though the more obvious vehicles for action would be trade unions and socialist parties rather than the new social movements. Although within most (but not all) western states the scope for beleaguered unions, with falling membership and reduced powers, is probably declining, unions are also being forced to confront the problems posed for themselves and others by economic globalization. The presence of trade unions at the Seattle protests against the WTO in 1999 and the Prague protests against the World Bank and IMF in 2000 may suggest moves towards a revived militancy.

Social democrats have proceeded through incremental reforms rather than strategies of revolution, and have therefore worked within a capitalist framework and given due recognition to the interests of business and finance. After 1945 social democracy became clearly associated with corporatism, but a corporatism that gave significant power to labour as well as business. Promoting social democratic policies was made possible both by the adopting of Keynesian economics and by the international financial framework provided by the 1944 Bretton Woods agreement, which enabled governments to control their domestic economies and their exchange rates. When faith in Keynesianism and the Bretton Woods monetary system both collapsed in the 1970s, the prospects for social democracy became less promising.

Whether states can still pursue genuinely social democratic goals in a context of neo-liberal orthodoxy and increasing economic globalization, which both challenge state autonomy, state ability to protect its own industries and the power of trade unions, is highly debatable. But some socialists challenge both the degree and the inevitability of globalization, suggesting that both are promoted by neo-liberal ideology. They also point to the explicit political role of governments endorsing neo-liberalism (as in Britain, Australia and New Zealand) in eliminating barriers to the unrestricted operations of global finance and multinational corporations. In addition, the policies adopted by the Reagan Administration also pressured international bodies like the IMF and World Bank towards imposing neo-liberal policies on poor debtor countries. Therefore a return to greater national economic autonomy based on state control is seen both as a realistic possibility and as the most effective means of combating global capitalism. (The policy adopted by the New Zealand Labour Government elected in 1999 to reverse the extreme neo-liberalism of the 1980s – to stop privatization, end deregulated labour markets and strengthen trade union rights – will be an interesting test case of whether this policy can work.[60]) This view is put forward by Manfred Bienefeld, who also argues the case for protectionism.[61] Göran Therborn notes that social democratic reform has always focused on the domestic state. Although Sweden, the ideal social democratic state, had problems in the 1990s, these were primarily national in origin, and there is still 'room to manoeuver in the world of globalization'.[62] Other theorists seeking to maintain social democratic policies argue that reimposition of state controls over trade and the flow of capital would have to be supplemented by international agreements and regulatory agencies.[63] This social democratic vision of an international, rather than a global, order is therefore opposed to the proposals for global democratic institutions and cosmopolitan democracy. Theories about the revival of social democracy also imply maintaining limited versions of global citizenship.

The alternative to creating social democracy within the state has been a revolutionary socialism. After the creation of the Soviet Union and the subordination of worldwide communist parties to Soviet interests, the revolutionary tradition became relatively weak and divided, but there still appeared to be some revolutionary potential in Asia, Latin America and Africa. However, the process of decolonization has, especially since the demise of the Soviet Union, left even those few developing countries formally committed to socialism vulnerable to control and exploitation by western governments and corporations. The rise of neo-liberalism and economic globalization has also seriously weakened the western labour movement. So by the beginning of the twenty-first century a Marxist analysis of the dynamics of an increasingly global capitalism can be made quite convincingly. But Marx's own vision no longer holds of a united working class arising out of the economic and sociological logic of capitalism to overthrow the system. Even his much debated prediction of captialism's demise as a result of its own internal contradictions might still prove to be ultimately correct. The instability of global financial markets, dramatized by the Asian crash of 1997, and the views of the arch-capitalist George Soros about the potential disintegration of the global capitalist system, indicate this possibility.[64] In the absence of social and political forces with a constructive alternative, however, disintegration suggests a spectre of worldwide poverty and famine, wars for scarce resources and political dictatorship or fascism.

A socialist perspective accepting the irreversibility of globalization tends therefore to be pessimistic. Looking to global civil society for an alternative politics seems very optimistic. Moreover, only certain groups within this civil society are genuinely oppositional, as Joachim Hirsch notes, although he does not rule out the possibility of developing cooperation between movements of the oppressed.[65]

Nevertheless, there are some signs of hope. Robert Cox argues in his 1992 paper 'Globalization, Multilateralism, and Democracy' that there is not 'one universal form of capitalism' and that there are still pressures within the EU for a 'social Europe'. He also comments on the growth of neighbourhood and self-help organizations, which are promoting social transformation even in the crisis-ridden continent of Africa, and suggests the scope for a participatory democracy based on civil society. Cox points to the responsibility of the UN to respond to such groups and discuss alternative forms of economic development.[66] In a later essay, after examining how economic globalization has damaged the environment and undermined the bases of the kind of civil society that used to underpin parliamentary institutions, he looks to new social movements and expressions of popular revolt, such as the Zapatistas in the Chiapas region of Mexico and the mass strikes in Paris in December 1995. He concludes that his strategy for a 'recomposition of civil society' will be 'elaborated less through intellectual concentration than by reflection upon the experience of an active citizenship'.[67] Like Falk, Cox believes that 'the new order will have to be built from the bottom up', especially 'when the present order falters in its attempt to hold things in place from the top down'.[68] In this perspective global citizenship is possible, but only through participation in movements resisting the dominant institutions and trends of today's capitalism.

Republican citizenship

Republicanism, which since 1989 has attracted some disillusioned socialists, is interesting here because republican values can not only promote a view of global citizenship, but also provide a basis for strongly criticizing the concept. Republicanism is a complex and secondary strand in western political thought, sometimes opposing and sometimes mingling with liberal beliefs in the eighteenth century. Republicanism as a separate tradition of thought, as we saw in Chapters 2 and 3, largely disappeared in the nineteenth and twentieth centuries, until its revival in recent years. In the discussion that follows I focus on republican thought that stresses citizen responsibility and activism, and that engages with issues of globalization.[69]

Early republicanism is drawn from the experience of the Greek city states, and republican Rome, which suggest the ideal of politically active citizens and citizen soldiers. In the eighteenth century Rousseau articulated the values and requirements of this original republican model. The association between republicanism and a cohesive community, as well as the link between republicanism and direct democracy, made it difficult to translate to the nation state. Where this transition took place, the role of community was likely to be replaced by nationalism.[70]

The modern version of republicanism, which emerged at the end of the eighteenth century in the Jacobins, did embrace the nation as its primary community. It also extended citizenship to the poor, often excluded from previous, more elitist versions, such as the aristocratic republicanism of English and Scottish writers in the seventeenth and eighteenth centuries. John Keane notes that Paine introduced a form of republicanism distinctively modern in two respects. It was 'dangerously democratic', including working people in the category of citizens, and it was not inspired by the classical Greek and Roman examples, but drew mainly on experience.[71]

The French Revolution stressed the status *citoyens* as opposed to subjects, and dissolved the social distinctions between aristocrats and common men. The Revolution also endorsed the ideal of the citizen soldier – famously introducing the *levée en masse* in place of the former professional armies – and the sentiment of patriotism. The emphasis of today's republicanism, however, is on forms of social rather than military service, and on voluntary social and political activity.

The tendency of some republican political theorists today to dismiss the possibility of global citizenship is a reversal of the position in the late eighteenth century, when Paine saw himself as a world citizen, but also urged republican patriotism on America and France. One reason for the change in emphasis is that in Paine's time republicanism was a transnational movement challenging the established order, like socialism a century later, so republicans shared a common cause and common principles. A second possible reason is suggested by Keane. He notes that in the late eighteenth century 'there was no contradiction between feeling oneself to be a citizen of the wider world ... and wanting to transform that little corner of the European world where one had been born'. But most of the *philosophes* wrote before the French Revolution, which, as Keane also notes, meant that a new kind of nationalism tended to supplant cosmopolitanism.[72]

However, republicans support a form of nationalism associated with allegiance to republican principles rather than allegiance to an ethnic identity. It is therefore still possible to believe that upholding republican principles at home will tend to coincide with upholding them abroad, by opposing oppressive regimes elsewhere and refusing to take part in unjust wars. This is the position suggested by the republican theorist of democracy Benjamin Barber.[73] But contemporary republican theorists like Miller, who emphasize communal membership within the nation state, and a demanding ideal of citizenship, deny the possibility of multiple levels of citizenship.

Davidson, on the other hand, espouses a republican ideal of citizen activity and civic virtue but rejects the centrality of the nation state and adherence to a strong communal national identity. Writing in an Australian context, he traces the evolution of Australians from 'subjects' in 1901 to a status of potential active citizenship by 1995. He also argues against a communitarian view of nationalism and claims that the reality today is mass migration and multi-ethnicity. Where Miller claims that foreign immigrants must either be educated into a national understanding of citizenship (as in France) or relegated to a non-citizen status (as in Germany), Davidson welcomes Australian multiculturalism. Communitarian concepts of nationalism are too narrow and have excluded too many who ought to have full citizen rights. Davidson suggests that newcomers must be able to engage in debate about the public good and have the possibility of 'reshaping the public space'.[74]

Davidson is also prepared to take a radical view on how easily resident aliens should acquire citizen rights. He cites the 1793 French Revolutionary Constitution, which, despite its nationalistic tone, allowed foreigners who had lived in France for a year to gain citizen rights.[75] He also envisages the future possibility of individuals moving from one country to another and acquiring citizen rights in each state, whilst recognizing that this is a distant ideal.[76] In the more immediate future the reality of mass migration of labour means that without a more open policy on granting citizen rights 'up to one fifth of the population of a state will be excluded from citizenship *ad infinitum*'.[77]

Davidson also explicitly refutes belief in the centrality of the nation state, arguing that it is being overtaken by regional and global trends. The pressures of the global economy are undermining the primacy of the state and promoting regional blocs. Davidson sees the development of regional economies and political organization as desirable as well as inevitable and makes a very positive assessment of developments in the EU. He recognizes that regionalism in the Asia Pacific faces much greater problems and that Australia has to cooperate with partners who are often very far from being liberal democracies. But in Australia, as elsewhere, the nature of citizenship is changing: in the twenty-first century national citizenship must be adapted to 'the requirements for a citizen appropriate to future regional economies in a global world'.[78] Whether regional citizenship can remain recognizably republican is more questionable.[79]

It would be possible to argue that since republicanism developed before the modern nation state, republican theory is not (as Miller acknowledges) easily adapted to it. So a new transnational order in which power is dispersed both downwards to provinces and cities within states, and upwards to confederal types of organization between states, allows for more genuinely republican politics at a more local level. A hint of this idea can be found in Rousseau's *Social Contract*, in which he envisages the possibility of confederation building on local democracy.[80] Anthony McGrew has suggested that one possible model of global governance is 'radical communitarianism', based on the creation of 'alternative forms of social, economic and political organization based on communitarian principles'. He refers to proposals for re-instituting forms of direct democracy suggested by John Burnheim.[81] Kenneth Baynes adopts a less radical approach, but suggests that promotion of world peace and a cosmopolitan world order requires a republican spirit absent in modern liberal states. Creating such a spirit could be linked to decentralization of state power and development of democratic controls in economic and social institutions. Baynes envisages differentiated sovereignty within the state corresponding to differentiated sovereignty at an international level, with multiple and overlapping sources of authority. The individual citizen would then have multiple allegiances, not a single overriding loyalty to the nation state.[82]

Republicanism, whether or not it is related closely to the nation state, is at present an ideal and far from a reality. In political theory republicanism serves primarily as a critique of liberalism, and of the lack of equality, community and active citizenship with liberal states. Republicanism (although it does not totally reject the market) has been critical of commercial society, which often leads to a huge gap between the rich and the poor, at odds with a cohesive community of citizens. Commercial society also fosters materialistic values at odds with the ideal of the virtuous citizen committed to the public weal. Although republicanism today repudiates the extreme emphasis on asceticism and virtue to be found in earlier writings, conspicuous consumption, pursuit of wealth and the tendencies to privatism that a consumer society fosters are still seen as a threat to active citizenship.

Critiques of cosmopolitanism and global citizenship

Despite the range of arguments for cosmopolitanism and an ideal of global citizenship, there are also cogent objections to them. Critics of cosmopolitanism are often republican and communitarian theorists, who have attacked liberalism for its individualist emphasis and its tendency to ignore how the social context shapes individual values, and also believe that liberalism has undervalued political participation. These objections may apply even more strongly to global citizenship. For example, the communitarian Michael Sandel argues that 'the cosmopolitan ideal is flawed, both as a moral ideal and as a public philosophy for self-government'.[83] Here we look briefly at the positions of Arendt, Miller and Walzer, before branching out into a more general discussion.

Hannah Arendt, despite her sympathy for Jaspers (and his description of her as a 'citizen of the world'[84]), totally rejects a vision of political unity at a global level. She does suggest that the conditions for 'negative solidarity' now exist. The technology that has created world communications has also created nuclear weapons that can ensure world destruction. But in this context an individual sense of responsibility to avert this disaster may be an 'unbearable burden' and the idealism of Enlightenment humanism looks like 'reckless optimism'.[85] Arendt also stresses that although philosophy may 'conceive of earth as the homeland of mankind', politics depends on plurality and diversity. 'A citizen is by definition a citizen among citizens of a country among countries.'[86] Arendt first voiced her critique of an empty cosmopolitanism, and of abstract human rights that are mocked by the reality of statelessness, in *The Origins of Totalitarianism*.[87] Her later writings develop a republican concept of politics rooted in the boundaries of a specific state, though she favours a federal rather than a unitary constitutional model. Despite her sympathy for non-violent social movements like Civil Rights as possible expressions of citizenship responsibility, and a generally positive response to the movement against the Vietnam War, the movements in the USA are seen as expressions of *American* citizenship, not of potential global citizenship.[88]

Arendt also sees the vision of world citizenship in a world federal state as simultaneously impossible and a nightmare prospect. 'A world citizen, living under the tyranny of a world empire, and speaking and thinking in a kind of glorified Esperanto, would be no less a monster than a hermaphrodite.'[89] She stresses that Jaspers' approach is not this inhuman uniformity, but a unity based on communication between those who recognize their inherited difference. But it seems clear that she rejects not only the concept of citizenship within a world state, but also the idea of a moral world citizenship that is expressed in forms of political action or solidarity.

David Miller sees the reciprocal bonds between citizens within the nation state as the necessary basis for a developed theory and practice of social justice. He also endorses a republican ideal of active citizenship that he does not believe can be realized without a shared culture and clearly defined constitutional boundaries. Moreover, the logic of a participatory democratic ideal requires a limit on the numbers involved – even nation states strain this requirement, but extension beyond the state makes it impossible. However, Miller also suggests that even a weaker liberal model of citizenship requires a degree of mutual sympathy and citizen responsibility incompatible with global citizenship. He also suggests that multinational states have been empires held together either by force or by allowing local self-determination but not genuine democracy. Therefore nationalism, in a cultural and not a narrowly ethnic sense, is necessary to create active citizens with a sense of their citizen identity.[90]

Republican theorists who repudiate the aim of global citizenship do not deny that there are claims of human solidarity and obligations towards those who are not fellow compatriots. Arendt clearly does not. *Eichmann in Jerusalem* in particular is eloquent about the moral and human importance of individuals resisting evils such as Nazism, which reject the bases of common humanity, and the permanent significance of such resistance, denying that even totalitarianism can create 'holes of oblivion'.[91] Miller in his defence of both nationalism and republicanism makes explicit that there are general humanitarian obligations beyond state borders.[92] What both deny is that the whole of humanity can constitute a true community, and that the specific and demanding criteria of a republican concept of citizenship can be extended to the category of global citizenship.

The position adopted by Michael Walzer is also relevant here. Walzer does not see himself as a republican and is unhappy with being labelled a 'communitarian', but he does stress the value of a concerned and responsible citizenship, the need to create greater equality between citizens, and how cultural contexts shape individual values and actions. He does therefore challenge some forms of universalism, for example that it is possible to deduce general principles of justice applicable to all societies and all spheres of life.[93] But Walzer, despite elements of relativism in his thought, does not wholly reject universalism. His important discussion of *Just and Unjust Wars* is based on a morality grounded philosophically in a doctrine of human rights, and draws on the just war tradition based on natural law.[94] Moreover, belief in human rights may justify intervention in other societies in the past and in the present where these rights are brutally violated.[95] Walzer distinguishes between a 'thin' universal morality and a 'thick' set of values and beliefs defined by a particular culture.[96] Individuals owe allegiance to both, although there is a crucial role for the social critic prepared to question some of the practices and beliefs of his or her own society.

Walzer's views on global citizenship are clearly stated in his response to Nussbaum's plea for cosmopolitanism and in his discussion of global civil society. He asserts, against Nussbaum, that he is not a world citizen because there are no institutions, procedures for decision-making or clear sets of rights and obligations to which he can subscribe.[97] He argues, however, that civil society is not fixed by state boundaries and voluntary bodies make links across borders. Walzer does believe that a global civil society now exists and that, together with international institutions, it challenges state sovereignty. But a role for the state remains. Moreover, participation in civil society is distinct from citizenship. Individuals can always choose to become members of civil society through joining existing groups or forming new ones. Citizenship is bounded. 'Citizenship has a different profile from civility: it can only be shared as the result of political decision.'[98] He also denies that commitments beyond state borders to those sharing cultural identity or ideological beliefs, or simply 'to people in trouble in far away countries', are 'citizen-like commitments'.[99]

The republican or communitarian criticisms of global citizenship, summarized here, therefore have two main elements examined below: a rejection of the moral adequacy of a pure cosmopolitanism; and the requirement of stringent criteria for the concept of citizenship. (These theorists also have serious reservations about the possibility or desirability of global institutions in which full global citizenship could be realized – this issue is addressed in detail in the next chapter.)

The moral adequacy of cosmopolitanism

The discussion of cosmopolitanism as the basis for a moral theory has two dimensions. The first is its adequacy for moral decisions at an individual level. The second is its implications for individuals as political beings linked to a variety of economic and political institutions, above all the state. The two are sometimes treated separately, but this is artificial, as in this area, beyond a degree of pure charity, moral obligations are also political. Criticism of moral cosmopolitanism can focus either on its inadequate social foundations and lack of inspirational power, or on the alleged deficiencies in its requirements and content. The brief discussion here refers primarily to the different viewpoints in the symposium *For Love of Country*, responding to Nussbaum's essay 'Patriotism and Cosmopolitanism', and also to the symposium on 'Duties Beyond Borders' in *Ethics*, July 1988.

Critics of cosmopolitanism often argue that morality is developed and understood originally in relation to immediate communities. Richard Rorty draws on Michael Oakeshott to suggest that we see morality in terms of membership of a common community, speaking a common language.[100] Walzer notes that Nussbaum quotes from Plutarch, 'We should regard all human beings as our fellow citizens and neighbours', thus extending by analogy a primary sense of moral fellowship.[101]

Another perceived problem with cosmopolitanism is that it can appear emotionally insipid, given the psychological difficulties of identifying with unknown people in distant lands. Nussbaum recognizes this problem, noting the much greater fervour which nationalism can induce. Robert Pinksy in his response comments that she fails to evoke a cosmopolitanism with the same attractions as nationalism, describing cosmopolitanism in abstract terms. He compares this to contrasting a real language with Esperanto.[102] Moreover, if cosmopolitanism is necessarily based on a very generalized concern for an abstract humanity, then perhaps it is insufficient to inspire acts of true human solidarity. Rorty has argued that those who risked their lives to save Jews from the Nazis were more likely to be inspired by a desire to help neighbours, or fellow members of a profession or union, rather than by a general commitment to fellow human beings.[103]

None of these objections rule out the possibility of a cosmopolitan morality. The fact that moral understanding evolves in relation to immediate communities does not mean that a fully developed morality cannot embrace universal categories. Indeed mainstream western moral philosophy, including both Kantian and utilitarian thought, has maintained that morality requires universality and impartiality – that all should be treated equally unless there are special reasons for discriminating. Robert Goodin claims that universality and impartiality are arguably 'defining features of morality itself'.[104] Walzer himself, in his distinction between thick (communal) and thin (universal) morality, suggests that morality can and should have a universal element.[105]

Walzer's concept of thinness does, however, seem to denote the emotional aridity of cosmopolitanism. Yet this is not really borne out by actual experience. In practice cosmopolitanism is not usually directed towards an abstract humanity, but to acting on behalf of individuals or groups with whom we can imaginatively identify: the starving, sufferers from an earthquake, victims of slavery or torture or people ravaged by war. Walzer agrees that he has 'commitments to people in trouble in far away countries'.[106] Human sympathy may also prompt action closer to home. Norman Geras has challenged Rorty's argument that taking extreme risks, such as helping persecuted Jews, depends on bonds of communal solidarity rather than those of common humanity. In a detailed study of why people say they helped Jews he notes the frequency with which they referred to obligations to help the helpless and oppressed, and a sense of a common humanity.[107]

There are, however, some serious questions about the adequacy of the morality entailed in a universal cosmopolitanism. Firstly, morality implies that individuals can actually fulfil the precepts it entails. If the demands it makes on individuals are impossibly high, then most, if not all, will fail to meet them.[108] This objection depends on how these requirements are interpreted. Peter Singer has posed extreme moral demands on individuals, although making a discretionary choice about whom we should help at a particular moment. In response to the famine in East Bengal in 1971 he argued that there is no distinction between duties to neighbours and duties to distant strangers, and that ideally we in the affluent West ought to give funds to relieve this suffering until our own standard of living is close to that of a Bengali refugee.[109]

Singer did not wholly ignore the responsibility of governments or the political role citizens could play in pressing for more generous government aid policies, but refused to see these as *alternatives* to direct personal action. Whilst his argument may be seen as partly rhetorical to illustrate the inadequacy of existing responses, he has continued to argue in this strain.[110] Singer's approach does not take into account what demands most people might accept. Henry Shue, on the other hand, whilst defending a cosmopolitan morality, stresses limits on obligation and the rights of the individual donor, and sees the role of institutions as buffers between the claims of suffering individuals and others.[111]

A more central objection is the lack of specificity in cosmopolitan claims. If an individual has obligations to everyone, which are impossible to fulfil, then this may suggest a lack of specific obligation to anyone. Shue illustrates this problem by suggesting that a universal right to food could be taken to mean that individuals ought to make some minimal contribution to every starving child – but even one penny per child is beyond the means of all except, perhaps, the fabulously wealthy.[112]

The claim that universal morality means there are only 'imperfect duties', which (unlike 'perfect duties') are not owed to anybody in particular, is also met by Shue. Drawing on another familiar distinction, between negative and positive duties, he claims that we all have a negative duty to abstain from actions that might directly deprive other people of their rights. Normally, however, this duty, if interpreted in terms of direct individual human interaction, does not require any effort from us.[113] Positive duties are more complex since any individual can only attempt to preserve the rights of a limited group of people. Shue argues that we do have 'highly stringent duties that are also indefinite'; we have discretion to choose whom to assist, and what means we use, but not to ignore altogether the rights of strangers to food or to be rescued from torture and arbitrary imprisonment.[114]

Exercise of positive duties is made feasible, and at least relatively effective, through the existence of intermediate institutions. If Shue's introduction of the role of institutions is pursued further, it could be argued that our negative duties also become more onerous, since we should avoid supporting institutions, such as many multinational companies, which inflict harm. We should also oppose policies by governments or international institutions, such as sale of arms to dictatorships or sanctions that deprive people of food and medicines. In that case a degree of discretion and of judgement is introduced into a rigorous attempt to perform our negative general duties. The role of institutions is, however, central since they provide, as Thomas Pogge argues, a way of holding 'the rich and mighty in today's developed world' accountable for harms resulting from institutions in which we participate.[115] But whether we focus on direct individual responsibility, or on a responsibility to work for institutional reform, a cosmopolitan morality does imply *a general* obligation to non-nationals.[116]

A central focus for criticism of global citizenship, as a purely moral individual commitment, is the assumption that this means giving *primary* allegiance to humanity as a whole, rather than to more immediate communities. Nussbaum does indeed at one point seem to suggest this, though elsewhere in the same essay she suggests an image of concentric circles radiating from the personal to the global.[117] How we interpret our general duties is clearly related to the scope of our particular duties to family, neighbours or colleagues at work. Accepting general duties does not entail denying the pressing claims of particular obligations and ties. A mother of small children is unlikely to spend long periods as a nurse or aid worker in dangerous parts of the world, whereas a woman without children, or a mother whose children have left home, can probably do so without a conflict of duties. There may, however, be crises when human obligations are thought to outweigh family commitments – some women with children took the grave risk of harbouring Jews fleeing Nazi persecution.

Patriotism, cosmopolitanism and global citizenship

The central issue is not in fact the respective claims of family, neighbours or workplace in relation to distant others, but the possible conflict between duties to compatriots and duties to foreigners. The nation state can also demand that citizens put aside their family commitments for the national good, most dramatically in wartime.

The claims of fellow citizens may draw on sentiments of patriotism, but the argument for giving compatriots priority depends on political considerations. So long as states constitute the primary political unit, if an implicit social contract is assumed, then compatriots have a strong claim upon us. For example, we ought to pay taxes towards ensuring the poor, the very old and the sick in our national society can live in dignity, and we also expect to receive benefits in turn. Goodin challenges this 'mutual-benefit society' model, pointing out that a notion of strict reciprocity between contributions and benefits cannot be maintained. He also notes the problems of deciding who should belong, for example the position of resident aliens. He proposes instead an 'assigned responsibility model', in which states should normally take special care of their own citizens, but which allows for recognition that some states lack the necessary resources. In this model there also remains a 'residual responsibility of all' towards those who lack the protection of a particular state.[118]

The critics of cosmopolitanism appeal to psychological and sociological considerations in stressing communal obligations. But the critics of cosmopolitanism cited here do all accept that we are also part of a wider global society, and therefore have *some* obligations within it, for example to those suffering from natural disasters and persecution. It is possible to be a good national citizen and also to pay some taxes willingly towards relief work and economic aid outside the country. This stance ties in with the concept of 'rooted cosmopolitanism', which tries to resolve the apparent conflict between cosmopolitanism and patriotism.[119] It also of course relates to the concept of global citizenship as an extension of national citizenship, discussed in relation to Rawls and social democracy.

There remain very real problems of priorities, and of both individual and governmental choices, when the interests of compatriots clash with those whose claim is that of common humanity. We examined this conflict in relation to refugees in Chapter 5. Since the growth of armed 'humanitarian intervention' in the 1990s it has become a serious issue whether governments should expect their soldiers to risk death in keeping the peace in foreign lands. A cosmopolitan position suggests that where the need is really acute, the interests of non-compatriots should have priority over fellow citizens.

In this context the concept of 'good international citizenship' as practised by states is relevant. This phrase was coined by the Australian Labor Foreign Secretary, Gareth Evans, and the concept was implicit in the early foreign policy commitments of the Blair Labour Government: to increase economic aid, refrain from selling arms to dictators, honour international human rights obligations.[120] There are, as experience has illustrated, dangers of hypocrisy and even dishonesty in promoting such a concept. There are also dangers that good international citizenship, or an 'ethical foreign policy', will be interpreted in ways that impose western values and economic and political interests.

The role of those who endorse cosmopolitan commitments is clearly to press their governments to pursue policies that take more seriously wider commitments. This seems indeed to be one goal of many advocates of cosmopolitan education, including Nussbaum herself. This task can often be pursued through both national and transnational campaigning bodies. Therefore the concept of global citizenship as an extension of national citizenship, and the concept of global citizenship as membership of global civil society, *can coincide*. Radicals deeply sceptical about existing governments will, however, interpret global citizenship as a more purely oppositional stance.

There are, of course, distinctions to be made between what we expect governments to do on our behalf with our support, and what individuals choose to do in addition with their own time and money. There is scope for *extra* voluntary action by individuals, for example in aid organizations, in which they can act directly as global citizens. This brings us to the objection that the term global citizenship is used too loosely.

Assessing arguments that global citizenship is not citizenship

A strong republican view of citizenship implies reciprocity of rights and duties; requirements of responsible and active citizenship; political and social equality between citizens; allegiance to a community and citizenship as a primary sense of identity. Miller recognizes that this tradition of active and virtuous citizens has to be modified to have relevance to modern pluralistic societies. But republicanism requires that people are 'engaged *at some level* in political debate, so that laws and policies of the state do not appear as alien impositions'.[121] The example he gives is of going to the aid of someone who collapses in the street, and he suggests that public service 'now is more likely to take place within civil society, in revamping the village hall ... restoring damaged wildlife habitats, and so forth'.[122]

Therefore, one might expect that the model of global citizenship as taking part in civil society movements would have some attractions for republican theorists. Membership of such groups is not only an important aspect of active citizenship within nation states, but also often the most effective means to display cosmopolitan concerns. Whether global citizenship is an appropriate description of supporters of transnational movements in any strict sense is, however, more contentious.

Miller argues that joining a global movement is not a form of global citizenship. He suggests that movement activists are often single-minded enthusiasts for a cause, who are not responsible to a clear community and who do not have to weigh up competing claims as citizens ideally should when adjudicating on policy.[123] Miller does indeed suggest that activists in social movements *within* the state may also not be willing to reach the fair compromises required by responsible citizenship within a community – there is an implied contrast between movements and other forms of participation in civil society.[124] This seems to conflict with Arendt's suggestion that social movements may be a repository of public spirit otherwise lacking, and a means of generating the kind of social power required for republican politics.[125] But both see some value in movements where power is unequal and democracy itself inadequately realized.

In that case, however, the need for social movements on a global scale is arguably much greater, and they provide one of the few channels for showing public spirit on cosmopolitan issues. Nor is it entirely correct that movement activists are blind to other interests, as the widening policies of these movements charted in Chapter 4 illustrates. It is of course true that social movements do not recognize the legitimacy of the interests of *all* organizations – for example logging firms or multinational chemical companies – operating at a global level. But then it is doubtful whether republicans would see their power as legitimate within the state.

Walzer, as noted earlier, distinguishes between civility and citizenship, and he also contrasts the voluntary character of engaging in civil society with the lack of choice entailed in citizenship. But Walzer himself in an earlier essay noted that 'the citizen governs himself most actively in groups other than the state, groups that sometimes play an informal, sometimes an official, role in determining state policy', such as churches, unions and parties. He quotes Hegel on the importance of providing men who only have a limited role in the 'public business of the state ... with business of a public character over and above their private business'.[126]

Because Walzer stresses membership of a plurality of groups, and advocates decentralization of power within the state, his approach seems open to an understanding of multiple identities and different levels of political allegiance.[127] But he does still link citizenship firmly to the nation state, though there may be circumstances where the obligations of national citizenship are loosened. In an interesting exploration as to whether prisoners of war have a patriotic duty to escape, Walzer concludes that they no longer have a duty to be combatants and it is important that this is recognized so that they are treated humanely. 'They ought to be treated, if not like "citizens of the world", at least like men entitled to rest for a while in limbo.'[128] This suggests a minimum understanding of people as 'world citizens' by virtue of being bearers of certain human rights.

Therefore both Miller and Walzer accept the importance of involvement in global civil society and recognition of universal rights. The issue is how narrowly citizenship is to be defined. A defence of extending the concept of citizenship to claim that obligations exist beyond national borders is provided by Albert Weale, although he notes that citizenship normally implies a limitation of duties.[129] He denies that 'the notion of citizenship is so tied to an exclusivist communitarian style of thought that it is intrinsically indifferent to duties beyond borders'.[130] He develops his argument in two key stages. He suggests first that, even if citizenship is understood as a combination of reciprocal rights and duties and as a form of communal identity, citizens have duties to future generations, and therefore citizenship implies duties that 'go beyond the borders of the present time'.[131] Secondly, he suggests that democratic citizenship implies representation. Since the state represents its citizens, but acts in an interdependent world to impinge on people outside state borders, citizens have a democratic duty to try to ensure that the government genuinely represents their own views on how duties outside national borders should be honoured. The fact of increasing interdependence in areas like the global economy and environment is an important element in Weale's analysis.

Ultimately the rejection of global citizenship by communitarians and republicans, who focus on the centrality of the nation state, must depend also on their view of the extent of globalization – Miller, for example, denies that globalization has significantly eroded national autonomy – and the nature of international politics (debated in the next chapter).

Conclusion

This chapter has examined how a wide range of political theories impinge on possible concepts of global citizenship. At one extreme is neo-liberalism embodied in the new class of businessmen and women who see themselves as citizens of the globe rather than one particular country, and in consumers enjoying the fruits of the earth. I have argued that a neo-liberal claim to global citizenship does not embody any of the moral or political connotations of citizenship and should not count. At the other extreme is the socialist resisting global capitalism. In between there is a spectrum of positions, in which global citizenship can be seen as an extra dimension (of more or less significance) of national citizenship, or can be interpreted as participation in networks and movements of global civil society. We noted that there are liberal and social democratic versions of both these models of global citizenship, which both have considerable force. I have also argued that these two models of global citizenship need not be opposed, but can (depending on one's ideological stance) be complementary.

Versions of global citizenship stressing engagement in cosmopolitan duties assume a universal morality. This does not exclude recognition of special duties at local and national levels, but suggests that in extreme circumstances the claims of humanity should come first.

Global citizenship can also be understood in terms of a minimum number of rights and duties held directly under international law, or in the context of membership in new institutions of global governance. These concepts of *direct* global citizenship need to be explored further in the context of theories of international relations. This is the focus of the next chapter.

8 Global citizenship and global governance

Perspectives in international relations theory

This chapter has two main goals. The first is to relate thinking about global citizenship to major approaches within international relations. The second is to consider critically contrasting theories about global governance and their implications for a theory of global citizenship. These two objectives are linked, as different perspectives on international politics suggest different forms of global order and global organization.

The distinction between political thought and international relations theory, never absolute, as the reference to Hobbesian, Grotian and Kantian models indicates, has become more blurred in recent years. In addition to the revived interest in Kant, reflected, for example, in theorizing about the link between the spread of liberal democracy and peace, in recent years some international relations practitioners have turned either to Habermasian critical theory or to poststructuralist or postmodern thinkers.[1] Habermas was discussed in the previous chapter, and Chapter 9 comments very briefly on some approaches influenced by Foucault or postmodernism. Therefore I focus here primarily on the mainstream theories in international relations.

I begin by examining the dominant theory in international relations since 1945 – realism. This provided a powerful rebuttal of the liberal or 'idealist' views dominant between 1919 and 1939, and focuses on the conflictual nature of politics between nation states with often opposing interests.[2] Realism draws on a Hobbesian concept of anarchy and a perpetual tendency to war in a state of nature where no sovereign power exists to impose order. The main criticism of this realist view of the world has, until recently, come from a group of theories usually labelled liberal, which do reflect key features of liberal political thought. Liberal theories can be fitted into an interpretation of the Grotian concept of international society, though the ambiguities in the Grotian model mean that it can contain a spectrum of views ranging from a modified realism at one end to a form of cosmopolitanism at the other. These three possible variations on a Grotian model are explored below.

Both realist and liberal theories of international politics are predicated on the Westphalian system of nation states, although liberal approaches also give weight to factors internal to states and to transnational economic and social linkages. I argue that increasing globalization by the beginning of the twenty-first century suggests that neither approach is wholly adequate, and summarize Alexander Wendt's attempt to supersede both in a constructivist analysis. I also note Andrew Linklater's discussion, drawing on Habermas's discourse ethics, of the transformation of political community.

A Kantian model of global politics has become rather more convincing than it was before, and is associated with reflections on democracy at an international or global level. Here political theorists like Norberto Bobbio and David Held have moved into the territory of international relations.

Much of the debate about strengthening global institutions focuses on reform of the UN. This chapter explores three possible approaches to global regulation and their implications for global citizenship: liberal internationalism, blending into cosmopolitanism, embodied in the Commission on Global Governance; world federalism; and cosmopolitan democracy as advocated by Held.

One major criticism of cosmopolitan theories is that the emphasis on creating a global market and economic interdependence is a form of economic imperialism. One of the key questions arising out of liberal theories and Kantian variants is, as I argued in the previous chapter, the role of trade and commerce. The liberal case that economic interdependence promotes peace is in many contexts persuasive. But the actual operations of the global economy, and the global power of large multinationals, demonstrably challenge the possibility of effective liberal democracy even in developed countries, and undermine any autonomy or hope of social justice for the poorer developing countries.

There are two liberal approaches to these problems. One is to promote oversight of economic activity by international bodies and encourage multinationals to adopt a globally responsible role – suggested by the Commission on Global Governance. The other is to turn to the more radical groups in civil society to help curb corporate excesses, as argued by Falk. Held's approach is to try to bring multinationals under legal and democratic controls. So a key question is whether reform of global institutions and proposals for cosmopolitan democracy could prevent abuse of corporate power.

It is necessary to avoid a glib optimism about cosmopolitan trends both by noting the continuing dangers of military preparations by the major powers, and by taking account of the ferocity of local national and religious conflicts that are challenging many states from within, and might suggest a new form of global anarchy. Whilst realism is unsatisfactory as a primary model of today's international politics, realist concerns do still have force. But I argue that the realist world view is, paradoxically, less equipped to respond to the new forms of anarchy than are cosmopolitan approaches.

Finally, one important objection raised against cosmopolitan policies is that they represent a western imperialist impulse to impose western values on the rest of the world, and serve the interests of the dominant western powers. I challenge this view, which has been put forward forcefully by the Italian legal and political philosopher Danilo Zolo.

Realist perspectives: a minimal role for global citizenship

The traditional realist perspective on international politics stresses the central role of nation states, which necessarily pursue their own interests, and the inevitable conflicts that ensue. Realists sometimes cite Machiavelli as a forebear, but the key theorist here is Hobbes. Some realists, for example Hans Morgenthau, have taken from Hobbes his pessimistic view of human nature.[3] But the central legacy is the logic of anarchy between states. This model sees states as entities controlling all affairs within their own borders, and therefore assumes national sovereignty. It also projects a world in which states only deal with other states, in which sustained cooperation is impossible and in which wars and preparations for war are inevitable. International politics is therefore a condition of pure anarchy, in the negative sense denoting lawlessness and violence.

One obvious way out of this kind of international anarchy is the Hobbesian solution of an overarching government, with sufficient concentrated military and legislative powers to enforce peace. In Hobbes' theory the standard dilemma is how individuals in a state of nature could overcome both their basic distrust of their fellows, and their desire to pursue individual gain and glory, to come together and agree to set up such a sovereign. Hobbes suggests that their individual vulnerability and rational awareness of the gains to be secured from peace will propel people to leave a state of nature and enter into a social order guaranteed by central power. But this stage in the argument about a hypothetical social contract becomes a real-life stumbling block to actual schemes for world government. After the Second World War the experience of appalling devastation, and the new threat of nuclear extinction, prompted many people to call for general disarmament and world government. Albert Einstein argued in February 1948 that world government was 'the only possible way ... of avoiding total destruction'.[4] But mutual fear and suspicion meant that, predictably for realists, both disarmament and world government were impossible.

Realist theory, especially when translated into the operations of foreign offices and war departments, has diverged somewhat from the Hobbesian model. In particular the actual world of international politics has diverged from Hobbes' assumption of effective equality of power and resources between individuals. A kind of order is imposed by the fact that some states have greatly superior power and therefore can impose their will on others. Great powers, in Hedley Bull's words, have the effect 'of simplifying the pattern of international relations'. In addition great powers make a contribution to order 'by managing their relations with one another', for example through crisis management, and by using their preponderance 'to impart a degree of central direction to the affairs of international society as a whole'.[5] One crucial way in which realists see the great powers promoting order is through managing the 'balance of power', that central principle of European statecraft in the eighteenth and nineteenth centuries, ensuring through shifting alliances – and if necessary through going to war – that no single state could predominate.[6]

After 1945 the concept of a balance of power between several great powers gave way to the much more inflexible system of two opposing power blocs and the 'balance of terror' created by nuclear weapons. This division of the world did create a kind of order, since the great powers imposed varying degrees of control over their own spheres of influence and developed an uneasy coexistence. But it also prevented other possible approaches to world order and peace. One of the reasons for the Soviet suspicion of international organizations, and any suggestion of supranational controls, was the well-founded view that existing international bodies like the UN were dominated by the West – though this position had altered slightly by the end of the cold war period. Therefore in the late 1940s the USSR rejected the Baruch Plan for international control of atomic energy, supported by some world federalists.

Realist theory has become more elaborate as the discipline of international relations has flourished in the last few decades. The crucial role of nuclear weapons led to increasingly sophisticated theories of deterrence and consideration of forms of arms control designed to reduce technological accidents and political miscalculation in maintaining a 'balance of terror'. Kenneth Waltz attempted to provide a 'neo-realist' structural interpretation of the interaction of states in a fundamentally anarchic world order.[7] Barry Buzan focused on the crucial concept of national security, exploring the individual and international as well as the statist dimensions involved, and the logic of the 'security dilemma', in which states' search for security through arms escalation tended to increase the insecurity of other states. He also examined problems of security complexes at a regional rather than a global level.[8] But these refinements are not relevant to the thrust of my argument here.

Realists suggest that a consistent set of moral principles cannot be applied in the context of international politics. Prudent pursuit of national interest and maintenance of international order through preserving the balance of power may often require states to act in ways contrary to ideas of morality and justice. There are, however, two possible versions of this thesis that morality is irrelevant to politics between states. The more extreme suggests a Machiavellian *realpolitik*, a wholly ruthless pursuit of national expansion and power. The second implies a kind of morality, since pursuit of national interest can be seen as promoting the welfare of the people of that state, and maintaining international order conduces to the welfare of all by avoiding unnecessary war and blocking oppression. Advocates of this kind of realism see appeals to morality as dangerously utopian or ideological, threatening violent revolution or policies that will undermine the fragile order achieved.[9]

A moderate realism is also linked to belief that international politics is not simply a state of permanent war or potential war, but also in at least a minimal sense an international society maintained by certain widely understood rules of the game, underpinned by formal agreements, and fostered by the evolution of diplomatic etiquette. There may even be a link between international law and the balance of power. Bull notes that maintaining such a balance often requires states to flout some of the rules of international law, such as those pertaining to just war, but that the balance of power can be seen as a prerequisite for the operation of international law. Therefore lawyers like Oppenheim have explicitly argued that international law can only exist if a balance of power is maintained.[10] Bull is proposing a Grotian version of realism.

Can global citizenship have any meaning or validity within a realist framework? If one adopts the *realpolitik* interpretation of realism, then the scope for global citizenship would indeed be bleak. For individuals who aspired to such citizenship there would be parallels with the Greeks who formulated this concept over 2,000 years ago: with the Cynics, who adopted an anarchist view of existing authority; or with that aspect of Stoicism that stressed withdrawal from the world and inner self-sufficiency. In contemporary terms a rigorous interpretation of being a world citizen within an international sphere dominated by *realpolitik* would imply living as independently of the state as possible, and an 'inner emigration'; or else it would require a more active anarchist resistance, such as non-payment of taxes and refusal of military service. Alternatively it might mean the kind of adventurous challenging of borders and state regulations undertaken by Garry Davis (see Introduction to Part III). The true home of a committed world citizen would be a national prison. There have been periods, and there are certainly countries, where this bleak interpretation seems the only one possible, but it is not universally convincing.

In a world where the milder version of realism predominated in the practice of states, there would be some scope for making personal and professional links across frontiers and attempting some joint political action. This was the position in the Enlightenment, when the ideal of world citizenship flourished. How far individual citizens of states can influence their government's external policies depends largely on the internal constitution. But from a realist standpoint internal politics are secondary. For example, realism suggests that popular attempts to alter foreign and defence policies are normally doomed to failure because the logic of the international system, in which states are embedded, means governments cannot rationally respond. If a popular peace movement is influential, then that country will suffer. So if realists are correct about the inevitably conflictual and fundamentally unchanging nature of international politics, global citizenship must remain either at the level of non-political communication across frontiers, be doomed to a politics of gesture rather than substance, or have wholly counter-productive results.

The alternative liberal perspective and global citizenship

For a more substantial understanding of global citizenship to emerge it is necessary to move from a Hobbesian to a Grotian conception of international politics. Though a Grotian model can be interpreted in different ways, from Bull's realist version at one extreme to a near-cosmopolitanism at the other, I am using it initially here to suggest a view of the international arena in which there is considerable scope for cooperation, a recognition of overarching common interests, a growing body of international law and acceptance in principle of universal moral principles that should influence states. This model allows for the existence of inhumane and aggressive regimes, and the need for national defence, but suggests a society of states linked by a network of economic interests and communications rather than a society maintained primarily by a precarious balance of military power.[11]

Grotius was writing at a time when states were generally ruled by monarchies and therefore also saw the responsibility for upholding international law resting on the shoulders of kings and their advisers, not ordinary citizens.[12] If his view of international politics is translated into the liberal internationalism of the nineteenth and twentieth centuries, then popular influence on government policies becomes part of the picture and this clearly increases the scope for individual action.

A liberal updating of Grotius also supplements international law with advocacy of international organization. This is one of the central legacies of earlier liberal thought, and is still an important strand in contemporary versions of liberalism in international relations theory. A wide range of approaches can be grouped under the label of 'liberal', including theories of interdependence and integration, Karl Deutsch's emphasis on the significance of communications theory and John Burton's 'world society' model incorporating sociological systems theory and psychological work on perception.[13] Recent theories also explore the potential for changing national perceptions as awareness of common interests and a common identity develop.[14] These approaches suggest the potential for both economic and political integration, but are more persuasive in relation to regional than global institutions. Scope for long-term cooperation between states with diverse interests and ideologies is also greater in relation to specific economic or functional issues than in upholding an agreed world order.

Maintaining peace is clearly the most difficult liberal goal to achieve, since in an imperfect world some states are liable to undertake unjust and aggressive wars. The liberal solution associated with the League of Nations, making concessions to realism, was the concept of collective security, whereby all those states that did respect international law would combine to deter and if necessary defeat an aggressor. The unhappy history of the League, and its inability to prevent blatant aggression, is often used to vindicate realist as against liberal theories of international politics. The frequent impotence of the UN also tells against liberal idealism. The end of the cold war, which suggested that divisions between the great powers would no longer automatically block agreement, has, however, led many previously sceptical about international bodies to believe that the UN can work more effectively.

Whereas realists focus on states as unitary actors, liberals argue that domestic politics impinge on how governments both perceive and conduct foreign and defence policy and look to international public opinion across borders. Liberals have generally relied on civil society institutions or public opinion to curb governments. Liberal influence has often been exercised through professional individuals like lawyers, scientists and academics and journalists applying their professional commitments and expertise to world problems, both in domestic politics and transnationally. In the sphere of peace interesting examples are provided – in the unpromising context of the cold war – by the role of Norman Cousins, editor of the *Saturday Review*, who created the Citizens' Committee for a Nuclear Test Ban in 1963 to lobby for ratification of the Partial Test Ban Treaty by the US Senate. He had earlier initiated a series of conferences in which American and Soviet citizens unofficially provided a basis for subsequent official agreements on a test ban and on establishing the 'hot line' between Moscow and Washington, as well as on trade and setting up a commercial air service between the Soviet Union and the USA.[15] Although public opinion is not always inclined to favour peace, the possibility of vigorous public campaigns, as against the Vietnam War, does provide a check on governments.

The spread of liberal institutions and beliefs within states, together with liberal perceptions and practices in international politics, clearly do enhance the scope for global citizenship. Global citizenship can first of all be realized as an additional dimension of national citizenship. Pressing governments to extend areas of cooperation and agreement, or to uphold international law, is not inherently doomed to failure if at least some sections of government share a liberal perception of the world.

But the effectiveness of those seeking to act as global citizens through their own states will still depend on the extent to which principles of international law are enshrined in agreements, and governments can be required to uphold treaties they have signed. Moreover, the existence of international institutions, even those beset by conflict and inefficiency like the UN, gives greater political substance to a model of active global citizenship exercised outside nation states through transnational groups. We saw in Chapter 4 how transnational groups can act in conjunction with international institutions to bring about change. The sheer existence of international bodies provides an important framework for strengthening global civil society, and global citizenship as participation within that global context.

Just as being an effective global citizen working within the state requires at least some scope for political organization and action from below, so transnational activity requires both a modicum of access to means of communication and freedom from state control. So the spread of liberal democracy tends to promote the number and influence of transnational pressure groups and movements. There is therefore a necessary relationship between the spread of liberal political institutions and the strengthening of global civil society.

Neither liberal nor realist theories have supplied a wholly satisfactory theory of international politics. Liberal theories have often suggested excessive faith in the potential for cooperation between states and the potential of international law and organization. But realist views have given too little weight to the importance of a network of international agreements and genuine common interests, the impact of institutions over time on perceptions and behaviour, and the fact that states are not unitary actors and that borders are permeable. The growing interest in the 1980s in the role of 'international regimes', centred on specific issues like nuclear weapons proliferation or control of new communications technology, indicated an attempt to recognize the liberal elements already embedded in actual practices, without giving way to excessive idealism.[16]

One central objection to realism at the beginning of the twenty-first century is that it is still strongly influenced by the realities of European politics two centuries ago and can no longer interpret adequately the world created by modern technologies, by increasing globalization of the economy and culture, and by shared vulnerability to environmental disaster. Some realist theorists like Buzan have responded by rethinking the concept of security, previously understood primarily in military and to a lesser extent in economic terms, to take account of environmental and social factors.[17] The range of liberal theories developed between the 1950s and 1980s (despite their roots in an earlier tradition) took much more account of these trends and in many cases provide a bridge to perceptions of a developing cosmopolitanism.

An emerging cosmopolitan order? Implications for global citizenship

Indeed both Grotian and liberal interpretations of international politics can logically move in a more cosmopolitan direction, and are now tending to do so. Governments are also much more willing to respond to environmental concerns (however inadequately in many cases) and to uphold individual and group human rights. The growth of 'humanitarian intervention' within states since the 1990s, and support for such action from some international lawyers and international relations theorists, indicates this shift.[18]

The increasing diversity and sophistication of international relations theory can also be conducive to underpinning a more cosmopolitan view of the world. One interesting attempt to transcend the debate between neo-realists and neo-liberals is provided by the 'constructivist' approach proposed by Alexander Wendt. Wendt starts from the apparently realist view that states are still the key units of analysis (despite the role of other bodies) and that states can often be treated as 'agents having identities, interests, rationality'.[19] But he also stresses the importance of 'shared understandings, expectations, and social knowledge' as well as economic or military capacities in determining the way states react to each other (nature of the systemic structure). He draws on integration theory to argue that state understandings of identity and interest are constructed by the international system, so that collective identities may emerge. Both trends towards economic and technological interdependence and the convergence of cultural or political values may encourage formation of a collective identity. Although Wendt is anxious to stress that this tendency is far from inevitable, he does conclude that the Westphalian system seems to be undergoing a fundamental transformation. Instead of independent sovereign states the world is moving towards 'transnational structures of political authority'. In the future, state functions may be performed at several different levels.

Wendt links this process to democratic theory, asking how democracy can be developed in this transnational setting and raising questions about the democratic deficit in the EU. He also explicitly refers to the work of Linklater and Held. Wendt is, however, sceptical about making the individual the basic unit of accountability in cosmopolitan democracy and therefore about a strong political concept of global citizenship.[20] (His response to Held is discussed further below.)

Linklater reconceptualizes international politics, starting with a critique of the neo-realist focus on the systemic anarchy between states. He discusses Kant's philosophy of world history and Marx's emancipatory project, which both envisage the possibility of transforming the boundaries of political community and new forms of transnational cooperation. But he notes that their 'universalist commitment ... left little scope for measures designed to promote cultural differences'. Instead Linklater looks to change that will create 'dialogic communities that are at pains to overcome the exclusion of marginal voices'.[21] He argues that there is still a role for the nation state, but stresses the significance of both globalization and fragmentation, and envisages new forms of political authority and citizenship, of the kind suggested by Held's cosmopolitan democracy.

One highly respected political and legal theorist who has stressed the connections between internal and international democracy and the centrality of peace to democracy at both levels is Norberto Bobbio. Bobbio argues that democracy internally is corrupted by conduct of foreign and defence policies, in particular because they foster secrecy, the enemy of democratic politics, and endorse immoral and illiberal practices. He suggests cautiously that the twentieth century saw moves towards arbitration as an alternative to war, international law enshrined in an international court and international institutions incorporating all states on an equal, and therefore democratic, basis. But he also notes the undemocratic nature of the Security Council within the UN and the absence of a genuine contract to maintain peace (the prerequisite of internal order) underpinning the UN. Bobbio elaborates on the Kantian inspiration of his reflections by suggesting that permanent peace is only possible among states with a similar liberal democratic form of government, and that the union of states must also embody liberal democratic principles. (Bobbio uses Kant's terminology of 'republican'.) His discussion stops well short of proposals for direct popular influence on international bodies or a political version of global citizenship.[22]

If we move from theory to actual cosmopolitan trends, recent developments in international law have had a significant impact on individuals and prospects for global citizenship. If international law is interpreted in a cosmopolitan mode, then the global citizen acting within the state has more leverage in resisting government policy that contravenes international law. For example, peace campaigners are using the advisory opinion by the International Court of Justice in July 1996 – that to use, or threaten to use, nuclear weapons would be generally contrary to international law – to justify civil disobedience before national courts.[23]

A cosmopolitan interpretation of the Grotian model also emphasizes that, although Grotius focuses primarily on relations between states, his theory includes specific obligations to individuals, such as a right to asylum and a right not to be subjected to extremes of cruelty. This concept of individual rights that should be protected was, as we saw in Chapter 1, embedded in early international law. Liberal belief in human rights has taken up this commitment.

Therefore a cosmopolitan slant either on Grotius or on liberal thought allows for a different concept of global citizenship, in which individuals are bearers of minimal rights directly derived from international law. This is a largely abstract and rhetorical position if the appeal is solely to principles of natural law and general declarations of rights, and if individuals have no means of asserting their rights. In international, as in national, society implementation of rights usually depends upon political organization and a legal system. It also depends upon international law being seen as a real constraint on governments. In the latter part of the twentieth century there were some moves in a Grotian direction of strengthening the legal rights of individuals. Thus rights to asylum can be upheld in national courts under the Convention on Refugees, and rights of migrants can be upheld under international law, as Yasemin Nuhoglu Soysal argues in her discussion of post-national citizenship (see Chapter 5). Where a supranational court exists, as in the case of the European Court of Human Rights, and national governments are prepared to recognize its judgments, individual rights are much more effectively underpinned.

But the fact that the international rights of *some* individuals can now be secured does not of course mean that *all* can be, even in liberal and constitutional states. Many would-be migrants or asylum seekers cannot escape conditions of dire poverty or oppression. Indeed, the great majority cannot, due to oppressive regimes barring emigration and increasingly due to the liberal and affluent countries limiting immigration and asylum rights. Therefore the idea that all individuals are global citizens with rights under international law is an ideal goal and very far from reality.

Maintaining rights often depends on others accepting certain duties, and a concept of a global citizenship underpinned by international law requires a minimum set of duties. Such duties are still far from being enforced under international law. But cooperation between state legislatures and police forces could deal with some serious abuses of human rights, such as enforced prostitution of women and children. Moreover, the recent creation of international courts to try individuals guilty of crimes against humanity or of genocide, and the use of national courts to pursue individuals guilty of such crimes (see Introduction), does indicate an embryonic framework of cosmopolitan law that may in the future hold individuals to account.

Whilst the development of international law with a cosmopolitan focus on individual rights and duties is necessary for a passive model of global citizenship, the stronger the web of agreements between states, the greater the scope for active global citizenship in an evolving global civil society. Falk suggests that the evolution of global civil society is changing the nature of the international order, endorsing the idea that civil society associations should be seen as composing a 'third system' alongside the system of states and the system of market forces.[24] The growing significance of civil society, therefore, indicates a move towards a more cosmopolitan order in which, Falk claims, the language of 'nongovernmental organizations' is misleading in suggesting a Westphalian model of dominant nation states. Civil society groups operate at a number of levels. At one extreme are the more radical activities of social movements, which may nevertheless include groups who lobby governments and international organizations. At another level is a network of unofficial and independent research bodies – such as peace research institutes – that provide alternative sources of information to the media but also have links with governments. Research is complemented by active unofficial attempts at mediation and conflict resolution by groups who also have connections to governments. Burton discusses the scope for this 'second-track diplomacy', citing examples from Cyprus and the Middle East.[25]

Civil society groups can also sometimes bring about desired changes in international law. For example, the decision by the UN General Assembly to refer the question of the legality of nuclear weapons to the International Court of Justice resulted from sustained campaigning and lobbying by the World Court Project set up in 1994, which secured support from sympathetic governments of non-nuclear states.[26]

Decisive moves towards cosmopolitanism depend, however, on changes in the existing international organizations and the creation of a transnational framework more suited to pursuing goals of peace, human rights, social justice and preservation of the environment. There are three main approaches. At one end of the spectrum is reform of the existing institutions along the lines suggested by the Commission on Global Governance, an approach dubbed 'liberal internationalism' by Falk and McGrew.[27] But it is a liberalism that also stresses the role of popular participation and so has a cosmopolitan slant. At the other end are proposals for federal world government. In between are the recent proposals for global or cosmopolitan democracy, which may start with changes to existing bodies, but aim to provide channels for direct democratic influence upon decision-making on key global issues. The image here is not of one central government, but of a range of global organizations to deal with different issues. The first model envisages stronger representation for civil society groups, thus enhancing the potential of global citizenship expressed through voluntary activism. The second and third also envisage direct representation of people throughout the world, thus creating global citizens in a stronger and more strictly political sense.

Liberal reform of existing international institutions

The most important target for reform is of course the United Nations, and perhaps specialized UN agencies. During the 1990s a number of groups began to urge reform of the UN, responding both to the possibilities opened up by the end of the cold war and to the fact that a review of the weaknesses as well as achievements of the UN would be appropriate in 1995, when it had been in existence 50 years.[28] But the most prestigious reform proposals in 1995 were produced by the Commission on Global Governance. This was a successor to the Brandt Commision on international development, the Palme Commission on security and disarmament, the Brundtland Commission on environmental issues and development and Julius Nyerere's South Commission, and drew on some of those involved in these earlier Commissions. The Commission itself, therefore, exemplified one recent trend in global politics: the creation of unofficial but authoritative bodies seeking to mobilize global public opinion and influence governments. It advocated numerous institutional reforms of the UN and other international bodies.

The issue of adequate geographical representation in key UN bodies such as the Security Council to reflect the increasing power and importance of non-western countries is an obvious starting point for debate. This question can be raised either from an anti-imperialist perspective, challenging the dominance of the US, the UK and France as permanent members of the Council, which dates from 1944, or from a realist desire to reflect the real centres of economic and potential military power by extending permanent Security Council seats to countries like Japan and Germany. There is a significant conflict between a realist approach that suggests giving *more* clout to countries with the most power and who contribute most financially to the UN – a view popular among right-wing governments in the 1980s – and a liberal approach stressing worldwide representation and a smaller role for the great powers.[29]

The Commission on Global Governance indicated its liberal preferences by arguing for an immediate increase in the number of standing members of the Security Council from five to ten, two to be significant industrial states and three of the larger developing countries to be drawn from Africa, Asia and Latin America, and an increase in the number of rotating members from nine to fourteen. The Commission also recommended phasing out the right of veto by permanent members. But it did accept that states acquiring increased power in the Security Council should have the capacity to assume commensurate responsibilities for UN tasks.[30]

The UN Charter from the outset reflected a tension between two tenets of liberal internationalist thought: respect for the sovereignty of individual states (enshrined in Article 2); and commitment to individual human rights, voiced originally in the UN Declaration of Human Rights. Respect for sovereignty was also of course a concession to realism, but has been central to liberal internationalism since sovereignty in principle guaranteed national autonomy and self-government. The tension between national sovereignty and individual rights (which can also be found in Rawls' essay on *The Law of Peoples*) has resulted in conflicting interpretations of the justification for UN 'humanitarian intervention' under international law.[31]

This tension between strict internationalism and a form of cosmopolitanism can be found in the report by the Commission on Global Governance, and the

Commission does incorporate significant elements of cosmopolitanism in its proposals. It endorses the proposal for an International Criminal Court with its own independent prosecutors to try individuals committing serious crimes that transcend state borders and break international law.

The Commission's suggestions for popular representation in, and access to, UN bodies are even more interesting from the standpoint of extending the political rights of global citizenship. It notes the increasing role of nongovernmental organizations in the work of the UN, and as a first step towards popular representation proposes a 'Forum of Civil Society', which would include between 300 and 600 groups, to meet annually before the UN General Assembly starts its own annual session. The Commission also viewed favourably the suggestions for an assembly of the peoples parallel to the General Assembly, which might initially be composed of parliamentarians selected by national parliaments and in the long run be directly elected. But the report stresses that such measures should not be a substitute for the General Assembly itself being revitalized as a forum.[32] The Commission also argues strongly for a right to be granted to both individuals and civil society groups to petition the UN directly in cases where people's security is at stake, and proposes the creation of a small Council for Petitions.

The Commission draws back, however, from the possibility of individuals paying taxes directly to the UN or from giving the UN any power to raise taxes. Instead it discusses the possibility of levying taxes on those engaging in the global economy, for example on multinational companies, or on foreign exchange transactions – which would have the benefit of penalizing short-term speculative trading. The Commission also favours taxing those engaged in activities with undesirable environmental effects, for example a small surcharge on international flights, fees for fishing in Antarctica and 'parking fees' for geostationary satellites.[33] Proposals for taxes or fees could be initiated within the UN, but should be formulated in international agreements and subject to endorsement by individual states.

Liberal belief in an international society composed of independent states and simultaneous reliance on international law and institutions does raise the question of how far states can go in committing themselves to international agreements without losing a substantial amount of sovereignty. This problem is most obvious when states endorse international principles, but hesitate to commit themselves to accept the decisions of an independent international body. The Commission on Global Governance explores the inadequacies of the existing International Court of Justice, which was set up to establish the rule of law between states. But as states had the freedom to decide whether or not to submit to the compulsory jurisdiction of the Court, many decided not to do so. There is also the problem of enforcing Court decisions in the rare but important cases where states refuse to recognize the Court's jurisdiction or ignore its rulings. The Commission, whilst unhappy about stressing enforcement, recommended that the existing provision for the Security Council to agree on means of enforcement should be resuscitated.[34]

The practices of liberal internationalism encourage discussion of possible supranational bodies for two apparently contradictory reasons. On the one hand, the weaknesses of the UN or the International Court of Justice suggest the need for much stronger global institutions, able at times to override the interests of states. On the other, the extent of actual cooperation, the growing number of treaties and engagement in a wide range of international organizations make moves towards supranationalism seem more realistic.

Is world federalism still on the agenda?

One might therefore expect that the idea of promoting a world federal government, which had widespread appeal 50 years ago, would again be the subject of serious debate. The end of the cold war and the example of the EU and its moves towards European federalism, now being openly urged by some leading figures, provide a much more promising starting point for thinking about world government. The revived emphasis on global citizenship might also appear to lead towards a global democratically elected body. Whereas in 1950 the case for world federalism had a Hobbesian slant, in the first years of the twenty-first century there is a Kantian case to be made. Experience of wars and near-war and prospects of global ecological disaster, on the one hand, and evidence of extensive inter-state cooperation and widespread formal commitment to liberal values, on the other, suggest stronger global institutions might be created.

The debates held by world federalists 50 years ago over the means of moving towards their goal also have resonance today. For example, the discussion considered whether to focus on amending the UN – the generally preferred solution – or to create a totally new body. When proposing UN reform, federalists addressed problems of balancing numerical representation of population in democratic elections with maintaining representation of regional and national interests. The well-known 1958 proposals by the American lawyers Grenville Clark and Louis Sohn suggested that the USA, the USSR, China and India should have 30 seats each in a reformed UN General Assembly, whilst states with a population under one million should only have one seat.[35]

World federalist proposals sometimes envisaged that world government could be created in stages. Clark and Sohn thought it would be necessary for the 12 largest states to agree to reform of the UN and that the support of almost all states would be required. But Henry Usborne's 1980s proposal for a 'Minifed' suggested that a core of middle-ranking states, initially excluding the great powers, could agree on significant arms limitation and create a federal 'police force', and hoped this security arrangement would gradually attract others, including the great powers.[36]

World federalists were divided on an issue very topical today: whether regional integration would promote global unity, enabling regional groupings to unite eventually in a world body, or whether European union would prove a further stumbling block. They were also divided over the best strategy to adopt: whether to focus on converting opinion-makers and governments, or to mobilize popular support by registering individuals as world citizens and promoting a representative world convention.[37]

Therefore a revived debate about world federalism would relate to present interest in the future of the EU and UN reform. World government in some form would also provide a clear political framework for creating global citizenship. Support for world federalism has not wholly disappeared. Keith Suter, an Australian lawyer and campaigner on global issues, notes that 'if nationalism keeps bouncing back, so does the idea of world federalism'.[38] World federalist and world citizen organizations still exist – particularly in the United States, where they have played a continuing role in promoting arms control, seeking to strengthen international law and in urging UN reform.[39] Renewed interest in world citizenship is sometimes linked explicitly to world federalism, and current debate about 'global governance' sometimes includes sympathetic examination of world government.[40] But most of the present literature and debate rejects world federalism as a solution.

There are a number of reasons for the reluctance to revive ambitious plans for world federalism. Some stem from the experience of the last 50 years. This history indicates not only the resistance of states to surrendering outright their national independence, but the apparently insurmountable difficulties of achieving what the exponents of world government saw as its necessary prerequisite: general disarmament. This experience also suggest that specific measures of arms control or institutional reform are more likely to be realizable and that cumulatively limited agreements can change the political context. Other doubts stem from a specifically Kantian concern about the despotic implications of concentrating military and political power in a world state, even one with a federal constitution.

Since 1950 the concept of a world federal state has also been subjected to devastating theoretical analysis within international relations theory.[41] Moreover, social movements, which are likely to be most sympathetic to the ideal of global citizenship, have rejected the world federalist approach. Peace movements and peace researchers have generally abandoned hopes for negotiated general disarmament, though the demand for total nuclear disarmament is still raised. But often peace activists have focused on negotiations for more limited goals such as non-proliferation of nuclear weapons, protested about issues like the arms trade, and campaigned for national unilateral measures of disarmament, or regional initiatives such as nuclear-free zones. Recent stress by social movements on linking peace, development and human rights, and on the idea of global citizenship (see Chapter 4), does suggest the possibility of a new focus on global institutions. But the radical idea that has become the focus of much of today's debate is cosmopolitan or global democracy. For example, Charter 99 launched its 'Charter for Global Democracy' in October 1999, demanding that 'all international decisions must be made accountable to the people of the World'.[42]

Cosmopolitan democracy

There are a number of possible models of global democracy stressing decentralization of power, popular initiative and direct democracy (these were referred to briefly in the previous chapter).[43] But these do not provide a convincing institutional framework. The most Kantian, and most influential model, is cosmopolitan democracy.

Cosmopolitan democracy, as elaborated by David Held, can be seen as a compromise between federalism and confederalism. Held notes the continuing relevance of Kantian arguments against both the practicality and the desirability of 'a single unified international state structure', and also notes that a world federation seems to presuppose a homogeneous culture and does not allow for the value of local diversity. But confederalism, 'a wholly voluntary treaty-based union, constantly renewed through voluntary agreements', would not be enough.[44] Cosmopolitan democracy should be based on initial consent, but then peoples would have to be bound by its laws. Cosmopolitan democracy indicates a world where citizens would 'enjoy multiple citizenships' in the national, regional and global contexts that affect them.[45]

Held starts from a commitment to maintain and promote democracy, noting that democratic theory has discussed exhaustively the obstacles to democracy within the nation state, but has not queried the centrality of the state itself as the forum for democracy. But the nation state is no longer the sole or even central focus for decisions that affect the people living within it, and therefore citizens can often no longer hold the real decision-makers to account. There is a 'disjuncture' between the formal political authority states still claim and the reality of the global economy, regional and international organizations, international law, environmental issues and global communications. Therefore it is necessary to reconstruct three of the key concepts arising from the Westphalian system: national sovereignty, a national community of citizens, and the definitive role of national territorial borders.[46]

Held suggests that the concept of state sovereignty should be superseded by the principle that people should be self-determining.[47] This does not mean that the nation state no longer has any power, or important political role. But Held does argue that it is necessary to extend democracy to the international and supranational organizations that already exist, and to devise new, democratic, means of dealing with issues that cross borders.

His specific proposals, which are inherently controversial, include the possibility of representative regional assemblies – the EU provides an advanced model – and the introduction of some form of direct popular representation within the UN. He also suggests the creation of supervisory boards of representatives elected from the relevant constituencies for functional bodies. As a form of direct democracy, Held raises the possibility of devising referenda, for example on environmental issues, which impinge on people in two or more states.[48]

Although Held's main emphasis is on extending popular democratic controls, he does give weight to the importance of enshrining individual rights in international, regional and national law. He argues for dethroning the concept of 'popular sovereignty' as well as national sovereignty, since an unrestrained rule by the people can override the rights of all individuals 'to be free and equal in the determination of the conditions of their own lives'.[49] Central to this goal is the creation of regional and international courts to which individuals can appeal and which can hold states or international bodies to account.[50]

The concept of 'cosmopolitan citizenship' that arises out of Held's model is both more complex and more attractive than the concepts arising from the Commission on Global Governance or world federalism. The former endorses the idea of all individuals as bearers of minimal rights and duties under international law and of self-selected individuals as active participants in global civil society. The latter suggests that the present attributes and loyalties of national citizenship should be transferred to a world state, which would have overarching power, despite a significant role for intermediate levels. But Held's ideal cosmopolitan citizen not only has a complex of rights and duties at multiple levels, and actively participates in civil society both locally and globally, but also has a 'mediating role'. Taking up themes from deliberative democracy, Held suggests the citizen should engage in 'dialogue with the traditions and discourses of others' to enlarge 'the scope of mutual understanding'.[51]

Whether cosmopolitan democracy is at all possible or desirable can be contested from socialist, communitarian and realist perspectives. (See previous chapter and later discussion in this chapter.) But if this model is taken seriously, its institutional complexity and the demanding nature of this view of cosmopolitan citizenship indicate some inherent problems. It raises the institutional question whether, as Dennis Thompson suggests, a multiplication of decision-making authorities reduces democratic accountability, and whether it is possible to avoid one level of government having primary power.[52] It also raises the psychological and sociological question whether most people need a primary political identity.

It could be argued that the logic of Held's proposals – despite his Kantian rejection of world government – suggests a bias towards eventual federalism. Although he refers to 'overlapping' authorities, his emphasis is primarily on different *levels* of government.[53] Moreover, he has drawn his ideas partly from the example of the EU with its increasingly strong supranational elements.[54] Within the EU increasing integration creates pressure for and expectations of a federal Europe.[55] Moreover, Held's ideal goal is a world in which an increasing proportion of states' military forces are transferred to transnational bodies, 'with the ultimate aim of demilitarization'.[56] Whereas world federalists in the 1950s looked to disarmament as the beginning of world government, Held sees it as an end goal. But like the federalists he envisages substantial military and police forces at the disposal of a global body. The federal implications of cosmopolitan democracy would only be relevant, however, if there were significant moves towards achieving it.

Some sympathetic critics argue that whilst Held is correct to identify the need to tackle issues that transcend boundaries, there are other ways of achieving this goal. Theorists of deliberative democracy argue that deliberation is suited to this task. John Dryzek suggests that Held does not pay enough attention to existing discursive contexts in international politics, such as negotiations on the ozone layer, biopiracy or sustainable development. He also stresses the communicative power of global civil society and its role in influencing the terms of discourse.[57] Michael Saward, who expresses scepticism about both the feasibility and advantages of regional and global democratic institutions, suggests cross-border issues could be dealt with by the states directly involved through a number of mechanisms. One is reciprocal parliamentary representation in which MPs sitting in the legislature of a neighbouring country might have a vote on environmental or other cross-border questions. Other possibilities include an extension of Held's own suggestions of cross-border referenda and transnational deliberative forums to recommend policy solutions.[58] Saward's approach is therefore close to that of deliberative democracy, with an emphasis on individual participation in a variety of forums.

Others claim that the nation state is still the natural locus of political community and loyalty. Wendt argues that although global trends are undermining the *de facto* autonomy of states, they are likely to be reluctant to relinquish *de jure* sovereignty for a considerable period, and therefore overarching global institutions are still a long way off. Wendt also expresses scepticism about how cosmopolitan popular opinion tends to be – citing isolationism in the United States – and suggests governments may be more likely than peoples to recognize the reality of transnational community. If a cosmopolitan democracy were possible, then Wendt queries whether it should be based on individual rights and individual votes for representatives in a global assembly, as this might lead to fear of majority tyranny by people in the most populous states. Instead 'group rights' based on nation states may be more likely to result in protection of legitimate interests and local culture, and states are more likely to enter a system in which these are preserved.[59] Wendt does not therefore endorse any concept of global citizenship.

Will Kymlicka is more sympathetic than Wendt to Held's emphasis on the positive role of groups in global civil society and their representation at the UN, and on enforcing individual human rights internationally. But he agrees with Wendt about the continuing importance of states and a sense of national community. He therefore queries Held's thesis that globalization is undermining a sense of a 'shared community of fate' within the state, arguing that there is still a strong sense of separate national identity. He is sceptical too about the realism of making global institutions directly accountable to individuals, and cites apathy about the European Parliament. He stresses the importance of a shared language for political participation (see argument in Chapter 6). Kymlicka suggests instead that international bodies should be accountable to state governments, and that the role for citizens is to discuss at a national level how they want their governments to act internationally. He suggests therefore 'that we should be quite modest in our expectations about transnational citizenship, at least in the foreseeable future'.[60]

A more fundamental challenge is posed by Robert Dahl's attack on the possibility of democracy in international organizations. Dahl's starting point is the difficulty of maintaining effective democracy, in terms of citizens' knowledge and interest in issues and their political participation, within the nation state. He then notes that foreign affairs is an area in which citizens notoriously tend to know and care less, though they may be mobilized on certain issues like the Vietnam War. Therefore the likelihood of citizens holding their governments to account for their role inside international organizations is low. If the aim is to give individuals some direct influence over a global body, then the problems are even greater. How can citizens in Sweden exercise as much control over Brussels as they do over their parliament in Stockholm? If a global democratic body were set up, 'the opportunities available to the ordinary citizen to participate effectively in the decisions of a world government would diminish to the vanishing point'.[61] Moreover, increasing numbers of people represented by an organization mean increased diversity and conflict of interests and make a concept of a common good even harder to achieve than nationally. Civic virtue is less likely to prevail over private interest.

Dahl does not reject the need for international organizations – they can fulfil important functions – but at best they can be seen as responding in some sense to the needs and wishes of those affected by their decisions. Dahl cites the EU and suggests that the 'democratic deficit' is likely to be the price for all international bodies with bureaucracies that make decisions affecting people collectively. The tenor of his argument suggests almost total pessimism about the possibility of global citizenship, whether exercised at a national or a transnational level.

Dahl's discussion ignores the role of transnational pressure groups and movements and the scope for influence provided by global civil society. Nor does he address the possibility of debate on specific issues affecting people across borders, or the dynamics whereby transfer of powers to a supranational level may also stimulate regional political activity. But he does point to the sheer difficulty of imposing democratic controls on international bureaucracies and the need to pause before trying to transfer representative democracy to a global level.

The comments on Held cited so far do not address one central problem: how adequately do his proposals address democratic control over the global economy? Wendt suggests that multinational capital is most 'conscious of its borderless quality', but does not pursue the implications of this claim.[62]

Liberal reform, cosmopolitan democracy and global capitalism

The Commission on Global Governance did address a range of issues relating to economic development, global monetary stability, trade and the role of international economic organizations like the IMF, the World Bank and the WTO. It commented optimistically on the need for business to 'act responsibly in the global neighbourhood and contribute to its governance'. The Commission also cited signs of such responsibility developing, for example proposals by the Business Council on Sustainable Development to the 1992 Rio Earth Summit. But the Commission's central message was to urge further liberalization of trade, to be balanced against negotiation of a UN code to prevent monopolistic practices, corruption and activities dangerous to both local people and the environment (giving as an example the escape of posionous gas at Bhopal in India).[63]

The Commission also stressed the need for greater transparency and effective oversight of the operations of corporations, banks and stock exchanges, and greater coordination of policies on international economic issues, including development. It recommended the creation of a new Economic Security Council and some democratization of the IMF and the World Bank – though it retained the principle that the voting power of countries should be geared to their economic power.[64] Falk criticizes the Commission for 'failing to clarify the challenges of globalization and the troublesome character of Bretton Woods approaches to world economic policy'. Therefore it fails to challenge the neo-liberal approach to economic globalization.[65]

Falk looks primarily to civil society, but suggests the need to develop consensus on 'normative democracy'. He wishes to encourage greater state action to control global capital and promote social equality, whilst encouraging transnational action on many issues. He therefore hopes democratic beliefs and practices will act as 'a counterweight to neo-liberalism'.[66] There are therefore some parallels with Held's reliance on cosmopolitan democracy, but a different institutional focus.

Held's rationale for moving beyond a form of democracy based on the territorial state rests, as we saw, on a number of 'disjunctures' – and the increasing power and scope of multinational corporations and impact of global financial markets is one of the most striking of these. His aim is to constrain neo-liberal globalism. Although he does consider sympathetically Friedrich Hayek's critique of central political control of the economy and emphasis on the rule of law and free markets as the basis of individual liberty, not only nationally but internationally, Held argues that 'Hayek's model of the liberal free-market order is fundamentally at odds with the modern corporate capitalist system.'[67] Business corporations and multinational banks shape national government policy and therefore undermine democracy. Held's suggested strategy has two main prongs: to strengthen global legal and political controls and to promote democratic processes within companies. A third approach implied at various points, particularly in discussions of public direction of investment, suggest asserting the role of national governments – or possibly regional authorities.[68]

At the global level Held advocates the development of 'cosmopolitan democratic law' to set out a framework within which economic bodies should operate. This framework should prohibit corporations from meddling in politics, for example influencing elections through funding, and should require that they respect the health and welfare of their workforce. Held notes that the Social Chapter in the EU aims to constrain companies, but that a regional arrangement is likely to be undermined if it is not extended to the rest of the world. These rules should be part of a new trade system, and as a sanction companies – or countries – that flouted them could be excluded. He also comments on the need to reorganize the IMF and the World Bank, and (like the Commission on Global Governance) suggests the need for a new coordinating body. But his proposals do not apparently envisage direct democratic controls over international economic organizations.

The strategy of democratizing the economic sphere from within – backed by a cosmopolitan law entrenching workers' rights – suggests both introducing mechanisms for giving a voice to workers, consumers, local communities and investment fund-holders in existing corporations, and encouraging cooperatives and community-based finanical institutions.[69]

One major challenge to international control is the extent to which multinationals can constrain or even dictate the decision-making of international organizations. An example is the role of the Transatlantic Business Dialogue, which pairs officials from major companies with leading officials from the US Government and the EU and has a long list of desired policy outcomes. The Dialogue prepared proposals and agenda items for the WTO for discussion at a meeting between President Clinton and Romani Prodi, the EU Commission President, in Portugal in June 2000. The Dialogue's list included, according to an article first printed in the British *Observer*, '33 environment, consumer and worker protection laws in selected nations that TABD wishes to defeat or water down'.[70] Even if a cosmopolitan democratic law along the lines that Held envisages could be agreed – at present unlikely in the teeth of corporate opposition – there would still be major questions about its effective implementation. This corporate influence extends even to the UN, dramatized by the Secretary General's controversial announcement in July 2000 that the UN had entered into partnership with 50 major corporations who could use the UN logo.[71]

Grahame Thompson provides an interesting assessment of possible ways of asserting democratic controls over multinationals.[72] He examines the three approaches: transnational controls, democratic processes within companies and national measures. He notes how work by the UN Economic and Social Council on a Draft Code of Conduct for Transnational Corporations, which started in the 1970s, petered out in the early 1990s. Commenting on recent proposals for a General Agreement on International Corporations, he suggests that at present such an agreement would be very difficult to achieve in the absence of consensus between key G7 states. For now the forms of limited international accountability that already exist may be all that is possible.

Thompson comments on proposals to move from formal accountability by companies to shareholders towards 'stakeholder' democracy, representing, for example, workers, consumers and local communities. But he sees considerable difficulties in the case of multinationals in identifying stakeholders and developing effective modes of cooperation between them, given their geographically dispersed nature. Cooperation between a number of states to strengthen control at the national level, through national monitoring of multinationals and agreeing joint measures, looks more promising.

In his book *Globalization in Question*, written jointly with Paul Hirst, Thompson argues strongly that nation states are still crucially important in the economy, and that, given the growth of international bodies, the state is vital in representing its population and acting as a 'pivot' between 'international agencies and subnational activities'.[73] This argument reinforces the views of Wendt and Kymlicka on the continuing role of the state. But Hirst and Thompson also agree with Kymlicka about the importance of campaigning groups in global civil society. Groups like Greenpeace and the Red Cross can rouse world opinion and assume some direct responsibilities.

Criticisms of the utopianism involved in applying cosmopolitan democracy to the economic sphere reflect the inherent difficulties of tackling the entrenched power of global corporations. Similar considerations arise in relation to Held's proposals on enforcing international law and ending the danger of military conflict between states.

Cosmopolitan democracy and security: realist perspectives

One of the disjunctures that Held addresses in his book on cosmopolitan democracy (though not in some of the shorter statements of his position) is between notional national sovereignty and the reality of hegemonic military powers. Since the end of the cold war the tight controls involved in the opposing blocs has been relaxed, but the US still plays a dominant role in NATO. The broader point that Held makes is that the security policy of one country impinges on the security of others, and today's weapons create global insecurity: 'proliferation of weapons systems of mass destruction radically increases the prospect of political instability and insecurity for all'.[74]

He says, however, remarkably little about specific approaches to promoting global security either in the short run or if cosmopolitan democratic institutions are achieved. It is possible to infer that Held hopes for a progressive development of a policy of common security under UN auspices, but in a world of nuclear, chemical and biological weapons this cannot be a total solution. It is also reasonable to guess that he supports the kind of arms control proposals put forward by the Commission on Global Governance on weapons of mass destruction. There are a number of obvious reasons for choosing not to discuss disarmament and security issues, including the impossibility of covering every relevant issue in detail and the counter-productive effect of composing too many wish lists. But virtual silence is significant. A realist might well argue that failure to confront the military obstacles to a developed cosmopolitan democracy indicates the fundamental implausibility of the idea.

When Held began to develop his ideas on cosmopolitan democracy in the early 1990s, it was possible to hope that substantial progress would continue on arms control, especially between the US and Russia. By the beginning of the twenty-first century the prospects are more bleak. India and Pakistan have both tested nuclear weapons, the breakdown of UN inspections in Iraq suggested that the Government is producing nuclear, chemical and biological weapons, and the US itself is threatening to launch a new anti-ballistic missile programme that would breach the 1972 Anti-Ballistic Missile Treaty with the then USSR.

Nevertheless, these threats to peace – serious as they are – do not prevent widespread negotiations and cooperation between states, including the US and Russia, on many other issues. (Iraq, which is being treated as a pariah state, is a partial exception.) Interdependence, perception of many common interests, and the institutional dynamics of international organizations help to create a context in which major wars are less likely. Held's implicit analysis is that major security problems may be easier to resolve if the bonds of international society become progressively stronger and globalization continues to erode national frontiers. There is a parallel here with negotiations to resolve historical conflicts, which often postpone the most difficult and symbolically divisive issues until towards the end of the process. A realist assessment of the central obstacles created by the search for military security certainly throws doubt on the goal of cosmopolitan democracy and an associated peace. But it does not prove that these goals are necessarily and permanently impossible.

Apart from orthodox realist objections to the possibility of cosmopolitan democracy, there are other obstacles to developing peaceful institutional cooperation arising out of current politics. The first is the breakdown of old empires and states into new national units. In favourable circumstances this can result in a positive assertion of national self-determination and creation of new relatively democratic regimes, but it is a process often accompanied by xenophobia and violence. The disintegration of the Soviet Union provided examples of both. But even where the political outcome is fairly peaceful and democratic, there are problems caused by the proliferation of the sheer number of states, which greatly enhances the difficulty of reaching effective international agreements. The dangers may be reduced where a semi-supranational regional organization is well established, as in the case of the EU, but no similar body is likely in the foreseeable future in more troubled parts of the world.

In addition to the challenge posed by the new nationalisms, the rise of religious fundamentalism threatens liberal values and practices internally and internationally. Both also challenge the rules of the international game as understood by realists.

Alongside these trends is the rise in flagrant corruption and use of lawless violence by some governments, so that the borderline between criminal gangs and allegedly legitimate governments is in quite a few states virtually non-existent. This overlap is not wholly new (we need only refer to the role of the Mafia in Italian politics), but the breakdown of the Soviet Union and Yugoslavia, and drug wars, diamond wars and prolonged civil wars in Latin America and Africa, have all tended to create the antithesis of peace and the rule of law in many areas. This is a development as unwelcome to realists as to cosmopolitans, since it tends in some regions to substitute virtually uncontrolled anarchy for the ordered anarchy envisaged by Bull. He does indeed note briefly the possible disintegration of states and rise of terrorism, but does not see it as a serious challenge to the state system.[75] Machiavelli might have found this scene more familiar, but he does not offer any solution, except the possible role of a ruthless but far-sighted dictator able to impose political unity on small warring states.[76]

A cosmopolitan view of the world may, paradoxically, be somewhat more sanguine about ethnic violence, religious passions and the criminalization of politics than a realist one. Cosmopolitan theorists today accept the thesis of increasing globalization. Although reassertion of cultural and religious identity can be seen as a reaction to aspects of economic and cultural globalization dominated by the West, in the longer run governments seeking economic growth and peoples influenced by global media (neither is necessarily true in dictatorships) may turn away from either political or religious extremes. China and Iran both illustrate this tendency. Whilst many cosmopolitan theorists deplore the extensive power of multinationals or the spread of the crasser forms of western materialism, they also see hope in the parallel extension of demands for human rights and democracy.

Secondly, although the record of atrocities in vicious civil wars of the 1990s is a reason for despair, the very savagery of these ethnic wars has served to strengthen pressures for cosmopolitan law and an increasing role for UN intervention. The Tribunals set up for former Yugoslavia and Rwanda underlined the need for a permanent International Court. Despite notable failures in UN operations, for example in Bosnia and Sierra Leone, so long as enough governments are willing to support UN operations with troops, police, observers and money the system of peace keeping or peace enforcement is being strengthened. The desperate need for an impartial and effective permanent international force, well publicized by the international media, *may* encourage governments to move towards providing it. This issue was discussed at the UN Millennium Summit in September 2000.

These crises also demonstrate the importance of civil society groups, both local and transnational. Although these unofficial groups are often not strong enough to *prevent* conflicts, they do play an important role in providing relief, campaigning for rights, publicizing abuses, and in some cases resisting war or promoting reconciliation. For example, the Centre for Peacemaking and Community Development in Moscow worked after the first Chechen war with other nongovernmental groups and UN agencies to give food, clothing and medical aid to refugees.[77] Transnational groups – although the impact of their work can create problems, such as indirectly providing resources to soldiers rather than civilians – often assist local activists and also work in parallel with international bodies. For example, in January 2000 Peace Brigades International established a presence in West Timor, where militias were terrorizing East Timorese in refugee camps and threatening local voluntary groups offering aid in the camps. The Brigades met with all political groupings, including the militias and the Indonesian Government, monitored the position and provided information to international organizations.[78]

These considerations suggest the extreme difficulty of promoting cosmopolitan values, but also the crucial role that can be played by the UN, by
governments with a commitment to internationalism and human rights, and by
local activists and transnational groups with cosmopolitan ideals. An important
question remains about the imperialist content of cosmopolitan thought and
practice – a criticism raised forcefully by Danilo Zolo.

Cosmopolitanism as imperialism

Danilo Zolo has made a vigorous case against cosmopolitan theorists like Bobbio
and Held.[79] He is highly critical of what he describes as western 'legal
globalism', leading to 'humanitarian intervention', to international courts to try
individuals, and towards world government. Much of Zolo's argument is based
primarily on a realist view of international relations, although in his own
proposals for a 'weak pacifism' he diverges from a strict realist path. Zolo
identifies himself primarily with the Hobbesian model, but expresses some
sympathy for Bull's Grotian neo-realism and for realist interpretations of 'regime
theory'.[80] But he also attacks the development of cosmopolitan law and
humanitarian intervention because they reflect western military and economic
power and cultural imperialism. In addition he views the UN as an organization
dominated by the West, and in particular the US, and emphasizes that the Gulf
War was a 'cosmopolitan' war endorsed by the UN, but effectively fought by the
US to support the New World Order.

The simplest aspect of Zolo's argument, and the most questionable, is the
suggestion that US foreign policy can be equated with 'cosmopolitanism'. He is
supported in this view by Edward Said, who suggests that the US during the cold
war had a sense of mission to create a world subject to the rule of law.[81] Said
believes that this analysis is even more true after the Gulf War. However, US
unilateral interventions in other countries have often been not only politically
controversial but also of very dubious legality under international law. So the
American Government's own interpretation of its role certainly does not make it
genuinely cosmopolitan. There is also a striking contrast between US claims to
moral superiority and America's effective undermining of international law – the
US has refused to accept the 1982 Law of the Sea, several human rights
conventions dating from the 1960s and 1970s and additional protocols to the
1949 Geneva Conventions – quite apart from the failure to sign or ratify several
key arms control agreements. Phyllis Bennis comments that 'The law of empire
takes the form of the US exempting itself from treaties and other international
agreements that it demands others accept.'[82] Moreover, although the US has
sometimes acted through the UN, in general, Congress, popular opinion and
even governments in the US are deeply suspicious of the UN and happier
operating outside its framework. Indeed, Zolo in his 'Postscript' to the English
edition of *Cosmopolis* puts forward the very different argument that in Europe the
US aim has been to sideline the UN, and use NATO to extend western political
influence.[83]

Zolo is more persuasive in his attack on what he calls 'legal globalism', which he suggests, 'despite its cosmopolitan aspirations ... remains firmly linked to the ... classic Christian doctrine of natural law'.[84] He also claims that moves to create international tribunals to judge individuals responsible for war crimes, crimes against humanity and genocide reflect not only western ideology, but also western power. 'Today the whole planet is gravitating around a single political, economic and cultural orbit comprising the industrial powers, with the United States as their focal point.'[85]

There is a possible case that the International Criminal Tribunal for the Former Yugoslavia has a western bias. But the enthusiasm of the US for international courts is limited. When it was agreed in 1999 to set up a permanent International Criminal Court, the US was one of the major opponents of the proposal and refused to sign the agreement, partly for fear that US nationals might be tried. President Clinton belatedly signed on 31 December 2000.

Support for applying principles of international law has, moreover, been clearly expressed in Africa. The government of Sierra Leone asked the UN in June 2000 to set up an international tribunal to try the rebel leader Foday Sankoh for crimes against humanity, although it was unlikely that this request would be met.[86] Indeed, contra Zolo, the West can be accused of *too little* concern with maintaining human rights or supporting international tribunals in Africa (the Tribunal for Rwanda was initially much less well staffed and funded than the Tribunal for Former Yugoslavia).

Zolo's suspicion of legal globalism stems partly from his fear that it is linked to a simplistic view that world law can create world peace and that it implies an impulse towards world government. The limited role of international tribunals, however, scarcely constitutes global government. Nor is it entirely clear which of Zolo's concerns are uppermost – belief that greater cosmopolitanism means a form of western imperialism, or a realist hostility to the goal of a unified world order.

There is in fact a very good case that moves towards increasing cosmopolitanism can *reduce* US and western influence. For example, moves to reform the UN that include bringing more non-western countries onto the Security Council and increasing the weight of developing countries in international economic bodies would limit the tendency for action by these bodies to reflect US foreign and economic policy. Moves to create a permanent UN peace-keeping force under independent command would make humanitarian intervention less dependent on western troops and less open to influence by western governments.

Moreover, cosmopolitan thinkers and activists in the West are generally among the strongest opponents of US attempts to act as an imperial power and flout the UN Charter. Zolo notes correctly that some cosmopolitan thinkers, including Bobbio, did support the Gulf War as a realization of the UN's original goal of collective action against aggression. But he does also recognize that others such as Falk were articulate critics of the war. More generally, as noted in Chapter 4, transnational movements try to hold governments to their obligations under international law and press them to take more action to preserve the global environment and reduce world poverty.

Zolo's broad case that theories of 'legal globalism' and human rights reflect western culture, that cosmopolitanism is influenced by Kantian morality, and that therefore cosmopolitan views constitute a form of western cultural imperialism does raise very interesting questions. These issues are addressed in the next chapter.

Conclusion

My own view of the opposing theoretical perspectives discussed in this chapter grants considerable force to the realist view of the irreducible conflicts involved in the pursuit of military security, but considers that realism cannot give a satisfactory account of contemporary international politics. Liberal arguments about the influence of internal political factors, the role of trade, and the significance of international institutions in creating a collective purpose and identity do have cogency. These factors constrain purely realist interpretations of national interest. I also share the view of cosmopolitan theorists that increasing interdependence and integration is eroding national boundaries, and that a fragile cosmopolitan order, which gives weight to the rights of individuals and sees an independent political role for non-state actors, seems to be emerging.

There are many possible scenarios that would destroy this emerging cosmopolitanism, including a major war, extreme environmental degradation and an entrenched struggle between the prosperous North against individuals, guerrilla groups and states in the impoverished South. It is also all too likely that if globalizing and cooperative trends do continue, they will do so in a framework primarily dictated by neo-liberal ideology and the power of multinationals.

But, as Kant argued over 200 years ago, no reliable prediction is possible in analysing international politics, and the ample grounds for pessimism are not in themselves a reason for despair. How individuals and governments act will help to shape what does actually happen in the future, and there is a moral and political obligation to act (within the bounds of reasonable prudence) in such a way as to promote cosmopolitan goals.

The concept of global citizenship as commitment to cosmopolitanism is therefore a relevant ideal, and conditions exist in many countries to act as a global citizen through global civil society. There are, moreover, openings for such action to have some positive results.

Global citizenship as a status under international law also has some validity today. It is still an embryonic status, but is being enlarged, partly by political groups appealing to international law to entrench their rights at a national level.

Global citizenship, understood as taking part in UN peace keeping, monitoring of elections or human rights, or working for UN agencies, is clearly possible, and, given the increasing importance attached to the UN, may become more signficant. If the UN moves towards an independent police and peace keeping force, for example, then the dual nature of national and global obligations will be superseded by a more clearly global responsibility.

Global citizenship as the right to vote for a world parliamentary assembly, on the other hand, still seems extremely remote. Other proposals for democratic forums that transcend national frontiers, such as cross-border deliberation and referenda, may be rather more likely. The desirability of a directly elected world assembly also remains questionable, for reasons suggested by some of Held's critics. Transparency and accountability, however, *are* crucial. One of the problems with international organizations, as both the EU and the UN amply illustrate, is that they are even more prone to bureaucratic inertia, waste of money and outright corruption than are many national governments. So there is a role for supervisory bodies independent of both national governments and international organizations.

The idea of global citizenship as a facet of national citizenship remains extremely important. In states where corruption, abuse of human rights and environmental degradation are rampant, the struggle to create a better national politics can coincide with cosmopolitan goals. Although an end to dictatorship may, as in Indonesia, unleash dangerous ethnic and religious antagonisms, new democratic governments are also more likely, as in the case of South Africa, to take seriously their international obligations.

Nation states enjoying reasonable stability, affluence and commitment to human rights and democratic principles play a crucial role in maintaining international institutions and promoting international agreements. A change of government can, however, result in a more cavalier attitude to international obligations – in general, conservative parties are less willing to subordinate national to global interest or to accept the application of international law to their domestic politics. Therefore citizens of these states can significantly influence achievement of cosmopolitan goals.

9 Cultural diversity, feminism and postmodernism

Challenges to global cosmopolitanism?

The concept of global citizenship depends upon the possibility of universally accepted norms of behaviour in international politics. Cosmopolitanism itself, however, is premised on the assumption of cultural diversity and tolerance for varied life styles. Where the lines should be drawn between universal principles, and beliefs and practices determined within particular cultures, may be morally and politically difficult, and certainly has to be discussed. But if there are insurmountable political and theoretical problems in asserting universal principles, then the ideal of global citizenship is unconvincing. It would still be open to individuals to identify themselves as global citizens as an act of purely personal choice, or as a reflection of their transcultural heritage, but it would be incoherent to argue that others should pursue a cosmopolitan politics.

There are three major theoretical challenges to both political and philosophical cosmopolitanism: rejection of universalism in the name of anti-imperialism and cultural diversity; some feminist theories that critique western liberalism and universalism; and poststructural and postmodern theories challenging the 'Enlightenment project'.

One response to western cultural imperialism is to assert the validity of diverse and incompatible cultural values. The main political impetus for this argument therefore comes from intellectuals and political leaders in the non-western world. But it has support in the West. We examined an explicit political critique of cosmopolitanism by Zolo in the previous chapter. Here the focus is on the relationship between rejection of western universal values and the more abstract concepts associated with postmodernism and postcolonialism. I use human rights as an example, and after exploring the debate about Asian values, I argue that the claims of a pure cultural relativism cannot be sustained either logically or politically.

The position of feminist politics and theory in relation to cosmopolitanism is more ambiguous than cultural relativism. Although there are strands of feminism influenced by belief in cultural diversity, feminist movements have generally asserted that women have common interests across cultures and that women's rights should be universal. This position is vigorously upheld today by 'radical' feminists. Although feminist movements themselves have in the past been biased by often unconscious western imperialist attitudes, the problems of accepting total cultural relativism in relation to human rights tend to be especially prejudicial to women's lives and women's autonomy and dignity, as many Asian and African women attest. The problems of reaching cross-cultural agreement on the rights essential for women, and the policies that should uphold these rights, have been at least partially overcome through a process of international dialogue between women.

Feminist thought has often been sympathetic to the ideal of global citizenship, and portrayed women as especially suited to promote peace and transnational cooperation. But these 'maternalist' views are challenged by postmodern feminists as 'essentialist', based on unsatisfactory theoretical foundations and leading to the wrong kind of political conclusions.

Postmodern philosophies and some feminist theories raise far-reaching questions about the bases of knowledge and the nature of the social world, and have also influenced understandings of international politics. Two important advocates of cosmopolitanism, Jürgen Habermas and Andrew Linklater, have adopted rather different strategies for responding to the challenges of postmodernism: Habermas has mounted a strong critique at a philosophical level; Linklater explores points of convergence between critical theory and postmodernism with a particular emphasis on political and moral concerns. I assess both briefly, and in this context examine several statements by leading poststructuralist or postmodern thinkers on human rights to see whether they suggest their theories can accommodate cosmopolitanism, or whether they have to abandon their theoretical position to pursue their political commitments. My general conclusion is that although many postmodern thinkers do accept Enlightenment values, the effect of postmodern arguments is to undermine cosmopolitan goals both theoretically and politically. This attack on cosmopolitanism tends to be borne out by at least some postmodern positions in international relations.

Cosmopolitanism as western imperialism: arguments from cultural diversity

Critics of cosmopolitanism, who see it as inherently imperialist, may either argue from a broad theoretical stance, which has political implications, or start from an explicitly political position. Contemporary 'postcolonial' critics of the cultural legacies of colonialism are often associated with the range of theories described as poststructural (for example Foucault and Derrida) or postmodern (for example Lyotard and Rorty), which became influential, especially in France and the USA, in the 1980s and 1990s. Despite the danger of conflating theorists who adopt varied approaches, and often disagree with one another, for present purposes of indicating a very broad approach it is simplest to use the popular term 'postmodern'.[1] A key claim in this body of thought is that, in Lyotard's words: 'The grand narrative has lost its credibility, regardless of what mode of unification it uses, regardless of whether it is a speculative narrative or a narrative of emancipation.'[2]

The implication for political theory is that both liberalism and Marxism as total ideologies should be rejected, because they constitute 'grand narratives' of inevitable historical progress and human emancipation, which rest on unsustainable foundations. It is also often argued by postmodernists that such ideologies tend to create repressive political and social systems. The repressive potential is obvious in the case of Marxism, given the nature of communist regimes; in the case of liberalism it rests on a more complex critique of the role of reason and the operations of power within western societies. (Not all postmodern theorists repudiate a more modest liberal politics – Richard Rorty calls for 'liberalism without foundations'.) More generally, postmodern philosophers and political theorists reject claims for the universal validity of concepts of rationality or morality, are sceptical about the claims of science and query 'discourses' claiming truth. They also tend to challenge the belief in individual autonomy and stress the fluidity of identity and the fragmentation of moral and social codes in society.

Theories undermining Enlightenment rationalism and universalism, on the grounds that knowledge and forms of thought constitute social power, and therefore subordinate other kinds of knowledge and experience, clearly have resonance with non-western intellectuals resisting a western culture that has often ignored or despised their own inheritance. The postmodern exploration of how privileging rationality necessarily excludes 'the Other', often defined as irrational, deviant and dangerous, also suggests how western thought has frequently feared and dismissed other races, either as incomprehensible ('the mysterious East') or as primitive and barbarous. Moreover, postmodern analyses of the claims to universality in western thought, which note that universality is identified with Europe (or some example of the European spirit), speak to Africans or Asians resisting the view that western culture is inherently universal in its significance, and that their own literature or art or philosophy is at best marginal.[3]

Rejection of 'totalizing' universal law and universal rights, as in Lyotard's later philosophy, in favour of recognition of individual and cultural difference also supports critiques of western assumptions about the universal validity of rights.

But cultural and political critiques of western imperialism first arose directly from the experience of intellectuals from parts of the world subject in the past to direct colonial rule and/or aware of the present impact of western economic and cultural power. Many important critics of western cultural imperialism developed their ideas long before the advent of the varieties of postmodernism. Nor are all of today's critics of western cultural imperialism enthusiastic about theorists such as Foucault or Lyotard. Edward Said, one of the key 'postcolonial' theorists, did draw on Foucault in his important work *Orientalism*, but in his later *Culture and Imperialism* compares Foucault unfavourably with Frantz Fanon, intellectual advocate for the Algerian Revolution, and sees both Lyotard and Foucault turning away from their earlier political radicalism and reflecting western intellectual disillusionment with anti-colonial struggles.[4] He also points out that whilst postmodern ideas may reflect the condition of western culture,

Arab intellectuals are often more concerned with the debate between tradition-alism and modernism.

For our purposes the sources of criticism of western universalism are less important than the key arguments. But first we need to clarify which arguments are relevant to discussion of cosmopolitanism. During the period of direct colonial rule western politics and culture were suffused with belief in European superiority and a corresponding intellectual arrogance, which (as noted in Chapter 3) extended to many liberals. But explicit racism and ideological justifications of imperial rule were resisted by cosmopolitan thinkers and social movements in the West, as we also saw in Chapters 2 and 3. Moreover, crude imperialism can more plausibly be seen as an extension of a certain sort of nationalism than of European cosmopolitanism. The nationalist focus is obviously true of the politics of empire, but even the cultural legitimations drew heavily on national traditions. These national traditions included universalist elements – the British claimed the general benefits of the rule of law and French colonialism drew on a nationalism significantly influenced by the Enlightenment and French Revolutionary ideology. But the fact that nationalist imperialism embodied a universalist impulse does not mean that genuine cosmopolitans endorsed empire.

A case can certainly be made that even committed cosmopolitans in the West are (often unconsciously) influenced by their imperial heritage (see Chapters 3 and 4). It is also true that European advocates of universal morality, global citizenship and global governance today can plausibly be charged with a European bias. Habermas is criticized by Said for explicitly admitting that he has nothing to say 'to anti-imperialist and anti-capitalist struggles in the Third World' and for his admitted Euro-centrism.[5] Held observed in an interview with Baogang He that he has been impressed by the example of the EU, and, as noted in the previous chapter, this model strongly influences his approach to cosmopolitan democracy.[6] American theorists of global citizenship like Falk are vividly aware of living in today's main imperial power, and that liberal universalist ideology can be misused to defend either military adventures or capitalist exploitation, but Falk's emphasis on world law might be construed as a reflection of American constitutionalism.[7]

It is, however, one thing to argue that even those committed to universal moral values and upholding an ideal of global citizenship do not wholly transcend their social and cultural contexts. It is quite another to claim that any attempt to promote universal values, and a politics that upholds these values, necessarily implies an imperialist impulse and should therefore be abandoned.

The obvious alternative to a philosophical or political quest for universal principles, and the approach adopted by some influenced by postmodernism, is to claim that the beliefs embedded within various cultures are necessarily diverse and all equally valid. Postcolonial criticism of the western Enlightenment naturally wishes to stress the values of non-western traditions and to demand respect for them. Western theorists have also in recent years debated the legitimacy of claims from indigenous peoples, migrants from former colonies and other immigrant groups that their right to maintain their religious beliefs, different customs and social institutions should be recognized within particular states. Thus the idea of a politics based on religious, cultural and ethnic difference has gained support. [8]

There are three major political and theoretical problems in abandoning belief in universal moral principles and accepting that all values are culturally relative. The first is that 'culture' is not a clear-cut or static social entity that can be simply identified – especially as most cultures have a complex history and embrace considerable diversity. Most religions include various schools of belief, scholars and religious leaders with contrasting doctrines and movements of reform or reaction – after all, Christianity covers both the Catholic and Orthodox Churches and Protestantism. How a culture is defined and elaborated is necessarily open to contest – what, for example, counts as an authentic interpretation of Islam or Hinduism?

Secondly, a political attempt to reassert particular cultural values against what are perceived as alien and contaminating influences may be reactionary – for example Hindu fundamentalism seeking to destroy the legacy of Islam – or may invest power in hierarchies claiming to protect cultural purity – as happened, for example, in Iran after the fall of the Shah.

Thirdly, although some religious and national traditions embody tolerance of differing religious or social beliefs and practices, others can be extremely intolerant. One response to diversity is to destroy other cultural monuments and practices and even the people who are associated with them. The last decade of the twentieth century provided numerous examples in the Balkans and the former Soviet Union. Pure cultural relativism cannot provide a coherent moral or political position. Nor can it provide a convincing critique of imperialism, explaining why it is wrong for one culture to impose its beliefs either by force of arms or by more subtle forms of power.

As it has been frequently noted, celebration of the value of cultural diversity relies simultaneously on an appeal to the universal principle that different cultures (and their adherents) should be respected and treated with tolerance. So some cultural attitudes promoting intolerance are incompatible with commitment to cultural variety, and should therefore logically be subordinated to an overarching requirement of tolerance. Nor is it satisfactory to make respect for the rights of socially organized groups to pursue their own beliefs and practices the sole cross-cultural principle. If groups can claim dignity and respect for their beliefs, this is surely more than an *aesthetic* claim that cultural variety is desirable. It suggests a moral respect for the people who adhere to these cultures. It then follows that individuals within these groups are also entitled to be granted respect. (Whether this argument should start with the group and extend to the individual, or vice versa as liberals believe, is not crucial here.) Moreover, societies interact with one another and individuals for various reasons and travel and settle in other cultures – these considerations influenced the early discussions of international law. This cultural interaction is very much greater today. Therefore rules for living together are needed that transcend one set of cultural beliefs.

How the rules and values of international society are created, and what legitimacy they have, raises further questions about imperialism and cultural diversity, however. This is well illustrated by the controversy over human rights. On the one hand, the idea of human rights has, as David Beetham argues, always been 'universalist in aspiration and global in its scope', resting on claims about common needs arising out of a shared human nature.[9] Human rights are also central to a concept of global citizenship and imply human duties. On the other hand, human rights have been the focus for polemical critiques of universalism.

Human rights

International human rights declarations clearly have their origins in the Enlightenment declarations of rights. The 1948 Declaration of Human Rights was framed when the US and Western Europe were dominant in the UN, though it did meet Soviet concerns about social and economic rights, and even the 1966 covenants, which reflected the input of newly independent Asian and African states, were still predominantly western in content and tone. The apparent western bias of human rights language is also suggested by the fact that western countries often criticize non-western governments for failing to respect civil and political rights, and the US Congress is inclined – though very selectively – to link trading relations to human rights standards. Moreover, safeguarding basic human rights provides the justification for armed 'humanitarian intervention', which (as noted in the previous chapter) is often pursued primarily by the West. So there is a plausible case that giving priority to individual human rights is either a subtle, or in some cases a fairly overt, form of western imperialism.

It is not surprising, therefore, that a number of Asian leaders in the 1990s rejected western-based individual human rights on the grounds that their own cultural traditions provided alternative values, stressing the priority of community over individualism and the importance of social welfare based on economic development. This claim could suggest that Asian values should supplant western values in international declarations. Leaders appealing to 'Asian values', who included the former Prime Minister of Singapore, Lee Kuan Yew, and Malaysian Prime Minister Mahathir bin Mohamad, also suggested the need for a revised UN Charter of Human Rights. Heiner Bielefeldt suggests that some Islamic declarations of rights (for example at the 1990 conference of the Organization of the Islamic Countries) claim superiority over other interpretations.[10] But discussion of these issues usually revolves round the need to recognize a plurality of values, and therefore the acceptance of cultural relativism.

Some western theorists have sympathy with the claim that Asian values provide a valid alternative to western versions of human rights. Zolo, for example, argues that the concept of individual liberty is 'foreign to Islamic culture', and notes that ideas of law and rights are so alien to Confucianism that a new word had to be invented to designate individual rights.[11] But the appeal to

Asian values was often suspect because of the governmental interests that underlay it. Governments eloquent about Asian values tended to be those also inclined to put troublesome trade unionists, journalists and intellectuals in jail. Asian activists in opposition have therefore often denounced Asian values as a smokescreen for oppression.[12] Interestingly Anwar Ibrahim, in his 1996 book *The Asian Renaissance*, written when he was Deputy-Prime Minister of Malaysia, argued that Asian values must include respect for the human person, and warned against appealing to cultural differences to prevent free speech or legitimate dissent.[13] In 1998 Mahathir jailed Ibrahim on trumped-up charges, and he was convicted of two separate charges in 1999 and 2000 in trials conducted with a clear political bias.[14]

Intellectuals from Asian cultures, who would dismiss governmental versions of 'Asian values', may nevertheless have sympathy with the claim that western individualism does conflict with important collective values in non-western cultures. Bhiku Parekh, for example, examines how liberal individualist interpretations can conflict with Asian or Islamic family and community-based concepts of duty. But he does not believe this need suggest that we should abandon belief in basic universal rights.[15]

One alternative to both a western version of universal human rights, and to pure cultural relativism, is to argue that, despite the variety of customs and social attitudes, a core of common values can be discerned across most cultures. Certainly it is unwarranted to suggest that belief in justice and rights, or concern for universal human welfare, are exclusively or even primarily to be found in the West. Amartya Sen, reacting against such an assertion, refers to 'the not insubstantial literature on these and related matters in Sanskrit, Pali, Chinese and Arabic'.[16] Islamic texts and tradition provide for rights to life and property, freedom of religion, equality before the law and social and economic rights.[17] Islam's general tradition of religious tolerance is illustrated by Moorish rule in Spain before 1492, when Christians and Jews worshipped freely and engaged in dialogue with Muslim scholars, and the willingness of the Ottoman Empire to offer asylum to Jews fleeing Christian persecution after the triumph of Catholicism in Spain in 1492.

But claims based on a historical or sociological comparison of major civilizations throw up difficult issues of interpretation. If the claim that there is a core of common values is made about all cultures past and present, it raises questions about, for example, human sacrifice in earlier cultures. If we focus only on the present, should all, or only some, existing cultures count in such an exercise? The usual approach is to focus on the major religious and ethical traditions in the world today.[18] Parekh suggests that 'respect for human life and dignity, equality before the law, equal protection of the law, fair trial and the protection of minorities' are valued 'in almost all societies'.[19] But this still creates difficulties: for example, what actual exceptions to respect for individual life and dignity can be recognized without jeopardizing the universality of the principle? Leaving aside the very major issue of the treatment of women – to be discussed later in this chapter – institutions central to some of these traditions, such as the Hindu caste system (which still includes systematic discrimination against lower castes, in particular the untouchables), are contrary to contemporary interpretations of human rights. Indeed, key figures in the Indian independence movement, in particular Mahatma Gandhi, campaigned to change the status of untouchables.

Another problem in looking for common values in varied cultures is (as noted earlier) the ambiguity in defining the cultures under discussion.[20] Reference to Asian values suggests drawing on the religious traditions and civilizations of Asia as they existed before they were significantly influenced by the West. (There is a further issue of how Asian cultures have impinged upon one another and the role of Islam, but the central issue today is western imperialism.) But Indian beliefs and values have been shaped by the experience of the British Raj and also by the secular socialism associated with the independence movement and early Congress governments. Arab governments rejecting western imperialism promoted – until the Iranian revolution – modernist secular nationalism.[21] China has a Confucian heritage, but it has engaged strongly with western culture since the early part of the twentieth century in pursuit of internal reforms, and in 1949 the new regime adopted Marxist ideology, even if a Maoist variant of it. Since the late 1980s in practice it has veered towards a capitalist economy. Moreover, the Chinese Government's insistence at the 1993 Vienna Conference on the priority of ending world poverty and debt seems to show a very western emphasis on economic growth.[22]

Western culture itself is of course very far from monolithic, even on the issue of human rights, and has also been changing. Within western political thought the relationship between rights and duties, and the range of rights that should be regarded as fundamental, is subject to ongoing debate. The right to property has been disputed by socialists, whilst neo-liberals view with alarm extension of social and employment rights. Moreover, western liberalism has in recent years become more sympathetic to the concept of the cultural rights of differing groups.

Rather than look for common values primarily in historical cultural traditions, it is more fruitful, therefore, to develop two other suggestions made by Parekh: that the world is becoming increasingly interdependent, and that there is a widening of moral consciousness. Growing interdependence means that different cultures are under pressure to find points of agreement. Bielefeldt suggests that 'we understand human rights as the center of a cross-cultural "overlapping consensus" on basic normative standards in our increasingly multicultural societies'. He draws a comparison with Rawls' concept of overlapping consensus on political justice.[23] Traditions of thought and belief, which are in any case inherently complex and open to diverse interpretation, are evolving and being influenced by a changing economy and technology, and also by transnational political movements and cultural trends.[24]

Widening moral consciousness is reflected in political pressure on governments, including western governments, to justify actions that contravene basic human rights and active transnational movements that publicize these abuses. It is arguable that, despite the ideological conflicts at conferences on human rights, and the compromise portmanteau nature of final documents and agreements, a common moral language is being created. The UN Secretary General claimed at the end of the 1993 Vienna Conference to draw up a new human rights document that human rights had become 'the common language of humanity'.[25] Whilst this could be seen as purely political rhetoric, it is also true that the 1993 Conference was based on extensive debate among all the members of the UN and preceded by regional conferences. It is certainly extremely significant that such diverse groups as indigenous peoples in Australia and Guatemala, asylum seekers in the West, and dissidents in China all appeal to human rights and the international law that articulates them. They may do so partly because this rhetorical appeal is politically effective (at least in the international media) or in some cases because they can actually go to court on this basis, so use of human rights does not necessarily imply consistent commitment to the underlying beliefs. But use of this language does have political implications.

Although in practice many governments do not respect or implement all these rights, there is a developing international regime focused on human rights sustained by a network of agreements and institutions.[26] In this context of growing interdependence and widespread recognition of the principle of human rights, it is certainly possible to argue, as John Vincent did,[27] that at a minimum there is widespread public agreement on a basic core of human rights.

The development of a worldwide language of human rights, which members of diverse cultures can draw on, suggests the potential for a growing cosmopolitan consciousness. Cosmopolitan aspirations have certainly been expressed by many non-westerners. Calls for world federalism and for world citizenship in the 1950s found, as we noted earlier, very strong support in Japan and to some extent in India. The Buddhist society Sokka Gakkai International, with over 12 million members in 128 countries, supports UN initiatives and peace campaigns. Its President, Daisaku Ikeda, calls for a global culture of peace and education for world citizenship. He was especially influenced by a Japanese pacifist, imprisoned during the Second World War, and draws primarily on Buddhism, but he also cites Arnold Toynbee's concept of 'unity in diversity', Yehudi Menuhin's 1962 essay anticipating eventual world citizenship, Tolstoy and Havel.[28]

One of the most distinguished exponents of a cosmopolitan world view was the Bengali poet, novelist and philosopher, Rabindranath Tagore, who lived through the Indian independence struggle. Tagore eloquently denounced the dangers of nationalism during the First World War. Whilst he particularly attacked nationalism in the West and in Japan, Tagore also warned against the dangers of developing Indian nationalism, and of elevating political goals above the urgent social and economic regeneration of India. On this issue, although they shared many beliefs, Tagore was one of the strongest critics of Gandhi, on whom Tagore had bestowed the title Mahatma (great soul). Tagore's lifelong cosmopolitanism was expressed in one of his best-known poems, in which he looks forward to international peace and freedom: 'Where the world has not been broken up into fragments by narrow domestic walls.'[29]

Tagore celebrated his own culture, but was also willing to draw on what he saw as the progressive elements in the West. In a 1921 lecture, 'The Call of Truth', he criticized the isolationist tendencies of turning to the past:

> Henceforth, any nation which seeks isolation for itself must come into conflict with the time-spirit and find no peace. From now onward the plane of thinking of every nation will have to be international. It is the striving of the new age to develop in the mind this faculty of universality.[30]

Gandhi, despite his commitment to Indian nationalism, was himself in many ways a cosmopolitan figure, inspiring later movements against colonialism, injustice and war. He relied heavily on Hindu tradition, whilst reinterpreting it and criticizing many aspects of Hindu practice, but also had deep respect for other religions and believed in an underlying common truth. Whilst he rejected western industrialization as a pattern for India, because of its social and economic effects, and was sceptical about western scientific knowledge, he drew on dissident western thinkers like Tolstoy and Ruskin to develop his critique. Contemporary denunciations of globalization that emphasize the dangers of domination by multinational companies, ecological disaster and the relevance of traditional knowledge of agriculture and medicine reflect a Gandhian spirit. But Tagore's sense that the world is becoming inextricably linked and needs corresponding cosmopolitan attitudes is closer to many of today's advocates of cosmopolitanism. It is to a novel by Tagore that Nussbaum turns to provide an example of cosmopolitanism in her essay 'Patriotism and Cosmopolitanism'.[31]

Whilst it is clear that belief in cosmopolitanism is far from being exclusively western, there may be a case that it privileges masculine interpretations of the world. With the exception of Nussbaum, all the cosmopolitan thinkers discussed in this book are men. Moreover, although some women, like Eleanor Roosevelt and South American women delegates in 1948, have had a role in shaping the language of human rights, it has predominantly been determined by men. Even though the UN General Assembly adopted the International Convention on the Elimination of All Discrimination Against Women in 1979, it has not been taken very seriously and numerous reservations have been entered against it.[32] Therefore we now turn to feminist critiques of universalism and to feminist debates about the more specific political issue of human rights.

Feminism: the dialectic between cultural diversity and the logic of universalism

There are several reasons for exploring feminist ideas and issues at this point. On the one hand, feminists have often been at the forefront of cosmopolitan movements and critiques of nationalism, and some feminist theorists have seen it as women's destiny to be citizens of the world by virtue of their gender. On the other hand, feminist theory since the 1980s has been quite strongly influenced by postmodernism, but has reinterpreted this critique to detect a specifically masculine domination embodied in the Enlightenment emphasis on rationality and a hidden exclusion of women in universalist pronouncements. These concerns have led to feminists supporting a politics of difference in their own countries. Suspicion of universalism has also made some western feminists very sympathetic to postcolonial theses about the western imperialism embedded in universalism and claims for the authenticity of non-western cultures, including customs and beliefs affecting women's social role.[33]

There is a paradox involved in the move among some feminists in the 1990s to adopt an anti-universalist stance and fall back on the value of cultural difference. The feminist movement that gained strength during the nineteenth century was combating the subordination of women entrenched in the conservative traditions of different cultures, often – though not always – endorsed by religious beliefs and practices. In the West, for example, Catholicism has generally hindered women's emancipation, but nonconformist Protestant Churches tended to encourage greater independence. Secular and universalist humanism, embodied in both liberalism and socialism, provided a basis for challenging cultural particularism oppressing women. This was so not only in the West, but also in modernizing regimes like those of Atatürk's Turkey or Mao's China. It is true that feminism has long been divided between those seeking to achieve equality for women by asserting their full status as human beings and those stressing women's difference from men. But until recently the latter, as in the maternalist branch of feminism, assumed a universality based on gender.

The second wave of feminism at the end of the 1960s drew initially on liberal or socialist universalism to demand full realization of women's equality. A diverse group of 'radical feminists', reflecting the militancy of the period, argued that liberalism and socialism could not challenge patriarchal structures, stressed the primacy and unique nature of women's universal oppression and the need for a universal liberation of women. The development at a theoretical level in the 1980s and 1990s of sophisticated versions of maternalism had a counterpart in sections of the feminist movement, particularly among anti-war campaigners. But here again claims about women's inherent difference, and their potential contribution to society, both nationally and globally, presupposed universal gender characteristics and universal values.

The appeal to culture is extremely problematic for feminists. Although the position of women in different cultures is nuanced and complex, in general it is striking how the subordination of women (even though it may take different forms) has been central to many traditional cultures. This does not mean that the modern West has always been more advanced in granting women rights. Radhika Coomaraswamy notes that western colonial law in Sri Lanka removed some of the traditional rights of married women. Colonial law dates from a period when women's rights in the West were still minimal; and the colonial legacy has sometimes influenced the law in a way unfavourable to women after decolonization.[34] For example, the Dutch interpretation of Sri Lankan Tamil law (which envisaged communal property) denied married women the right to dispose of their property, a right they still do not possess. Nevertheless, the appeal to human equality and universal rights has, both in the West and in modernizing regimes, tended to remove the most obvious legal and political forms of oppression. Feminist gains depend of course partly on changing economic contexts and on effective political support for women's rights, but they need a source of moral legitimation to combat rooted beliefs in women's inherent mental and spiritual inferiority.

It is also revealing that revolutionary liberation movements, which have also often rejected traditional cultural attitudes, have tended to liberate women incorporated in the struggle. The Chinese communist movement is an obvious example, and women have been involved in both fighting and wider forms of resistance in many African countries, including South Africa.[35] After victory there has often been some tendency to revert to more traditional attitudes.

Religious and ethnic traditions are open to markedly different interpretations. Therefore some feminists have been able to appeal to elements in their cultural heritage that support equality. In particular, Muslim feminists, combating western stereotypes about the oppression of women in Islam, have argued that the original doctrines of their religion are favourable to women's equality and have been overlaid by reactionary elements in various ethnic cultures that have adopted the Muslim faith.[36] There are, however, limits on women's equality and freedom inherent in appealing back to the Koran. A more radical approach is to question whether literal interpretation of the Koran is always appropriate, given the changes in modern life.[37] But this suggests a potential challenge to tradition from a modernist perspective.

The example of Islam illustrates how bitterly contested the position of women is among those adhering to traditionalist Islamic beliefs. Some Islamic regimes have struck a compromise between granting women certain modern rights, such as the right to education and the vote (though the latter is still denied to women in Kuwait), and maintaining tradition in dress and family matters. But extreme fundamentalism requires an extreme denial of women's rights: the Taliban in Afghanistan illustrate how confining women to the home can be a symbolic test of Islamic purity. Twenty years after the success of the Islamic revolution in Iran, which imposed extremely strict limits on women and authorized male zealots to enforce these rules with violence, there are moves towards women regaining some of the independence they had previously enjoyed.

Moreover, the position of women and their role in the family are often central to the conflict between universal principles and cultural rejection of what are seen as western, urban and intellectual values. This is a debate not simply between the West and other cultures, but also within many countries and continents. Practice of 'female circumcision' or 'genital mutilation' (the choice of words itself denotes a political position) is now being strongly criticized by articulate women within Africa as well as by western feminists. To take an example from India, Radhika Coomaraswamy discusses the highly controversial case of Roop Kanwar, an 18-year-old student who, in September 1987, died on her husband's funeral pyre. Sati (or suttee) had been outlawed by the British and was against Indian law. The federal and the state government sided with the outraged feminist movement and Roop Kanwar's husband's family was arrested for abetting suicide. However, Kanwar's 'sacrifice' prompted mass popular support on religious grounds in Rajasthan, and Hindi-language newspapers tended to support sati as an expression of traditional Indian religion and to celebrate her heroic act. Whether in fact she genuinely chose to die or was coerced into doing so by her husband's family was also hotly disputed.[38] Cooraswamy suggests that unless universal rights and international law have support within society and local traditions they will remain fragile. Women's rights in India have also become entangled with the revival of Hindu fundamentalism, which challenges tolerance of other religions and beliefs, and cosmopolitan principles at all levels.

Does the compromise position of looking for a core of common universal values have any relevance to reconciling women's basic rights with respect for cultural diversity? The obvious danger is that rights specifically relating to women will be assigned to the category of the non-universal. Parekh, for example, suggested in his 1993 essay that rights to unlimited freedom of expression and to private property, and the right that marriage should be based on the full and free consent of both parties, count as specifically western and not universal rights – though more recently in a specific discussion of women's rights he has abandoned this latter position.[39] The issue here is not romantic love versus arranged marriages, but whether the woman has a real choice. If women are forced into marriage, this is a basic denial of freedom, especially as it suggests women may also be forced into a subordinate position within marriage and young girls can be forced to marry much older men. Moreover, it fails to deal with the problems arising for young women who belong to two cultures – forced marriages of Asian women in Britain, tricked into visiting their fathers' countries, has become a significant human rights issue. Here the British response has, eventually, been to extend the concept of core human rights. In June 2000, a Home Office report based on a working group including Asian women argued: 'We must value ... our diversity [but] we must not excuse practices that compromise or undermine the basic rights accorded to all people.' The report was a belated response to a campaign by Asian women's groups.[40]

Achieving women's rights and dignity depends upon a willingness to reinterpret or modify an inherited culture in the light of awareness of other cultures and international principles. There are active feminists in most of the world now, including some countries where religious fundamentalism, whether Islamic or Hindu, is politically powerful. But the struggle of these women is aided by awareness of greater equality elsewhere, of the possibility of appealing to universal principles and of the role of international law and international institutions. For example, the Organization of African Unity adopted the African Charter of Human and People's Rights in 1981, which included a commitment (under Article 1893) to eliminate discrimination against women. Because there is a regional African declaration that has binding force on member states, the courts may refer to the charter in adjudicating cases concerning women's rights.

Therefore the High Court in Tanzania, after a series of legal hearings and appeals, ruled in 1989 that Haya customary law, which denied women the right to inherit and dispose of clan land, should be overridden by the principles of the Tanzanian Constitution and international conventions that Tanzania had signed.[41]

International declarations and covenants are important, partly because governments often sign them for a variety of reasons, even if they also often intend to disregard them. Soviet and Eastern European dissidents made good use of the 1975 Helsinki Agreement with its 'third basket' of human rights. But international human rights charters and covenants themselves have been criticized by feminists for failing to take real account of women's rights. There are a number of issues. One central concern reflects the feminist critiques of the distinction between the public and private realms upheld by mainstream liberalism, since the oppression of women is often based in the structure of the family.[42] In relation to international law domestic violence is a central issue: for example, Rhonda Copelon argues that it should be understood as torture.[43] Women lawyers have also argued vigorously for rape during war to be treated as a war crime.[44] In response to the systematic Serbian rape of Muslim women in Bosnia, the first case before the International Criminal Tribunal for the former Yugoslavia dealing exclusively with sexual crimes began at the Hague in March 2000.[45]

Feminist attempts to extend international law do not, however, in practice challenge the universal nature of human rights. Rather their intent is to make rights more genuinely universal by taking into account the particular ways in which women are often abused. Women's groups had some success in this enterprise in 1993 when at the UN Vienna Conference they influenced the content of the final document, and in March 1994 the UN Commission on Human Rights called for the monitoring of women's human rights through the UN Human Rights Centre.[46]

There are other rights of women that cannot be addressed by changing international law, but require major changes in national and international social and economic policies. The universal tendency of women to be poorer than men, and their restricted access to even primary education in many developing countries – in 2000 about 90 million girls of primary school age were not in school – and much lower rates of secondary and higher education indicate these problems.[47] There is widespread agreement among many feminists, aid agencies and international governmental organizations about the urgency of tackling women's deprivation, both as a matter of justice and as a means of improving the society and economy in many of the poorest regions.

Most feminist groups around the world recognize the need to establish universal rights and worldwide polices to reduce women's inequality. This does not, however, mean that there is total agreement. Cultural diversity and strikingly different levels of economic development both mean that there is scope for considerable disagreement. The priorities of a liberated western feminist are markedly different from those of a woman in a poor village in Africa. There are also deep ideological divisions on emotive issues, such as abortion, and sensitivities about imposition of western standards on traditional practices. But feminist groups and governmental representatives have found that it is possible through dialogue to reach agreement on general principles, such as seeking to combat violence against women, and to relate these principles to varying social circumstances. (See the discussion of the 1995 Beijing Conference in Chapter 4.)

In western feminist theory the continuing inequality of women (though measured at a qualitatively different level from the fate of the majority of women in many parts of Asia and Africa) has since the 1980s quite often been framed by an exploration of the meanings of citizenship. The search for specifically feminist conceptions of citizenship also opens up the question whether feminist approaches are sympathetic to the idea of global citizenship.

Citizenship and global citizenship in feminist thought

There are many varieties of feminist thought and diverse approaches to the topic of citizenship, so simple generalizations are not possible. Earlier feminists usually embraced either liberal or socialist ideas, although insisting on full recognition of women's rights and women's equality. Second wave feminists in the West initially also accepted broadly liberal or socialist ideologies, though underlining how far both liberal and socialist states had failed to deliver fully on women's liberation. Socialist feminist critiques centred on the existing socialist states. This discussion has been overtaken by the demise of almost all these states, although the impact of unrestrained capitalism on the former Soviet Union, Eastern Europe and even in China suggests that women have tended to become more unequal economically, socially and politically.

The strategy suggested by liberal feminists involved extending the rights of women through eliminating barriers to higher education and employment, granting married women full independent legal status, and policies of affirmative action. To tackle the special problems of single mothers, of women carers of the disabled or elderly, of widows or women pensioners, feminists generally looked to the state to provide more generous benefits. This strategy built on Marshall's concept of social rights as a crucial element of citizenship and meshed with the ideas and values of social liberalism. A possible danger, discussed by feminists, is that women's behaviour may be regulated and they may be treated as weak and dependent by state policies.[48] But emphasis on rights, and eliminating bureaucratic tendencies to treat women as dependants of men, could tilt the balance towards strengthening women's equal citizenship. This social liberal strategy in relation to women's rights also fitted well with the ethos and laws of the EU, and, as noted in Chapter 6, both the European Court of Human Rights and the European Court interpreting EU law have generally strengthened the position of women.

On a global scale a social liberal policy that incorporates specific rights for women is much harder to implement. The priority is to promote change in the global economy in ways that will strengthen developing countries and specifically empower women. The goal, however, is to extend women's social and economic rights and to make it possible for women to become equal citizens. In the meanwhile, as argued above, emphasis on women's rights as individuals under international law does strengthen their independent status and citizenship within their own countries. If the appeal is to international law, in this sense women become global citizens as bearers of transnational rights if the appeal can be enforced.

Many feminists since the 1970s have, however, concluded that liberalism, including social liberalism, cannot enable women to become genuinely independent and equal citizens. This school of thought was originally labelled radical feminism, though more recently feminists have been wary of this and other labels. The fundamental claim of these theorists was that women's oppression was much more deep-rooted than liberal feminists had recognized and that patriarchal structures shaped all societies and even apparently egalitarian and emancipatory ideologies. Andrea Dworkin and Catherine MacKinnon focused on violence against women, rape and pornography as instruments of masculine control.[49] Shulamith Firestone reinterpreted Marxist categories to claim that the fundamental class conflict is between men and women.[50] Carole Pateman drew on Freud to argue provocatively that the liberal social contract overthrowing patriarchal political rule was simultaneously a fraternal contract to share and subordinate all women. Pateman, writing as a political theorist with a long-term interest in social equality and democracy, was particularly interested in relating women's subordination in sexual and family life to their lack of full citizenship.[51]

This focus on women's common vulnerability and inequality is universalist in approach. For example, women universally face the threat of domestic violence (including being killed by husbands or relatives) and the threat of rape, including systematic rape in war.[52] Pateman's analysis is focused on western political thought and social practices in the English-speaking world, but its thrust has wider implications. She suggests that the subordination of women and the failure to take note of women's major contribution to society, because much of it takes place within the private sphere, does have implications for women in developing countries. She notes that the UN System of National Accounts makes exactly the same assumptions about the division between public and private, production and housework, as in the West. The UN system excluded not only all domestic work but other women's activities such as carrying water, gathering firewood and subsistence crop production – as opposed to commercial agriculture.[53] Pateman concludes that to take account of women's contribution to the economy would require questioning patriarchal institutions just as taking account of women's contribution to the welfare state would in the West.

Theorists who fall into this loosely defined school of 'radical feminism' tend therefore to suggest that women share common forms of oppression that cross both class boundaries and national frontiers. The factors that unite women can be politically transformed into belief in global sisterhood, and might therefore suggest that subordinate citizenship at home encourages transnational action. But focusing on women's wrongs does not necessarily suggest a broader concept of women as global citizens acting on other world issues.

The idea that class or groups may from the very fact of their subordination see more clearly what is wrong with the world, and see their own emancipation as part of a wider transformation of society, is, however, deep-rooted. As we noted in the Introduction to this part of the book, Virginia Woolf, writing in the 1930s, did suggest that women, excluded from patriarchal institutions, were better placed to see through the dangerous myths of nationalism and the passions leading to war. Because women have 'no country', their 'country is the world'.[54] Moreover, because through their roles as sweethearts, wives, mothers and sisters, and their quasi-domestic jobs, such as nurses, they nurtured not only men's bodies but also their self-esteem, Woolf argued that women had a duty to refuse cooperation in time of war and to withdraw those essential support systems on which men and warriors rely.

The cultural conditioning that is linked to women's biological roles has been seen as a positive basis for women's global citizenship by a group of feminist theorists stressing the differences between women and men, and women's distinctive moral and political attitudes. These theorists include Carol Gilligan, well known for arguing that women tend to adopt an ethic of care rather than stressing impartial justice, and Sara Ruddick, who argues that the role of mothering gives women a more nurturing and cooperative outlook on political issues than men.[55] Women activists in the peace and environmental movements have also sometimes argued that women are inclined to value peace highly, whereas men are more likely to be drawn to both the violence and the technology of warfare. The best-known symbol of this stance was the 1980s' women-only peace camp at the Greenham Common missile base in England.[56]

There have also been striking examples of women acting specifically as mothers intervening in politics on behalf of their children, for example Russian mothers protesting against the Chechen War in the mid-1990s.[57] The mothers (and grandmothers) in Argentina and Chile, demonstrating on behalf of their children who were kidnapped, tortured and murdered – the 'disappeared' – under the reign of terror of military regimes, have also had a potent impact on campaigns for human rights in these countries.[58]

Some feminist political theorists have developed the view that women think and act differently to delineate a new concept of citizenship. Posing a radical challenge to the public/private divide of orthodox political thought, Jean Bethke Elshtain in her earlier writings suggested that maternal thinking could alter public political values. She did, however, stress that maternal thinking needs to be transformed by feminist consciousness.[59] Many other feminists have, however, argued strongly against using a model of maternalism as the basis for suggesting women have a different kind of morality from men or that they approach politics quite differently. Some have queried the reliability of the research suggesting women think differently about moral issues.[60] Others have argued that the role of mothers as traditionally defined has been shaped by patriarchal domination and is not the best starting point for a feminist politics. It is also relevant that traditional styles of mothering vary considerably in different cultures with different family structures. Theorists concerned about the nature of politics and citizenship, notably Mary Dietz, have argued that both the unequal relationship between mother and child, and the nature of intimate relationships, are both unsuited to an ideal of political activity based on equality and a more general approach to collective issues.[61] There is also ample evidence that women can be very nationalistic and strongly support war, endorsing the role of men fighting to protect their families and celebrating male heroism. The famous example in Britain is women handing out white feathers, symbolizing cowardice, to men who did not enlist early in the First World War. Moreover, states have often successfully drawn on maternal images to promote the war effort.[62] This suggests that traditional maternal roles can result in very different political responses.

Whilst all these objections are cogent, it can nevertheless be argued that in practice many women still engage in politics in a rather different way from men. Research suggests that women in the West still tend to be more active in groups within civil society rather than political parties and parliaments.[63] These also tend to be the kind of groups which form transnational links. So women's interests and values do often lead them towards a particular version of citizen activity and one that quite often relates to identification as global citizens.

Critiques of a maternalist version of women's universally shared attitudes and commitments can appeal to a republican version of citizenship. This is true of Dietz, who refers back not to the more explicitly masculine and warlike strands in republicanism, but to Aristotle and to Arendt. But this kind of feminist republicanism, whilst it rejects nationalism, does not lend itself either to a theory of global citizenship. (See brief discussion of Arendt in Chapter 7.)

The more usual criticism of maternalism, however, is based both on rejection of the category of 'women' having a universal meaning and on repudiation of liberal and republican concepts of citizenship that assume a single ideal of citizenship and a single set of political values within the state. The best-known theorist of a politics of difference as the basis for citizenship is Iris Marion Young. Young illustrates how earlier American republicanism was based on both racist and masculinist assumptions, excluding native Americans, African-Americans and Chinese immigrants, and also excluding women. Her response is to argue for a politics based on recognition of racial, ethnic and gender difference, and also differences due to age and disabilities. Each group has its own needs, values and often its own cultural heritage, and therefore it is necessary to represent these differences in the public realm and to promote a dialogue between them. Young's focus is on politics in the USA, and despite her rejection of elements of republicanism her ideal is a highly participatory politics. Her concept of citizenship does not therefore naturally extend to global citizenship.

On the other hand, the group basis of the politics Young recommends does suggest transnational connections between groups. Where these connections are simply with the land of origin of immigrants, a significant feature already in mainstream American politics, the result may simply be to enshrine outdated nationalist images and to bias US foreign policy. But transnational links between indigenous peoples, gays or women may promote transnational campaigns for social justice, and may sometimes involve embracing wider global causes.

Postmodern theories provide the inspiration for a range of feminist criticisms of the universalist assumptions of both radical feminism and maternalism. Young herself, whose theoretical influences are eclectic, draws on Foucault's concept of the 'normalizing gaze' to explain how whiteness and masculinity, identified with reason, repudiate racial and sexual difference, categorized as inferior. But other feminists adopt a more explicitly postmodern stance, influenced by thinkers such as Foucault and Derrida and their critiques of the forms of domination inherent in the Enlightenment. However, feminist postmodernism also emerged out of a wide-ranging feminist interrogation of inherited social theory, including epistemology. Universalism and the emphasis on rationality could be seen as an abstraction from a dominant masculine view of the world, which suppressed the interpretations of subordinated women.

Postmodern feminists argue that radical feminist concepts of patriarchy are oversimplified and 'essentialist', ignoring the diversity of women's actual positions and sometimes unduly pessimistic about the options for change. Moira Gatens and Wendy Brown have applied this kind of criticism to Pateman's concept of a fraternal sexual contract.[64] Secondly, theories such as maternalism, which are rooted in women's gendered identity, appear to restrict women's freedom, whereas theories that reject predetermined identities as creations of male-dominated social power structures suggest women's freedom to define their own identities. There is therefore no universal category of 'women'. Julia Kristeva, the French poststructuralist and feminist, argues that: 'A woman cannot be; it is something which does not even belong in the order of being.'[65]

Postmodern feminists therefore cannot logically see women generically as global citizens, although they certainly do not see them primarily as national citizens. Emphasis on pluralism and difference need not exclude transnational politics. Kimberley Hutchings suggests that even in the case of theories 'which are explicitly critical of moral and political universalism, feminism is committed to being more sympathetic to the cosmopolitan conception of citizenship' than to a 'bounded' national citizenship.[66]

Despite the apparent cogency of postmodern feminist critiques of universalism, other feminists feared that postmodern scepticism challenged the bases of feminist politics both nationally and globally. If there are no valid interpretations of social reality and no objective moral and intellectual bases for claiming justice and rights, what grounds do women have for challenging oppression? Seyla Benhabib argues that a strong postmodernism suggests there are no autonomous individuals (the death of man), no coherent historical narratives for groups seeking political change (the death of history) and no objective grounds for criticizing society (the death of metaphysics). But this would mean that 'women's agency and sense of selfhood, ... the reappropriation of women's own history in the name of an emancipated future, and ... the exercise of radical social criticism which uncovers gender' would be impossible.[67] Linda Alcoff, noting that Kristeva concludes that 'a feminist practice can only be negative, at odds with what already exists', asks how feminists can mobilize a movement based solely on negative struggle. She also argues that deconstruction of the female subject 'threatens to wipe out feminism itself'.[68]

It is in this context interesting to note that when Kristeva confronts the problems of resurgent neo-Nazism in Germany and increasing resentment of North African immigrants in France – a resentment mobilized by the National Front – she turns to two French Enlightenment thinkers, to Montesquieu in particular and also to Diderot, to provide a theoretical basis for attacking racism and advocating recognition of difference.[69] She claims to speak 'as a cosmopolitan' and suggests that the French Declaration of the Rights of Man and Citizen, despite its limitations, upholds 'a universal, transnational principle of Humanity ... a continuation of the Stoic and Augustinian legacy, of that ancient and Christian cosmopolitanism that finds its place among the most valuable assets of our civilization' that we must 'go back to and bring up to date'. This can form 'a rampart against a nationalist, regionalist, and religious fragmentation'.[70]

Kristeva also appears to generalize about the special role of women as 'boundary subjects: body and thought, biology and language, ... nation and world', which has psychological dangers and can turn women into 'accomplices of religious fundamentalisms and mystical nationalism', but also affords opportunities. So the 'maturity of the second sex will be judged in coming years according to its ability to modify the nation in the face of foreigners, to orient foreigners confronting the nation toward a still unforeseeable conception of a polyvalent community'.[71]

Postmodernism and cosmopolitanism

There are a number of possible strategies that those believing in cosmopolitanism can adopt in response to poststructuralist and postmodern critiques. Two of the main strategies of argument are either to focus on perceived incoherencies in the logic of postmodern theories, or to focus on their alleged reactionary or even nihilist political implications. An alternative approach, adopted by Linklater in his book *The Transformation of Political Community*, is to suggest that the gulf between cosmopolitan universalism and postmodernism has been greatly exaggerated.

In his defence of the Enlightenment and modernity Habermas has argued that various postmodern theorists who engage in 'the radical critique of reason ... can and want to give no account of their own position'. They avoid being identified with clear categories of thought or giving grounds for their position. Foucault 'refuses to draw conclusions from manifest contradictions' and Derrida flees 'into the esoteric' or fuses 'the logical with the rhetorical'.[72] Secondly, Habermas argues that (poststructuralist) theorists like Foucault and Derrida implicitly use normative criteria that they do not acknowledge in their explicit theories.[73] Habermas has not directly commented on Lyotard, but other thinkers have compared the two to conclude that Lyotard's argument 'depends on a form of shared rationality that it wishes to deny'.[74]

Postmodern theorists tend to claim that they are espousing individual freedom and resistance against 'totalizing' theories and totalitarian political tendencies. But theories that dissolve the concept of the self, and treat explanations of the social world as incompatible discourses, are not well placed to provide a coherent understanding of freedom. Linklater, examining the claim by postmodern international relations theorists Richard Ashley and Rob Walker to espouse an ethic of freedom, comments that 'if the aim is to question established meanings … to disturb all efforts to speak with a sovereign voice … then it is difficult to know why an ethic of freedom should be preferred to an ethic of domination'.[75] Habermas has indeed argued that postmodernists lack a moral or theoretical basis from which to oppose structures of power and that therefore their theories in effect are conservative. Benhabib, cited above, makes a similar point about the implications of postmodernism for feminist politics.

But Linklater's basic strategy towards postmodern critics of universalism is to argue that they do in fact embrace universalism of a sort. He bases this argument partly on the insistence of critics that postmodernists rely, in Richard Bernstein's words, on 'a hidden form of universality', and partly on a distinction between exclusionary and non-exclusionary forms of universalism. The latter is not defined but presumably relates to recognition of difference. Linklater also observes that Foucault and Derrida are, like Habermas, exploring what is still relevant in the thought of Kant and Marx and 'offer variations on the theme of the Enlightenment project'.[76] He notes too that Habermas himself rejects the grand historical narratives of Hegel and Marx, and is concerned to recognize the importance of difference, and suggests that both critical theorists and postmodernists like Lyotard support 'the ideal of communities of discourse'.[77]

Convergence seems improbable, given the gulf between Habermas's view that language can ideally lead to consensus and *either* Derrida's deconstructive view that language is 'ineradicably marked by instability and indeterminacy of meaning', *or* Lyotard's insistence that language 'begins and ends with dissension'.[78] Linklater is not alone, however, in seeing some linkage between Habermas and Derrida. Michael Naes, in his introduction to Derrida's *The Other Heading*, comments that Derrida argues for the necessity of working for Enlightenment values of liberal democracy 'while recalling that these values are never enough to ensure respect for the other'.[79] Christopher Norris rejects the view that Derrida is promoting 'a species of last-ditch irrationalism', and argues instead that he is operating 'within the tradition of Kantian enlightened critique, even while pressing that tradition to the limits (and beyond) of its own self-legitimizing claims'. Norris then suggests that Derrida has begun to show 'signs of convergence' with Habermas, even though there is no 'simple equivalence of method or aim' between them. In pursuing this argument, however, Norris suggests that there is total disagreeement between Lyotard and Derrida.[80] Linklater's approach, therefore, does tend to iron out too neatly significant disagreements between all the theorists he is discussing.

The most illuminating way to pursue the discussion in this chapter, however, is to follow up the final line of argument pursued by Linklater, in which he cites evidence to demonstrate that a number of postmodern thinkers have specifically endorsed cosmopolitanism at some point. The issue I wish to examine is whether these political interventions arise coherently from their wider theory, or illustrate a break between theory and specific political argument. My examples, which overlap with Linklater's, are: Foucault's 1981 appeal to the rights and duties of international citizenship in relation to the plight of Vietnamese boat people; and the lectures by both Lyotard and Rorty for Amnesty International in 1993.

Given Foucault's understanding of power, it is hard to see, as many critics have pointed out, how it can be resisted and what scope there is for political action to bring about change. But Foucault did suggest that power generates resistance – 'There is no power without potential refusal or revolt'[81] – and noted the importance in contemporary society of resistance based on individual experience – resistance of women to men or of the mentally ill to psychiatry. Foucault himself supported such localized resistance, and was active with a group campaigning for the rights of prisoners.

But, given his rejection of liberal ideas and general theoretical approach, it is startling to discover that Foucault, attending a UN conference on piracy in 1981 with friends from *Médecins du Monde*, gave a brief speech about the plight of the Vietnamese boat people (affected by piracy). He said:

> There is such a thing as an international citizenship which has its rights, which has its duties and which implies a commitment to rise up against any abuse of power. ... One of the duties of international citizenship is to reveal human misery to the eyes and ears of government.

Foucault also claimed that bodies like Amnesty International and *Médecins du Monde* have created a new right: 'the right of private individuals to intervene effectively in the order of international policies and strategies'.[82] David Macey, who quotes this document, suggests that Foucault's address can be seen as the basis for asserting a general right to intervene in other countries in the name of human rights – though whether Foucault himself would have accepted this generalization is questionable. Foucault does rest his claim to human solidarity on the fact that 'After all, we are all governed, and by that token, our fates are bound together', suggesting a negative bond rather than an appeal to what human beings have in common. But otherwise this sounds like a cosmopolitan manifesto, making liberal distinctions between individuals and governments. Even allowing for the changing emphasis of Foucault's later theory,[83] his adoption of the language of international citizenship and rights suggests a gap between his general theorizing and this particular political stance, which might also suggest that his theory did not provide a satisfactory basis for his political commitments.

Lyotard is the most extreme postmodern sceptic – Peter Beilharz comments that 'Lyotard (more so than, say, Foucault) is plainly Habermas's opponent' despite the fact Habermas does not directly mention Lyotard in his *Philosophical Discourse*.[84] So it is particularly interesting to see how Lyotard approaches the Amnesty lectures. He starts from Hannah Arendt's reflections on human rights in *The Origins of Totalitarianism*: 'It seems that a man who is nothing but a man has lost the very qualities which make it possible for others to treat him as a fellow man.'[85] Lyotard then develops the argument that a sense of common humanity depends upon recognition of difference, and that human language involves the ability to distinguish both similarity and disparity – as in 'I' and 'you'. He then pursues the Arendtian theme that citizenship presupposes the republican principle that the citizen has a recognized right to address others. But this principle can be made universal so that it is possible 'to extend interlocution to any human individual whatsoever, regardless of natural or national idiom' – different languages can be translated. Lyotard suggests that the capacity to speak to others is 'perhaps the most fundamental human right'.[86] To be forcibly silenced is to be excluded from human community. In politics silence is associated with despotism and being forgotten associated with terror. The role of Amnesty International is to 'restore the victim to the community of speakers'.[87]

Although Lyotard's philosophy is concerned with language, the thrust of his Amnesty lecture runs counter to his emphasis on competing 'language games' and irresolvable conflicts. James Williams gives an example from Lyotard's study of the conflict between legal language in court and the plight of a plaintiff who cannot testify to the wrong suffered because there is no adequate language – for example to prove rape where a culture does not recognize the concept. He then comments on the conflict between the language game of human rights and the language game of reasons of state, which might justify internment without trial.[88] Lyotard suggests these language games are necessarily 'incommensurable' – they cannot be resolved into a common overarching language or be resolved by common criteria of judgement. In his Amnesty lecture, however, he seems to appeal to a unifying capacity for speech as a basis for universal human rights. Moreover, his general position is to reject the possibility of any fixed political programme or values; instead the philosopher can only bear witness to unpredictable events.[89] There does therefore seem to be a significant conflict between Lyotard's general postmodern philosophy and approach to politics, and his particular reflections in support of Amnesty International.

Rorty and Lyotard are in agreement in repudiating 'grand narratives' and the search for absolute truths. But, unlike Lyotard, Rorty does not believe that this casts doubt on 'the possibility (as opposed to the difficulty) of peaceful social progress'.[90] There is no gap between general theory and specific politics in Rorty's Amnesty lecture, but this lecture, which relies heavily on the need for a 'sentimental education' to extend support for human rights, reveals how unsatisfactory his own theory is to support his belief in human solidarity and cosmopolitanism.

Rorty is well known for advocating that we stop worrying about the philosophical foundations of our political and ethical beliefs. Ironists like himself face up to the inevitable contingency of their beliefs – there are no final answers to moral questions. Although Rorty is seen as the leading American exponent of postmodernism, he draws on a much earlier American philosophical tradition of Deweyan pragmatism, which upheld liberalism whilst abandoning the attempt to find transhistorical foundations for it.

Rorty dismisses the search for a human essence – such as a common ability to reason – when supporting the goal of human solidarity, and denies the possibility of 'identification with "humanity as such" '.[91] He believes 'that our sense of solidarity is strongest when those with whom solidarity is expressed are thought of as "one of us" ' – for example a fellow American. Therefore he rejects the kind of universalism that suggests that we should feel as strongly about a slum dweller in India as a neighbour. But he does see moral progress as extending 'our sense of "we" to people whom we have previously thought of as "they" '.[92] This extending identification involves a sense that feeling pain or humiliation transcends differences of religion, race or culture. Awareness of the suffering of others is promoted by an appeal to emotions, and therefore both art and journalism are more relevant to fostering this sentiment of identification than is philosophy. Rorty is arguing in particular against Kant's rigorous account of unemotional moral obligation to other rational beings.

Many cosmopolitan thinkers would not disagree with Rorty that our response to the pain of others is an important element in human solidarity. (See the discussion in Chapter 7.) But they are likely to argue for the necessity of a universalist and reason-based approach to morality. Vincent draws on J.S. Mill to argue for

> a view of the discussion of human rights in international politics as appeal-
> ing to the empire of reason and not merely that of power ... no human
> being can seriously hold some ethical principle to be right, or imperative,
> without wishing that others too deem it right or imperative.[93]

If we follow Rorty, why should we uphold the human rights of those for whom we feel *no* emotional sympathy? Rorty clearly believes that we should feel such sympathy for all human beings, but also stresses the tendency to categorize groups of people as subhuman.

Rorty does suggest that since the Holocaust a 'human rights culture' has developed, and sees it as a sign of progress. Although it 'may be just a blip', it may also mark the beginning of true human solidarity.[94] But it is not clear whether Rorty thinks this human rights culture, which he relates to the historical extension of liberalism, has moral purchase outside the West. Since he explicitly seeks to uphold an Enlightenment spirit whilst rejecting most Enlightenment philosophy (he approves of Hume's approach to morality), his writings do not really challenge cosmopolitanism. But in rejecting arguments from universalism and the political relevance of reasoned justification, he tends to undermine it.

How, then, should cosmopolitan theorists respond to the challenge from postmodernism? Linklater is correct in pointing out the variety of 'postmodern' responses to cosmopolitanism, and the political sympathy of noted postmodern theorists for Enlightenment and cosmopolitan values. But it is surely misleading to suggest that there is a significant theoretical convergence between any of these thinkers and Habermas. It is also misleading to suggest that French poststructuralists or postmodernists can offer *theoretical* support for cosmopolitan political conclusions. Rather they are cosmopolitans *malgré eux*.

Moreover, the issue is not only what ideas the most influential postmodern theorists have actually articulated, but what the much wider group of those drawing on postmodernism think are the major conclusions, and the resultant implications for attitudes to truth, morality and political responsibility. Postmodernism can suggest either a radical scepticism, or academic frivolity in playing with language, or greater interest in 'cultural politics' than in issues of oppression.[95] Some postmodern theorists in international relations are also explicitly sceptical about cosmopolitanism and global citizenship.

Postmodernism, international relations and global citizenship

The poststructuralist and postmodern critics of mainstream approaches in international relations tend to be particularly critical of the theory underlying the realist concept of systemic international anarchy. In the case of James Der Derian this analytical demolition job is designed to rescue an older strand of 'Ulyssean' realism based on prudential political experience and a sense of the moral tragedy underlying public life – he names Reinhold Niebuhr, George Kennan and Hans Morgenthau.[96] But others see their undermining of existing theory promoting a radical politics.

Ashley and Walker urge a radical scepticism concerning historical and analytical judgements about the nature of international politics, as well as about criteria for moral judgements. They suggest that this opens up 'a space of freedom – freedom for thought, for political action'. They also suggest that dissident feminist, ecological and peace movements are reflected in the new theoretical questioning of how to study international relations.[97] But whilst they offer prospects of radical change, Ashley and Walker do not offer much support for cosmopolitanism or global citizenship.

Indeed, Walker criticizes Linklater's arguments for global citizenship. He comments on the inevitable tensions in trying to reconcile our national citizenship with our cosmopolitan humanity, and agrees with Linklater that national citizenship as understood in modern political thought is inadequate 'to reconcile our political being with our being as humans'.[98] But he does not accept what he sees as Linklater's solution, which locates citizenship within an account of an emerging cosmopolitan community with a hierarchy of international and national political units. Whilst admitting this interpretation makes sense of the EU, and also allows for a 'thin' cosmopolitanism (as envisaged by Walzer) that may become 'thicker' over time, Walker does not believe that it solves the problems of identity in the contemporary world. He cites feminist, postcolonial and poststructuralist critiques of the modern liberal concept of 'the individual/human subject' and queries the relationship between the individual subject and both other subjects and 'some common or even universal humanity'. He suggests both individual identity and collective identities such as the nation state 'are being unbundled and differentiated'.[99] New forms of inclusion and exclusion, which may not be defined by territorial boundaries, are being created. Walker dismisses the idea of 'some half-remembered, half-foreseen cosmopolis' that harks back to the premodern era.[100] Although he is specifically commenting on Linklater, his observations apply more directly to Held's advocacy of global institutions of cosmopolitan democracy, based on the concept of 'autonomy, both for individuals as citizens, and for the collectivity'.[101] Linklater's position, which stresses recognition of difference and the role of dialogic communities, is, in his own view, somewhat closer to postmodernism.

A specific attack on cosmopolitanism occurs in an article by Michael Dillon and Julia Reid in a special issue on postmodern theorizing of international relations in the journal *Alternatives*. Dillon and Reid attack the disciplinary implications of the term 'global governance' and the associated concepts of liberal (or democratic) peace, global civil society and the rule of international law. They contend that 'the liberal peace of global governance' has to be understood as 'a complex hybrid form of power', which 'has no single source that might be located and cut off'.[102]

They are explicitly drawing on Foucault, who explores in his writings on madness, modes of punishment and the history of sexuality the thesis that power is not something that can be seized or acquired and is not located in a single 'headquarters' or governing caste, but is 'immanent' in economic relations, sexual relations and relations of knowledge.[103] Therefore, although the state is important, it rests on other power relations. Foucault argued: 'The State is superstructural in relation to a whole series of power networks that invest the body, sexuality, the family, kinship, knowledge, technology and so forth.'[104] Power, therefore, is all-pervasive, creating social definitions of normality, and 'discourses' defining truth and rationality are modes of constraint.

Dillon and Reid comment on 'discourses' emerging out of 'liberal peace': 'No political formulation is therefore innocent. None refers to a truth about the world that pre-exists the truth's entry into the world through discourse.'[105] They also follow Foucault in interpreting civil society as a medium for exercising disciplinary power – not an arena of creative resistance – and therefore dubbing global civil society as part of the power complex of global governance. Dillon and Reid do distinguish between Kantian and 'technocratic-capitalist variants' of global governance, but the general thrust of their article is to see the two approaches as complementary. They cite Falk's analysis of the Commission on Global Governance, but effectively deny the validity of his emphasis on the role of global civil society in combating the power of global corporations and neo-liberal ideology. Whilst there may be occasions when the language of human rights organizations, for example, does promote a rhetoric that helps legitimize the more questionable examples of humanitarian intervention, Dillon and Reid do not recognize the critical role such bodies also adopt. Cosmopolitanism therefore becomes an undifferentiated 'discourse' justifying coercive processes of globalization, not a basis for political change.

Conclusion

The central thesis of this chapter is that in a world of increasing interdependence a fragile, but nevertheless socially significant, moral consciousness is developing across cultures and influencing international politics. This consciousness, and the international agreements that both reflect and help create it, are the outcome of political debate and compromise between governments of states, but most crucially between representatives of civil societies within states creating transnational understanding. I have argued that this is true both in relation to human rights in general and in relation to the rights of women. This emerging consciousness is a historical political and legal construct, but it appeals to universal principles. Without this universality it would lose its moral and political force, and insofar as it is based on debate it rests upon reasoned argument and agreement. This debate can also distinguish, as Habermas suggests, between justification of general principles and the precise application of these principles to differing circumstances.[106]

This sense of an evolving acceptance of universal norms is challenged by theories associated with postmodernism, which claim to reject the Enlightenment heritage and its confidence in the possibility of objective truth, the role of reason, moral universalism and historical progress.

I have suggested that poststructural or postmodern theorists, if they engage seriously in politics, also tend to fall back on Enlightenment values and rights claims. Moreover, even postcolonial or postmodern feminist writers, sensitive to forms of thought that assume western or masculine superiority, and so operate to exclude the culturally different, often find a genuine cosmopolitanism and cultural openness in some Enlightenment theorists, notably Montesquieu. Enlightenment thought needs to be related to our present understanding and circumstances, but it is an important contribution to global political practice and underpins a concept of global citizenship.

Conclusion

This book has charted the evolution of cosmopolitan thought in the social context of a trend towards globalization and the growth of a global civil society. It suggests that we are moving beyond an international society of increasing intergovernmental cooperation towards a more cosmopolitan world, in which individuals have rights and duties under international law, and political activity increasingly transcends national frontiers.

It would be neat, therefore, to propose a metanarrative of cosmopolitanism emerging out of modernity; but such a claim would be misleading in a number of crucial ways. It would ignore the extent to which globalization also encourages anti-cosmopolitan reactions, such as an exclusive nationalism. It would also ignore the extraordinarily destructive potential of technological changes, which are at some levels creating global unity, but could also end up destroying the world. Although common threats add an extra impetus for global cooperation, it is no longer possible to believe in necessary progress.

Moreover, the forces that have tended to unify the world have often simultaneously been politically and economically oppressive. Direct and indirect imperialism has served to create some of the social conditions that favour cosmopolitanism – for example the present emergence of English as a global language. But it has also imposed the interests of the West on other peoples and brought not only oppression but also destruction. The present suspicion that cosmopolitan ideals are a guise for western imperialism is a response to this past – though I have argued that a truly cosmopolitan commitment to respect individual rights and cultural diversity entails opposition to all forms of imperialism.

Even more importantly, the present processes of globalization tend to favour the interests of powerful multinational corporations at the expense of the well-being of the vast majority of people and of the natural environment. A neo-liberal theory of the global economy celebrates a free market and the breaking down of national barriers, but justifies a system that results in extremes of wealth and poverty. Despite its global scope and internationalist claims, neo-liberalism as it is applied through international institutions such as the International Monetary Fund and the World Trade Organization tends to be opposed to a cosmopolitanism based on belief in human equality. The criticisms of neo-liberal policies by governments of developing countries and transnational movements have had a limited impact on international organizations such as the World Bank, but have not so far fundamentally altered policy.

Prediction of the future is impossible because of the role of contingency, but also because of the scope for autonomous political action to influence events. Such action may take unexpected turns and in some cases is likely to constitute rebellion against global trends. On the other hand, political action provides the greatest hope that globalization will lead to a world in which cosmopolitan values are respected. Many individuals do choose to take part in transnational politics to promote human rights, reduce poverty, preserve the environment and limit conflict. Participation in global social movements, or in agencies offering relief or aid, is at present the most obvious expression of active global citizenship.

Global citizenship suggests that all should enjoy not only moral but also legal rights. The extension of international law, which has an influence on judicial decisions within countries – especially if international conventions are incorporated in national law – is beginning to create such rights, though as yet very imperfectly. The process is most advanced in Europe, where individuals can appeal directly to the European Court of Human Rights in Strasbourg or to the EU European Court of Justice in Luxemburg. National governments may also be criticized by international bodies such as the UN Human Rights Committee.

The plight of refugees fleeing oppression and desperate to secure a place to live illustrates the attempt to entrench minimum rights in law, but also underlines the political difficulties of both preventing oppression and ensuring that all those in need do find asylum. The continuing debate about migration indicates tentative moves towards extending citizen rights to non-nationals and creating a form of transnational citizenship. But it also highlights national resistance in affluent areas to the very poor being allowed to enter and seek work. Skilled and professional workers are often more welcome immigrants. But this also raises ethical problems, if those trained in poorer countries are enticed by higher salaries to fill jobs in the most developed societies. Cosmopolitanism does imply freedom of movement, but freedom to live and work anywhere in the world can only be practicable if there is not a huge gulf between rich and poor, and it can only conduce to general welfare if the same conditions apply. So migration policies need to be linked to economic development.

Given the central role still played by national governments, issues relating to asylum and migration must be satisfactorily resolved by cooperation between states and through international agreements that are honoured. This suggests that the concept of states as 'good international citizens' is extremely relevant. It also suggests that a view of global citizenship that sees it as an extra dimension of national citizenship, holding governments to account for their international policies, is critical to achieving cosmopolitan goals.

Stressing the role of national governments within international society is not incompatible with seeking to ensure human rights, prevent or limit wars, maintain the environment and promote greater wealth in the less developed regions. Indeed, as theorists such as Wendt, Kymlicka and Hirst and Thompson have stressed, effective international action to achieve such goals depends on competent and responsible states. Even theorists of cosmopolitan democracy, who emphasize the erosion of national borders and state competencies, still see states as, in Daniele Archibugi's words, the political institutions that 'constitute the world's major depositories of power'.[1]

Emphasis on the continuing role of nation states is also compatible with the development of international law that holds individuals, including leading government figures, accountable for flagrant breaches of international law. The International Tribunals for ex-Yugoslavia and Rwanda focused on genocide and crimes against humanity, but in the future this principle might be extended to mass destruction of the environment. Recognizing the importance of states is also compatible with willingness to contribute to UN peace keeping, to apply sanctions or to intervene within states if major violations of human rights occur – though how sanctions should be applied, and what methods of military intervention are justifiable, need to be rigorously debated.[2] But international society between states need not rest on strict state sovereignty, and can coexist with a cosmopolitan layer focused on the rights and responsibilities of individuals.

Civil society bodies, and in particular social movements, are well equipped to operate simultaneously within the state and within international society by lobbying and cooperating with international organizations, and to focus on individual rights and responsibilities at a global level. Moreover, given the importance of global economic activity, individuals as consumers and investors can play a consciously political role in seeking economic justice, preserving the environment or boycotting companies that sell arms.

Republican and communitarian critics of the idea of global citizenship argue that such activities fall well short of what is implied by citizenship. Global citizenship in the strong sense of having supranational political rights would be possible if there were moves towards an elected UN world assembly, recommended by advocates of cosmopolitan democracy. Even if a world parliament were possible – which at present seems very unlikely – there is a danger that such a body would amplify the negative aspects of national assemblies and be too huge, remote and unwieldy to realize the benefits of parliamentary institutions. The example of the European Parliament, which indicates mass apathy among electors and a strong tendency among elected members to amass the perquisites of office, is not so far encouraging. The monitoring of the finances and performance of international organizations can probably be done much better by small and specialized bodies, which could issue public reports. Redress of individual and group complaints can be met by international versions of the ombudsman or in some cases by courts.

The cosmopolitan democrats are, however, correct to point to the potential for increasing transnational political action – by political parties and trade unions as well as by social movements or oppressed groups like indigenous peoples. There may also be much greater scope for *ad hoc* popular assemblies to debate particular issues, for cross-border advisory referenda or for permanent sub-national institutions to promote transnational cooperation on issues such as transport and the environment.

The role of regional bodies like the EU is of particular interest. Regional organization can potentially promote area interests, create greater stability where nation states are disintegrating into much smaller ethnic entities, and provide forums for political decision-making and transnational citizenship. Regional measures of arms limitation can also pave the way for more general agreements. But regional bodies may also encourage economic and migration policies designed to defend their members' interests to the exclusion of the needs of other parts of the world, and therefore obstruct international goals. Despite the existence of a number of regional organizations, they are not likely, for a range of reasons, to move towards the degree of economic and political integration accomplished by the EU.

Citizenship within the EU does approximate to a strong concept of citizenship, incorporating not only legally guaranteed civil and social and economic rights, but also political rights and at least minimal symbols of citizen identity. But many commentators deny that it constitutes citizenship in the fullest sense, particularly as it involves no specific European duties and no real sense of a shared community. Therefore it is even less likely that a status of global citizenship can ever fulfil rigorous criteria of citizenship. By definition it cannot meet one criterion suggested by some theorists – exclusivity of rights and duties.

But, as I have argued throughout the book, the concept of global citizenship is far from meaningless. It captures the trend in international law and politics to move beyond exclusive focus on sovereign states to the rights and responsibilities of individuals. It also indicates the increasing role of individuals acting through a range of organizations within global civil society and the increasing political significance of this transnational phenomenon. In addition it serves as an ideal of individual concern and commitment at a global as well as a national and local level. Global citizenship challenges earlier distinctions between the public and private, since, as theorists of ecological citizenship have noted, effective action can be taken as consumers and householders, as well protesters and voters, to promote environmental and other goals.

Theoretical support for the idea of global citizenship can be traced in the western tradition to the Stoics, is underpinned by natural law and found expression in the early modern era in theorists like Erasmus and exponents of European or world organization. Cosmopolitanism received its strongest expression in the Enlightenment. But from the nineteenth century until today, ideas and values conducive to global citizenship have been developed in strands of liberalism, socialism and feminism and more recently environmental thought, as well as in the more explicitly cosmopolitan thought of those influenced by Kant and in Habermas's discourse ethics and theory of deliberative democracy. In international relations theory, liberal and Kantian approaches that reject realism usually underpin the concept of an international society between states or a cosmopolitan connection between individuals.

There are ideological positions totally opposed to the possibility of global citizenship. These include some forms of conservatism and nationalism and exponents of realism. From these perspectives the role and the particular interests of the nation state are still paramount. Republican and communitarian critics of cosmopolitanism, on the other hand, may query the extent and implications of globalization, and focus on membership of a cultural community, but do not deny that there are transnational moral claims. Even the poststructuralist and postmodern critics of Kant and the Enlightenment, or those intellectuals who see cosmopolitan claims acting as a form of imperialism, often tend – despite their theoretical scepticism – to endorse a politics suggesting belief in human dignity and equality.

There is not a single political theory of global citizenship or a single model of what global citizenship entails. Rather there is a spectrum of theories, with somewhat different interpretations of global citizenship and overlapping interpretations of cosmopolitanism. What global citizenship can mean in terms of different kinds of activity is still emerging in the realm of transnational politics.

Notes

Introduction

1 *Peace News*, no. 2424, April 1998, p. 3.
2 *Guardian*, 3 December 1999, p. 15.
3 Amanda Meade, 'Global Citizen Seeks Compassion for Refugees', *The Australian*, 24 June 1996, p. 2.
4 See Emily Moore, 'Going Global', *Guardian Education*, 21 September 1999, p. 9. A range of materials promoting a global dimension to the teaching of citizenship in schools is now available. See *Oxfam GC Link Bulletin: Keeping in Touch with Global Citizenship Issues*, no. 6, September 2000, pp. 1–2.
5 *Global Citizen: The International Newsletter of Charter 99*, no. 1, March 2000, p. 1.
6 See, for example, Charles Beitz, 'Cosmopolitan Ideals and National Sentiments', *Journal of Philosophy*, vol. 80, 1983, pp. 591–600; Onora O'Neill, 'Transnational Justice', in D. Held, ed., *Political Theory Today*, Cambridge, Polity, 1991; J. Thompson, *Justice and World Order: A Philosophical Enquiry*, London, Routledge, 1992.
7 John Rawls, *The Law of Peoples*, Cambridge, Mass., Harvard University Press, 1999.
8 Derek Heater, *Citizenship: The Civic Ideal in World History, Politics and Education*, London, Longman, 1990; *World Citizenship and Government: Cosmopolitan Ideas in the History of Western Political Thought*, Basingstoke, Macmillan, 1996; R.A. Falk, 'The Making of Global Citizenship', in B. Van Steenbergen, ed., *The Condition of Citizenship*, London, Sage, 1994, pp. 127–40.
9 See Martha C. Nussbaum, 'Patriotism and Cosmopolitanism', in Martha C. Nussbaum *et al.*, *For Love of Country*, edited by Joshua Cohen, Boston, Beacon Press, 1996, pp. 3–17 and 'Kant and Stoic Cosmopolitanism', *Journal of Political Philosophy*, vol. 5, no. 1, 1997, pp. 1–25; Andrew Linklater, 'Citizenship and Sovereignty in the Post-Westphalian State', *European Journal of International Relations*, vol. 2, no. 1, 1996, pp. 77–103.
10 David Held, *Democracy and the Global Order*, Cambridge, Polity, 1995.
11 Jürgen Habermas, 'Citizenship and National Identity: Some Reflections on the Future of Europe', *Praxis International*, vol. 12, no. 1, April 1992, pp. 1–19, and 'The European Nation-State and the Pressures of Globalization', *New Left Review*, no. 235, May/June 1999, pp. 46–59.
12 Immanuel Kant, 'Perpetual Peace', in Hans Reiss, ed., *Kant: Political Writings*, 2nd enlarged edition, translated by H.B. Nisbet, Cambridge, Cambridge University Press, 1991, pp. 98–9.
13 For a recent interpretation of cosmopolitanism see Catherine Lu, 'The One and Many Faces of Cosmopolitanism', *Journal of Political Philosophy*, vol. 8, no. 2, June 2000, pp. 244–67. Lu 're-imagines' cosmopolitanism to denote the fragility of being human, with an emphasis on opposing cruelty; solidarity with others; and active opposition to injustice.
14 See, for example, Andrew Hurrell, 'Kant and the Kantian Paradigm in International Relations', *Review of International Studies*, vol. 16, pp. 183–205; Mark N. Franke, 'Immanuel Kant and (Im)possibility of International Relations Theory', *Alternatives*, vol. 20, 1995, pp. 279–322; Wade L. Huntley, 'Kant's Third Image: Systemic Sources of the Liberal Peace', *International Studies Quarterly*, vol. 40, 1996, pp. 45–76. Kant has figured particularly prominently in the debate about whether democratic states are inherently more peaceful and whether liberal democracies fight each other.

15 For discussion of these three models see Hedley Bull, *The Anarchical Society*, Basingstoke, Macmillan, 1977.

16 Michael Randle, 'Ploughing a Deep Furrow', *Guardian Society*, 7 August 1996, p. 5. The women were part of the transnational 'Ploughshares' campaign involving direct action against weapons.

17 *Guardian Weekly*, 26 July 1998, p. 3.

18 'The Pinochet Verdict', *Guardian*, 25 March 1999, pp. 8–9.

19 Elizabeth Nash, 'Spanish Inquiry into Guatemalan Leaders' Crimes', *Independent*, 24 March 2000, p. 17. The human rights campaigner and Nobel Prize-winner Rigoberta Menchu lodged the accusations in December 1999.

20 See W. Kymlicka and W. Norman, 'Return of the Citizen: A Survey of Recent Work on Citizenship Theory', *Ethics*, vol. 104, January 1994, pp. 352–81.

21 Derek Heater, 'Citizenship: A Remarkable Case of Interest', *Parliamentary Affairs*, vol. 44, no. 2, 1991, pp. 140–55, discussing British Conservative ministers' statements about 'active citizenship' within the local community, and the Commission on Citizenship chaired by the Speaker of the House of Commons, which reported in 1990.

22 Habermas, 'Citizenship and National Identity'.

23 Fred Steward, 'Citizens of the Planet Earth', in Geoff Andrews, ed., *Citizenship*, London, Lawrence and Wishart, 1991, pp. 65–88.

24 David Miller, 'Bounded Citizenship', in Kimberley Hutchings and Roland Dannreuther, eds, *Cosmopolitan Citizenship*, Basingstoke, Macmillan, 1999, p. 60.

25 T.H. Marshall, *Citizenship, Social Class and Other Essays*, Cambridge, Cambridge University Press, 1950.

26 See Miller, 'Bounded Citizenship' for useful brief summary. See also J.G.A. Pocock, 'The Ideal of Citizenship since Classical Times', *Queen's Quarterly*, vol. 99, 1, 1992, pp. 33–55.

27 Carole Pateman, *The Disorder of Women: Democracy, Feminism and Political Theory*, Cambridge, Polity, 1989.; Sara Ruddick, 'Maternal Thinking', *Feminist Studies*, vol. 6, no. 2, 1980, pp. 342–67; Mary Dietz, 'Citizenship with a Feminist Face: The Problem with Maternal Thinking', *Political Theory*, vol. 13, no. 1, February 1985, pp. 19–35; Iris Marion Young, 'Polity and Group Difference: A Critique of the Ideal of Universal Citizenship', *Ethics*, vol. 99, January 1989, pp. 250–74.

28 For example, Britain withdrew citizenship rights from many residents in its former Empire, notably in Hong Kong, despite agreeing to transfer Hong Kong to China in 1997.

29 See Alastair Davidson, 'Citizenship, Sovereignty and the Identity of the Nation-State', in Nancy Fraser, Anna Yeatman and Alastair Davidson, eds, *Critical Politics: From the Personal to the Global*, Melbourne, Arena Publications, 1994, pp. 111–23.

30 Reiss, ed., *Kant: Political Writings*.

31 Bryan S. Turner, 'Outline of a Theory of Human Rights', in B.S. Turner, ed., *Citizenship and Social Theory*, Thousand Oaks, Calif. Sage, 1993, p. 178.

32 See Roger Scruton, *Dictionary of Political Thought*, London, Macmillan, 1982, p. 100 for a definition of the cosmopolitan 'as a kind of parasite' and Jeremy Waldron, 'What is Cosmopolitan?' *Journal of Political Philosophy*, vol. 8, no. 2, June 2000, pp. 227–43, for a discussion of these issues and defence of cosmopolitan culture.

33 Richard Falk, 'The Making of Global Citizenship', in Bart van Steenbergen, ed., *The Condition of Citizenship*, London, Sage, 1994, p. 134.

34 Steven Connor, 'UK Companies Sell Toxic Soap to African Women' and Andrew Mullins, 'Lethal Goods Find a Global Market', *Independent*, 11 May 2000, p. 7. *Common Cause (Action Aid Magazine)*, Summer 2000, p. 4. reports on a case before the European Patent Office, which revoked a patent granted in 1994 to an American multinational, W.R. Grace, for a product derived from the seed of the neem tree in India. Indian campaigners, Greens in the European Parliament, the Belgian Environment Minister and Action Aid had brought the case. But about 70 other patents have already been taken out on the neem tree, which traditionally has been used for medicinal and contraceptive purposes and as an insecticide. See also Vandana Shiva, 'Poverty and Globalisation', in *Respect for the Earth*, The Reith Lectures, London, Profile Books, 2000, pp. 64–79.

35 Joseph A. Camilleri and Chandra Muzaffar, *Globalisation: The Perspectives and Experience of the Religious Traditions of Asia Pacific*, Selangor, International Movement for a Just World, 1998.

Part I: Introduction

1 Cited in H.C. Baldry, *The Unity of Mankind*, Cambridge, Cambridge University Press, 1965, p. 159. For a recent brief survey of Stoic social and political ideas see Malcolm Schofield, 'Social and Political Thought', in Keimpe Algra, Jonathan Barnes and Jaap Mansfeld, eds, *The Cambridge History of Hellenistic Philosophy*, Cambridge, Cambridge University Press, 1999, pp. 739–70.

2 See T.A. Sinclair, *A History of Greek Political Thought*, London, Routledge and Kegan Paul, 1961. But other scholars have queried the extent both of the decline of the city state and of the search for meaning in this period. See F.H. Sandbach, *The Stoics*, 2nd edition, Bristol, Bristol University Press, 1989, p. 23. For a disputed thesis that Alexander anticipated Stoic attitudes, see W.W. Tarn, *Alexander the Great*, 2 vols, Cambridge, Cambridge University Press, 1948.

3 The Stoic concept of natural law was subjected to a damaging critique by the Sceptical philosopher Carneades, who argued for the primacy of self-interest over justice. Cicero attempted to refute these criticisms. Today's 'postmodern' theorists can be seen as sceptics – see N.J. Rengger, *Political Theory, Modernity and Postmodernity*, Oxford, Blackwell, 1995, pp. 83–91.

4 Stoic philosophers tended to urge masters not to treat their slaves as possessions, but to recognize that they should also be treated justly. Epictetus urged that they should be recognized as 'brothers'. See Baldry, *Unity of Mankind*, p. 85 and Sandbach, *The Stoics*, p. 168.

5 See, for example, L. Edelstein, *The Meaning of Stoicism*, Cambridge, Mass., Harvard University Press, 1966. Moses Finley, *Ancient Slavery and Modern Ideology*, Harmondsworth, Penguin, 1980, p. 121 challenges this view, arguing that Stoic comments on slavery that urged masters to avoid extreme cruelty 'preached obedience to the slaves'.

6 William Stephens, 'Stoic Naturalism, Rationalism, and Ecology', *Environmental Ethics*, vol. 16, 1994, p. 277, fn. 9 claims: 'All of the *ancient* Stoic authors conceived of the Stoic sage as exclusively male.' C.E. Manning, 'Seneca and the Stoics on the Equality of the Sexes', *Mnemosyne*, vol. 26, 1973, pp. 170–7 argues that the Stoics relegated women to a secondary status, and that this was consistent with Stoic principles. M. Schofield, *The Stoic Idea of the City*, Cambridge, Cambridge University Press, p .43 provides some cautious evidence that Greek Stoics did believe 'the same virtue belongs to both a man and a woman'. Martha Nussbaum, 'Kant and Stoic Cosmopolitanism', *Journal of Political Philosophy*, vol. 5, no. 1, 1997, p. 14 claims that the Greek and even the Roman Stoics respected 'the equal personhood and dignity of women'.

7 Zeno in fact sent two of his pupils to join a circle of Stoics close to the King of Macedon. Sandbach, *The Stoics*, p. 140. In general, Stoic philosophy was understood to advocate political participation, unless political corruption or personal unsuitability made it inadvisable.

8 Martha C. Nussbaum, 'Lawyer for Humanity: Theory and Practice in Ancient Political Thought', in I. Shapiro and J. DeCew, eds, *Theory and Practice, Nomos*, vol. 37, New York, New York University Press, p. 192. For a detailed study of Seneca exploring his political role, see Miriam T. Griffin, *Seneca: A Philosopher in Politics*, revised edition, Oxford, Clarendon Press, 1992.

9 Panaetius is credited with the belief that 'Reason is the law for all men, not merely for the wise.' Cited by G.B. Sabine and S.B. Smith, eds, *Cicero on the Commonwealth*, New York, Macmillan, 1976, p. 25. See also Baldry, *Unity of Mankind*, pp. 177 and 181, who agrees about the switch in emphasis by the Middle Stoa.

10 Baldry, *Unity of Mankind*, pp. 108–9. E. Zeller, *The Stoics*, London, Longman, 1892, p. 327 comments that for Cynics citizenship of the world did not denote 'the brotherhood of all men' but 'the philosopher's independence of country and home'.

11 J.L. Males, 'The Cynics and Politics', in A. Laks and M. Schofield, eds, *Justice and Generosity: Studies in Hellenistic Social and Political Philosophy*, Cambridge, Cambridge University Press, 1995, p. 138.

12 Plutarch, writing in the first century AD, and Sextus Empiricus, writing in the second century AD, are the main sources for knowledge of Zeno and Chrysippus. The quotation from Zeno that 'we should regard all men as our fellow-countrymen' has been translated somewhat differently by different scholars and it is even contested whether Plutarch was referring to Zeno's book *The Republic*. See Baldry, *Unity of Mankind*, p. 211 endnote 27 and alternative translation in Sandbach, *The Stoics*, p. 25.

13 R.W. Hall, *Plato*, London, Allen and Unwin, 1981, p. 144 traces natural law back to Plato.

14 Cited in Edelstein, *The Meaning of Stoicism*, p. 73.

15 Schofield, *The Stoic Idea of the City*, p. 103.

16 See A.P. D'Entreves, *Natural Law*, London, Hutchinson, 1967. Neither Cicero nor other Stoic thinkers achieved a level of theoretical rigour required by twentieth-century philosophers, but that did not prevent their ideas having political significance in the period after the Nuremberg trials. See Gerald Watson, 'The Natural Law and Stoicism', in A.A. Long, ed., *Problems in Stoicism*, London, Athlone Press, 1971, pp. 216–38.

17 Peter Kropotkin, 'The State: Its Historic Role', in P. A. Kropotkin, *Selected Writings on Anarchism and Revolution*, edited by Martin A. Miller, Cambridge, Mass. MIT Press, 1973, pp. 222–3.

18 Paul Ghils, 'International Civil Society: International Non-Governmental Organizations in the International System', *International Social Science Journal*, no. 133, August 1992, p. 418.

1 Citizens of Christendom or of the world?

1 Emeric Crucé, *The New Cyneas*, extract in Peter Mayer, ed., *The Pacifist Conscience*, Harmondsworth, Penguin, 1966, p. 68, translated by Peter Mayer.

2 Immanuel Kant, 'Perpetual Peace', in Hans Reiss, ed., *Kant: Political Writings*, 2nd enlarged edition, translated by H.B. Nisbet, Cambridge, Cambridge University Press, 1991, p. 103. Kant dismisses Grotius, Pufendorf and Vattel because they are 'quoted in *justification* of military aggression' and because their precepts, he claims, can have no legal force between independent states.

3 See A. Bance, 'The Idea of Europe: from Erasmus to ERASMUS', *European Studies*, vol. 22, 1992, p. 1. Bance described Erasmus as 'the cosmopolitan Renaissance scholar, whom Stefan Zweig called the "first European" '.

4 See Michael Screech, Foreword to the English translation of Léon-E. Halkin, *Erasmus: A Critical Biography*, Oxford, Blackwell, 1987, p. viii. (*Erasme parmis nous*, translated by John Tonkin.)

5 See Frederick Seebohm, *The Oxford Reformers: John Colet, Erasmus and Thomas More*, 3rd edition, London, Longman, 1913; and Robert P. Adams, *The Better Part of Valor: More, Eramus, Colet and Vives. On Humanism, War and Peace, 1496–1535*, Seattle, University of Washington Press, 1962, who argues that these four scholars shared key ideas and had a common English programme linked to Henry VIII.

6 John P. Dolan, ed., *The Essential Erasmus*, New York, New American Library (Meridian), 1983, p. 196.

7 James D. Tracy, *The Politics of Erasmus: A Pacifist Intellectual and His Political Milieu*, Toronto, University of Toronto Press, 1978, p. 8. He cites as sources Erasmus's letters 1417, 2375 and 2645.

8 Cited by Halkin, *Erasmus*, p. 281 quoting from letter to Ulrich Zwingli, 1523.

9 Cornelis Augustjin, *Erasmus: His Life, Work and Influence*, translated by J.C. Grayson, Toronto, University of Toronto Press, 1991, p. 183. Augustjin takes the letter to Zwingli referring to world citizenship to say: 'I wish to be a citizen of the world, to belong to everyone or rather to be alien to everyone,' p. 183.

10 See E. Cameron, 'Humanists, Reformers and Scholastics', Review Article, *European History Quarterly*, vol. 26, 1996, p. 127. Cameron notes that Erasmus refuses to 'fit in' with the conventions of sixteenth-century life.

11 Tracy, *Politics of Erasmus*, p. 5.

12 See Quentin Skinner, *The Foundations of Modern Political Thought*, vol. I, *The Renaissance*, Cambridge, Cambridge University Press, 1978, pp. 101–12 and 193–243. The humanists attacked the earlier 'scholastic' learning derived from medieval traditions as arid, trivial and irrelevant to practical life. Whilst accepting the classical cyclical view of history, the humanists believed they were promoting a revival of classical glory.

13 See Philip C. Dust, *Three Renaissance Pacifists: Essays in the Theories of Erasmus, More and Vives*, New York, Peter Lang, 1987; and Adams, *The Better Part of Valor*.

14 For example in the debate with Martin van Dorp, who on behalf of the conservative Catholic theologians of Louvain attacked both *In Praise of Folly* and Erasmus's translation of the New Testament into Greek. See R.J. Schoek, 'Telling More from Erasmus: An *essai* in Renaissance Humanism', *Moreana*, vol. 23, November 1986, pp. 11–19; and E.E. Reynolds, *Thomas More and Erasmus*, New York, Fordham University Press, 1965, pp. 73–4 and 101–5.

15 See Richard Marius, *Thomas More*, London, Dent, 1984, also C.A. Patrides, 'Erasmus and More: Dialogues with Reality', *The Kenyon Review*, vol. 8, no. 1, 1986, p. 45, who calls him a 'fanatic' in his opposition to heresy. Peter Ackroyd, *The Life of Thomas More*, London, Vintage,

1999, pp. 291–303 discusses More's reasons for severely repressing seditious heresy. Ackroyd points out that some stories of More personally whipping heretics were propaganda, but confirms his belief (shared by most of his contemporaries) in the necessity of burning unrepentant heretics.

16 See Marius, *Thomas More*, p. 212. Marius also cites More's criticism of the expense of Wolsey's interventionist foreign policy.

17 Seebohm, *The Oxford Reformers*, pp. 261–65, citing Erasmus as a source.

18 Cited in Halkin, *Erasmus*, p. 150. When eventually Erasmus addressed the issues raised by Luther, he concentrated on defending free will, which Luther acknowledged in his reply 'On the Bondage of the Will' was the central issue.

19 'Letter to Anthony à Bergis', reproduced in Mayer, ed., *The Pacifist Conscience*, p. 55.

20 Cited in Daniele Archibugi, 'Erasmus on War and Peace', *END Journal of European Nuclear Disarmament*, no. 17, December 1985–January 1986, p. 23.

21 See John Mulryan, 'Erasmus and War: The *Adages* and Beyond', *Moreana*, no. 23, February 1986, pp. 15–17.

22 See José A. Fernandez, 'Erasmus on the Just War', *Journal of the History of Ideas*, vol. 34, no. 1, 1973, pp. 218–19.

23 See James T. Johnson, 'Two Kinds of Pacifism: Opposition to the Political Use of Force in the Renaissance–Reformation Period', *Journal of Religious Ethics*, vol. 12, no. 1, 1984, pp. 46–8.

24 Erasmus polemicized against the Italian authors adopting a purely secular humanism in a 1528 dialogue *Ciceronianus*, arguing that a Ciceronian in the sixteenth century should speak within a Christian context. See Richard Tuck, *Philosophy and Government 1572–1651*, Cambridge, Cambridge University Press, 1993, p. 21.

25 Machiavelli's *Prince* was drafted in 1513, three years before Erasmus's book was published, and was specifically directed at earlier Italian humanist books of advice to rulers.

26 See Tracy, *Politics of Erasmus*, pp. 60–3. NB: Machiavelli is *also* undermining the advice given by Cicero and Seneca, and hence the humanist precepts of the Stoics, in key chapters of *The Prince*. See Skinner's Introduction in Q. Skinner and R. Price, eds, *Machiavelli, The Prince*, Cambridge, Cambridge University Press, 1988.

27 Cited in Halkin, *Erasmus*, p. 102.

28 Tracy, *Politics of Erasmus*, pp. 26–8.

29 Donald M. Frame, *Montaigne: A Biography*, London, Hamish Hamilton, 1965, pp. 315–16.

30 R.A. Sayce, *The Essays of Montaigne: A Critical Exploration*, London, Weidenfeld and Nicolson, 1972, pp. 1–2.

31 Quentin Skinner, *The Foundations of Modern Political Thought*, vol. 2, *The Age of Reformation*, Cambridge, Cambridge University Press, 1978, p. 279.

32 Michel de Montaigne, 'On Cannibals', in *Essays*, translated by J.M. Cohen, Harmondsworth, Penguin, 1958, p. 113.

33 Sayce, *Essays of Montaigne*, p. 93. See also pp. 89–93 and p. 142.

34 Frame, *Montaigne*, p. 321.

35 'J'estime tous les hommes mes compatriotes, et embrasse un Polonois comme un Francois', cited in Sayce, *Essays of Montaigne*, p. 98.

36 Tuck, *Philosophy and Government*, pp. 52–3. Senecan Stoicism can also be seen as compatible with element in Scepticism.

37 Rudolf Kirk, ed., *Two Bookes of Constancie Writen in latine by Iustus Lipsius. Englished by Sir John Stradling*. New Brunswick, NJ, 1939, p. 90. Cited in A.A. Bromham, ' "Have You Read Lipsius?" ', *English Studies*, vol. 5, 1996, p. 409.

38 Epictetus claims that Socrates always described himself as a citizen not of Athens but of the world. See *The Golden Sayings of Epictetus*, translated by Hastings Crossley, London, Macmillan, 1957, p. 12.

39 See Tuck, *Philosophy and Government*, p. 45.

40 See Skinner, *Foundations*, vol. 2, p. 279.

41 Cited in ibid., p. 283.

42 *Politicorum*, 1589, published in English 1594 as *Six Books of Politics*, cited in Tuck, *Philosophy and Government*, p. 60.

43 R.J. Collins, 'Montaigne's Rejection of Reason of State in "De Utile et de l'honneste" ', *Sixteenth Century Journal*, vol. 23, no. 1, 1992, pp. 71–94.

44 Tuck, *Philosophy and Government*, pp. 57–8.

45 Grotius gives particular mention to Gentili and to Balthazar Ayala (1548–84), a Spanish jurist who wrote on the laws of war.

46 See Cornelius F. Murphy, 'The Grotian Vision of World Order', *The American Journal of International Law*, vol. 76, 1982, pp. 477–98, citing Suárez, *De Legibus ac Deo Legislatore*, bk 2, chap. 19, para. 9.

47 J.C. Rolfe, ed., *De Juri Belli Libri Tres*, Carnegie, translated 1933, p. 122, cited in T. Meron, 'Common Rights of Mankind in Gentili, Grotius and Suárez', *American Journal of International Law*, vol. 85, 1991, p. 114.

48 Gentili also wrote on the law of the sea, anticipating Grotius. See Meron, 'Common Rights of Mankind', pp. 115 and 114.

49 See Tuck, *Philosophy and Government*, pp. 179–90.

50 *De Jure Belli et Pacis*, bk II, chap. 20, s. 46, cited in Benedict Kingsbury and Adam Roberts, 'Introduction: Grotian Thought in International Relations', in Hedley Bull, Benedict Kingsbury and Adam Roberts, eds, *Hugo Grotius and International Relations*, Oxford, Clarendon Press, 1990, p. 45, fn. 154.

51 Hugo Grotius, *Prolegomena to The Law of War and Peace*, translated by Francis W. Kelsey, New York, Liberal Arts Press, p. 21.

52 Ali Khan, 'The Extinction of Nation States', *American University Journal of International Law and Policy*, vol. 7, 1992, pp. 202–5.

53 *De Jure Belli et Pacis*, bk II, chap. 25, s. 8, cited in Kingsbury and Roberts, 'Introduction', p. 41.

54 Gentili, *De Jure Belli Libri Tres*, cited in Meron, 'Common Rights of Mankind', p. 115. Meron argues that Suárez and Vitoria did not uphold humanitarian intervention.

55 See Hedley Bull, *The Anarchical Society*, Basingstoke, Macmillan, 1977, pp. 24–7.

56 *The Law of Prize* is in Latin *De Jure Praedae*, originally entitled *De Indiis*, of which a chapter, *Mare Liberum*, was published in 1609.

57 Grotius, *Prolegomena*, pp. 25–6.

58 Ibid., pp. 8–9.

59 See Knud Haakonssen, 'Hugo Grotius and the History of Political Thought', *Political Theory*, vol. 13, no. 2, 1985, pp. 248–9 and A.P. D'Entreves, *Natural Law*, London, Hutchinson, 1967, p. 71.

60 D'Entreves, *Natural Law*, p. 71.

61 See Hedley Bull, 'The Importance of Grotius in the Study of International Relations', in Bull *et al.*, eds, *Hugo Grotius and International Relations*, p. 82.

62 W.P. George, 'Looking for a Global Ethic? Try International Law', *The Journal of Religion*, vol. 76, 1996, p. 366.

63 Cited in Rosalyn Higgins, 'Grotius and the United Nations', *International Social Science Journal*, vol. 37, no. 1, p. 122. Grotius addressed *On the Truth of the Christian Religion* to Jews and Muslims, arguing the moral superiority of Christian practices on some issues – though he can also be seen as developing a minimal common religion. See Tuck, *Philosophy and Government*, p. 195.

64 See Herbert F. Wright, *The Controversy of Hugo Grotius with Johan de Laet on the Origin of the American Aborigines*, Bibliotheca Visseriana, vol. vii, p. 211, cited in C.D. Wallace, 'The Foundation of International Law: A Four Hundred Year Tribute to Hugo Grotius', *Connecticut Bar Journal*, vol. 57, 1983, p. 92.

65 See Kingsbury and Roberts, 'Introduction', p. 36 on Grotius's reference to Inca social mores and also p. 48 on his drawing on Islam.

66 Cited in ibid., p. 14, fn. 41.

67 Cited in ibid., p. 14, fn. 39.

68 Cited in Murphy, 'The Grotian Vision', p. 481.

69 Grotius, *De Jure Belli et Pacis*, bk II, chap 2, ss. 6–7, cited in L.C. Green, 'Is World Citizenship a Legal Practicality?' *Canadian Yearbook of International Law*, 1987, p. 168.

70 Rousseau attacks Grotius:

> Grotius denies that all human government is established for the benefit of the governed, and he cites the example of slavery. His characteristic method of reasoning is always to offer facts as a proof of right. It is possible to imagine a more logical method, but not one more favourable to tyrants.

Jean-Jacques Rousseau, *The Social Contract*, translated by M. Cranston, Harmondsworth, Penguin, 1968, p. 51.

71 Kingsbury and Roberts, 'Introduction', p. 48.

72 Grotius, *De Jure Belli et Pacis*, bk I, chap 23 ss. 7–8, noted in Kingsley and Roberts, 'Introduction', pp. 27–8.

73 Cited in F.H. Hinsley, *Power and the Pursuit of Peace: Theory and Practice in the History of Relations between States*, Cambridge, Cambridge University Press, 1967, p. 18.

74 Cited in ibid., p. 200. See also Derek Heater, *World Citizenship and Government: Cosmopolitan Ideas in the History of Western Political Thought*, Basingstoke, Macmillan, 1996, pp. 65–70.

75 Quoted in Murphy, 'The Grotian Vision', p. 482.

76 Hinsley, *Power and the Pursuit of Peace*, p. 23.

77 William Penn, *The Peace of Europe*, London, Dent (Everyman), 1993, p. 12.

78 Ibid., p. 18.

79 Hinsley, *Power and the Pursuit of Peace*, pp. 34–5.

2 Enlightenment cosmopolitanism and world citizenship

1 Montesquieu, *The Spirit of the Laws*, translated by T. Nugent, ed. F. Neumann, New York, Hafner, 1949, bk XXIV, chap. 10, p. 33. Voltaire admired Marcus Aurelius and Franklin admired Cicero: see Derek Heater, *World Citizenship and Government: Cosmpolitian Ideas in the History of Western Political Thought*, London, Macmillan, 1996, p. 73.

2 Julia Kristeva, *Nations Without Nationalism*, translated by Leon S. Roudiez, New York, Columbia University Press, 1993, pp. 27–8.

3 See John Macmillan, 'Democracies Don't Fight: A Case of the Wrong Research Agenda?', *Review of International Studies*, vol. 22, 1996, pp. 275–99.

4 John Keane, *Nations, Nationalism, and the European Citizen*, University of Westminster Press, CSD Perspectives, Centre for the Study of Democracy, Research Papers, Number 2, Autumn 1993, p. 24. John Keane, *Tom Paine: A Political Life*, London, Bloomsbury, 1995. See esp. Prologue: 'A Citizen Extraordinary', pp. ix–xiv.

5 Thomas J. Schlereth, *The Cosmopolitan Ideal in Enlightenment Thought: Its Forms and Functions in the Ideas of Franklin, Hume and Voltaire 1694–1790*, Notre Dame, Ind., University of Notre Dame Press, 1977. NB: The inclusion of Hume, often seen as a conservative figure, has been criticized (see review by A. Owen Aldridge, *William and Mary Quarterly*, vol. 35, no. 3, 1978, pp. 578–80). But Hume was explicitly hailed as a cosmopolitan figure by Diderot, as noted later in this chapter.

6 Michel Foucault, *Discipline and Punish: The Birth of the Prison*, translated by Alan Sheridan, London, Allen Lane, Penguin Press, 1977; and *Madness and Civilization: A History of Insanity in the Age of Reason*, translated by R. Howard, London, Tavistock, 1977.

7 Peter Gay, *The Party of Humanity: Essays in the French Enlightenment*, Part Three 'Unfinished Business', New York, W.W. Norton, 1971, pp. 185–290.

8 Peter Gay, *The Enlightenment: An Interpretation*, London, Weidenfeld and Nicolson, 1967, p. 17.

9 Andrew Vincent, 'Kant's Humanity', *Political Theory Newsletter*, vol. 7, no. 2, 1995, pp. 35–50.

10 On Franklin, see Esmond Wright, 'Benjamin Franklin, the Old England Man', *Contemporary Review*, vol. 256, April 1990, pp. 169–77.

11 *Encylopédie ou dictionnaire Raisonné des Sciences, des Arts et des métiers* [1750–80], vol. 4, Stuttgart/Bad Canstatt, Fredrich Fromann Verlag, 1966, p. 297. The original quotations are: 'un homme qui n'a point de demeure fixé' and 'un homme qui n'est étranger nulle part'.

12 The Encyclopaedia referred to Socrates, drawing on Montaigne and references in Cicero, Plutarch and Epictetus. See Schlereth, *The Cosmopolitan Ideal*, p. 47.

13 Montesquieu's *pensée* is quoted by Kristeva, *Nations Without Nationalism*, p. 28. Translated it reads:

> If I knew something useful to myself and detrimental to my family, I would reject it from my mind. If I knew something useful to my family but not to my homeland, I would try to forget it. If I knew something useful to my homeland and detrimental to Europe, or else useful to Europe and detrimental to Mankind, I would consider it a crime.

14 Cited in Gay, *The Enlightenment*, p. 13.

15 Tom Paine, *The Rights of Man*, Harmondsworth, Penguin, 1969, p. 250.
16 Immanuel Kant, *Anthropology from a Pragmatic Point of View*, translated by Mary J. Gregor, The Hague, Martinus Nijhoff, 1974, p. 4.
17 Ibid., p. 193; see p. 3. for reference to man as member of a species.
18 Hans Reiss, ed., *Kant: Political Writings*, 2nd enlarged edition, translated by H.B. Nisbet, Cambridge, Cambridge University Press, 1991, pp. 107–8.
19 Schlereth, *Cosmopolitan Ideal*, p. 39.
20 Montesquieu, *Persian Letters*, translated by Harmondsworth, Penguin, 1973, p. 135, Letter 67.
21 Gay, *The Enlightenment*, p. 15.
22 Frank E. Manuel, *The Prophets of Paris*, New York, Harper and Row, Harper Torchbooks, 1962, p. 84.
23 Jean-Jacques Rousseau, *The Government of Poland*, translated and introduced by Wilmoore Kendall, Indianpolis, Bobbs-Merrill, 1972, pp. 11–12.
24 Hannah Arendt, *The Origins of Totalitarianism*, 2nd enlarged edition, London, Allen and Unwin, 1958, p. 21.
25 Hannah Arendt, *The Jew as Pariah: Jewish Identity and Politics in the Modern Age*, New York, Grove Press, 1978, pp. 67–95.
26 Alan Arkush, *Moses Mendelssohn and the Enlightenment*, New York, State University of New York Press, 1994, p. xi.
27 See E. Jospe, ed. and trans., *Moses Mendelssohn: Selections from His Writings*, New York, Viking Press, 1975, 'Introduction', pp. 3–5 and 27–9.
28 Cited in Schlereth, *Cosmopolitan Ideal*, p. 107.
29 David Williams, ed. and trans., *Voltaire: Political Writings*, Cambridge, Cambridge University Press, 1994, p. 29.
30 Ibid., p. 29.
31 Gay, *The Enlightenment*, p. 13.
32 Williams, ed., *Voltaire: Political Writings*, 'On the Serfdom of Minds', p. 140.
33 Reiss, 'Postcript' to *Kant: Political Writings*, p. 253.
34 Ronald Grimsley, *From Montesquieu to Laclos*, Geneva, Libraire Droz, 1974, p. 6.
35 Montesquieu, *Persian Letters*, pp. 164–6, Letter 85.
36 Williams, ed., *Voltaire: Political Writings*, p. 216.
37 Gregory Claeys, *Thomas Paine: Social and Political Thought*, Boston, Unwin Hyman, 1989, p. 91.
38 Michael Foot and Isaac Kramnick, eds, *The Paine Reader*, Harmondsworth, Penguin, 1987, pp. 52–6.
39 Cited in Schlereth, *The Cosmopolitan Ideal*, p. 92.
40 Montesquieu, *Persian Letters*, p. 152.
41 Montesquieu, *Spirit of the Laws*, p. 137.
42 See Reiss, ed., *Kant: Political Writings*, pp. 172–3.
43 Ibid., p. 106.
44 Cited in Henry Reynolds, *This Whispering in Our Hearts*, St Leonards, New South Wales, Allen and Unwin, 1998, p. xii.
45 Foot and Kramnick, *Thomas Paine Reader*, pp. 57–62.
46 Keane, *Tom Paine*, pp. 147–50. The fact that many native Americans sided with the British in the War of Independence also antagonized revolutionary leaders.
47 Charles M. Wiltse, *The Jeffersonian Tradition in American Democracy*, New York, Hill and Wang, 1960, pp. 183–4.
48 Edward W. Said, *Culture and Imperialism*, London, Vintage, 1994, p. 290.
49 Reiss, ed., *Kant: Political Writings*, p. 106.
50 Cited in Schlereth, *Cosmopolitan Ideal*, p. 105.
51 Reiss ed., *Kant: Political Writings*, p. 160.
52 Wiltse, *Jeffersonian Tradition*, pp. 184–6.
53 See Alastair Davidson, *From Subject to Citizen*, Melbourne, Cambridge University Press, 1997, pp. 43–4; and Jürgen Habermas, 'Citizenship and National Identity: Some Reflections on the Future of Europe', *Praxis International*, vol. 12, no. 1, April 1992, p. 17.
54 L.C. Green, 'Is World Citizenship a Legal Practicality?', *Canadian Yearbook of International Law*, vol. 25, 1987, pp. 167–9.
55 Schlereth, *Cosmopolitan Ideal*, p. 101.

56 John Bryant, 'Citizens of a World to Come: Melville and the Millennial Cosmopolite', *American Literature*, vol. 59, no. 1, 1987, p. 21.

57 See F.A. Hayek, 'Adam Smith's Message in Today's Language', in *New Studies in Philosophy, Politics, Economics and the History of Ideas*, London, Routledge, 1978, pp. 267–9.

58 Montequieu, *Spirit of the Laws*, pp. 316–17.

59 T.L. Pangle, *Montesquieu's Philosophy of Liberalism*, Chicago, University of Chicago Press, 1973, pp. 211–12.

60 Donald Winch, 'Adam Smith: Scottish Moral Philosopher as Political Economist', *The Historical Journal*, vol. 35, no. 1, 1992, pp. 91–113.

61 Reiss ed., *Kant: Political Writings*, p. 107.

62 Robert Housman, 'A Kantian Approach to Trade and the Environment', *Washington and Lee Law Review*, vol. 49, no.4, 1992, pp. 1378–88.

63 Montesquieu, *Persian Letters*, p. 176.

64 Reiss, ed., *Kant: Political Writings*, p. 103.

65 Montesquieu, *Persian Letters*, p. 178.

66 Reiss, ed., *Kant: Political Writings*, pp. 167–70. See also Thomas Mertens, 'War and International Order in Kant's Legal Thought', *Ratio Juris*, vol. 8, no. 3, 1995, pp. 296–314, who argues that Kant partly fits into the just war tradition.

67 The different interpretations of Montesquieu are charted by Mark Waddicor, *Montesquieu and the Philosophy of Natural Law*, The Hague, Martinus Nijhoff, 1970.

68 Reiss, ed., *Kant: Political Writings*, pp. 98–9.

69 W.B. Gallie, *Philosophers of Peace and War*, Cambridge, Cambridge University Press, 1978, p. 33.

70 Williams, ed., *Voltaire: Political Writings*, pp. 150 and 152.

71 Isaac Kramnick, ed., *The Portable Enlightenment Reader*, Harmondsworth, Penguin, 1995, p. 551.

72 Jeremy Bentham, 'Plan for a Universal and Perpetual Peace', reprinted in M.C. Jacob, ed., *Peace Projects of the Eighteenth Century*, New York, Garland, 1974, pp. 3–95; see also F.H. Hinsley, *Power and the Pursuit of Peace*, Cambridge, Cambridge University Press, 1967, pp. 81–91.

73 Cited by Claeys, *Thomas Paine*, p. 103.

74 See Hinsley, *Power and the Pursuit of Peace*.

75 Rousseau's critique of Saint-Pierre has been interpreted as 'realist' by Kenneth Waltz, *Man, the State and War*, New York, Columbia University Press, 1959. But it can equally be seen as a republican argument about the impossibility of kings interested in extending their individual power coming to such an agreement.

76 See Andrew Hurrell, 'Kant and the Kantian Paradigm in International Relations', *Review of International Studies*, 1990, vol. 16, pp. 183–205; and Georg Cavallar, 'Kant's Society of Nations: Free Federation or World Republic?', *Journal of the History of Philosophy*, vol. 32, 1994, pp. 461–82.

77 Hannah Arendt, *On Revolution*, Harmondsworth, Penguin, 1973 charts the republican elements in both.

78 For a discussion of the background to republican thought and its development in the eighteenth century, see: J.G.A. Pocock, *The Machiavellian Moment: Florentine Republican Thought and the Atlantic Republican Tradition*, Princeton, NJ, Princeton University Press, 1975; and Quentin Skinner, *Liberty before Liberalism*, Cambridge, Cambridge University Press, 1998. For the Jacobins see Istvan Hont, 'The Permanent Crisis of a Divided Mankind: "Contemporary Crisis of the Nation State" in Historical Perspective', *Political Studies*, vol. 42, 1994, pp. 166–231. See also J. Robertson, *The Scottish Enlightenment and the Militia Issue*, Edinburgh, John Donald, 1985.

3 Internationalism, cosmopolitanism and challenges to them, 1815–1914

1 See Edward Acton, *Alexander Herzen and the Role of the Intellectual Revolutionary*, Cambridge, Cambridge University Press, 1979, p. 128.

2 See Denis Mack Smith, *Mazzini*, New Haven, Conn., Yale University Press, 1994, p. 12. Mazzini was not a free market liberal, but leaned towards socialism and his supporters were involved in founding the First Socialist International.

3 For information on international cooperation in the nineteenth century see: F.S.L. Lyons, *Internationalism in Europe 1815–1914*, Leyden, A.W. Sythoff, 1963. Many of the details in the Introduction to this chapter are drawn from Lyons. For a recent study of the rise of

international bodies see John Boli and George M. Thomas, eds, *Constructing World Culture: International Nongovernmental Organization Since 1875*, Stanford, Calif., Stanford University Press, 1999.

4   Article 1 of the Statutes, cited by Lyons, *Internationalism*, p. 219.

5   F.H. Hinsley, *Power and the Pursuit of Peace*, Cambridge, Cambridge University Press, 1967, p. 127.

6   See S. Prakash Sinha, *Asylum and International Law*, The Hague, Martinus Nijhoff, 1971, p. 28.

7   See for more detail Evan Schofer, 'Science Associations in the International Sphere, 1875–1990: The Rationalization of Science, and the Scientization of Society', in Boli and Thomas, eds, *Constructing World Culture*, pp. 249–66.

8   Robin Blackburn, 'Anti-Slavery and the French Revolution', *History Today*, vol. 41, November 1991, pp. 19–25.

9   Harold J. Laski, *The Rise of European Liberalism*, London, Allen and Unwin, Unwin Books, 1962, p. 154.

10   Cited in Hugh Tinker, *A New System of Slavery: The Export of Indian Labour Overseas, 1830–1920*, London, Oxford University Press, 1974, p. 239.

11   Cited in D. Read, *Cobden and Bright: A Victorian Partnership*, London: Edward Arnold, pp. 210–12.

12   John Stuart Mill, *Essays on Politics and Culture*, edited by Gertrude Himmelfarb, New York, Doubleday Anchor, 1963, p. 36.

13   Tinker, *New System of Slavery*, p. 65.

14   Judith M. Brown, *Gandhi: Prisoner of Hope*, New Haven, Conn., Yale University Press, 1989, pp. 25–6.

15   See C.L.R. James, *The Black Jacobins: Toussaint l'Ouverture and the San Domingo Revolution*, New York, Vintage, 1963.

16   Eric Williams, *Capitalism and Slavery*, London, André Deutsch, 1964.

17   Stéphane Dion, 'Durham et Tocqueville sur la colonisation libérale', *Revue d'études canadiennes*, vol. 25, no. 1, 1990, p. 67. Dion argues against the view of Todorov that Tocqueville rejected the idea of empire as a civilizing force: Tzetvan Todorov, 'Tocqueville et la doctrine coloniale', in Alexis de Tocqueville, *De la colonie en Algérie*, Brussels, Complexe, 1988, pp. 9–34.

18   David L. Schalk, 'Reflections *D'Outre Mer* on French Colonialism', *European Studies*, vol. 28, 1998, pp. 9–12.

19   See Max Beloff, 'Tocqueville and Gobineau: On Race, Revolution and Despair', *Encounter*, vol. 67, no. 1, 1986, pp. 29–31.

20   Charles DeBenedetti, *The Peace Reform in American History*, Bloomington, Indiana University Press, 1980, pp. 71–7.

21   Britain did legislate in times of emergency to allow governments to control entry of aliens or expel them. Such laws operated from 1793 to 1826 during and after the Napoleonic Wars and in 1848–50 during the wave of revolutions in Europe (though not then used). But for almost all the nineteenth century there were no laws at all on entry into Britain. See Bernard Potter, *The Refugee Question in Mid-Victorian Politics*, Cambridge, Cambridge University Press, 1979, p. 3.

22   See: Maldwyn Allen Jones, *American Immigration*, Chicago, University of Chicago Press, 1960; and Lucy Sayler, 'Captives of Law: Judicial Enforcement of the Chinese Exclusion Laws, 1891–1905', *Journal of American History*, vol. 76, no. 1, 1989, pp. 91–117.

23   Quoted in Jones, *American Immigration*, p. 259.

24   Manning Clark, *Short History of Australia*, 4th revised edition, Ringwood, Victoria, Penguin, 1995, p. 216.

25   Cited in Lyon, *Internationalism*, p. 312.

26   Ibid., p. 16.

27   Cited in David Thomson, *England in the Nineteenth Century*, Harmondsworth, Penguin, 1950, p. 103.

28   Cited in Lyons, *Internationalism*, p. 317.

29   J.S. Mill, 'England's Maritime Power', in *The Collected Works of John Stuart Mill*, vol. 28, Toronto, University of Toronto Press, 1988, pp. 222–3.

30   Herbert Spencer, *The Man versus the State*, edited by E. Mack, Indianapolis, Liberty Classic, 1981.

31   Cited in Lyons, *Internationalism*, p. 384.

32   Cited in DeBenedetti, *Peace Reform*, p. 38.

33   William Cobden, *Three Panics*, cited in Read, *Cobden and Bright*, p. 110.

34   Cited in Read, *Cobden and Bright*, p. 113.

35 Cited in DeBenedetti, *Peace Reform*, p. 53. See also Charles Chatfield, *The American Peace Movement: Ideals and Activism*, New York, Twayne Publishers, 1992, p. 13.

36 Jill Liddington, *The Long Road to Greenham*, London, Virago, 1989, pp. 25–26.

37 Cited in Peter Mayer, ed., *The Pacifist Conscience*, Harmondsworth, Penguin, 1966, p. 117.

38 Cited in Hinsley, *Power and the Pursuit of Peace*, p. 104.

39 Jill Liddington, 'The Women's Peace Crusade', in Dorothy Thompson, ed., *Over Our Dead Bodies*, London, Virago, 1983, pp. 180–98.

40 Yukiko Matsukawa and Kaoru Tachi, 'Woman's Suffrage and Gender Politics in Japan', in Caroline Daley and Melanie Nolan, eds, *Suffrage and Beyond: International Feminist Perspectives*, Armadale, New South Wales, Pluto Press, 1994, pp. 171–4.

41 See Ian Tyrell, *Woman's World, Woman's Empire: The Woman's Christian Temperance Union in International Perspective, 1880–1930*, Chapel Hill, University of North Carolina Press, 1991.

42 Deborah Stienstra, *Women's Movements and International Organizations*, New York, St Martin's Press, 1994, pp. 48–50.

43 Cited in Tyrell, *Woman's World*, p. 35.

44 See Hannah Bailey's speech to the 1895 peace conference in America on a mother's duty to 'make peace in her family where contentions exist or better still, to prevent them by timely care', cited in ibid., p. 174.

45 Cited in DeBenedetti, *Peace Reform*, p. 211 fn. 13. Willard was quoting Paine.

46 Philip N. Cohen, 'Nationalism and Suffrage: Gender Struggle in Nation-Building America', *Signs*, vol. 21, no. 3, Spring 1996, pp. 707–27.

47 Ellen Carol DuBois, 'Woman Suffrage Around the World: Three Phases of Suffrage Internationalism', in Daley and Nolan, eds, *Suffrage and Beyond*, p. 259.

48 Leila J. Rupp, 'Challenging Imperialism in International Women's Organisations, 1884–1945', *National Women's Studies Association Journal*, vol. 8, no. 1, 1996, pp. 8–27.

49 Karl Marx and Friedrich Engels, 'Manifesto of the Communist Party', in Harold J. Laski, ed., *Communist Manifesto: Socialist Landmark*, London, Allen and Unwin, 1961, p. 124.

50 For an eminently readable account of socialism up to 1917, see Edmund Wilson, *To the Finland Station*, London, Collins/Fontana, 1960.

51 G.D.H. Cole, *A History of Socialist Thought*, vol. 3, part 1, *The Second International*, London, Macmillan, 1963, pp. 7–9.

52 Ibid., p. 58.

53 Ibid., pp. 69–70.

54 Ibid., p. 69.

55 Richard J. Evans, *Comrades and Sisters: Feminism, Socialism and Pacifism in Europe 1870–1945*, Brighton, Wheatsheaf, 1987, p. 133.

Part II: Introduction

1 Paul Hirst and Grahame Thompson, *Globalization in Question*, 2nd edition, Cambridge, Polity, 1999 is a frequently cited exposition of this critique of economic globalization.

2 John Tomlinson, *Globalization and Culture*, Cambridge, Polity, 1999 provides an overview of cultural globalization, including a discussion of the possibility of cosmopolitanism.

3 This term was used by the Australian Foreign Secretary, Gareth Evans, during the early 1990s to indicate the ideal which Australian policy should follow. See G. Evans and B. Grant, *Australia's Foreign Relations in the World of the 1990s*, Melbourne, Melbourne University Press, 1991. See also Andrew Linklater,, 'What is Good International Citizenship?' in P. Keal, ed., *Ethics and Foreign Policy*, Sydney, Allen and Unwin, 1992, pp. 21–43.

4 Global civil society

1 Lawrence S. Wittner, *Resisting the Bomb*, Stanford, Calif., Stanford University Press, 1997, pp. 33–7.

2 There is a large literature on the concept of civil society. For the revival of the idea in Eastern Europe, see John Keane, ed., *Civil Society and the State: New European Perspectives*, London, Verso, 1988. For an overview from a western political science perspective, see L. Diamond, 'Rethinking Civil Society: Towards a Democratic Consolidation', *Journal of Democracy*, vol. 5, no. 3, 1994, pp. 4–17.

3 Václav Havel, *Living in Truth*, edited by Jan Vladislav, London, Faber and Faber, 1987, pp. 36–122.

4 See, for example, Danilo Zolo, *Cosmopolis: Prospects for World Government*, Cambridge, Polity, 1997, pp. 127–35.

5 On global civil society see: R.D. Lipschutz, 'Reconstructing World Politics: The Emergence of Global Civil Society', *Millennium*, vol. 21, no. 3, 1992, pp. 389–430; Michael Walzer, ed., *Toward a Global Civil Society*, Providence, RI, Berghahn Books, 1995; Richard Falk, 'Global Civil Society and the Democratic Prospect', in Barry Holden, ed., *Global Democracy: Key Debates*, London, Routledge, 2000, pp. 162–78; and Paul Ghils, 'International Civil Society: International Non-Governmental Organizations in the International System', *International Social Science Journal*, no. 133, August 1992, pp. 417–31.

6 Richard Falk, 'The World Order between Inter-State Law and the Law of Humanity: The Role of Civil Society Institutions', in Daniele Archibugi and David Held, eds, *Cosmopolitan Democracy*, Cambridge, Polity, 1995, p. 164.

7 Barbara C. Crosby, *Leadership for Global Citizenship: Building Transnational Community*, Thousand Oaks, Calif., Sage, 1999, p. viii.

8 Liam Mahony and Luis Enrique Eguren, *Unarmed Bodyguards: International Accompaniment for the Protection of Human Rights*, West Hartford, Conn., Kumarian Press, 1997. See also Mary Matheson, 'Bullet-Proof Companions', *Guardian Weekly*, 5 July 1998, p. 24.

9 Amnesty International, *Amnesty International and the Death Penalty*, London, 1979.

10 Crosby, *Leadership*, p. 164.

11 Ibid., pp. 135–6.

12 David Held, Anthony McGrew, David Goldblatt and Jonathan Perraton, *Global Transformations*, Cambridge, Polity, 1999, p. 67.

13 Crosby, *Leadership*, p. 136.

14 Quoted in Held *et al.*, *Global Transformations*, p. 65.

15 Quoted in Crosby, *Leadership*, p. 110.

16 Deborah Stienstra, *Women's Movements and International Organizations*, Basingstoke, Macmillan, 1994, pp. 78–9.

17 Ibid., pp. 96–7.

18 Crosby, *Leadership*, p. 2.

19 Stienstra, *Women's Movements*, p. 101.

20 Steven Mufson, 'Women of the World Make Common Cause', *Guardian Weekly*, 24 September 1995, p. 19. Extracted from *Washington Post*. For more detailed information and analysis see: *Women's Studies Quarterly* (symposium in Beijing), vol. 24, Spring/Summer 1996, pp. 16–298.

21 Stienstra, *Women's Movements*, pp. 138–9.

22 Maggie Black, *A Cause for our Times: Oxfam the First 50 years*, Oxford, Oxfam/Oxford University Press, 1992, pp. 4–5. The USA was a neutral until 1917.

23 See, for example, Raymond Whitaker, 'Overseas Aid is a Self-Perpetuation Industry That Needs Greater Public Scrutiny', *Independent International*, 10–16 June 1998, p. 15 on the latter criticism.

24 Coskun Usterci and Omer Turkes, 'What Remained Under the Ruins is the Government', *Peace News*, no. 2437, December 1999, pp. 7–8.

25 Justin Huggler, 'UN Urged to Set Up Rapid Reaction Unit for Disasters', *Independent*, 23 September 1999, p. 14.

26 Roy Medvedev and Guiletto Chiesa, *Time of Change*, translated by Michael Moore, New York, Pantheon Books, 1989, p. 236.

27 See, for example, Kevin Toolis, 'Africa's Famine is Very Big Business', *Guardian Weekly*, 6 September 1996, p. 20; and John Pomfret, 'Charities Get Caught Up As Tools of War', and 'Agencies Helped Spark Congo Conflict', *Guardian Weekly*, 5 October 1997, p. 17.

28 Black, *A Cause*, pp. 172–3.

29 Ian Black, 'Aid Agency Wins Nobel Peace Prize', *Guardian*, 16 October 1999, p. 3.

30 Black, *A Cause*, p. 195.

31 These issues are covered by ibid., pp. 167–99.

32 Dick Bird, *Never the Same Again: A History of VSO*, Cambridge, Lutterworth Press, 1998.

33 Larry Elliott, 'G8 Fails Test of Leadership', *Guardian Weekly*, 27 July–2 August, 2000, p. 1.

34 Peter van Tuijl, 'NGOs and Human Rights: Sources of Justice and Democracy', *Journal of International Affairs*, vol. 52, no. 2, Spring 1999, pp. 493–512.

35 Andrew Gumbel, 'The Apathy Generation Has a Reason to be Angry', *Independent*, 2 December 1999, p. 5; Vandana Shiva, 'This Round to the Citizens', *Guardian Society*, 8 December 1999, pp. 4–5.

36 Ed Vulliamy, 'Seattle Fears "GreenRage" ', *Observer*, 28 November 1999, p. 21.

37 Larry Elliot, 'Activists Trigger Security Scare', *Guardian*, 30 November 1999, p. 14.

38 Lipschutz, 'Reconstructing World Politics', p. 393.

39 Paul Wapner, *Environmental Activism and World Civic Politics*, Albany, New York, State University of New York Press, 1996.

40 *Peace News*, no. 2436, September–November 1999, p. 31. NB: Purist eco-activists deplore this switch to a central organization reliant on supporters providing funds, rather than a network of small groups trying to live in accordance with green principles.

41 Peter Popham, 'Arundhati and the Dam', *Independent Wednesday Review*, 12 January 2000, pp. 1 and 8.

42 Walter Schwarz, 'Prize Fighters Who Push for Change', *Guardian Weekly*, 22–8 July 1999, p. 19.

43 Lipschutz, 'Reconstructing World Politics', p. 393.

44 John Vidal, 'The Seeds of Wrath', *Guardian Weekly*, 8–14 July 1999, pp. 16–17.

45 Fred Steward, 'Citizens of Planet Earth', in Geoff Andrews, ed., *Citizenship*, London, Lawrence and Wishart, 1991, p. 68.

46 Andrew Dobson, 'Ecological Citizenship: A Disruptive Influence?', *Europa Mundi*, paper for Conference in Santiago di Compostella, May 2000, pp. 61 and 55. A slightly different version of this paper is available in C. Pierson and S. Tormey, eds, *Politics at the Edge*, London, Macmillan, 2000, pp. 40–62.

47 See, for example, Sarah Boseley, 'Manila Jails Child Sex Tour Boss', *Guardian Weekly*, 20 October 1996, p. 7. Jean-Michel Dumay, 'Paedophile and Thai Sex Tourism Go on Trial in Paris', *Le Monde*, excerpt reprinted in *Guardian Weekly*, 9–15 November 2000, p. 34. The Australian Government has prosecuted Australians engaged in child sex in countries abroad.

48 Rob Harrison, 'Bare-Faced Cheek: Can We as Consumers Really Make Business More Ethical?', *New Internationalist*, April 1997, p. 26.

49 'The Bank That Likes to Say Yes', *The Big Issue*, 26 November 1999, pp. 12–13 Extract from *Scientific American*, November 1999. A British-based scheme is Shared Interest, founded in 1990.

50 See Peter Marshall, *Riding the Wind: A New Philosophy for a New Era*, London, Cassell, 1998 for a critique of green consumerism and ethical investment. (Excerpt in *Peace News*, no. 2436, September–November 1999, p. 28.)

51 See John Vidal, 'Power to the People', *Guardian G2*, 7 June 1999, pp. 2–3.

52 Anthony Browne, 'Buy a Chair on the High Street and You Put the Amazon at Risk', *Observer*, 23 July 2000, p. 3.

53 Mary Braid and Stephen Castle, 'How A Little Band of London Activists Forced the Diamond Trade to Confront the Blood on its Hands', *Independent*, 24 July 2000, p. 6.

54 See Nicholas Foulkes, 'Real Diamond Geezer Who Guards the Gems of Choice', *Financial Times, Weekend FT*, 12/13 August 2000, p. 4.

55 Stephen Castle, 'UN-Backed Code on Diamond Trade Could be Meaningless, Warns Minister', *Independent*, 18 July 2000, p. 12.

56 Oxfam, 'Change, Challenge and the Curriculum: Bringing Global Citizenship into the Classroom', Agenda for Conference 30 June–2 July 2000 at the Univesity of Hertfordshire.

57 Severin Carrell, 'How to Watch the World Falling Apart', *Independent*, 21 August 2000, p. 20.

58 Chris Rose, 'Is the Golden Age of Pressure Groups Coming to an Abrupt End?', *Independent, Friday Review*, 11 August 2000, p. 4.

59 Kevin Bales, *Disposable People: New Slavery in the Global Economy*, Berkeley, University of California Press, 1999.

60 Saira Shah, 'West African Parents Sell Children into Slavery', *Independent*, 21 February 2000, p. 13. This article draws on a report by Anti-Slavery International and was also broadcast on Channel 4 News, 21 February 2000.

5 Global or multinational citizens?

1 Cited in L. Green, 'Is World Citizenship a Legal Practicality?', *Canadian Yearbook of International Law*, vol. 25, 1987, pp. 167–8.

2 Cited in ibid., pp. 166–7.

3   Ernst Tugendhat, 'The Moral Dilemma in the Rescue of Refugees', *Social Research*, vol. 62, no. 1, Spring 1995, p. 137.

4   Steve Boggan, 'Appeal to Chinese Community over Lorry Deaths', *Independent*, 21 June 2000, p. 5; Rory Carroll, 'In Rotterdam it is Another Vanishing, Another Consignment Gone Wrong', *Guardian*, 24 June 2000, p. 5; Ted Plafker and John Pomfret, ' "Snakeheads" Feed Off a Culture of Migration', *Washington Post*, reprinted in *Guardian Weekly*, 29 June–5 July 2000, p. 31. These news stories indicated that many other illegal migrants have died trying to reach the United States or Western Europe.

5   See Claudia M. Skran, *Refugees in Inter-War Europe: The Emergence of a Regime*, Oxford, Clarendon Press, 1995, p. 6.

6   J.H. Simpson, *The Refugee Problem: Report of a Survey*, London, Oxford University Press, 1939, p. 10.

7   UNHCR, *The State of the World's Refugees*, Harmondsworth, Penguin, 1993.

8   Hannah Arendt, *The Origins of Totalitarianism*, 2nd enlarged edition, London, Allen and Unwin, 1958, pp. 276–87.

9   Pierre Hassner, 'Refugees: A Special Case for Cosmopolitan Citizenship?', in Daniele Archibugi, David Held and Martin Köhler, eds, *Re-imagining Political Community: Studies in Cosmopolitan Democracy*, Cambridge, Polity, 1998, p. 274.

10 Otto Graf Lambsdorff, 'The Human Rights of Refugees', *UN Chronicle*, vol. 35, no. 4, 1998, p. 51.

11 See Arendt, *Totalitarianism*, pp. 277–9.

12 Skran, *Refugees*, pp. 23 and 27.

13 Ibid., pp. 74–6.

14 Ibid., pp. 104–8; see also Green, 'World Citizenship', p. 181.

15 Skran, *Refugees*, pp. 104–14.

16 Ibid., p. 108.

17 Ibid., p. 78.

18 UNHCR, *State of World's Refugees*, 1993, pp. 11–12.

19 Yasemin Nuhoglu Soysal, *Limits of Citizenship: Migrants and Postnational Membership in Europe*, Chicago, University of Chicago Press, 1994, p. 158.

20 UNHCR, *The State of the World's Refugees: In Search of Solutions*, Oxford, Oxford University Press, 1995, p. 12.

21 Ibid., p. 16.

22 Sarah Collinson, *Beyond Borders: West European Migration Policy towards the 21st Century*, London, RIIA, 1993, p. 66, fn. 9.

23 John Gittings, 'Gate Slams on the Last of the Boat People', *Guardian Weekly*, 8–14 June 2000, p. 5.

24 Sita Bali, 'Migration and Refugees', in Brian White, Richard Little and Michael Smith, eds, *Issues in World Politics*, Basingstoke, Macmillan, 1997, pp. 200–1.

25 Collinson, *Beyond Borders*, p. 69.

26 Ibid., p. 71.

27 Paul Close, *Citizenship, Europe and Change*, Basingstoke, Macmillan, 1995, p. 133.

28 See A. Travis, 'Straw Wants Curb on Liberal Judges', *Guardian*, 12 October 1999, p. 10.

29 Clare Dyer, 'Asylum Seekers Wrongly Jailed', *Guardian Weekly*, 5–11 August 1999, p. 9.

30 Collinson, *Beyond Borders*, p. 85.

31 Katherine Butler and Frances Kennedy, 'Human Traffickers Held for 100 Deaths', *Independent*, 28 August 1999, p. 12.

32 Increasing numbers of nation states also mean that what was once internal migration becomes international – though there is still very large migration within countries, for example from the countryside to the cities.

33 See Elaine Eliah, 'Northern Exposure', *New Internationalist*, September 1998, pp. 12–13 on failure of the West to live up to expectations of African students and job seekers.

34 Bali, 'Migration and Refugees', pp. 203–5.

35 *Keesing's Record of World Events*, 1998, pp. 42136–7.

36 Duncan Campbell, 'Tough US Border Controls "Breach Human Rights" ', *Guardian*, 25 November 1999, p. 16; Jan McGirk and Andrew Gumbel, 'UN Envoy is Sent to Investigate Rio Grande shootings by Posses of Vigilantes', *Independent*, 24 May 2000, p. 16.

37 Soysal, *Limits of Citizenship*, p. 131.

38 Bali, 'Migration and Refugees', pp. 211–12.

39 See Soysal, *Limits of Citizenship*, and on Germany see William Drozdiak, 'Germany's New Multicultural Citizens', *Guardian Weekly*, 13–19 January 2000, p. 27. Excerpted from *Washington Post*.

40 Alastair Davidson, 'Citizenship, Sovereignty and the Identity of the Nation-State', in Nancy Fraser, Anna Yeatman and Alastair Davidson, eds, *Critical Politics: From the Personal to the Global*, Melbourne, Arena Publications, 1994, p. 120.

41 See: Rogers Brubaker, 'Membership without Citizenship: The Economic and Social Rights of Noncitizens', in Rogers Brubaker, ed., *Immigration and Politics of Citizenship in Europe and North America*, Lanham, Maryland, University Press of America; and Zig Layton-Henry, 'Citizenship or Denizenship for Migrant Workers?', in Zig Layton-Henry, ed., *The Political Rights of Migrant Workers in Western Europe*, London, Sage, 1990, pp. 188–95.

42 Rainer Bauböck, 'Changing the Boundaries of Citizenship: The Inclusion of Immigrants in Democratic Politics', in Rainer Bauböck, ed., *From Aliens to Citizens: Redefining the Status of Immigrants in Europe*, Aldershot, Avebury, 1994, pp. 199–232.

43 Tomas Hammar, *Democracy and the Nation State*, Aldershot, Avebury, 1990, p. 115.

44 Ibid., p. 106; moreover only nine had ratified the entire convention, p. 112.

45 Ibid., pp. 112–13.

46 Ibid., p. 119.

47 Soysal, *Limits of Citizenship*, p. 205.

48 Ibid., p. 26;

49 Mark J. Miller, 'Dual Citizenship: A European Norm?', *International Migration Review*, vol. 23, 1989, pp. 945–50.

50 Quoted in Soysal, *Limits of Citizenship*, p. 153.

51 Hammar, *Democracy and the Nation State*, p. 215.

52 Monique Chemillier-Gendreau, 'Should Outsiders Have the Vote?', *Le Monde diplomatique*, January 2000, p. 16.

53 Soysal, *Limits of Citizenship*, pp. 122–3.

54 Ibid., pp. 126–7.

55 Ibid., pp. 65–118.

56 Ibid., pp. 132–4.

57 Ibid., pp. 130–1.

58 Ibid., pp. 139 and 147.

59 Ibid., pp. 154–5.

60 Ibid., p. 161.

61 Ibid., p. 166.

62 Ann Dummett, 'The Acquisition of British Citizenship', in Bauböck, ed., *From Aliens to Citizens*, p. 81.

63 Ibid., p. 82.

64 Hammar, *Democracy and the Nation State*, p. 206.

65 See, for example, David Miller, *On Nationality*, Oxford, Oxford University Press, 1995, pp. 24, 83–5, 89.

66 Soysal, *Limits of Citizenship*, p. 159.

67 Ibid., p. 142.

68 Ibid., p. 158.

69 Collinson, *Beyond Borders*, pp. 74–5.

70 A leaked Austrian 'Strategy paper on Asylum and Immigration Policy' presented to the EU in July 1998 called for the EU to show 'political muscle' to prevent a flow of refugees and suggested 'direct influence and presence is necessary' to contain conflicts and create stability for refugees to return. See Nicholas Busch, 'Fortress Europe', *Peace News*, no. 2427, December 1999–February 2000, pp. 20–2.

71 Jan Willem Honig and Norbert Both, *Record of a War Crime*, London, Penguin, 1997. The figure of 7,000 men killed is regularly quoted in newspaper reports.

72 Collinson, *Beyond Borders*, p. 98.

6 European citizenship

1 Larry Siedentop, *Democracy in Europe*, London, Allen Lane, 2000 has argued this forcefully in his well-regarded book.

2 The Court of Justice at Luxemburg (often referred to as the European Court) interprets EC/EU Treaties and legislation and is quite distinct from the European Court of Human Rights at Strasbourg, created by the Council of Europe in 1949 to adjudicate on the European Convention of Human Rights.

3 Richard Owen and Michael Dynes, *The Times Guide to 1992*, London, Times Books Ltd, 1989, p. 44.

4 Technically the EC was three Communities, as the ECSC, EEC and Euratom were merged in 1967.

5 *Keesing's Record of World Events, News Digest*, March 1999, p. 42864.

6 The Swiss Government withdrew its application for membership in the light of public doubts expressed in a referendum.

7 Stephen Castle, 'Historic Bid to Merge Europe's Armies into United Force', *Independent*, 20 November 2000, p. 4.

8 John Hooper and Ian Black, 'Showdown Over Europe', *Guardian*, 23 June 2000, p. 1; but see also John Lichfield, 'Chirac spurns "Premature" German Vision of the United States of Europe', *Independent*, 31 May 2000, p. 18; and Martin Woollacott, 'We Need Vigour and Rigour at the Heart of Europe', *Guardian Weekly*, 6–12 July, 2000, p. 12, arguing that despite pressing for a group of European states to move more rapidly towards integration, German and French leaders do not agree on the details of a new Europe and are politically weak at home.

9 Two useful recent guides to the evolution of the EU are: John Pinder, *The Building of the European Union*, 3rd edition Oxford, Oxford University Press, 1998; and Timothy Bainbridge, *The Penguin Companion to European Union*, new edition, London, Penguin Books, 1998.

10 See Stephen Castle, 'Big Four Emerge Triumphant After Diplomatic "Coup" ', *Independent*, 12 December 2000, p. 4 (see also other articles on this page).

11 Siofra O'Leary, *European Citizenship: The Options for Reform*, London, Institute for Public Policy Research, 1996, pp. 55–57.

12 Ibid., p. 58 and fn. 33, p. 85.

13 See Bainbridge, *Penguin Companion*, p. 274.

14 Elizabeth Meehan, *Citizenship and the European Community*, London, Sage, 1993, p. 89.

15 Ibid., pp. 87–8.

16 The Directives remain operative until secondary legislation is adopted to enshrine the principle of free movement reiterated in the Maastricht Treaty.

17 O'Leary, *European Union Citizenship*, pp. 51–2.

18 For example, in the 1985 Gravier case the Court ruled that Belgium wrongly charged migrants registration fees for vocational education, which were not paid by nationals; in the Cowan case in 1989 the Court found that a Briton assaulted in France was entitled to the same compensation as a French citizen.

19 Ray Koslowski, 'Intra-EU Migration, Citizenship and Political Union', *Journal of Common Market Studies*, vol. 32, no. 3, September 1994, pp. 369–402.

20 Cited in O'Leary, *European Union Citizenship*, p. 96.

21 Meehan, *Citizenship and the European Community*, p. 21.

22 Bainbridge, *Penguin Companion*, p. 451.

23 See: Pinder, *Building of the European Union*, pp. 135–6; and Paul Marginson and Keith Sissons, 'European Collective Bargaining: A Virtual Prospect?', *Journal of Common Market Studies*, vol. 36, no. 4, December 1998, p. 506.

24 Marginson and Sisson, 'European Collective Bargaining', pp. 505–28.

25 John Grahl and Paul Teague, 'Economic Citizenship in the New Europe', *Political Quarterly*, vol. 65, 1994, pp. 379–96.

26 Meehan, *Citizenship and the European Community*, p. 108.

27 Evelyn Ellis, 'Recent Developments in European Community Sex Equality Law', *Common Market Review*, vol. 35, 1998, p. 381.

28 Ibid., pp. 379–408.

29 Ursula Vogel, 'Emancipatory Politics between Universalism and Difference: Gender Perspectives on European Citizenship', in Percy B. Lehning and Albert Weale, eds, *Citizenship, Democracy and Justice in the New Europe*, London, Routledge, 1997, p. 148.

30 Jürgen Habermas, 'Citizenship and National Identity', in Bart van Steenbergen, ed., *The Condition of Citizenship*, London, Sage, 1994, pp. 27–8.

31 O'Leary, *European Union Citizenship*, p. 45. See the Micheletti case, 1992. O'Leary speculates that this might mean national policies on citizenship could be queried in future.

32 Cited in ibid., p. 90.

33 Bainbridge, *Penguin Companion*, p. 406.

34 Ibid., p. 126.

35 J.H.H. Weiler, 'The Reformation of European Constitutionalism', *Journal of Common Market Studies*, vol. 35, no. 1, 1997, pp. 97–131.

36 Karlheinz Neunreither, 'Citizens and the Exercise of Power in the European Union: Towards a New Social Contract?', in Allan Rosas and Esko Antola, eds, *A Citizens' Europe: In Search of a New Social Order*, London, Sage, 1995, pp. 1–18.

37 Martin Walker, 'Voter Apathy Leaves Left Feeling Glum', *Guardian Weekly*, 20 June 1999, p. 6. Details of the 1999 electoral turnout can be found in *Keesing's Record of World Events, News Digest*, June 1999, pp. 43022–3.

38 O'Leary, *European Union Citizenship*, p. 92.

39 Percy B. Lehning, 'European Citizenship: A Mirage?' in Lehning and Weale, *Citizenship, Democracy and Justice*, p. 189.

40 Raymond Aron, 'Is Multinational Citizenship Possible?', *Social Research*, vol. 41, no. 4, 1974, pp. 638–56.

41 'Conscription: It's Had Its Day', *Economist*, 10 February 1996, pp. 52–3; David Fairhall, 'Death of the Draft: Europe Falls Into Step on New Model Army', *Guardian*, 2 March 1996, p. 14.

42 Martin Shaw, 'Theses on a Post-Military Europe: Conscription, Citizenship and Militarism after the Cold War', in Chris Rootes and Howard Davis, eds, *A New Europe? Social Change and Political Transformation*, London, UCL Press, 1994, p. 63.

43 Hans Ulrich Jessurun d'Oliveira, 'Union Citizenship: Pie in the Sky?', in Rosas and Antola, eds, *A Citizens' Europe*, pp. 58–84, see esp. pp. 77–81.

44 Jürgen Habermas, 'The European Nation State. Its Achievements and Limitations. On the Past and Future of Sovereignty and Citizenship', *Ratio Juris*, vol. 9, no. 2, June 1996, pp. 125–37.

45 Lehning, 'European Citizenship; A Mirage?', p. 189.

46 Ibid., p. 195.

47 P. Pierson and S. Liebfried, 'The Dynamics of Social Policy Integration', in S. Liebfried and P. Pierson, eds, *European Social Policy: Between Fragmentation and Integration*, Washington, DC, The Brookings Institution, 1995, p. 433. Cited in Lehning, 'European Citizenship: A Mirage?', p. 194.

48 John Kincaid, 'Confederal Federation and Citizen Representation in the European Union', *West European Politics*, vol. 22, no. 2, April 1999, pp. 34–58.

49 Meehan, *Citizenship and the European Community*, p. 152.

50 Ulrich K. Preuss, 'Citizenship in the European Union: A Paradigm for Transnational Democracy', in Daniele Archibugi, David Held and Martin Köhler, eds, *Re-imagining Political Community: Studies in Cosmopolitan Democracy*, Cambridge, Polity, 1998, p. 149.

51 Maurice Roche, *Rethinking Citizenship: Welfare, Ideology and Change in Modern Society*, Cambridge, Polity, 1992, p. 192.

52 Ibid., p. 218.

53 Meehan draws on Derek Heater, *Citizenship: The Civic Ideal in World History, Politics and Education*, London, Longman, 1990, p. 16.

54 Heater gives the example of Paul of Tarsus claiming the rights of Roman citizenship.

55 Meehan, *Citizenship and the European Community*, p. 8.

56 Elizabeth Meehan, 'Citizenship and the European Community', *Political Quarterly*, vol. 64, no. 2, 1993, p. 186.

57 John Keane, *Nations, Nationalism and Citizens in Europe*, Oxford, Blackwell, 1994, pp. 182–3.

58 Etienne Tassin, 'Europe: A Political Community?', in Chantal Mouffe, ed., *Dimensions of Radical Democracy*, London, Verso, 1992, pp. 169–92.

59 Dieter Grimm, 'Does Europe Need a Constitution?', *European Law Journal*, vol. 1, no. 3, November 1995, pp. 295 and 296.

60 Will Kymlicka, 'Citizenship in an Era of Globalization', in Ian Shapiro and Casiano Hacker-Cordón, eds, *Democracy's Edges*, Cambridge, Cambridge University Press, 1999, p. 121.

61 Jürgen Habermas, 'Comment on Grimm', *European Law Journal*, vol. 1, no. 3, November 1995, p. 307.

62 G.J. Buitendijk and M.P. C.M. Van Schendelen, 'Brussels Advisory Committees: A Channel of Influence?', *European Law Review*, vol. 20, no. 1, 1995, pp. 37–56.

63 Roche, *Rethinking Citizenship*, p. 219.

64 Kincaid, 'Confederal Federalism', p. 47.

65 Heater, *Citizenship*, p. 18.

66 See Koslowski, 'Intra-EU Migration', p. 377.

67 Marco Martiniello, 'Citizenship of the European Union: A Critical View', in Rainer Bauböck, ed., *From Aliens to Citizens*, Aldershot, Avebury, 1994, p. 36.

68 Richard Falk, 'Regionalism and World Order after the Cold War', in Björn Hettne, András Inotai and Osvaldo Sunkel, eds, *Globalism and the New Regionalism*, Basingstoke, Macmillan, 1999, p. 228.

69 Full application of the WTO rule that all members should be granted tariff concessions on an equal basis was waived until 2000, but in the dispute over the EU's preferential treatment of Caribbean banana producers over those in Central and South America the WTO ruled against the EU.

70 Preuss, 'Citizenship in the European Union', p. 149.

71 See Ian Ward,' Law and the Other Europeans', *Journal of Common Market Studies*, vol. 35, no. 1, March 1997, p. 82.

72 Ibid., pp. 84–5.

73 Claude Moraes, 'Definite Article', *Guardian Society*, 8 December 1999, p. 7.

74 See, for example, Alastair Davidson, *From Subject to Citizen*, Melbourne, Cambridge University Press, 1997, pp. 280–6 discussing problems for Australia hoping that APEC will emulate the EU, given the widespread lack of democracy and abuse of human rights in the region and lack of common public norms.

75 Jürgen Habermas, 'The European Nation-State and the Pressures of Globalization', *New Left Review*, no. 235, May/June 1999, p. 58.

Part III: Introduction

1 Muriel Lester, *Gandhi: World Citizen*, Allahabad, Kitab Mahal, 1945.

2 Virginia Woolf, *Three Guineas*, London, Hogarth Press, [1938] 1947, p. 197.

3 Norman Cousins, 'World Citizenship – When?', in Lyman Bryson, Louis Finkelstein and Robert M. Maciver, eds, *Approaches to World Peace* (4th symposium), New York, Conference on Science Philosophy and Religion in their Relation to the Democratic Way of Life, 1944, pp. 522–6.

4 Louis Wirth, 'The Bearing of Recent Social Trends Upon Attainable Programs for Peace and World Organization', and Bingham Dai, 'Some Problems of Inter-cultural Collaboration for World Peace', in ibid., pp. 110–23 and 124–42.

5 Lawrence S. Wittner, *One World or None*, Stanford, Calif., Stanford University Press, 1993, pp. 71, 113 and 118.

6 Ibid., pp. 160 and 163.

7 Garry Davis, *The World Is My Country*, New York, G.P. Putnam, 1961, pp. 21–35.

8 Wittner, *One World or None*, pp. 114–15 and 163.

9 Davis, *World Is My Country*, pp. 241–3.

10 For a good summary of continuing proposals for world citizenship and world government up to the mid-1960s and alternative policy approaches, see Hanna Newcombe, ed., 'Alternative Approaches to World Government', *Peace Research Reviews*, vol. 1, no. 1, April 1967, pp. 1–55.

11 *Global Citizen*, No. 2 May 2000, p. 1. published by One World Trust, London.

12 Linda Longmire, 'Lighting up the Small Places', *UN Chronicle*, vol. 35, no. 4, 1998, p. 71 referring to an international conference in New York, 30 September–2 October 1998.

7 Global citizenship in contemporary political thought

1 Jürgen Habermas, 'The European Nation-State and the Pressures of Globalization', *New Left Review*, no. 235, May/June 1999, p. 51.

2 John Locke, *Two Treatises of Civil Government*, Cambridge, Cambridge University Press, [1690] 1988. See also Locke, 'A Letter Concerning Toleration', in M. Cranston, ed., *Locke on Politics, Religion and Education*, New York, Collier Books, 1965, pp. 104–46.

3 Social liberalism has roots in J.S. Mill, *On Socialism*, Buffalo, NY, Prometheus Books, [1879] 1976; and T.H. Green 'Liberal Legislation and Freedom of Contract', [1880] essay in R.L. Nettleship, ed., *The Works of Thomas Hill Green*, vol. 3, London, Longmans, Green, 1888. L.T. Hobhouse, *Liberalism*, New York, Oxford University Press, [1911] 1964 sets out the case in full at the beginning of the twentieth century.

4 See F.A. Hayek, *The Constitution of Liberty*, London, Routledge and Kegan Paul, [1960] 1976 and *Law, Legislation and Liberty*, 3 vols, London, Routledge, 1973–82.

5 J.A. Schumpeter, *Capitalism, Socialism and Democracy*, London, Allen and Unwin, 1943, chaps 21–2.

6 See Anthony Downs, *The Economic Theory of Democracy*, New York, Harper, 1957. For an interesting comparison between Schumpeter and Downs, see David Miller, 'The Competitive Model of Democracy', in Graeme Duncan, ed., *Democratic Theory and Practice*, Cambridge, Cambridge University Press, 1983, pp. 133–55.

7 Herman R. van Gunsteren, 'Admission to Citizenship', *Ethics*, vol. 98, no. 4, July 1988, p. 741.

8 See John Browne, 'Business', in *Respect for the Earth: Sustainable Development*, The Reith Lectures, London, Profile Books, 2000, pp. 36–48.

9 This ideal was articulated by J.S. Mill, *Considerations on Representative Government*, Chicago, Henry Regnery, [1861] 1962. It was this ideal that was challenged by the American voting studies of the 1940s and 1950s that stressed the role of automatic allegiances and apathy, and the elitist theorists of democracy, such as J.S. Schumpeter, saw voters as relatively ignorant and prejudiced.

10 There is a large literature on this topic. An early formulation, drawing heavily on Kant, is M.W. Doyle, 'Kant, Liberal Legacies, and Foreign Affairs', Parts 1 and 2, *Philosophy and Public Affairs*, vol. 12, no. 3, pp. 205–35, and vol. 12, no.4, pp. 323–53. An incisive realist critique is provided by Christopher Layne, 'Kant or Cant: The Myth of the Democratic Peace', *International Security*, vol. 19, no. 2, Fall 1994, pp. 5–49.

11 John Rawls, *The Law of Peoples*, Cambridge, Mass., Harvard University Press, 1999, see pp. 37 (for eight principles of justice between peoples) and 119–20.

12 For an interesting critique of Rawls's essay see Thomas McCarthy, 'On the Idea of a Reasonable Law of Peoples', in James Bohman and Matthias Lutz-Bachmann, eds, *Perpetual Peace: Essays on Kant's Cosmopolitan Ideal*, Cambridge, Mass., MIT Press, 1997, pp. 201–18.

13 Rawls, *Law of Peoples*, p. 36.

14 Ibid., pp. 56–7.

15 For elitist theories of democracy and their critics, see Henry S. Kariel, ed., *Frontiers of Democratic Theory*, New York, Random House, 1970. Carole Pateman, *Participation and Democratic Theory*, Cambridge, Cambridge University Press, 1970 (written before she became a feminist theorist) was an important defence of participatory democracy, including worker participation.

16 See Michael Walzer, ed., *Toward a Global Civil Society*, Providence, Rhode Island, Berghahn Books, 1995; Paul Hirst, *Associative Democracy*, Amherst, Mass., University of Massachusetts Press, 1994.

17 Richard Falk, 'Global Civil Society and the Democratic Prospect', in Barry Holden, ed., *Global Democracy: Key Debates*, London, Routledge, 2000, p. 163.

18 Ibid., pp. 171–74.

19 Richard Falk, 'The Making of Global Citizenship', in Bart von Steenbergen, ed., *The Condition of Citizenship*, London, Sage, 1994, p. 139.

20 Kant, 'Perpetual Peace: A Philosophical Sketch', in Hans Reiss, ed., *Kant: Political Writings*, 2nd enlarged edition, translated by H.B. Nisbet, Cambridge, Cambridge University Press, 1991, pp. 105–8, 'Third Definitive Article of Perpetual Peace: Cosmopolitan Right shall be Limited to Conditions of Universal Hospitality.'

21 Immanuel Kant, 'The Metaphysical Elements of the Theory of Right', in ibid., pp. 174, 175.

22 Kant, 'Perpetual Peace', pp. 108–14. 'First Supplement: On the Guarantee of a Perpetual Peace'. Kant also suggests that in the past wars have helped to populate the whole globe by encouraging migration.

23 Ibid., p. 114.

24 Martha C. Nussbaum, 'Kant and Stoic Cosmopolitanism', *Journal of Political Philosophy*, vol. 5, no. 1, March 1997, p. 13, fn. 39.

25 Martha C. Nussbaum, 'Patriotism and Cosmopolitanism', in Martha C. Nussbaum *et al.*, *For Love of Country: Debating the Limits of Patrotism*, edited by Joshua Cohen, Boston, Beacon Press, 1996, p. 7.

26 Ibid., pp. 12–13.
27 Martha Nussbaum, 'Lawyer for Humanity: Theory and Practice in Ancient Political Thought', in I. Shapiro and J. DeCew, eds, *Theory and Practice, Nomos*, vol. 37, New York, New York University Press, pp. 189–98.
28 See Lawrence S. Wittner, *Resisting the Bomb*, Stanford, Calif., Stanford University Press, 1997, p. 118, and Translator's Note to Karl Jaspers, *The Atom Bomb and the Future of Man*, Chicago, University of Chicago Press, 1961, p. v. As well as being attacked by the left for giving support to Chancellor Adenauer, Jaspers was later attacked by the right for criticizing the goal of German reunification.
29 Karl Jaspers, 'Philosophical Memoir', in *Philosophy and the World*, translated by E.B. Ashton, Chicago, Henry Regnery, 1963, p. 277.
30 Ibid., p. 302.
31 Karl Jaspers, 'Kant's Perpetual Peace', in *Philosophy and the World*, pp. 116–17. It is debatable whether Jaspers' interpretation of Kant's 'secret article' requiring governments to listen to philosophers is correct, but Jaspers indicates his own approach.
32 Hannah Arendt, 'Karl Jaspers: Citizen of the World?', in *Men in Dark Times*, New York, Harcourt Brace and World Inc., 1968, pp. 81–94.
33 Japsers, 'Philosophical Memoir', p. 296.
34 Arendt, 'Karl Jaspers', p. 85. 'Truth is what binds us together' is quoted from Jaspers, 'Vom bebedigen Geist der Universitat', 1946, in *Rechenschaft und Ausblick*, Munich, 1951, p. 185.
35 Japsers, 'Kant's Perpetual Peace', p. 123.
36 Jaspers, *The Atom Bomb*, p. 233.
37 Arendt, 'Karl Jaspers', p. 93. See also Jaspers, *The Atom Bomb*, pp. 332–5.
38 Jaspers, *The Atom Bomb*, p. 315.
39 Ibid., p. 22.
40 Ibid., p. 159.
41 Andrew Linklater, 'Cosmopolitan Citizenship', in Kimberley Hutchings and Roland Dannreuther, eds, *Cosmopolitan Citizenship*, Basingstoke, Macmillan, 1999, p. 39.
42 Andrew Linklater, 'Citizenship and Sovereignty in the Post-Westphalian State', *European Journal of International Relations*, vol. 2, 1996, p. 91.
43 Linklater, 'Cosmopolitan Citizenship', pp. 43–4.
44 Ibid., p. 43.
45 Jürgen Habermas 'On the Cognitive Content of Morality', in *Proceedings of the Aristotelian Society*, London, Aristotelian Society, 1996, pp. 352–3. The most comprehensive reworking of Habermas's position on morality, politics and law is *Between Facts and Norms: Contributions to a Discourse Theory of Law and Democracy*, translated by William Rehg, Cambridge, Polity, 1996.
46 Discourse is understood at a number of levels. At its most abstract it provides a basis for justifying norms (William Rehg, Translator's Introduction to ibid., p. xxvi), whilst moral discourse is based on validity claims everyone could in principle understand and 'ethical discourse' refers to claims relevant to and understood only within specific groups (ibid., p. xv).
47 Jürgen Habermas, 'Three Normative Models of Democracy', in Seyla Benhabib, ed., *Democracy and Difference*, Princeton, NJ, Princeton University Press, 1996, pp. 21–30.
48 Ibid., p. 29.
49 Jürgen Habermas, 'Remarks on Dieter Grimm's "Does Europe Need a Constitution?" ', *European Law Journal*, vol. 1, no. 3, November 1995, p. 306.
50 I am grateful to Martin Leet for this point.
51 Jürgen Habermas, 'The European Nation State. Its Achievements and Limitations. On the Past and Future of Sovereignty and Citizenship', *Ratio Juris*. vol. 9, no. 2, June 1996. p. 131.
52 Jürgen Habermas, 'Citizenship and National Identity: Some Reflections on the Future of Europe', *Praxis International*, vol. 12, no. 1, April 1992, p. 8.
53 Ibid., p. 12.
54 Habermas, 'Comment on Grimm', p. 307.
55 Jürgen Habermas, 'The European Nation-State and the Pressures of Globalization', *New Left Review*, no. 235, May/June 1999, pp. 57–8.
56 Habermas, 'Citizenship and National Identity', p. 18.
57 Habermas, 'The European Nation State', p. 137.
58 Jürgen Habermas, 'Kant's Idea of Perpetual Peace, with the Benefit of Two Hundred Years' Hindsight', in Bohman and Lutz-Bachmann, eds, *Perpetual Peace*, pp. 134–5.

59 James Bohman, 'The Public Spheres of the World Citizen', in Bohman and Lutz-Bachman, eds, *Perpetual Peace*, pp. 179–200.

60 For an enthusiastic survey of the possibilities in New Zealand see Jonathan Freedland, 'The Future is Kiwi', *Guardian*, 3 May, 2000, p. 19. For background see Jane Kelsey, *Reclaiming the Future: New Zealand and the Global Economy*, Wellington, N.Z., Bridget Williams Books, 1999.

61 Manfred Bienefeld, 'Capitalism and the Nation State in the Dog Days of the Twentieth Century', in Ralph Miliband and Leo Panitch, eds, *The Socialist Register 1994*, London Merlin Press, 1994, pp. 94–129.

62 Göran Therborn, 'Social Democracy in One Country', *Dissent*, Fall 2000, p. 64.

63 Paul Hirst and Grahame Thompson, *Globalization in Question*, 2nd revised edition, Cambridge, Polity, 1999.

64 George Soros, *The Crisis of Global Capitalism*, London, Little Brown & Co., 1998.

65 Joachim Hirsch, 'Nation-State, International Regulation and the Question of Democracy', *Review of International Political Economy*, vol. 2, no. 2, Spring 1995, p. 281.

66 Robert Cox, 'Globalization, Multilateralism, and Democracy', in Robert W. Cox with Timothy J. Sinclair, *Approaches to World Order*, Cambridge, Cambridge Univesity Press, 1996, pp. 534–5.

67 Robert Cox, 'Democracy in Hard Times: Economic Globalization and the Limits to Liberal Democracy', in Anthony McGrew, ed., *The Transformation of Democracy?*, Cambridge, Polity, 1997, p. 70.

68 Cox, 'Globalization, Multilateralism and Democracy', p. 535.

69 I have therefore ignored the historical and contemporary versions of what Quentin Skinner calls 'neo-roman theory', which is focused particularly on individual liberty and its relation to a free state. See Quentin Skinner, *Liberty before Liberalism*, Cambridge, Cambridge University Press, 1998.

70 Rousseau in *The Social Contract* suggests that the ideal unit is on the scale of a Swiss canton, but Rousseau has also been seen as paving the way for nationalist ideology in his *Constitution for Poland*.

71 John Keane, *Tom Paine: A Political Life*, London, Bloomsbury, 1995, p. xx.

72 John Keane, 'Nations, Nationalism and European Citizens', in S. Periwal, ed., *Notions of Nationalism*, Budapest, Central European University Press, 1995, p. 203.

73 Benjamin Barber, *Strong Democracy*, Berkeley, Calif., University of California Press, 1984.

74 Alastair Davidson, *From Subject to Citizen*, Melbourne, Cambridge University Press, 1997, pp. 257–58.

75 Ibid., pp. 43–4.

76 Alastair Davidson, 'Citizenship, Sovereignty and the Identity of the Nation State', in Nancy Fraser, Anna Yeatman and Alastair Davidson, eds, *Critical Politics: From the Personal to the Global*, Melbourne, Arena Publications, 1994, pp. 111–23.

77 Ibid., pp. 262–3.

78 Ibid., p. 45.

79 Alastair Davidson, 'Globalism, the Regional Citizen and Democracy', in B. Galligan and C. Sandford, eds, *Rethinking Human Rights*, Sydney, Federation Press, 1997, pp. 215–33, which stresses the role of experts and of communication by internet.

80 Jean-Jacques Rousseau, *The Social Contract*, translated by Maurice Cranston, Harmondsworth, Penguin, 1968, p. 143 (bk III, chap. 15). In a footnote relating to the dangers of a very small republic being subjugated, Rousseau comments that he had intended to deal with foreign relations and 'the subject of confederation', which is entirely new 'and its principles have yet to be established'.

81 Anthony McGrew, 'Democracy Beyond Borders', in Anthony McGrew, ed., *The Transformation of Democracy*, pp. 245–7. For Burnheim's theory of 'demarchy', which stresses functional forms of organization, see John Burnheim, *Is Democracy Possible?*, Cambridge, Cambridge University Press, 1985. Burnheim extends the concept of demarchy across borders in John Burnheim, 'Democracy, Nation States and World Systems', in D. Held and C. Pollitt, eds, *New Forms of Democracy*, London, Sage, 1986, pp. 218–39.

82 Kenneth Baynes, 'Communitarian and Cosmopolitan Challenges to Kant's Conception of World Peace', in Bohman and Lutz-Bachman, eds, *Perpetual Peace*, pp. 219–34.

83 M. Sandel, *Democracy's Discontent*, Cambridge, Mass., Harvard University Press, 1996, p. 342 (cited in McGrew, 'Democracy Beyond Borders', p. 253).

84 Jaspers, 'Philosophical Memoir', pp. 273–4. 'An emigrant since 1933, having roamed the earth with her spirit unbroken by difficulties. ... Her inner independence made her a world citizen; her faith in the singular strength of the American Constitution ... made her a citizen of the United States.'

85 Arendt, 'Karl Jaspers', pp. 83–4.

86 Ibid., p. 81.

87 Hannah Arendt, *The Origins of Totalitarianism*, 2nd revised edition, London, Allen and Unwin, 1958, pp. 290–302 on 'The Perplexities of the Rights of Man'.

88 Hannah Arendt, *Crises of the Republic*, New York, Harcourt Brace Jovanovich, 1972, which includes her essays on 'Civil Disobedience' and 'Thoughts on Politics and Revolution'. See also Hannah Arendt, *On Violence*, London, Allen Lane/Penguin Press, 1970 for her criticisms of the move by protest movements towards a rhetoric of violence. On the republican element in non-violent social movements, see Jeffrey C. Isaac, 'Oases in the Desert: Hannah Arendt on Democratic Politics', *American Political Science Review*, vol. 88, no. 1, March 1994, pp. 156–68.

89 Arendt, 'Karl Jaspers', p. 89.

90 David Miller, 'Bounded Citizenship' in Hutchings and Dannreuther, eds, *Cosmopolitan Citizenship*, Basingstoke, Macmillan, 1999, pp. 68–69.

91 Hannah Arendt, *Eichmann in Jerusalem: A Report on the Banality of Evil*, revised and enlarged edition, Harmondsworth, Penguin, 1994, pp. 232–3.

92 David Miller, 'The Ethical Significance of Nationality', *Ethics*, vol. 98. no. 4, July 1988, pp. 647–8; Miller, 'Bounded Citizenship', p. 60; David Miller, *On Nationality*, Oxford, Oxford University Press, 1995.

93 Michael Walzer, *Spheres of Justice: A Defense of Pluralism and Equality*, New York, Basic Books, 1983.

94 Michael Walzer, *Just and Unjust Wars*, Harmondsworth, Penguin, 1980, pp. xv–xvi and xiv. Walzer leaves it open, however, whether his moral arguments here are truly universal or drawn from a (western) world view which will be shared by all his readers (see p. 20).

95 William A. Galston, 'Community, Democracy and Philosophy: The Political Thought of Michael Walzer', *Political Theory*, vol. 17, no. 1, February 1989, p. 124, citing Walzer, *Interpretation and Social Criticism*, Cambridge, Mass., Harvard University Press, 1987, p. 45, discussing Vitoria's invocation of natural law against the Aztec custom of human sacrifice.

96 Michael Walzer, *Thick and Thin: Moral Arguments at Home and Abroad*, London, University of Notre Dame Press, 1994.

97 Michael Walzer, 'Spheres of Affection', in Nussbaum *et al.*, *For Love of Country*, p. 125.

98 Walzer, 'Introduction', in Walzer, ed., *Toward a Global Civil Society*, p. 4.

99 Walzer, 'Spheres of Affection', p. 126.

100 Richard Rorty, *Contingency, Irony and Solidarity*, Cambridge, Cambridge University Press, 1989, pp. 58–60.

101 Walzer, 'Spheres of Affection', p. 126. See also Michael W. McConnell, 'Don't Neglect the Little Platoons', in Nussbaum *et al.*, *For Love of Country*, pp. 78–84.

102 Robert Pinksy, 'Eros Against Esperanto', in Nussbaum *et al.*, *For Love of Country*, p. 85.

103 Rorty, *Contingency, Irony, and Solidarity*, pp. 189–91.

104 Robert E. Goodin, 'What Is So Special About Our Fellow Countrymen?', *Ethics*, vol. 98, no. 4, July 1988, p. 664.

105 Walzer, *Thick and Thin*.

106 Walzer, 'Spheres of Affection', p. 126.

107 Norman Geras, 'Richard Rorty and the Righteous among the Nations', in Miliband and Panitch, eds, *The Socialist Register 1994*, pp. 32–59. Some of the respondents also referred to Christian beliefs that required giving help to fellow human beings. What people say is not necessarily an accurate reflection of motivation, but does suggest how they think about their actions. For a more detailed study see Kristin Renwick Monroe, *The Heart of Altruism: Perceptions of a Common Humanity*, Princeton, NJ, Princeton University Press, 1996.

108 John Rawls, *A Theory of Justice*, Oxford, Oxford University Press, 1972, p. 176 suggests that in formulating principles of justice it is necessary to consider whether people can reasonably be expected to accept the consequences of observing a principle. Hence the need to consider 'the strains of commitment'.

109 Peter Singer, 'Famine, Affluence, and Morality', *Philosophy and Public Affairs*, vol.1, 1972, pp. 229–43.

110 See Peter Singer, *Practical Ethics*, Cambridge, Cambridge University Press, 1979, chap. 8. For a reconsideration of these arguments and references to a wider literature, see Garrett Cullity, 'International Aid and the Scope of Kindness', *Ethics*, vol. 105, Oct. 1994, pp. 99–127.

111 Henry Shue, 'Mediating Duties', *Ethics*, vol. 98, no. 4, July 1988.

112 Ibid., p. 689.

113 Ibid., pp. 688–700.

114 Ibid., p. 704.

115 Thomas W. Pogge, 'Cosmopolitanism and Sovereignty', *Ethics*, vol. 103, October 1992, p. 52.

116 For an argument against prioritizing compatriots, see also Goodin, 'What Is So Special about Our Fellow Countrymen?'

117 Nussbaum, 'Patriotism and Cosmopolitanism', pp. 7 and 9.

118 Goodin, 'What Is So Special About Our Fellow Countrymen?' pp. 675–86. Nussbaum also adopts a version of the assigned responsibility model in relation to family duties.

119 Kwame Appiah, 'Cosmopolitan Patriots', in Nussbaum *et al.*, *For Love of Country*, pp. 21–9. Another argument for 'rooted cosmopolitanism' is Bruce Ackerman, 'Rooted Cosmopolitanism', *Ethics*, vol. 104, April 1994, pp. 516–35. Ackerman's reflections are closely tied to his own previous writings and differing interpretations of the US Constitution.

120 See Gareth Evans, *Cooperating for Peace: The Global Agenda for the 1990s and Beyond*, Sydney, Allen and Unwin, 1993; Andrew Linklater, 'What is Good International Citizenship?' in P. Keal, ed., *Ethics and Foreign Policy*, Sydney, Allen and Unwin, 1992, pp. 21–43.

121 David Miller, 'Citizenship and Pluralism', *Political Studies*, vol. 53, 1995, p. 448.

122 Miller, 'Bounded Citizenship', pp. 62 and 63.

123 Ibid., p. 78. Miller's argument is skewed by focusing on a phrase from Falk suggesting movement activists are 'citizen pilgrims' and stressing the elements of 'pilgrimage'.

124 Ibid., p. 66.

125 Arendt, 'Civil Disobedience' in *Crises of the Republic*, pp. 94–102.

126 Michael Walzer, 'The Problem of Citizenship', in *Obligations: Essays on Disobedience, War and Citizenship*, Cambridge, Mass., Harvard University Press, 1970, p. 219, citing Hegel's *Philosophy of Right*, para. 255.

127 Baynes contrasts Walzer's pluralism with Charles Taylor's form of republicanism and 'unmediated conception of public life' suggesting an indivisible republic. See Baynes, 'Communitarian and Cosmopolitan Challenges to Kant's Conception of World Peace', p. 222.

128 Michael Walzer, 'Prisoners of War; Does the Fight Continue After Battle?', in *Obligations*, p. 166.

129 Albert Weale, 'Citizenship Beyond Borders', in Ursula Vogel and Michael Moran, eds, *The Frontiers of Citizenship*, Basingstoke, Macmillan, 1991, pp. 155–65. Weale notes alternative approaches based on moral philosophy to duties beyond borders, citing in particular Goodin in the issue of *Ethics*, vol. 98, no. 4, July 1988, discussed earlier in this chapter.

130 Weale, 'Citizenship Beyond Borders', p. 157.

131 Ibid., p. 161.

8 Global citizenship and global governance

1 See: Kimberley Hutchings, *International Political Theory*, London, Sage, 1999; Andrew Linklater, *The Transformation of Political Community: Ethical Foundations of the Post-Westphalian Era*, Cambridge, Polity, 1998; Chris Brown, ' "Turtles All the Way Down": Anti-Foundationalism, Critical Theory and International Relations', *Millennium*, vol. 23, no. 2, 1994, pp. 213–36; Jürgen Haacke, 'Theory and Praxis in International Relations: Habermas, Self-Reflection, Rational Argumentation', *Millennium*, vol. 25, no. 2, 1996, pp. 255–89.

2 Two classic realist statements are: E.H. Carr, *The Twenty Years' Crisis*, London, Macmillan, 1939; and Hans Morgenthau, *Politics Among Nations*, New York, Knopf, 1948.

3 Morgenthau, *Politics Among Nations*.

4 International Steering Committee of Peoples' World Convention, *Peoples' World Convention: The Plan in Outline*, London, June 1950, p. 2.

5 Hedley Bull, *The Anarchical Society*, London, Macmillan, 1977, pp. 206–7.

6 A well-known analysis of the ambiguities of the balance of power is Martin Wight, 'Balance of Power', in Wight, *Power Politics*, Harmondsworth, Penguin, 1979, pp. 165–85. See also Bull, *Anarchical Society*.

7 Kenneth N. Waltz, *Theory of International Politics*, Reading, Mass., Addison-Wesley, 1979.
8 See: Barry Buzan, *People, States and Fear: The National Security Problem in International Relations*, Brighton, Wheatsheaf, 1983; and Barry Buzan, 'Regional Security as a Policy Objective: The Case of South and Southwest Asia', in A.Z. Rubinstein, ed., *The Great Game: The Rivalry in the Persian Gulf and South Asia*, New York, Praeger, 1983, chap. 10.
9 See Bull, *Anarchical Society* on justice in international politics. See also Geoffrey Goodwin, 'An International Morality?', in Bhiku Parekh and R.N. Berki, eds, *The Morality of Politics*, London, Allen and Unwin, 1972, pp. 99–113.
10 Bull, *Anarchical Society*, pp. 108–9. Bull cites Lassa Oppenheim, *International Law*, 1st edition, London, Longmans, 1905, vol. 1, p. 73.
11 See Michael Banks, 'The Evolution of International Relations Theory', in Michael Banks, ed., *Conflict in World Society: A New Perspective on International Relations*, Brighton, Wheatsheaf, 1984, p. 20.
12 At the beginning of *The Social Contract*, Rousseau attacked Grotius as a supporter of tyrants.
13 Karl W. Deutsch, *The Nerves of Government*, New York, Free Press, 1957; Banks, ed., *Conflict in World Society*. See also John W. Burton, *Global Conflict: The Domestic Sources of International Crisis*, Brighton, Wheatsheaf, 1984; Michael Smith, Richard Little and Michael Shackleton, eds, *Perspectives on World Politics*, London, Croom Helm/Open University Press, 1981, s. 2: 'The Politics of Interdependence and Transnational Relations'.
14 See Mark W. Zacher and Richard A. Matthew, 'Liberal International Theory: Common Threads, Divergent Strands', in Charles W. Kegley, ed., *Controversies in International Relations Theory: Realism and the Neoliberal Challenge*, New York, St Martins Press, 1995, pp. 107–49.
15 See Lawrence S. Wittner, *Resisting the Bomb*, Stanford, Calif., Stanford University Press, 1997, pp. 426–7. The White House saw 'support from the grassroots as key'. On the 'Dartmouth Conferences', see Gale Warner and Michael H. Shuman, *Citizen Diplomats: Pathfinders in Soviet–American Relations*, New York, Continuum, 1987, pp. 157–88.
16 See, for example, Stephen D. Krasner. ed., *International Regimes*, Ithaca, NY, Cornell University Press, 1983.
17 See Barry Buzan, Ole Waever and Jaap de Wilde, *Security: A New Framework for Analysis*, Boulder, Colo., Lynne Rienner Publishers, 1998.
18 For an argument that the Westphalian system is gradually being replaced by an evolving world legal order, see Allan Rosas, 'State Sovereignty and Human Rights', *Political Studies*, vol. 63, 1995, pp. 61–78.
19 Alexander Wendt, 'Collective Identity Formation and the International State', *American Political Science Review*, vol. 88, no. 2, June 1994, pp. 384–96.
20 Alexander Wendt, 'A Comment on Held's Cosmopolitanism', in Ian Shapiro and Casiano Hacker-Cordón, eds, *Democracy's Edges*, Cambridge, Cambridge University Press, 1999, pp. 127–33.
21 Linklater, *Transformation of Political Community*, p. 43.
22 Norberto Bobbio, 'Democracy and the International System', in Daniele Archibugi and David Held, eds, *Cosmopolitan Democracy: An Agenda for a New World Order*, Cambridge, Polity, 1995.
23 Daniel Warner, 'The Nuclear Weapons Decision by the International Court of Justice: Locating the *raison* behind *raison d'état*', *Millennium*, vol. 27, no. 2, 1998, pp. 299–324. The opinion did not reject possession of nuclear weapons for deterrence or totally exclude their use as a last resort.
24 Richard Falk, 'Global Civil Society and the Democratic Prospect', in Barry Holden ed., *Global Democracy: Key Debates*, London, Routledge, 2000, p. 163.
25 Burton, *Global Conflict*, pp. 153–60.
26 Kate Dewes and Robert Green, 'The World Court Project: How a Citizen Network Can Influence the United Nations', *Pacifica Review*, vol. 7, no. 2, October/November 1995, pp. 17–38.
27 The Commission on Global Governance, *Our Global Neighbourhood*, Oxford, Oxford University Press, 1995. See: Richard Falk, 'Liberalism at the Global Level: The Last of the Independent Commissions', *Millennium*, vol. 34, no. 3, 1995, pp. 563–78; and Anthony McGrew, 'Democracy Beyond Borders? Globalization and the Reconstruction of Democratic Theory and Practice', in Anthony McGrew, ed., *The Transformation of Democracy?*, Cambridge, Polity, 1997, pp. 242–5.

28 See, for example, Frank Barnaby, ed., *Building a More Democratic United Nations*, London, Frank Cass, 1991 (drawing on diverse proposals made by the US-based Campaign for a More Democratic United Nations); and Ramesh Thakur, ed., *The United Nations at Fifty: Retrospect and Prospect*, Dunedin, New Zealand, University of Otago Press, 1996.

29 See Mark Imber, 'Geo-Governance Without Democracy? Reforming the UN System', in McGrew, ed., *Transformation of Democracy?*, pp. 201–30.

30 Commission on Global Governance, *Our Global Neighbourhood*, pp. 233–41.

31 Jarat Chopra and Thomas G. Weiss, 'Sovereignty Is No Longer Sacrosanct: Codifying Humanitarian Intervention', *Ethics and International Affairs*, vol. 6, 1992, pp. 95–117; Christopher Greenwood, 'Is There a Right of Humanitarian Intevention?', *The World Today*, vol. 49, no. 2, 1992, pp. 34–40; Adam Roberts, 'Humanitarian War: Military Intervention and Human Rights', *International Affairs*, vol. 69. no. 3, 1993, pp. 429–49.

32 Commission on Global Governance, *Our Global Neighbourhood*, pp. 254–60.

33 Ibid., pp. 217–21.

34 Ibid., pp. 303–34.

35 Grenville Clark and Louis B. Sohn, *World Peace Through World Law*, 3rd edition, Cambridge, Mass., Harvard University Press, [1958] 1966.

36 John C. de Vere Roberts, *World Citizenship and Mundialism*, Westport, Conn., Praeger, 1999, pp. 75–6; and Keith Suter, 'Towards a Federal World State?', in Michael Salla, Walter Tonetto and Enrique Martínez, eds, *Essays on Peace*, Rockhampton, Central University of Queensland Press, p. 210.

37 International Steering Committee of Peoples' World Convention, *Peoples' World Convention*.

38 Suter, 'Towards a Federal World State?', p. 210.

39 Joseph P. Baratta, 'The International History of the World Federal Movement', *Peace and Change*, vol. 14, no. 4, October 1989, pp. 383–5.

40 See Roberts, *World Citizenship*; and Suter, 'Towards a Federal World State?' Derek Heater, *World Citizenship and Government: Cosmopolitan Ideas in the History of Western Political Thought*, Basingstoke, Macmillan, 1996, pp. 187–212 provides a good summary of earlier aspirations to and criticisms of the idea of world government, and comments briefly on today's thinking about cosmopolitan democracy.

41 Inis L. Claude, *Swords Into Plowshares*, New York, Random House, 1956.

42 *Global Citizen*, no. 1, March 2000, p. 1.

43 See: McGrew, 'Democracy Beyond Borders?'; and Hutchings, *International Political Theory*, pp. 153–79. Hutchings suggests a theoretically diverse category of 'radical democratic pluralism as a preferred form of political cosmopolitanism' (p. 166).

44 David Held, *Democracy and the Global Order*, Cambridge, Polity, 1995, pp. 230 and 231.

45 Ibid., p. 233.

46 David Held, *Models of Democracy*, Cambridge, Polity, 1996, chap. 10.

47 Held, *Democracy and the Global Order*, p. 147.

48 Held, *Models of Democracy*, p. 355.

49 Held, *Democracy and the Global Order*, p. 147.

50 Held, *Models of Democracy*, pp. 355 and 358.

51 David Held, 'The Changing Contours of Political Community: Rethinking Democracy in the Context of Globalization', in Holden, ed., *Global Democracy*, pp. 29–30.

52 Dennis Thompson, 'Democratic Theory and Global Society', *Journal of Political Philosophy*, vol. 7, no. 2, 1999, pp. 111–25. Thompson sees deliberative democracy as a partial solution to institutional and other problems.

53 See Michael Saward, 'A Critique of Held', in Holden, ed., *Global Democracy*, p. 37.

54 See Baogang He and David Held, 'Democracy, Transnational Problems and the Boundary Question: Challenges for China', *Social Alternatives*, vol. 16, no. 4, October 1997, p. 35. Held comments: 'I have developed my ideas partly in the context of the European Union.'

55 See, for example, speech by Joschka Fischer, German Foreign Secretary, in May 2000 urging progress towards federal Europe. John Hooper and Ian Black, 'Showdown Over Europe', *Guardian*, 23 June, 2000, p. 1.

56 Held, *Models of Democracy*, p. 359.

57 John S. Dryzek, 'Transnational Democracy', *Journal of Political Philosophy*, vol. 7, no. 1, 1999, pp. 30–51.

58 Saward, 'A Critique of Held', pp. 32–46.

59 Wendt, 'Comment on Held's Cosmopolitanism'.

60 Will Kymlicka, 'Citizenship in an Era of Globalization: Commentary on Held', in Shapiro and Hacker-Cordón, eds, *Democracy's Edges*, p. 119.
61 Robert Dahl, 'Can International Organizations be Democratic? A Skeptic's View', in ibid., p. 22.
62 Wendt, 'Comment on Held's Cosmopolitanism', p. 128.
63 Commission on Global Governance, *Our Global Neighbourhood*, pp. 172–4.
64 Ibid., chap. 4, pp. 135–224.
65 Falk, 'Global Civil Society and the Democratic Prospect', p. 170.
66 Ibid., p. 175.
67 Held, *Democracy and the Global Order*, p. 245.
68 Ibid., pp. 26–61.
69 Ibid., pp. 253 and 262.
70 Gregory Palast, 'How US Business Sets the Globalisation Agenda for the World Trade Organisation', *Guardian Weekly*, 26–31 May 2000, p. 14.
71 Katherine Butler, 'UN Offers Firms "Logo for Human Rights" Deal', *Independent*, 26 July 2000, p. 14. The companies included Nike, Shell and Rio Tinto, accused in the past of human rights violations. Greenpeace and 19 other NGOs protested. The UN argued that this move would reduce corporate abuses and that companies would be monitored by the UN and by NGOs.
72 Grahame Thompson, 'Multinational Corporations and Democratic Control', in McGrew, ed., *Transformation of Democracy?*, pp. 149–70.
73 Paul Hirst and Grahame Thompson, *Globalization in Question*, 2nd revised edition, Cambridge, Polity, 1999, p. 276.
74 Held, *Democracy and the Global Order*, p. 118.
75 Bull, *Anarchical Society*, pp. 266–70.
76 See Niccolò Machiavelli, *The Prince*, edited by Quentin Skinner and Russell Price, Cambridge, Cambridge University Press, [1532] 1988, pp. 87–91: 'Exhortation to Liberate Italy from the Barbarian Yoke'.
77 Chris Hunter, 'Taking Responsibility', *Peace News*, no. 2439, June–August 2000, p. 8.
78 PBI Team, 'Protecting Peace', *Peace News*, no. 2439, June–August 2000, p. 9.
79 Danilo Zolo: *Cosmopolis: Prospect for World Government*, Cambridge, Polity, 1997; and 'The Lords of Peace: From the Holy Alliance to the New International Criminal Tribunals', in Holden, ed., *Global Democracy*, pp. 73–86.
80 Zolo, *Cosmopolis*, p. xv and 'Lords of Peace', p. 81.
81 Edward Said, *Culture and Imperialism*, London, Chatto and Windus (Vintage) 1994, p. 345. Said quotes from Richard J. Barnet, *The Roots of War*, New York, Atheneum, 1972, p. 21.
82 Phyllis Bennis, 'US Undermines International Law', *Le Monde diplomatique*, December 1999, p. 2.
83 Zolo, *Cosmopolis*, p. 177.
84 Zolo, 'Lords of Peace', p. 79.
85 Ibid., p. 78.
86 Chris McGreal, 'UN Urged to Try Leader of Rebels', *Guardian*, 19 June 2000, p. 11.

9 Cultural diversity, feminism and postmodernism

1 See Jean-François Lyotard, *The Postmodern Condition: A Report on Knowledge*, translated by Geoff Bennington and Brian Massumi, Manchester, Manchester University Press, 1984. For a discussion of the problems of defining postmodernism and its relation to French feminism, see Judith Butler, 'Contingent Foundations: Feminism and the Question of "Postmodernism" ', *Praxis International*, vol. 11, no. 2, July 1991, pp. 150–65.
2 Lyotard, *The Postmodern Condition*, p. 37, cited in James Williams, *Lyotard: Towards a Postmodern Philosophy*, Cambridge, Polity, 1998, p. 33.
3 For exploration of European claims to universality, see Jacques Derrida, *The Other Heading: Reflections on Today's Europe*, translated by P.A. Brault and M.B. Naes, Bloomington, Indiana University Press, 1992. For a general discussion of postcolonialism and its links to postmodernism, see Leela Gandhi, *Postcolonial Theory: A Critical Introduction*, St Leonards, New South Wales, Allen and Unwin, 1998.
4 Edward Said, *Culture and Imperialism*, London, Chatto and Windus (Vintage), 1994, pp. 335–6 and 31–2.

5 Ibid., p. 336.
6 Baogang He and David Held, 'Democracy, Transnational Problems and the Boundary Question: Challenges for China', *Social Alternatives*, vol. 16, no. 4, October 1997, p. 35.
7 See, for example, Richard A. Falk, Robert C. Johansen and Samuel S. Kim, *The Constitutional Foundations of World Peace*, Albany, State University of New York Press, 1993.
8 Western recognition of cultural differences may still be explicitly framed by liberal principles. See, for example, Will Kymlicka, *Multiculural Citizenship: A Liberal Theory of Minority Rights*, Oxford, Clarendon Press, 1995. But multiculturalism may also challenge liberalism itself. See Bikhu Parekh, *Rethinking Multiculturalism: Cultural Diversity and Political Theory*, Basingstoke, Macmillan, 2000. Parekh does not adopt an extreme relativist position. He argues that all cultures deserve some respect but not *equal* respect, emphasizes pluralism within cultures and stresses the need for dialogue between them.
9 David Beetham. 'Human Rights as a Model for Cosmopolitan Democracy', in Daniele Archibugi, David Held and Martin Köhler, eds, *Re-imagining Political Community: Studies in Cosmopolitan Democracy*, Cambridge: Polity, 1998, p. 59.
10 Heiner Bielefeldt, ' "Western" versus "Islamic" Human Rights Conceptions? A Critique of Cultural Essentialism in the Discussion on Human Rights', *Political Theory*, vol. 28 no. 1, 2000, pp. 91 and 103.
11 Danilo Zolo, *Cosmopolis*, Cambridge, Polity, 1997, p. 119.
12 See, for example, Angela Lee Nga Kam, 'Sticks, Stones and Smokescreens', *New Internationalist*, no. 298, January/February 1998, pp. 34–5.
13 Anwar Ibrahim, *The Asian Renaissance*, Singapore, Times Books International, 1996, pp. 20–8.
14 Richard Lloyd Parry, 'Malaysia Risks International Isolation Over Anwar Sentence', *Independent*, 9 August 2000, p. 11.
15 Bhiku Parekh, 'The Cultural Particularity of Liberal Democracy', in David Held, ed., *Prospects for Democracy*, Cambridge, Polity, 1993, pp. 156–75.
16 Amartya Sen, 'Humanity and Citizenship', in Martha C. Nussbaum *et al.*, *For Love of Country: Debating the Limits of Patriotism*, edited by Joshua Cohen, Boston, Beacon Press, 1996, p. 117.
17 L.P. Fitzgerald, *The Justice God Wants: Islam and Human Rights*, Melbourne, Collins Dove, 1993.
18 See, for example, Joseph A. Camilleri and Chandra Muzaffar, *Globalisation: Perspectives and Experiences of the Religious Traditions of Asia Pacific*, Selangor, Malaysia, International Movement for a Just World, 1998.
19 Parekh, 'Cultural Particularity of Liberal Democracy', p. 174.
20 This point is made forcefully in Ken Booth, 'Human Wrongs and International Relations', *International Affairs*, vol. 71, no. 1, 1995, pp. 103–26, which argues for the universality of human rights and cosmopolitan politics.
21 Roland Dannreuther, 'Cosmopolitan Citizenship and the Middle East', in Kimberley Hutchings and Roland Dannreuther, eds, *Cosmopolitan Citizenship*, Basingstoke, Macmillan, 1999, p. 155.
22 Noted by Zolo, *Cosmopolis*, p. 119.
23 Bielefeldt, ' "Western" versus "Islamic" Human Rights Conceptions?', p. 114.
24 The possibility that global human rights arise out of a cosmopolitan structure of modernity is explored in R.J. Vincent, *Human Rights and International Relations*, Cambridge, Cambridge University Press, 1986.
25 Cited in Joseph A. Camilleri, 'Human Rights, Cultural Diversity and Conflict Resolution: The Asia Pacific Context', *Pacifica Review*, vol. 6, no. 2, 1994, p. 18.
26 Jack Donnelly, 'International Human Rights: A Regime Analysis', *International Organization*, vol. 40, no. 3, 1986, pp. 599–642.
27 Vincent, *Human Rights and International Relations*.
28 Daisaku Ikeda, *Humanity and the New Millennium: From Chaos to Cosmos*, Tokyo, The Soka Gakkai, 1998.
29 Cited in Dennis Dalton, *Mahatma Gandhi: Nonviolent Power in Action*, New York, Columbia University Press, 1993, p. 68.
30 Cited in ibid., p. 74.
31 Martha C. Nussbaum, 'Patriotism and Cosmopolitanism', in Nussbaum *et al.*, *For Love of Country*, pp. 5–6, 15–16.
32 Georgina Ashworth, 'Promoting Women's Human Rights in the International Arena', paper for December 1994 British International Studies Association Conference, cited by Marysia

Zalewski, 'Well, What is the Feminist Perspective on Bosnia?', *International Affairs*, vol. 71, no. 2, 1995, p. 345.

33 See Martha C. Nussbaum, *Sex and Social Justice*, New York, Oxford University Press, 1999, pp. 35–7 for a satirical account of western intellectuals celebrating premodern cultural pratices.

34 Radhika Coomoraswamy, 'To Bellow like a Cow: Women, Ethnicity, and the Discourse of Rights', in Rebecca J. Cook, ed., *Human Rights of Women: National and International Perspectives*, Philadelphia, University of Pennsylvania Press, 1994, p. 45.

35 See, for example, Carol B. Thompson, 'Women in the National Liberation Struggle in Zimbabwe: An Interview of Naomi Nhiwatiwa', *Women's Studies International Forum*, vol. 5, no. 3–4, 1982, pp. 247–52.

36 For a re-reading of verses of the Koran (Qur'an) to favour women's equality, see Riffat Hassan, 'On Human Rights and the Qur'anic Perspective', in Arlene Swidler, ed., *Human Rights in Religious Traditions*, New York, Pilgrim, 1982, pp. 51–65.

37 See Nikki R. Keddi, 'The Rights of Women in Contemporary Islam', in Leroy S. Rouner, ed., *Human Rights and the World's Religions*, Notre Dame, Ind., University of Notre Dame Press, 1988, pp. 99–100.

38 Cooraswamy, 'To Bellow Like a Cow', pp. 48–50.

39 Parekh, 'The Cultural Particularity of Liberal Democracy', p. 174. For his later thoughts, see Bhiku Parekh, 'A Varied Moral World', in Susan Moller Okin and Respondents, *Is Multiculturalism Bad for Women?*, Princeton, NJ, Princeton University Press, 1999, p. 70.

40 Yasmin Alibhai-Brown, 'The Truth About Forced Marriages', *Guardian*, 3 July 2000, p. 7.

41 See Chaloka Beyani, 'Toward a More Effective Guarantee of Women's Rights in the African Human Rights System', in Cook, ed., *Human Rights of Women*, pp. 285–6 and 292–3.

42 Spike Peterson, 'Whose Rights? A Critique of the "Givens" in Human Rights Discourse', *Alternatives*, vol. 15, no. 3, 1990, pp. 303–44.

43 Rhonda Copelon, 'Intimate Terror: Understanding Domestic Violence as Torture', in Cook, ed., *Human Rights of Women*, pp. 116–52.

44 Judith G. Gardam, 'A Feminist Analysis of Certain Aspects of International Humanitarian Law', *Australian Yearbook of International Law*, vol. 12, 1992, pp. 265–78. Rhonda Copelon, 'Surfacing Gender: Reconceptualizing Crimes against Women in Time of War', in Lois Ann Lorentzen and Jennifer Turpin, eds, *The Women and War Reader*, New York, New York University Press, 1998, pp. 63–79.

45 Ian Black, 'Serbs "Enslaved Muslim Women at Rape Camps" ', *Guardian*, 21 March 2000, p. 13.

46 Fred Halliday, *Rethinking International Relations*, Basingstoke, Macmillan, 1994, pp. 164–5.

47 See Nussbaum, *Sex and Social Justice*, pp. 30–2; and Victoria Brittain and Larry Elliot, 'Educating Girls is a Real Life-saver', *Guardian Weekly*, 9–15 March 2000, p. 27.

48 See, for example, Linda Gordon, ed., *Women, the State and Welfare*, Madison, University of Wisconsin Press, 1990.

49 Andrea Dworkin, *Woman Hating*, New York, E.P. Dutton, 1974 and *Pornography: Men Possessing Women*, New York, Perigee/G.P. Putnam's. 1981; Catherine MacKinnon, 'Sexuality, Pornography, and Method: "Pleasure under Patriarchy" ', *Ethics*, vol. 99, January 1989, pp. 314–46.

50 Shulamith Firestone, *The Dialectic of Sex: The Case for Feminist Revolution*, New York, Bantam Books, 1970.

51 Carole Pateman, *The Sexual Contract*, Cambridge, Polity, 1988 and *The Disorder of Women: Democracy, Feminism and Political Theory*, Cambridge, Polity, 1989.

52 Catherine MacKinnon, 'Crimes of War, Crimes of Peace', in S. Shute and S. Hurley, eds, *On Human Rights: The Oxford Amnesty Lectures 1993*, New York, Basic Books, 1993, pp. 83–109.

53 Carole Pateman, 'Citizen Male', *Australian Left Review*, March 1992, p. 33.

54 Virginia Woolf, *Three Guineas*, London, Hogarth Press, [1938] 1947, p. 197.

55 Carole Gilligan, *In A Different Voice*, Cambridge, Mass., Harvard University Press, 1982; and Sara Ruddick. *Maternal Thinking: Towards a Politics of Peace*, London, Women's Press, 1990.

56 Alice Cook and Gwen Kirk, *Greenham Women Everywhere*, London, Pluto Press, 1983. For a wider discussion, see Elisabeth J. Porter, *Women and Moral Identity*, London, Allen and Unwin, 1991, chap. 7, 'Affirmation of Difference'; and Alison Bailey, 'Mothering, Diversity and Peace Politics' (Review Essay), *Hypatia*, vol. 9 no. 2, 1994, pp. 188–98.

57 See Andrew Higgins, 'Trouble for Yeltsin on the Home Front', *Independent* , 12 January 1995, Section Two, p. 1.

58 See Ruddick, *Maternal Thinking*, pp. 225–34.

59 Jean Bethke Elshtain, *Public Man/Private Woman*, Princeton, NJ, Princeton University Press, 1981, and Elshtain, 'On Beautiful Souls, Just Warriors and Feminist Consciousness', *Women's Studies International Forum*, vol. 5, no. 3–4, 1982, pp. 341–8. For a rather different emphasis, drawing on Arendt, see Elshtain, *Women and War*, New York, Basic Books, 1987.

60 Jean Grimshaw, *Philosophy and Feminist Thinking*, Minneapolis, University of Minneapolis Press, 1986; Catherine C. Greeno and Eleanor M. Maccoby, 'How Different is the "Different Voice"?', *Signs*, vol. 11, 1986, pp. 310–16.

61 Mary G. Dietz, 'Citizenship with a Feminist Face: The Problem with Maternal Thinking', *Political Theory*, vol. 13, no. 1, February 1985, pp. 19–37.

62 Lorraine Bayard de Volo, 'Drafting Motherhood: Maternal Imagery and Organizations in the United States and Nicaragua', in Lorentzen and Turpin, eds, *Women and War Reader*, pp. 240–53.

63 Vicky Randall, *Women and Politics*, London, Macmillan, 1982; L. Weir, 'Limitations of New Social Movement Analysis', *Studies in Political Economy* no. 40, 1993, pp. 73–101; G. Kaplan, *Contemporary Western European Feminism*, London, University College of London Press, 1992.

64 See Barbara Sullivan, 'Carole Pateman: Participatory Democracy and Feminism', in April Carter and Geoffrey Stokes, eds, *Liberal Democracy and its Critics*, Cambridge, Polity, 1998, p. 189.

65 Julia Kristeva, 'Woman Can Never be Defined', in Elaine Marks and Isabelle de Courtivron, eds, *New French Feminism*, New York, Schocken, 1981, p. 137, cited in Linda Alcoff, 'Cultural Feminism versus Post-Structuralism: The Identity Crisis in Feminist Theory', *Signs*, vol. 13, no. 3, Spring 1988, p. 418.

66 Kimberley Hutchings, 'Feminist Politics and Cosmopolitan Citizenship', in Hutchings and Dannreuther, eds, *Cosmopolitan Citizenship*, p. 140. Hutchings' discussion is within the context of the debate between Linklater and Miller that frames the book.

67 Seyla Benhabib, 'Feminism and Postmodernism: An Uneasy Alliance', *Praxis International*, vol. 11, no. 2, July 1991, p. 146.

68 Alcoff, 'Cultural Feminism versus Post-Structuralism', pp. 418–419.

69 Julia Kristeva, *Nations Without Nationalism*, translated by Leon S. Roudiez, New York, Columbia University Press, 1993, on Montesquieu: pp. 27–8, 40–1, 53–8, and on Diderot: pp. 27–9.

70 Ibid., pp. 26–7.

71 Ibid., p. 35.

72 Jürgen Habermas, *The Philosophical Discourse of Modernity*, translated by Frederick Lawrence, Cambridge, Polity, 1987, p. 336.

73 Ibid., p. 337, and Lois McNay, *Foucault: A Critical Introduction*, Cambridge, Polity, 1994, p. 158.

74 Williams, *Lyotard*, pp. 136–7.

75 Andrew Linklater, *The Transformation of Political Community: Ethical Foundations of the Post-Westphalian Era*, Cambridge, Polity, 1998, p. 71.

76 Ibid., p. 73.

77 Ibid., p. 98.

78 See: Stuart Sim, *Derrida and the End of History*, Cambridge, Icon Books, 1999, p. 31; and Peter Beilharz, 'Critical Theory – Jürgen Habermas', in David Roberts, ed., *Reconstructing Theory: Gadamer, Habermas, Luhmann*, Melbourne, Melbourne University Press, 1995, p. 61.

79 Michael B. Naes, 'Introduction' to Derrida, *The Other Heading*, p. xlv.

80 Christopher Norris, *Derrida*, London, Fontana, 1987, p. 169.

81 Michel Foucault, *Politics, Philosophy, Culture: Interviews and Other Writings 1977–1984*, edited by Lawrence D. Krizman, New York, Routledge, 1988, p. 84.

82 David Macey, *The Lives of Michel Foucault*, London, Vintage, 1993, pp. 437 and 438.

83 See the discussion of Foucault's changing understanding of power in his concept of 'governmentality' in McNay, *Foucault*, pp. 113–33.

84 Beilharz, 'Critical Theory – Jürgen Habermas', p. 60.

85 Jean-François Lyotard, 'The Other's Rights', in Shute and Hurly, eds, *On Human Rights*, p. 136.

86 Ibid., pp. 139 and 141.

87 Ibid., p. 141.

88 Williams, *Lyotard*, pp. 104–5.

89 Ibid., p. 114.
90 Richard Rorty, 'Cosmopolitanism Without Emancipation', in *Objectivity, Truth and Relativism*, Cambridge, Cambridge University Press, 1991, cited in N.J. Rengger, *Political Theory, Modernity and Postmodernity*, Oxford, Blackwell, 1995, p. 92.
91 Richard Rorty, *Contingency, Irony, and Solidarity*, Cambridge, Cambridge University Press, 1989, p. 198.
92 Ibid., pp. 191 and 192.
93 Vincent, *Human Rights and International Relations*, p. 56.
94 Richard Rorty, 'Human Rights, Rationality and Sentimentality', in Shute and Hurley, eds, *On Human Rights*, p. 134.
95 This last point is made by Rorty in 'Intellectuals in Politics: Too Far In? Too Far Out?', *Dissent*, Fall, 1991, pp. 483–90. See also Michael T. Gibbon. 'The Ethic of Postmodernism', *Political Theory*, vol. 19, no. 1, 1991, pp. 96–102.
96 James Der Derian 'A Reinterpretation of Realism: Genealogy, Semiology, Dromology', in *International Theory: Critical Investigations*, Basingstoke, Macmillan, 1995, pp. 363–96.
97 See R. Ashley and R.J.B. Walker, 'Reading Dissidence/Writing the Discipline: Crisis and the Question of Sovereignty in International Studies', *International Studies Quarterly*, vol. 34, no. 3, 1990, pp. 367–416. Cited in Hutchings, *International Political Theory*, p. 78.
98 R.B.J. Walker, 'Citizenship After the Modern Subject', in Hutchings and Dannreuther, eds, *Cosmopolitan Citizenship*, p. 191.
99 Ibid., pp. 196–7.
100 Ibid., p. 198. Walker suggests that underlying Linklater's approach is a return to the hierarchical 'Great Chain of Being that modern subjectivities, modern states, and modern citizens were supposed to undermine' (p. 196).
101 David Held, *Democracy and the Global Order*, Cambridge, Polity, 1996, p. 146.
102 Michael Dillon and Julia Reid, 'Global Governance, Liberal Peace and Complex Emergency', in Jenny Edkins and R.B.J. Walker, eds, Special issue: 'Zones of Indistinction: Territories, Bodies, Politics', *Alternatives*, vol. 25, January–March 2000, pp. 124 and 139.
103 Barry Smart, *Michel Foucault*, London, Routledge, 1988, pp. 122–3.
104 Michel Foucault, 'Truth and Power', in *Power/Knowledge: Selected Interviews and Other Writings 1972–1977 by Michel Foucault*, edited by C. Gordon, Brighton, Harvester Press, 1980, p. 122, quoted in ibid., p. 124.
105 Dillon and Reid, 'Global Governance', p. 123.
106 See Jürgen Habermas, *Justification and Application: Remarks on Discourse Ethics*, translated by C.P. Cronin, Cambridge, Polity, 1993. A political example is the way in which the Beijing Conference endorsed the general principle of opposing violence against women, but focused on different forms of such violence in differing cultures.

Conclusion

1 Daniele Archibugi, 'Cosmopolitical Democracy', *New Left Review*, no. 4, second series, July–August 2000, p. 137.
2 Sanctions against Iraq and the NATO war against Serbia to protect Kosovan Albanians show that international action can harm the most vulnerable or even contravene international law itself.

Index

Note on indexing 'global' and 'world citizenship': Since the concept of global citizenship is the subject of the whole book, I have not indexed it as a separate item. Instead I have followed the logic of the overall argument, indexing it as a subsection of schools of thought espousing the idea, such as the Stoics and Enlightenment philosophy, and under individuals who have contributed especially to developing the idea in the past and today. Global citizenship is also indexed under concepts of cosmopolitanism, cosmopolitan democracy, global civil society, world federalism, as well as under transnational movements, human rights, refugees and international law. In addition it is indexed in relation to national citizenship and the varying strands of political theory and international relations which provide support for, or critiques of, the idea of global citizenship. The author's own summary definitions can be found on pp. 7, 8, 49, 96–7, 174–6, 203–4, 233–6. As noted in the Preface, the original term world citizen was largely (but not wholly) replaced in the 1990s by the terms global or cosmopolitan citizen. Both in the text and the index I have generally used world citizen for earlier periods and global citizen for contemporary debates. Cosmopolitan citizenship is subsumed under global citizenship. Transnational citizenship, which is indexed, denotes more limited forms of citizenship across borders.